Nixon in the White House

Nixon in the White House:
The Frustration of Power

ROWLAND EVANS, JR., & ROBERT D. NOVAK

VINTAGE BOOKS

A Division of Random House, New York

Copyright © 1971, 1972 by Rowland Evans, Jr., and
Robert D. Novak

All rights reserved under International and Pan-American
Copyright Conventions. Published in the United States by
Random House, Inc., New York, and simultaneously
in Canada by Random House of Canada Limited, Toronto.
Originally published by Random House, Inc., in 1971.

Library of Congress Cataloging in Publication Data

Evans, Rowland, 1921–
    Nixon in the White House.

    Reprint of the 1971 ed., brought up to date with a new
chapter.
    1. Nixon, Richard Milhous, 1913–   2. U.S.—Politics
and government—1969–   I. Novak, Robert D., joint
author.   II.   Title.
E855.E9   1972   973.924'092'4 [B]   72-1430
ISBN 0-394-71803-8

Manufactured in the United States of America

Vintage Books Edition, September 1972

ACKNOWLEDGMENTS

The definitive account of the Nixon administration will not, of course, be written for many years, not until the Presidential papers and personal memoirs are available. For now, however, we believe that as journalists we can shed significant light on the great events of this administration, its principal figures and, most important, on the thirty-seventh President of the United States.

Our sources of information have been varied: the regular, daily reporting for our syndicated column; approximately fifty special interviews in depth with officials and former officials, high and low, of the Nixon administration whose assistance, candor and patience were absolutely indispensable to this book. For obvious reasons we shall not name them, but we shall never forget their help under often difficult circumstances.

Helen M. McMaster, our assistant, was invaluable as the principal researcher, typist and copy reader for the manuscript. We also appreciate the help of Cynthia Johnston, who performed research work, and Geraldine Williams Novak and Julie A. Cleary, who assisted with the typing.

The librarians of the Washington Bureau of *Newsweek* and the *Washington Post* were particularly cooperative. We also appreciate the assistance we received from staff members of the Washington Public Library; the library of the Washington Bureau of the *New York Times; Congressional Quarterly;* the Washington bureaus of *Time, Newsday,* the *Des Moines Register and Tribune* and the *Los Angeles Times;* the Washington Star Syndicate; television station WBTV of Charlotte, N.C.; and particularly our office neighbors—the Washington bureaus of the *Boston Globe* and the Newhouse Newspapers.

Our thanks, too, to the White House Press Office, the White House Press Releases Office, the White House Office of Records and the Department of Defense Press Office.

We appreciate the wise counsel of our long-time editor and partner, Robert A. Gutwillig, and of James H. Silberman of Random House.

And, finally, our deep gratitude to our wives, Katherine and Geraldine, whose patience was exemplary, as always, and whose culinary arts were indispensable in our numerous evening interviews at home.

R. E., Jr., and R. D. N.

Contents

Nixon in the White House

I

The President

A President cannot have problems which are personal to him alone. His troubles are the troubles of the nation and if they become disastrous, the nation is in peril.

—George E. Reedy, in
The Twilight of the Presidency

In the second week of January 1971 the Republican National Committee was assembling in Washington for its midwinter meeting. It was nearly two years since the inauguration of Richard Milhous Nixon, the first authentic Republican politician to become President of the United States since Calvin Coolidge was elected in 1924, the heyday of the Grand Old Party. Whatever Nixon's identification problems with the rest of the country, he should have had none whatever here with the members of the National Committee, so many of whom he knew so well.

One Western committeeman, in particular, was a tried-and-true Nixon man, a party man who was called a member of the Old Guard in an earlier day and who now backed Richard Nixon as he once backed Robert Alphonso Taft. But on the evening of January 13, 1971, as members of the National Committee gathered for cocktails at the Washington Hilton Hotel, this Westerner was preoccupied with thoughts about a most-un-Republican letter to the editor published in that morning's *Washington Post* and signed by the distinguished historian and biographer Irving Brant. It was typical of the hard, sometimes brutal criticism that the academic community had leveled at Richard Nixon for a generation.

"Richard Nixon," wrote Brant, "in spite of his tremendously hard work and overwhelming ambition to be well thought of, is at bottom a synthetic figure." By contrast, he continued, each of the first five American Presidents had faults, but "each man was a genuine person—himself—presenting a definite personality and clear-cut character. Who and what is Richard Nixon?"

The Western Republican politician, an unquestionably loyal Nixon man, remarked that he thought the author of that letter was a little unfair, a little rough, but still, that fellow had something. "I wonder myself," he said slowly. "Who and what *is* Richard Nixon?"

That Irving Brant should have asked the question was neither surprising nor significant. That a conservative member of the Republican National Committee should agree was both surprising and significant. Nor was he alone, and therein lay the central irony of Richard Nixon, who had swept to office, after so many years of frustration, as Mr. Republican, successor to Taft, comrade-in-arms to party workers.

Never having made his reputation as a politician emotionally wedded to controversial or powerful causes—as, by contrast, Barry Goldwater made his reputation as ideologue of the right—Nixon came to the Presidency curiously unfathomed as a human being even by the party stalwarts who composed his base of support. For Nixon the politician, far more than Lyndon Johnson or John F. Kennedy or Dwight Eisenhower, concealed Nixon the man, and the man was, even to some of his close friends, an unbelievably complex, shy, remote and tense figure whose iron control seldom permitted anyone to glimpse the tumult inside. He was also a man cursed to live without the appearance of charm. He waged an endless battle to overcome that lack, but the effort usually fell short. At the root of this incapacity was his loneliness, and the loneliness was partly an inheritance of birth in a poor and undistinguished family, partly his environment as a poor boy, partly the harsh way politics had dealt with him. Having never attached himself to powerful causes, he lacked the political intimacies and camaraderies that so often joined politicians in common undertakings. His closest friends were not great leaders in the academic, business or political worlds or childhood pals, but a newly rich real estate speculator in Florida and the millionaire inventor of the aerosol valve.*

*Charles (Bebe) Rebozo and Robert Abplanalp.

But this was no Warren Harding, bewitched by vulgar wealth. His idols were not captains of industry but heroes of state—Winston Churchill, above all. Late one evening the last week of November 1970, at a low point in his Presidency, he had finished writing the finishing touches for a speech (working as ever on a yellow legal pad), and turned to an aide to talk about the kind of President he admired and would like to emulate. He eliminated the recent past: they were too close at hand to judge. But looking back, he mentioned these as Presidents who *did* something: Andrew Jackson, nemesis of the banks; Abraham Lincoln, who saved the Union; Grover Cleveland, who restored the power of the Presidency after all those stalwart Republicans; Theodore Roosevelt, who fought the trusts; Woodrow Wilson, the great reformer and internationalist; Franklin D. Roosevelt, who engineered a peaceful revolution. Four Democrats and two Republicans—one of whom bolted his party—scarcely a pantheon for Mr. Republican.

Richard Nixon's personal reputation was that of a hard man, bordering on meanness. It was bolstered as stories leaked out of the inner sanctum of the White House about his intemperate attitude toward his greatest nemeses: liberal Republicans who did not support their President, and the press. Oddly, he could have been a good newspaperman himself, with a taste for journalistic voyeurism in observing and, from a detached viewpoint, analyzing sports events and politics alike. But his wife, Pat, and his two daughters, Tricia and Julie, had never sought to hide the anguish induced by a story critical of him, and that had its effect on the President himself, adding to his own annoyance.

That ill temper, in bygone days, had displayed itself frequently and publicly, as during his 1956 campaign for reelection as Vice President when a mass resignation of his staff threatened. On the last day of campaigning for President in 1960, on the eve of defeat, a fatigued, worried Richard Nixon lashed out in a television studio at his staff in front of press and television technicians. But now, as President, not once had he lost his temper—never castigating an underling, except perhaps in the inmost intimacy of his personal staff and his family. He was, moreover, almost compulsively unable to fire or dress down an aide, whether Cabinet member or middle-level policy-maker. Although a college debater, he now detested confrontation with an opponent and would do anything to avoid it. To blow off steam at an aide or to confront an enemy was the soul and substance of the political life of a Harry Truman or a Lyndon Johnson or a Huey Long or even of a John F. Kennedy. But not President Richard Nixon.

His lack of wit and humor was a cliché both in and outside the White House, but he was capable of practical jokes of a rather high order, one of which he pulled off following his European trip in early 1969, when he ordered the White House police force to wear elegant ceremonial uniforms like the household guard in a European court. The first appearance of the costumes, which were straight from Central European comic opera, unleashed a public torrent of abuse, and the President quickly retreated. A few days later his two most intimate White House aides, H. R. (Bob) Haldeman and John Ehrlichman, both of whom had thought the new uniform a great idea, each received an embossed hat box tied in gold ribbon and decked out like a Christmas tree. Inside was one of the new gold-ribboned stovepipe hats with the patent-leather visor. There was no note, and the President never mentioned his little gifts to Bob and John. Considering Nixon's genuine love for ceremony and ritual, that bit of humorous self-deprecation was remarkable.

There were, too, many midnight telephone calls, friendly and intimate, to close aides, friends and occasionally a journalist. They would come sometimes as late as two in the morning, and could go on for many minutes and on a variety of subjects. In one such call to Donald Rumsfeld, a Presidential Counsellor, Nixon mentioned his great friend Whittaker Chambers, whose help had been indispensable to Nixon in breaking the Alger Hiss case, and Rumsfeld sought to learn more about him. The President discoursed brilliantly on Chambers, the tortured intellectual who had joined and then deserted the Communist Party. It was one of many midnight chats that revealed a side of Nixon the public knew nothing about.

Often the precise idiom or choice of words to make a point or to make an apt response seemed just beyond the President's grasp, —a fault that badly hurt his public reputation. That was true when, during his campaign in St. Petersburg, Fla., in October 1970, a motorcycle policeman was thrown from his vehicle in the Presidential caravan and severely injured. Leaving his limousine, Nixon rushed to the injured policeman and expressed his sympathies. The policeman replied that *he* was the one to be sorry that the motorcade had been delayed. Then, embarrassing silence—the President speechless for seconds. Finally he blurted out: "Do you like the work?"

Despite this inability to relate to individuals in specific, ordinary life situations, he prided himself on his skill as a master of mass communications. He worked his press conferences with neither notes nor podium; his steel-trap mind could comprehend difficult concepts and memorize great quantities of facts. Yet, no President ever prepared so diligently for a press conference as Richard Nixon, and he treated each as if it were his first exposure to the naked eye of the camera, with nerves taut as airtime neared. He would sit in a cool, dark room collecting his thoughts and calming himself, but when he entered the East Room of the White House for the press conference, he would often be bathed in sweat. He had fewer press conferences than any President since Herbert Hoover.

That added to his isolation, which was more pronounced than any President's since Hoover—isolation from the press, from most of his aides, from his Cabinet. Reclusive by nature, the Presidency heightened that characteristic and added difficulties to his Presidency.

Yet, all in all and now well into the third year of his Presidency, Richard Nixon had changed remarkably little in office. He was still, in essence, the same man who had, after so long and hard a chase for power, awaited its assumption at the Pierre Hotel in New York in November 1968.

II

Prelude
at the Pierre

*There was to be no Hundred Days or Great Society
to mark the beginning of the Nixon Administration;
the style of the Presidency and its goals would become
apparent only as the years wore on.*

— Theodore White, in
The Making of the President 1968

Having brooded, dreamed and schemed for the Presidency for the
last sixteen of his fifty-five years, President-elect Richard M. Nixon
in November 1968 set up his transition headquarters at Manhattan's
elegant Pierre Hotel, opposite Central Park, with only the vaguest
intentions of what he would do with the immense power he had
craved so long.

His knowledge of foreign affairs was encyclopedic and in the
weeks just ahead would astonish those who had not known him
before. And no President had had so detailed an understanding of
the mechanics of American politics—such significant trivia as knowing whether a Wisconsin state rally should be held in Milwaukee or
Madison, and precisely how platform arrangements should be made.
But there were deep and obvious gaps, surprising for one so long on
the national scene, in his knowledge of the federal government and
the Congress. From the gaps came the appalling vacuum of advance
planning on how to organize and operate one of the biggest and most
intricate governments in the world.

Those eight years as Dwight D. Eisenhower's Vice President

had not helped much. Surrounded by enemies bent on his destruction, Nixon had little time for self-education. He had told close associates in the past that *his* White House would have no Sherman Adams and no James Hagerty—no single assistant so all-powerful as Adams had been under Eisenhower and no press secretary so free to speak as Hagerty had been. But these axioms were based more on personalities than governmental theory. A man with an infinite capacity for keeping a permanent mental ledger of the ills done him over the years, Nixon had never forgiven or forgotten the way Adams and Hagerty had slighted him as an unnecessary appendage to the Eisenhower administration. Less personal but no less explicit was his conviction that the new Secretary of State would be no John Foster Dulles. Nixon was too engrossed in the business of foreign policy to give any Secretary the grant of power that Eisenhower had bestowed on Dulles. Thus, what Nixon mainly carried away from the Eisenhower administration was some deeply ingrained feelings about what *not* to do.

Nor had his long political career uncommonly enlarged his knowledge of government. His tenure on Capitol Hill, four years in the House and two in the Senate, was much too brief and too frenetic for a detailed grounding in the legislative process. He spent those six years and the eight that followed as Vice President, as he revealed clearly in his *Six Crises,* vastly more interested in his own personal development and the interplay of personalities in political confrontations than in microscopic probing of the governmental process. The succeeding eight years in the political wilderness, with the seemingly fatal defeat for the governorship of California in 1962, and the stunning resurrection were an epic in self-survival that left little time for creative political thought.

Even more surprising, Nixon entered the Pierre after his victory with very little in the way of specific plans for his administration. His much publicized "plan" to end the Vietnam war was more myth than reality. His campaign proposals for using tax incentives as a substitute for government social-welfare spending disintegrated under the first careful analysis. On the economy, the environment and civil rights, there was a total absence of planning.

Although a Presidential campaign may generate programs for the incoming administration, Nixon's did no such thing. Its content was at heart schizophrenic, split between rally speeches on the stump and an unusual series of paid speeches delivered over network radio.

The rally speeches, with their strong emphasis on law and order, infuriated liberals, particularly the attacks on the federal judiciary's civil libertarian decisions. But mainly they were filled with partisan generalities, intended merely to maintain the advantage inherited from intense public animosity toward the Democratic administration of Lyndon B. Johnson and his anointed candidate, Vice President Hubert H. Humphrey. The radio speeches, considerably more liberal and vastly more interesting, were designed chiefly to polish Nixon's image with the liberal press. Few key figures in the Nixon administration took them seriously, and Nixon clearly did not regard them as pertinent to his Presidency.*

Moreover, on the day the President-elect took up transitional residence in the Pierre Hotel, he could count on fewer close associates to help him run the government than any recent predecessor. The handful of his trusted lieutenants and advisers would, of course, take up key positions in the White House and administration. But almost to the man, they were sadly inexperienced in the ways of Washington, government, public affairs and politics. To supplement them, Nixon would have to call on outsiders that would make his, at the beginning, an administration of strangers.

He did, however, carry into the Pierre a short list of notions— some to endure, some to be quickly discarded; some interconnected, some contradictory—about the way he would run his government. They were articulated only raggedly, if at all. Unmistakably, however, they were in the President-elect's consciousness.

1. The President must run foreign affairs and let his Cabinet handle the humdrum of domestic affairs. "I've always thought this country could run itself domestically without a President," he told an interviewer in November 1967. "All you need is a competent Cabinet to run the country at home. You need a President for foreign policy; no Secretary of State is really important; the President makes foreign policy."

2. That "competent" Cabinet should be magnified in power,

---

*The radio speeches were incomparably better reading than the rally speeches but often far removed from political reality. For example, Nixon's speech over the CBS radio network on May 16, calling for a "new alignment" in politics, suggests that "the Republicans, the new liberals, the new South [and] the Black militants . . . are talking the same language" in preferring individual action to government action and, therefore, could form the basis of a new political grouping. Nixon's closest political advisers viewed the idea as sheer nonsense.

while the White House staff should be reduced in size and influence. Not only was there not to be another Sherman Adams; there was to be no spiritual successor to Joseph Califano, President Johnson's top domestic aide of his latter years in power. Nixon lieutenants and Nixon himself had heard stories of Joe Califano, the tough young lawyer from Brooklyn by way of Harvard, harassing and riding herd on distinguished Cabinet members many years his senior. There would be no repetition of this in the Nixon administration, where power would flow back to the Cabinet-level departments.

3. No significant amount of legislation was desirable or necessary. The glut of social-welfare bills passed under Johnson's Great Society had left more than enough laws on the books. The Nixon administration would be concerned with the conduct of foreign policy and management of government, not with an enervating and ultimately heartbreaking struggle to pry legislation out of a Democratic Congress.

4. There would be no repeating the irremediable failure of the Eisenhower administration sixteen years earlier to clean out the Democrat-infested federal bureaucracy. This time would be different. Nixon, infinitely more partisan than the old general, would root out Democratic civil servants and replace them with Republicans, thereby broadening the base for the emergence of the Republican Party as the nation's majority party.

Even these vague notions were not to endure. The first Nixon held to, in part at least, for the first two years of his Presidency, helped along by the special nature of his mental process. Quick, analytic and absorbent though it is, Nixon's mind is uncomfortable concentrating hard on more than two or three large issues at the same time, and the points of concentration in 1969–70 concerned international affairs. The President's interest in domestic affairs would be intermittent and secondary, until the harmful results of the 1970 midterm election sharply dictated otherwise. The other three assumptions were stillborn: victims of fuzzy conception, bad planning and the tyranny of governmental reality over the rainbow fantasies of the campaign trail.

The incompleteness of these early notions by the President-elect was typified by one startling contradiction. If Nixon were really to concentrate on foreign affairs to the virtual exclusion of domestic matters, some aide at the White House would have to be ceded vast powers. But that would conflict squarely with Nixon's intention to downgrade and decapitate the White House staff.

So it was that in those early winter weeks at the Pierre Hotel, while word was being put out that there would be no Nixon aide holding Sherman Adams' lofty title of *The* Assistant to the President and that all top aides would be more or less equal, Nixon was privately making a somewhat contradictory proposition to one of his oldest and least typical advisers: Dr. Arthur Burns, Professor of Economics at Columbia University.

Burns, an Austrian-born Jew whose nasal twang unintentionally imitated W. C. Fields, was a distinguished economist who had chosen to concentrate his career on the intersection of politics and economics rather than on pure economics (though he had won scholarly acclaim for his original theories on business cycles). "Arthur would have been a great economist," Milton Friedman, the conservative economic theoretician, once told a friend, "if he hadn't been so interested in politics." That interest brought him to Washington in 1953 as chairman of the Council of Economic Advisers under Eisenhower and into contact for the first time with the young Vice President.

The contact was favorable. Nixon's tendency to summarize and analyze arguments put forth at the Cabinet table, annoying to the big guns of the Eisenhower administration who regarded Dick Nixon as a pipsqueak, won Arthur Burns' deep admiration. Their friendship began in disagreement over an increase in the minimum wage—Burns arguing in Cabinet that it would be folly, Nixon favoring it as an attempt to woo the workingman. Afterward, however, Nixon told Burns privately: If you can convince me with your economic arguments, I'll put political arguments aside. The older man was deeply impressed. Their alliance thickened after Burns left the administration. During the economic recession of 1958 that proved so politically disastrous for the Republican Party, Burns and Nixon were allies in an unsuccessful fight for a stimulative tax reduction. In 1960 they again attempted, again unsuccessfully, to get the Eisenhower administration to pump up the economy to stave off another economic downturn. Had Eisenhower followed Burns' advice on either occasion, Nixon always felt, the winner in the 1960 Presidential election would not have been John F. Kennedy but Richard M.

Nixon. The friendship continued during Nixon's years in the wilderness. To Burns, they both held roughly the same political philosophy —essentially conservative but strongly tempered with pragmatism. Beyond that, Nixon and Burns each felt himself a self-made man who had by his own drive and intellect forced himself into the upper reaches of power. They frequently compared the similarity of their backgrounds.

Even before he was elected in 1968, Nixon had decided, but not announced, that Burns would replace William McChesney Martin on January 31, 1970, when his term expired after two decades as chairman of the Federal Reserve Board—thus becoming the first professional economist and the first Jew to run the country's central bank, a post long preserved for Protestant bankers. In the interim, Burns expected to be out of government.

Consequently, he was surprised when the President-elect summoned him to the Pierre and offered him a post on the White House staff with Cabinet rank, the only Presidential assistant to be given that status. In intimate discussions, such as this one, what Richard Nixon says is convoluted, circuitous and frequently open to multiple interpretations. Burns thought he was being offered a post equivalent to Deputy President for Domestic Affairs, filling the gap to be left by Nixon's emphasis on foreign policy. Some Nixon assistants said later that could not be what the President-elect intended. In any event, Burns said no, telling the President-elect that he had had enough of the White House staff nearly twenty years ago with Eisenhower and was not about to get back into that snakepit at age sixty-four. He did accept the President's request that he take overall charge of several then-unpublicized task forces covering many areas of policy, a job lasting some six weeks, and to be concluded in any event by Inauguration Day.

Had Burns said yes to the original staff offer with his conception of a Deputy President's mandate, the confusion that was to grip White House policy-making through 1969 would have been elevated to sheer chaos because of simultaneous overtures then being made to a very different kind of academician, Professor Daniel Patrick Moynihan of Harvard.

Moynihan had received a Ph.D. in political science from Tufts University's Fletcher School of Law and Diplomacy in 1961, but far more than Burns, Pat Moynihan had geared his career not to the academic life, but to politics: Assistant to Governor Averell Harriman of New York, Assistant Secretary of Labor in the Kennedy and Johnson administrations, unsuccessful candidate in 1965 for president of the New York City Council. A poor Irish boy from Hell's Kitchen, Moynihan's credentials were impeccably Democratic and liberal.

At least on the surface, that is. In the 1960s, after the death of John F. Kennedy, Moynihan and other old-style liberals were appalled by the neo-anarchistic tendencies of those liberals who uncompromisingly took up the banners of militant blacks and youth. In Moynihan's case, this alienation was given traumatic velocity by the vicious personal attack on him by Negro leaders over his publication of *The Negro Family: The Case for National Action,* a Labor Department staff study analyzing illegitimate births and other forms of social disintegration in the black ghetto. That abuse reached hysterical proportions in Moynihan's unhappy quest for public office in 1965. On returning to academic life, Moynihan found that his ideas and those of other old-style liberals whose work often appeared in *The Public Interest,* were increasingly finding common cause with innovative new Republican thinking. In 1967 one of the Republican innovators, Representative Melvin Laird of Wisconsin, asked Moynihan to contribute to a selection of writings on public affairs to be called *Republican Papers.* With Republicans concentrating then on the removal of Lyndon B. Johnson from the White House, the written word of Democrat Moynihan could not displease Republican Nixon: "The true task of American liberals would seem to be clear. We cannot do anything without the President, and the President seems determined to do nothing."

By the fall of 1967, Nixon noted to author Theodore White that he had been reading "this fellow Moynihan" and it was "very good stuff." In a paid speech over the CBS radio network on May 16, 1968, Nixon referred to Moynihan as a "thoughtful liberal," whose "insistence on more personal freedom and less government domination" was bringing him close to conservative doctrine. Laird, traveling aboard the campaign plane as a senior adviser, urged Nixon to give Moynihan a high post in the administration. Similar advice came from speech writers Raymond Price and William Safire and Lieutenant Governor Robert Finch of California, Nixon's long-time confidant who was traveling aboard the campaign plane. Finch was telling reporters the last week of the campaign that they could speculate with impunity on Pat Moynihan's winding up somewhere on the Nixon team.

Nixon had never met Moynihan. In conversations with aides, Nixon acknowledged that Moynihan's reputation was that of a tempestuous iconoclast, not easy to work with. But the President-elect expressed strong hope that he could be inveigled into the White House and channeled into constructive work there. Indeed, the idea of this voluble, charming Irishman among the buttoned-up Christian Scientists of the campaign staff appealed to the President-elect's hunger for novelty. Lacking any consistent ideology, Nixon was easily entranced by a novel idea or a bewitching personality.

As an omen of the future, the only objection at the Pierre to co-opting Moynihan came from Arthur Burns. Candid, confident of the correctness of his own views and not in the slightest concerned with currying favor with the President-elect, the crusty old economist thought the imminent Moynihan appointment was a bad idea and told Nixon exactly that, when asked for an opinion. Embracing anybody so clearly a partisan Democrat, Burns lectured Nixon in his deliberate tones, raised two serious questions. First, would Moynihan be so foreign to the rest of the White House staff as to constitute a disruptive influence? For instance, when he entered the White House Mess, would conversation subside? Second, and more ominously, could he really be a loyal member of the team or was his heart back in his ancestral party? Could this Hell's Kitchen Irishman work in harness with the methodical Germans and the lace-curtain Irishmen in the White House? Richard Nixon listened and, as is so often the case with this champion college debater, who actually loathes debating, made no substantive response. It was not the last time that Arthur Burns would give advice to the administration that was neither welcomed nor followed.

Moynihan first learned he was being considered at the Pierre when *Newsweek* reported in its November 18 issue that he might be named to the Cabinet. Moynihan suspected that this might be more than mere speculation when a week later, on November 25, *Newsweek* reported he was in line to become Secretary of Housing and Urban Development. Contacting friends at the Pierre, Moynihan found that he was indeed to be offered a high position. What followed was a series of meetings in New York with Nixon and his aides. No

Cabinet spot was offered. Instead, Moynihan was invited to take a place of high importance on the White House staff.* But again, the President-elect's lack of precision about what he wanted in domestic-policy staffing obscured exactly what, at that point, he envisaged for Moynihan, just as it had with Burns. Some Nixon men felt then and later that the President-elect was seeking no more than a liberal Democratic totem. But Moynihan himself, in analyzing his conversations with Nixon, got the clear impression that he was to be in charge of all domestic-policy formulation at the White House outside the economic sphere—an impression supported by other staffers.† Wonder enough that Nixon would consider a liberal Democrat for this assignment. Wonder even more that at the same moment he was still trying to persuade Burns to become Deputy President for Domestic Affairs, with Burns still refusing. How he thought Moynihan and Burns would coexist in the White House under these terms can only be guessed at.

The rationale for the role Moynihan fitted into came from Roy Ash, president of Litton Industries, already tapped by Nixon to run a study for massive reorganization of the federal government. It was Ash's notion at that time, later discarded, that appropriate Cabinet members should form into several "councils" to formulate policy, each with an executive secretary from the White House staff. The first of these was to be an Urban Affairs Council, and Moynihan was the automatic choice as secretary. It seemed to Moynihan that this mechanism, announced at the Pierre on December 10, could transcend urban affairs and approach in the domestic area what the National Security Council had become in the foreign—that is, surveying *all* domestic policy.

Nixon simply could not rid himself of his desire to give Burns a role. Robert F. Ellsworth, a former Congressman from Kansas who had been on Nixon's campaign team since 1967, proposed to Nixon a Cabinet-rank post of Counsellor—a generalist who would

*Although it had been leaked to the press, Nixon never seriously considered putting Moynihan at Housing and Urban Development, which went to Governor George Romney of Michigan.

†Moynihan was given the impression by Nixon that he would be a staff co-equal of Dr. Henry Kissinger in national security affairs as Director of the National Security Council staff and Dr. Paul McCracken in economic affairs as Chairman of the President's Council of Economic Advisers.

advise the President on a broad area of policy but have no administrative responsibilities. Ellsworth, himself a generalist of great capacity, not unnaturally had himself in mind for the role. Nixon jumped
at the idea, but his candidate to fill it was not Ellsworth but Burns.
Here was the very thing for Arthur Burns until he took over the
Federal Reserve post. In Nixon's mind, he would be the Cabinet
member without portfolio used widely in the European parliamen-
tary systems.

Arthur Burns came to Washington for Richard Nixon's inauguration on January 20, carrying with him the task-force reports to
be presented to the new President the next day. On that morning
he was ushered into the Oval Office and confronted for the first time
his old ally as President of the United States. He was impressed by
Nixon's new confidence, and had an odd feeling that the mystique
of the office was already at work. In that mood, Nixon for the first
time offered him the post of Counsellor, a role wholly different from
the previously offered Deputy President job. Burns scarcely had a
chance to refuse. The President ushered him into the Cabinet room
to show him the chair Burns would use at the long Cabinet table,
and then started a conversation about issues coming up. Burns
knew protest was useless. He was back on the White House
staff.

Thus, on January 23, the President surprised and mystified
nearly everybody by announcing the "major appointment" of Dr.
Burns—described as "a long-time friend and trusted adviser"—to
become the Counsellor to the President with Cabinet rank. There
immediately followed, inside and outside the White House, all manner of speculation. The *Wall Street Journal,* calling Burns "coordinator of domestic policy," wondered whether he "could
overshadow Cabinet officers." Press Secretary Ronald Ziegler clarified little when he explained that Moynihan would deal with specific
issues, while Burns would work on overall programs. In truth, nobody—not Burns, not Moynihan, not even Nixon—knew their relationship at this point.

To Pat Moynihan, the sudden emergence of Arthur Burns was
a most unpleasant surprise. He correctly perceived that the new
President, for some reason, had put Moynihan and Burns in adversary positions, competing for control of domestic policy. But for
what reason? Contrary to the explanation of some of his aides,

Richard Nixon was no Franklin Roosevelt placing opposites in positions of overlapping jurisdiction to achieve, through disorder, a creative synthesis. When his mind was on a problem, Nixon preferred to achieve results through far more orderly means. All the evidence is that his mind, fully engaged on foreign policy, simply was not clearly focused on domestic policy during those vague transitional days at the Pierre. The Moynihan-Burns confusion reflected a lack of direction in policies, organization and personnel by the man who had so long fought to be President.

In truth, there had been no hard thought about how domestic policy would be shaped, the relative roles of Moynihan and Burns in shaping it or even whether *either* of them was best equipped to run domestic policy. The confusion was costly, insuring that much of 1969 would be spent simply getting organized while the great course of events rushed on.

There was no such indecision in the foreign policy area. Here Nixon had the ready-made staff machinery of the National Security Council which had been evolving since Truman days. He also had a clear conception of whom he wanted to head it, and the identity of that individual was to prove the greatest surprise of all his appointments, with implications for his foreign policy then wholly unimaginable.

Henry Kissinger, a young son in a German-Jewish family which fled the Nazi terror, eventually became professor of government at Harvard, with periodic service to both Presidents Kennedy and Johnson as a foreign policy adviser. But he was best known for his intimate association with Governor Nelson Rockefeller of New York, blood enemy of Richard Nixon in one of the Republican Party's great vendettas. As a regular member of Rockefeller's vast stable of advisers over the years, Kissinger had heard Nixon's capabilities downgraded in a way that dovetailed with his own prejudices as a member of the Eastern academic establishment. To Kissinger, Nixon's foreign policy was grounded in gimmickry and shallowness. They had never met until December 1967, when they exchanged a few words at the Christmas party given in Manhattan by former Ambassador Clare Booth Luce. If Kissinger had summed up his feeling about Nixon in those earlier days, the word would have been "anathema."

But Kissinger, the laconic intellectual, fascinated Nixon as a remote figure who traveled in the highest intellectual and establishment circles and whose mind had turned out some of the most original thinking on the nuclear age. When Kissinger's landmark *Nuclear Weapons and Foreign Policy* was published in 1957, Vice President Nixon sent him a note of congratulations. He also sent Kissinger a letter of praise for his article in the *New York Times Magazine* of September 6, 1959, just before the 1959 summit meeting, warning of the perils of summitry with the Russians.

A decade later, during the 1968 campaign for President, Kissinger was asked to join Nixon's foreign policy advisory committee. He declined. Kissinger put no great store in a telephone call shortly after the 1968 election from the President-elect's personal aide, Dwight Chapin. Accepting Chapin's invitation to chat with Nixon at the Pierre, Kissinger assumed that the President-elect wanted his opinion on various members of the foreign policy crowd Kissinger knew so well.

Nixon certainly wanted that from Kissinger. But halfway through their conversation, Kissinger realized he wanted much more. In his indirect, convoluted way, Nixon was offering this virtual stranger the foremost staff job in foreign policy, Director of the National Security Council staff. As with Moynihan, here was a respected intellectual who under no conditions would have joined forces with Candidate Nixon but now was responding to the call of President-elect Nixon. Like other skeptical intellectuals meeting Nixon for the first time, Kissinger was startled and deeply impressed by his command of foreign affairs and his incisive mind. The formal offer came from Nixon at a second meeting two days later, and was accepted after another three days, during which Kissinger consulted Rockefeller and his other anti-Nixon friends.*

Richard Nixon had chosen as chief foreign policy adviser a man he barely knew and who had been associated most intimately with his political enemies. Ever the loner, in all his years of concentration

---

*Kissinger's appointment had the effect of reassuring some liberal Democrats who had wrongly regarded Nixon as nothing more than a saber-rattling cold warrior, much indeed as Kissinger had. For instance, Professor Arthur Schlesinger, Jr., of the City University of New York, a former colleague of Kissinger's at Harvard, delivered public and lavish praise of the Kissinger appointment.

on foreign policy, Nixon had failed to develop either a tutor or a protégé he could quickly place in this sensitive post once he was elected to the Presidency. Four weeks after his first serious conversation with Nixon, Henry Kissinger was to become the second most powerful figure on foreign policy—a remarkable development enhanced no little by the peculiar way in which Nixon named his Secretary of State.

In mid-October 1968, while the campaign for President raged, William P. Rogers seemed isolated from it all as he attended a Georgetown dinner party given by Mrs. Philip L. Graham, publisher of the *Washington Post* and *Newsweek*. He was absolutely certain, said Rogers in table conversation, that he would play no part in any Nixon administration. Indeed, he went on, he was taking no part then in the Presidential campaign of his old friend Dick Nixon.

There was a note of poignancy in that disavowal. As a Communist-hunting young Congressman in the late 1940s, Nixon had met young Bill Rogers, then counsel for a Senate investigating committee, and liked him immensely. In 1952, Nixon asked Rogers to travel on his Vice Presidential campaign plane as a political aide, a seemingly trivial decision that may have changed the course of history. By his calm and shrewd advice, Rogers, as much as anybody else, salvaged Nixon from his desperate crisis in that campaign when the exposure of a Nixon political fund back in California very nearly forced him off the ticket. After that, Rogers ranked high in that small company of Americans and even rarer company of public figures who are truly friends of Dick Nixon. When President Eisenhower suffered his heart attack in 1955, Rogers, then Deputy Attorney General (under Herbert Brownell), was the first person Vice President Nixon called. Later that day, Nixon moved into Rogers' house to be at the side of this sage counselor at a moment when a false step seeming to lean toward usurpation of power could destroy him forever.

Although they still talked frequently on the telephone, Rogers and Nixon were seeing much less of each other by the campaign of 1968, and the veracity of Rogers' disavowals at Mrs. Graham's dinner party is not to be doubted. Gregarious, charming and getting rich in the practice of law in New York and Washington (with such

clients as Mrs. Graham's publishing and broadcasting interests),
Rogers certainly was not looking for a reentry into national politics.
Nor did Nixon seem to be planning one for him. If Nixon had even
thought of Rogers as a prospect for Secretary of State, he confided
to no one.

His first choice was a strange figure in American politics: William Warren Scranton of Scranton, Pennsylvania, former Governor
of Pennsylvania, an aristocrat with liberal leanings, who, four years
after seeking office for the first time, became a Presidential prospect
in 1964, failed, and then left elective politics, vowing never to return.
His foreign policy experience was slight—as a low-level State Department aide briefly during the Eisenhower administration—but his
abiding interest in world affairs and forceful personality made him
a strong prospect for the post and eminently acceptable to the foreign
policy establishment. Nixon delegated Brownell to sound out Scranton. But Scranton sensed what Brownell was up to, and not wanting
the President-elect to be put in the position of being refused, stopped
him before the question was asked. Under no condition, said Scranton, would he accept any full-time job in any administration—not
Nixon's, not anybody's.

With Scranton eliminated, the foreign policy establishment (in
particular, the prestigious Council on Foreign Relations) turned to
C. Douglas Dillon, the urbane ex-diplomat now reigning in the Wall
Street house of Dillon Read. Dillon, a major contributor to the
Republican Party over the years, had, as Eisenhower's Under Secretary of State, known Nixon well. But he never had a chance. He had
been entered twice on that invisible ledger of past wrongs kept so
meticulously by Richard Nixon. First, Dillon had failed to ask Nixon's approval in advance before becoming the resident Republican
in John F. Kennedy's Cabinet as Secretary of the Treasury in 1961.
Second, and perhaps more important, Nixon felt that Dillon had
joined the Republican elite of Manhattan in snubbing him at the low
point of his life when he moved to New York following his defeat
in the race for governor of California in 1962. Instead of inviting
Nixon into their clubs and homes, the rich Republicans, who had
never liked him anyway, now ignored him as a has-been beneath
their notice. That was something the poor boy from Yorba Linda,
California, could never forget. The opposition to Dillon as Secretary
of State from Congressman Mel Laird, expressed personally and

forcefully to Nixon at the Pierre, only reinforced his own determination.

But if not Scranton or Dillon, then who? The cupboard was bare. Incredibly, the President-elect so immersed in foreign policy had a far better idea of whom he did *not* want than whom he did want. Into the vacuum came those two hoary Republican practitioners, former Governor Thomas E. Dewey of New York and his old lieutenant Herb Brownell. They strongly recommended Rogers to Nixon, and Nixon was receptive. Rogers' weakness—the fact that his foreign policy experience was limited to a brief term on the U.S. Mission team at the United Nations and that his interest in the field was minimal—was overlooked in the broader context of finding a Secretary of State with whom Nixon would feel comfortable and who would be absolutely trustworthy in carrying out the President's orders. After all, this was a President who believed in being his own Secretary of State. The problems, bound to be magnified in the weeks ahead, of an unqualified Secretary of State were scarcely perceived at the Pierre.

But there is something even more puzzling. William Scranton, fiercely independent, would have been a forceful figure at the State Department and a dominant personality in the Cabinet, as Nixon was well aware. He was selected, then, not for his compatibility with or loyalty to the President-elect, but for his intrinsic capability. Why, then, would the second choice be selected for apparently opposite reasons? The answer can only be found in the broader question of Nixon's Cabinet, selected without pattern or theme, first laboriously and finally in haste.

Flying aboard *Air Force One*, supplied by President Johnson, from New York to Key Biscayne, Fla., for a vacation soon after his victory, the President-elect was tossing around names in a casual bull session with aides. Somebody mentioned David Rockefeller, head of the Chase Manhattan Bank, for Secretary of the Treasury, but then demurred on the assumption that Nelson Rockefeller would surely be in the Cabinet, either at State or Defense.

"I guess," said the aide, "that David is out because you can't have two Rockefellers in the Cabinet."

"There is no law," replied Nixon quietly, "that you have to have *one.*" Having resurrected himself fighting the Rockefellers every step of the way, Nixon wanted no Rockefeller in his Cabinet. And having said that, precisely what he *did* want in his Cabinet was fundamentally an open question. Not surprisingly, then, the Cabinet selections proved an exercise in confusion, revealing once again the lack of any clear purpose as the administration began.

First, there was dawdling. Next came refusals for the Cabinet's most prestigious positions. Scranton turned down Secretary of State. Far more shattering was the refusal by Senator Henry M. (Scoop) Jackson of Washington to become Secretary of Defense. Laird had proposed him for the Pentagon shortly after the election, and it was appreciated by Nixon at the Pierre as a stroke of political genius. Jackson was that high-level Democrat Nixon had been seeking for his Cabinet. A one-time Democratic National Chairman (during the 1960 campaign lost by Nixon), Jackson voted liberal on domestic issues and hard anti-Communist in international affairs. His contacts at the Pentagon were superb and his knowledge of the military establishment unmatched on Capitol Hill. What's more, he wanted the job. His prospects for national office had dimmed with the Democratic Party's moving leftward on foreign policy, and this seemed a way to cap a distinguished career. He gave Nixon a tentative yes. But when word leaked out, Democratic senators pressured Jackson in brutal fashion. One of them, Senator Edward M. Kennedy of Massachusetts, warned that Jackson's old colleagues in the Democratic cloakroom would make the Senate a living hell for him as Richard Nixon's Defense Secretary. Jackson regretfully declined, and another vacancy remained unfilled.

And thanks to a public relations gimmick, Nixon was laboring under a stringent deadline. The press had been grumbling that Nixon was far behind the pace set by John F. Kennedy during the last transition eight years earlier in naming his Cabinet. In reply, Frank Shakespeare, a Columbia Broadcasting System vice president who had been a communications consultant for Nixon during the campaign and was to become director of the U.S. Information Agency, thought up the idea of an unprecedented television spectacular over a nationwide hookup at which Nixon would present *all* Cabinet nominees at once. In order to get everybody ready for the cameras the evening of December 11, fast footwork was necessary.

Rogers was selected without much deliberation. When Scoop Jackson gave Nixon the bad news, the President-elect instinctively

turned to one of his chief talent scouts, Mel Laird, and talked him
into leaving his place of enormous power in the House. Nixon's real
choice for Secretary of the Interior, Representative Rogers C. B.
Morton of Maryland, proved unacceptable to Western Republicans
strictly for reasons of geography, and Nixon turned to Governor
Walter Hickel of Alaska. Two telephone calls nailed Hickel into the
Cabinet. Arthur Burns recommended a fellow economist, George
Shultz, Dean of the University of Chicago Graduate School of Business, to become Secretary of Labor. Nixon met him for the first time
at the Century Plaza Hotel in Los Angeles, engaged in a little talk
and approved him.*

The Cabinet selection process seemed even more haphazard
than under John F. Kennedy. Never deeply interested in economic
questions, Nixon was elected without the slightest idea whom he
wanted for the vital Treasury portfolio. Maurice Stans, the New
York financier who was Eisenhower's Budget Director and a fantas-
tically able money-raiser for Nixon's Presidential campaign starting
in the early days when it seemed quixotic, desperately wanted the job
himself. Against him was the weight of the financial community,
which felt that Stans lacked sufficient stature for this traditional
position of power. So it was that Dr. Charls Walker, lobbyist for the
American Bankers Association, picked up his telephone the day after
Nixon's election and placed calls to two Republican pillars of Wall
Street: Banker George Champion (David Rockefeller's predecessor
as top man at Chase Manhattan) and financier Robert Anderson
(Secretary of the Treasury under Eisenhower). "I hear Maurice Stans
is going to be Secretary of the Treasury," Walker told each. When

---

*Shultz had earlier turned down a request by Nixon to coordinate all the task
forces because he was on a fellowship at the Center for Advanced Study of Behav-
ioral Sciences at Stanford University, Palo Alto, California, to finish work on a book
in collaboration with Albert Rees (later published in 1969 as *Workers and Wages
in an Urban Labor Market*). Economist Milton Friedman, Shultz's colleague at the
University of Chicago who was helping to establish the task force operation, grumbled to friends about Shultz's rejection. Friedman's point was that Shultz was not
a serious macro-economist engaged in vital academic research—a theme that would
be echoed time and again two years hence inside the administration by Shultz's
critics—and therefore had no valid reason to turn down the assignment for his
California study. When later asked to join the Cabinet, Shultz did not hesitate in
giving up his California sojourn.

they expressed disbelief, he shot back: "Well, that's the word I hear." What could be done about it? Walker was asked. "Well, you can't beat something with nothing."

He then unveiled his "something": Chicago banker David Kennedy, a moderate Republican who could have had Treasury in the Johnson administration, and, based largely on his excellent work as head of a Presidential commission named by Johnson to reform the budget, commanded widespread bipartisan respect on Capitol Hill. Within hours, Champion and Anderson had fed Kennedy's name to John Mitchell, Nixon's law partner and campaign manager. By week's end, David Kennedy was selected.* As with every other Cabinet post, there was no effort to relate nominee to policy, for the policy on almost everything—including Treasury—was an unfathomable void.

Kennedy brought with him one of his fellow executives at the Continental Illinois Bank, Robert Mayo, suggesting that he could work well with him and that he would make a splendid Director of the Budget. The easy acquiescence to this by Nixon and Mitchell revealed their ignorance of the operation of the Executive Office of the President. The Director of the Bureau of the Budget is not a subordinate of the Secretary of the Treasury but is, rather, a Cabinet-level officer with vastly *more* power than most members of the Cabinet. The fact that Mayo had rapport with Kennedy but not with Nixon, a fact ignored at the Pierre, would have repercussions long after Mayo and Kennedy had both left the administration.

There was, however, one member of the Cabinet who was there not by chance or expediency but because Richard Nixon insisted that he be there. In John Mitchell, Richard Nixon at long last, after twenty-two years, countless campaigns and two shattering defeats, had found a campaign manager. More than that, he had found the first man in his political life who could tell Nixon what to do— strong, decisive, tough. Nixon was not about to let that man leave him now that he was entering the White House.

In early 1968 with a long, hard campaign still before him, Nixon had already gone through two campaign managers and was on his third—Bob Ellsworth—with no telling how many more would be

---

*A month later, Kennedy selected Walker as his Under Secretary, but there was no political deal involved.

run over before election day or how much damage this would do his Presidential prospects. It was then that Mitchell, a millionaire bond lawyer new to Nixon's law firm in New York, entered the picture. With a speed and agility that dismayed Nixon's old political friends, Mitchell not only seized power from Ellsworth and all other rivals but did what Leonard Hall, Robert Finch, Bob Ellsworth and many others had failed to do over the years: get Richard Nixon to listen and obey the man he put in charge of his political campaign.

By the spring of 1968, Mitchell was confident enough in his position to bluntly inform a luncheon of pro-Nixon Congressmen in a private dining room of the Capitol that there was now a new manner of doing things for Richard Nixon: "You people know Dick Nixon perhaps better than I do, and you think he can't have a campaign manager. I've got news for you: I'm his campaign manager, and I'm running the show. I bring more business into the law firm than he does. When I tell Dick Nixon what to do, he listens. I'm in charge. So, if you have questions about the campaign, call me. But you won't be able to reach me because I'll be busy electing a President of the United States. I'll get your message. But call *me,* don't call *him* [Nixon], because *I'm* running this campaign." Dumbstruck at this lecture by a Wall Street lawyer, the twenty or so Congressmen sat in awed silence.

The way Mitchell performed at that luncheon revealed much about the reasons for his success in handling Nixon, and those reasons were more psychological than political. A political novice when he entered the Nixon law firm in 1966, Mitchell never gained full mastery over the political names and faces in 1968; his strategy of rejecting the liberal Democratic vote that defected from Hubert Humphrey at the Chicago convention, not to mention his deliberate shunning of the black vote, very nearly proved fatal for Richard Nixon. But political genius or not, Mitchell as no one before him fulfilled an unmet need in Nixon. Perhaps, as in that luncheon performance, he was the man Nixon himself had always wanted to become, and sometimes pretended to be: saturnine, totally self-assured, hard, domineering, steely-eyed, insulting or charming as the occasion required. Not ever could Nixon have managed so insulting a lecture to anybody, much less Congressmen never met before. Nixon, who hated face-to-face confrontations with his enemies and literally could not bear to criticize a subordinate to his face, could only look with awe at his dour campaign manager. "Nixon in 1968," explained a mutual friend, "was a man of deep uncertainties, and here in Mitchell was this fellow who didn't have any uncertainties at all and was able, smart. Nixon needed him."

Nixon, reviled by a generation of liberals as a man of no conviction, in truth has a Utopian and idealistic streak running through him. His hero is Woodrow Wilson, the martyred President, and his decisions in the Presidency were often to be predicated on his strong concepts of national pride and prestige. None of that in Mitchell, the supreme pragmatist. Does John Mitchell believe in anything? "Yes," replied one of his enemies on the Nixon staff, "he believes in the advancement of John Mitchell, his family and his friends." Perhaps Richard Nixon perceived this; more likely not. But in any case, it did not matter. What was good for Richard Nixon in 1968 was good for John Mitchell, and the other way around as well.

So it was that at the Pierre, Nixon turned most often to his pipe-smoking, unsmiling law partner for advice. When Bob Finch, Nixon's protégé and alter ego, chose to be Secretary of Health, Education and Welfare instead of Attorney General (a choice fraught with fateful consequences), Nixon insisted that Mitchell take the Justice portfolio. Mitchell had told friends that under no circumstances would he uproot his family from Rye, New York, and move them to Washington, and perhaps he meant it. But when the time came, he did not say no to the President. He was, everybody understood, to be a very great deal more than Attorney General.

Placing John Mitchell in his Cabinet was, then, no afterthought for Nixon. It was the highest imperative in any personnel decision he made in those early days. There was one other personnel decision Nixon made that was also an imperative, but with a reverse twist. That was to get Ray C. Bliss out as Republican National Chairman. The Bliss imperative and why Nixon felt so strongly about firing him as the party chairman revealed almost as much about the new President as did the Mitchell imperative.

In that era of good feeling when General Eisenhower served with magisterial nonpartisanship, the Republican Party's state and county leaders yearned for the day when one of their own—Richard M. Nixon—would be President. At long last, they felt, the party structure would then be given its place in the sun and federal patronage would be used to advance Republicanism. Certainly, not since William McKinley entered the White House had a Republican President enjoyed such lavish confidence on the part of the party faithful. Thanks to modern communications and transportation, no previous Republican President had been in contact so many times with so many party factotums across the country.

Yet, even before Richard Nixon was inaugurated, that warm glow had disappeared, never to return. Two acts, explicable not in rational terms but only in terms of human relationships, soured the old intimacy between the new President and his party with astounding speed.

The first was a horrendous beginning in the business of dispensing federal patronage. John Sears, a twenty-eight-year-old lawyer in Nixon's firm who had been traveling the country in search of delegates for him since the beginning in 1967, was to be the political aide in the White House, providing liaison between the President and Republican national headquarters, state chairmen and party politicians generally. Sears had proposed to Nixon that his duties include surveillance of patronage to make sure it served the best political advantage, and the President-elect agreed. Tough, bright and gregarious, Sears had become well known and well liked among the party pros. They liked the arrangement.

But not John Mitchell. Sears had made the fatal error of crossing the man that younger Nixon workers had come to call *El Supremo*. A hard-boiled Irishman from Notre Dame, Sears was neither impressed nor intimidated by the Mitchell hauteur and showed no compunction in contradicting him in staff meetings.* Even before the Miami Beach convention, Sears' stock had begun to fall. Typically, there was not a word of criticism from Nixon himself, but Mitchell's hostility hung heavy. The word was spread that Sears spent far too

*The most intense of these came in New York early in 1968 when the Nixon staff was searching for a press secretary. Mitchell suggested Frank Shakespeare, the hot-tempered CBS vice president on leave as Nixon's television consultant. Shakespeare's contacts with the working press tended to be stormy, and Sears shot back that the idea was disaster. Sears then went on to charge that Mitchell was not looking for an effective press spokesman but a network executive whose ability to offer or deny high-paying television news jobs in the future might influence some correspondents. Mitchell dropped the idea but thereafter intensified his hostility toward Sears.

much time talking and drinking with news correspondents, the hallmark of unreliability to the manager of a candidate who had never
forgiven the press for its indignities, particularly when the manager
nurtured the candidate's prejudices. By campaign time in 1968,
Mitchell had managed to banish Sears to the lowly level of traveling
with the Vice Presidential candidate, Spiro T. Agnew. Clearly,
Mitchell, growing in power with each passing day, would not permit
Sears to have the patronage plum.

While Sears and other political aides were cooling their heels,
with little to do after the election, in Nixon's Washington headquarters on Pennsylvania Avenue one block from the White House,
Mitchell acted at the Pierre. Without consulting Nixon, he designated a patronage chief in the White House: Harry Flemming, a
twenty-eight-year-old former City Council member from Alex-
andria, Va., and son of Arthur Flemming, president of Macalester
College and Secretary of Health, Education and Welfare in Eisenhower's day. With no knowledge of the convoluted federal job structure and scarcely less expertise in Republican Party affairs,
Flemming was handed a nightmarish task that, incredibly, had been
ignored until the last minute. For all the talk of taking over the
federal establishment, the Nixon planners had no idea how to go
about it. Flemming was clearly understood to be Mitchell's man in
the White House, but Mitchell was engrossed in so many details of
the transition that he had no time to help his lieutenant set up a
patronage system.

As for Nixon's agreement that Sears handle the political aspects
of patronage, it was soon forgotten. The President-elect, unlike Lyndon B. Johnson, could not keep all such minutiae in place. To the
party politicians, the Flemming appointment and the exclusion of
Sears seemed filled with ill omens.

It was the second act, the purge of Ray Bliss, that particularly
dismayed the state party leaders. To most of them, Bliss was the
quintessence of professionalism, the symbol of ideological neutrality
that had led the party back from the abyss, following the debacle of
1964 when conservative ideologues had been permitted to run rampant. There had been a time when Richard Nixon agreed. Writing in
1962, Nixon called Bliss, then Ohio state chairman, "one of the best
political craftsmen in the nation [who] sets an example . . . that I wish
all Republican State Chairmen would follow. He always kept in

mind Will Hays' simple axiom that it is the responsibility of a party chairman 'not to eliminate but to assimilate.' " In 1965 Nixon helped arrange the difficult transfer of power from Barry Goldwater's campaign staff, then controlling the Republican National Committee, to Bliss, the overwhelming party choice to be new national chairman.

Bliss' unexciting style, emphasizing nuts-and-bolts political techniques and ignoring ideology, was precisely what was needed by a party sapped by doctrinal struggles. His popularity soared with the remarkable Republican comeback in the midterm elections of 1966, but it was precisely that moment of triumph which brought the costly split with Nixon that was to terminate Bliss' career in national politics.

Nixon was traveling the country in behalf of Republican Congressional candidates, and as the only national party figure making such a tour, felt that the Republican National Committee should supply a plane or at least share the costs. Bliss refused on the wholly defensible grounds that the National Committee should not supply special aid to a potential candidate for the 1968 Presidential nomination when his rivals were paying their own expenses in races for governor elsewhere. Stung by Bliss' refusal, Nixon came back with one more request of Bliss. During the closing days of the 1966 campaign, President Johnson momentarily lost his self-control and delivered a tirade against Nixon that did the Republicans far more good than harm. Nixon proposed that Bliss scrap a dreary election-eve program and substitute for it a film of Johnson's attack, followed by Nixon's reply. Again Bliss refused, on grounds that this would be a boost for Nixon financed by the National Committee. Nixon was outraged and bitter in his private invective against Bliss. To Bliss himself, Nixon characteristically said nothing. A black mark was quietly entered against him on that invisible ledger.

That was the determining factor in 1968, though not the only one. Nixon and his political operatives now began to feel that Bliss' reputation as a nuts-and-bolts mechanic was grossly overblown, a sharp contradiction of Nixon's own words in 1962. Whether or not this was a rationalization, Nixon now decided he needed an articulate spokesman (which Bliss decidedly was not), instead of a technician in the national chairmanship, usually a requirement for the party without a spokesman in the White House. The Nixon high command discussed the feasibility of purging Bliss when Nixon was nominated at Miami Beach in July but decided it would be too divisive on the eve of a campaign. After the election would be soon enough.

Thus, the proper scenario was obvious. Soon after the election, Nixon could telephone Bliss, explain his feelings and ask him to resign by a certain date. An old political soldier, Bliss of course would comply without a whimper and, much to Nixon's and Mitchell's satisfaction, Ray Bliss would be packed up for his way back to Ohio. But, astonishingly, that call to Bliss was never placed—partly a sign of the lack of planning and organization by the supposedly superefficient Nixon forces at the Pierre, partly because Nixon was concentrating on something else and had no time for politics, partly because of Nixon's habitual disinclination for face-to-face confrontations of an unpleasant nature. No President has had more difficulty drawing himself up to fire somebody.

Predictably, word that Nixon wanted Bliss replaced leaked to the press in late November, and just as predictably Republican politicians were outraged. Republican state chairmen began organizing a lobbying campaign to keep Bliss in the chairmanship. When the President-elect attended the winter meeting of the Republican Governors Association at Palm Springs, Calif., in early December, he was greeted by individual pleas from the governors to keep Bliss on as National Chairman; a formal resolution followed. By their incompetence, Nixon and Mitchell had done exactly what they most wanted to avoid: a public debate, barely one month after election day, over whether the new President ought to purge his respected party chairman. But Nixon was adamant that Bliss go.

Some two months too late, on January 10, Bliss was finally summoned to the Pierre for a meeting with Nixon. For two hours Nixon, Bliss and Bryce Harlow, a senior political adviser to the President, talked politics. It was made clear that Nixon wanted Bliss out of the national chairmanship, and replaced by a party spokesman. But as so often would prove to be the case, when Richard Nixon was trying to fire somebody, there was confusion. Nixon wanted Bliss out just as soon as possible—immediately, that is—to close the nasty chapter. But he buttered up Bliss with so much praise (calling his organizational work "superb") that the chairman thought the President-elect was letting him write his own departure ticket—later, when things had calmed down, perhaps June or July or some other time.

The resulting newspaper stories, based on Bliss' account, were sheer disaster. "Bliss Agrees to Stay as Chairman," read the headline in the *Washington Post*. The story said Bliss had agreed to "continue indefinitely," hinting his tenure might even last through the 1970 elections. To counter these stories, Nixon aides leaked reports that Bliss would go, and would go soon. Things were back to where they had been right after the election, with party leaders justifiably angry that Richard Nixon was treating a true and loyal party functionary with undeserved shabbiness. When the Nixon team moved from the Pierre to the White House, the matter remained unresolved with yet greater difficulties ahead. The new President, champion of the party pros, had gotten off to a surprisingly bad start as party leader that was to prove prophetic.

On October 22, 1968, Vicki Lynn Cole, thirteen, daughter of a Methodist minister, was on her way to the train station in her home town of Deshler, Ohio, to see Richard M. Nixon's whistle-stop campaign. Vicki carried a Nixon-for-President sign, but as she entered the crush she was jostled and pushed into the crowd, and lost her sign. She then noticed a poster lying on the ground reading "Bring Us Together Again." For something to hold, she picked it up and pushed her way close to the speaker's platform, setting off a chain of events that pointed to the philosophic formlessness of the Nixon administration.

Nixon noted Vicki's sign in the crowd and told his staff about it, remembering it as "Bring Us Together." Speech writer William Safire wrapped the idea into a victory statement for Nixon, prepared on Election Day but not given to Nixon until his victory was assured. As worked over by Nixon, the victory statement delivered early the next morning concluded with these words:

> I saw many signs of this campaign, some of them were not friendly, some of them were very friendly. But the one that touched me the most was one that I saw in Deshler, Ohio, at the end of a long day of whistle-stopping.
>
> A little town. I suppose five times the population was there in the dusk. It was almost impossible to see, but a teen-ager held up a sign: "Bring us together."
>
> And that will be the great objective of this administration at the outset, to bring the American people together. This will be an open administration, open to new ideas, open to men and women of both

parties, open to the critics as well as those who support us. We want to bridge the generation gap. We want to bridge the gap between the races. We want to bring America together. And I am confident that this task is one that we can undertake, and one in which we will be successful.

These words of reconciliation were taken to heart after a bitter year of unrelieved recrimination and hostility. Indeed, the Nixon Inaugural Committee was so impressed that it was about to adopt "Bring Us Together" as the theme for Richard Nixon's inauguration. Immediately recognizing that Nixon was in danger of creating a Frankenstein monster in the Safire-composed victory statement, Safire was appalled. "That wasn't the theme of the campaign," he reminded Nixon's right-hand man, H. R. (Bob) Haldeman. As a result, Haldeman managed to get the theme changed to "Forward Together." But the damage had been done. Every time the new President said or proposed something that was not intended to bring all of America together again, the slogan in his victory statement would be tossed back in his teeth by the press and his political opposition.*

And built into the Nixon campaign were proposals based on campaign pledges that by their very nature were either divisive or at least nonconciliatory: Southern conservative judges on the Supreme Court for the benefit of the South; mandatory quotas for the benefit of the textile industry; retention of special trade and tax benefits for the benefit of the oil industry.

Indeed, "Bring Us Together" was antithetical to the doctrine of John Mitchell. His conviction was that a certain definable constituency elected Richard Nixon, and the correct political course of the President now was to satisfy its needs, not those of his enemies who would never vote for him anyway. To Mitchell, a second Nixon term depended on keeping his own vote of 1968 and being able to win over the vote of segregationist third-party candidate George Wallace should Wallace not run again. Apart from their personal differences, this was a point of contention between Mitchell and vast numbers of Republican professionals, including John Sears. Sears felt that

---

*It also provided the title for the first inside exposé by a former Nixon administration official. *Bring Us Together,* by Leon Panetta, who had been fired as chief of the civil rights section of the Department of Health, Education and Welfare, was published on April 21, 1971.

policy should be softened to defuse, though not necessarily win over, the enemy. Sears' ideas were a minority view at the Pierre. Soon Sears was on his way back to private life, while Mitchell was reaching new heights of power.

But that is not quite the whole story. Richard Nixon believed in *both* Mitchellism and "Bring Us Together." In the next two years, he would reserve his greatest enthusiasms for hurling thunderbolts —at the Senate for Supreme Court nominations rejected, at the Congress for spendthrift money bills vetoed, at the liberal establishment for ignoring the Silent Majority (which he extolled), at collegiate "bums"—all of which mocked the theme on the little girl's placard. But there was another aspect to Nixon, the starry-eyed Wilsonian who talked movingly to his staff about exactly where Woodrow Wilson had sat and worked and slept in the White House. That Nixon, wanting desperately to be something indefinable that he wasn't—to be admired? respected? understood?—privately authorized studies and surveys on college campuses to try to understand what it was about him that students so obviously scorned. That Nixon went strolling to the Lincoln Memorial in the small hours to reach out his hand to the students, but couldn't find the right words and ended up talking football.

There was, then, a deep ambivalence of purpose, the darker side of which was far more damaging than confusions over domestic policy-making or the slapdash selection of a Cabinet. Nixon projected an alternating image of mailed fist on one side, occasional olive branch on the other. That was the worst brand of politics, infuriating his enemies and disturbing his friends, because it seemed based on expediency. That ambivalence surfaced in the precise hour of his great election triumph when Richard Nixon cried "Bring us together"—just once; never before, nor after.

III

The President's Men

The first impression that one gets of a ruler and of his brains is from seeing the men that he has about him.
—Niccolò Machiavelli, in
The Prince

Some [assistants] . . . acknowledge, that if the [staff] system as it has evolved to date is judged by some of the results, the President ought to be even more dissatisfied than he is said to be.
—John Osborne, in
The Nixon Watch

On the morning of April 7, 1969, the Cabinet-level Urban Affairs Council convened at the White House, Richard M. Nixon presiding, to engage in a dialogue that would not have been faintly conceivable a few months before. At issue was the Model Cities program, and nothing symbolized more clearly Lyndon B. Johnson's Great Society at its worst: a program grandiose and euphoric in its conception, raising lavish hopes, but undernourished in its planning and financing. In theory, Model Cities was supposed to select certain poor neighborhoods of certain cities for an infusion of federal funds for projects that would then serve as a "model" for other communities. In practice, the program was a shambles. When the Republicans took over on January 20, they found an unwelcome legacy left them by the Democrats at the Department of Housing and Urban Development (HUD). There was no clear blueprint of either how the money was to be spent or how the "models" would be used else-where. Far worse, the Johnson administration had not decided *which* cities would receive the new federal subsidy. It did not even have a rationale for choosing them. Thus, the Nixon men entering HUD confronted hundreds of mayors, hard-pressed for money, clamoring for inclusion in the Model Cities program. To satisfy even half of them would cost far more than the $750 million budgeted for Model Cities by Johnson during the forthcoming fiscal year.

Surely, if any Great Society nostrum was a candidate for oblivion under Nixon, it was Model Cities. Professor Edward Banfield of Harvard, the distinguished conservative urbanologist, who headed Nixon's postelection task force on the cities, considered it feckless. Daniel Patrick Moynihan, ranking Democrat and urbanologist in the White House, regarded it as trivial. And as for Richard M. Nixon, if he gave it any thought at all, he must have assumed that Model Cities would be junked. Among the very few threads of substance in his campaign was the very strong impression that just such ill-conceived programs of the Great Society would be dismantled forthwith.

Yet, on that early spring morning in Washington, President Nixon and the Urban Affairs Council were to receive a very different recommendation. George W. Romney, the liberal Republican Governor of Michigan who had made a spectacularly inept attempt to win the 1968 Presidential nomination from Nixon and had wound up as his Secretary of Housing and Urban Development, had brought to the meeting a staff paper that recommended a continuation of the Model Cities program. To be sure, it would be given a new sheen: greater emphasis on private enterprise, less (but only 4 percent less) federal spending, extension to *all* poverty neighborhoods instead of just selected neighborhoods, more efficient procedures. But, polished or not, it was still Model Cities, now to be given a Nixon imprimatur.

That did not please Nixon. Preoccupied though he was with foreign affairs, he assumed that his administration would be quick in shedding excess baggage of the Great Society. Typically, however, he did not directly challenge Romney's recommendation. Also typically, he began his questioning of Romney by attacking a wholly tangential aspect of the question. "What is the attitude of the governors toward the Model Cities program?" asked the President. Implicit in the question was a notion widely held at the White House in 1969 that the Nixon administration should ignore the overwhelmingly Democratic mayors and concentrate instead on the state governors, preponderantly Republican after the elections of 1966 and 1968. And, obvious to all, these governors were not the slightest bit interested in the Model Cities program.

Obvious though it might have been, however, ex-Governor Romney would not concede it was. The governors, he replied to Nixon, are "very anxious to participate."

"How do we bring [the Governors] in?" Nixon persisted. "We know the jealousies between the cities and many states."

Romney replied in bureaucratese about states possibly being represented on review boards passing on Model Cities applications.

Now drowning in procedural details, Nixon—working as usual from the outside toward the center on a problem—began moving toward his real objections to Model Cities, while maintaining typical balance between his criticism of the program and praise for Romney's report: "My concern—though the study is excellent—is about going for broke on a program at best experimental. This is putting a lot of eggs in this basket. The cautionary notes in here about going step by step are well taken. The main thing you have to look at is the question of whether this is the right thing, whether this is where we put the money."

In reply, Romney gave the President the same line he would give the press: The revised program is designed to "get us off the money kick" by concentrating on procedures.

Clearly unsatisfied, Nixon continued to voice his concerns about overinvestment in the program: "Consider Model Cities and homes or housing. There is only so much energy and effort we are capable of. I'd be concerned to have an inordinate amount thrown into this, compared to the more tangible things. You could go hog-wild on this, as Congress did."

Floyd Hyde, who had quit as mayor of Fresno, Calif., to become Assistant Secretary of HUD, with responsibility for Model Cities, commented that a few cities—notably Seattle—had plans for using Model Cities money that had been fairly well thought out.

"Don't raise hopes we will dash," responded Nixon, moving ever closer to the heart of his real opposition and to the language that might have been used by any Republican county chairman in talking of Great Society spending programs. "I can see in Model Cities one of the most horrible boondoggles in history. You mention Seattle, but have you seen some Model Cities committees in other cities? Pretty sad."

Romney responded with what would become a favorite ploy in the Nixon administration: masking essentially liberal programs with conservative Republican rhetoric. The revised Model Cities program, said Romney, "places responsibility at the local and not the Washington level."

His objections growing more pointed, Nixon was now traveling rapidly toward the conventional Republican view of overeducated social engineers disrupting the delicate balance that otherwise would have prevailed under laissez faire. "God knows," said the President, "you turn the social planners loose and it is sorry."

The response was more protective Republican rhetoric. Back home in Fresno, Hyde told the President, the Model Cities committee was run not by those "social planners" but with deep involvement from the business community (described by Hyde as people "who don't screw around").

That only pushed Nixon deeper into the language of the county chairmen: "In most other cities, there is apathy, leaving it to the dregs and social reformers. We must keep from putting too many eggs in this basket. After this year, we hope to have more money; then the question of priorities comes up. Where is it the surest? Lots of places are sure now—hunger, the first five years of life, housing. But Model Cities?"

When the President then asked what the program would show after a year's operation, Hyde gave Seattle as an example of what could be accomplished. "Yes," shot back Nixon, a bit edgy, "pick the best one."

Romney, hot-tempered and unaccustomed to working under anybody, was getting restive about all the Presidential nit-picking. "We're late already on the development of our policy," he said impatiently. "We have to know *you* want to pull this together. It isn't going to work if you don't. No Cabinet officer can pull it together."

Before the President could reply, Dr. Moynihan intervened as executive secretary of the Urban Affairs Council with a bureaucratic ploy intended to end the discussion. "We see the line of your questioning," he told the President, " and will get you staff papers on these points."

For his part, Nixon responded with another ploy, changing the topic from discussion of substance to the name of the programs—thereby implying his acquiescence in continuation of Model Cities. "On the name," asked the President, "since it is a different program, have you strong feelings about what it should be?"

"I'd ride it through on 'Model Cities' since if we try to change it," replied Romney, "we'll get into a battle with charges that we're killing it. It is not as important as the concept and selling it."

Moynihan closed with a piquant note: "Shall we make the rule that we change the name only when we don't change the program?"

Thus did President Nixon acquiesce, perhaps to his own astonishment, in Model Cities. Romney's role in forcing that acquiescence stemmed from his Mormon missionary zeal of adopting whatever he found in the cupboard when he arrived at HUD. But Moynihan's patronage of HUD, far more influential with the President than Romney's, was based on a conscious grand strategy of government.

When Pat Moynihan arrived at the Pierre Hotel fresh from Harvard in November 1968, he had carried with him one overriding concept: the violence, disillusionment and instability of the late 1960s had so divided the nation that the very legitimacy of government was in question. To buttress that legitimacy, Moynihan wanted to impress upon Nixon the axiom of government that had become thoroughly established in British practice but somewhat less so in American: A conservative government coming into power does not undo the really important programs of a preceding liberal government. From his reading of 1968 campaign statements, Moynihan feared a wholesale dismantling of the Great Society by Richard Nixon that would threaten further divisions in America. To convince the new President of the unwisdom of this move became Moynihan's top priority, a Moynihan Doctrine.

The most important Great Society program vulnerable to elimination was the antipoverty program carried on by the Office of Economic Opportunity (OEO), the first new domestic program initiated by Lyndon Johnson in 1964 after John Kennedy's death and the target for endless harangues from conservative Republicans the past five years. The campaign oratory of Richard Nixon promised an early end to one part of the program, the Job Corps (which ran camps to train unemployed youths), and hinted broadly that the entire program was in jeopardy. An Assistant Secretary of Labor in the Johnson administration, Moynihan had been in on OEO's con-

ception, and although he had been publicly critical of what it had
evolved into, he was unwilling under terms of the Moynihan Doctrine to preside over its evisceration.* Following Moynihan's advice,
Nixon made an early decision to continue the antipoverty program.
In a February 19 message to Congress, Nixon not only proposed a
renewal of legislation authorizing OEO but even reprieved the seemingly doomed Job Corps (while transferring it from OEO to the
Labor Department).

Having decided to keep OEO alive, Nixon set off in search of
not any social reformer but a Republican manager to run it. His
selection was Donald Rumsfeld, a thirty-six-year-old Congressman
from the rich North Shore suburbs of Chicago whose conservative
voting record included a vote against OEO when it first came up in
1964. Surrendering his safe seat in Congress after insistent urging
from Nixon, Rumsfeld on April 21 was named Director of OEO and
Presidential assistant with Cabinet rank. He immediately embraced
the spirit of the Moynihan Doctrine. While attempting to systema-
tize OEO and make it an engine for helping the poor instead of
restructuring the system, Rumsfeld proposed few radical changes.
He even went against his erstwhile Republican colleagues in the
House and a great many of his new colleagues in the White House
by opposing an absolute veto for governors over poverty projects,
long a tenet of Republican policy.†

To keep the poverty program going in some major form was not
all that much of a surprise. Retaining the Model Cities program,
however, stretched the Moynihan Doctrine to its outer limits. From
the ivied isolation of Harvard, Moynihan had felt Model Cities was
a worthless program whose passing would find few mourners. Arriving in Washington, he was amazed to find that Model Cities had been
transmogrified into a symbol of federal commitment to saving the
cities. Only for that reason, he concluded, should it survive. Moynihan's candid advice to Nixon: Worthless though it is, continue
Model Cities.

He did. No Great Society program of any magnitude, either

---

*Moynihan's sharp criticism of the Johnson war against poverty is contained in
Maximum Feasible Misunderstanding, written before he joined the Nixon administration but published in 1969.

†Rumsfeld's difficulties over this with the White House lobbying staff are discussed in Chapter V.

substantive or symbolic, perished. Perhaps, as Moynihan theorized, this helped restore the eroded legitimacy of government. For certain, it helped give the new President at least a few months of grace before liberals opened against him in full fury.

But there was a price. Having come to office with so vaporous a concept of what he wanted to do domestically, Richard Nixon now had added a further note of ambivalence and ambiguity by embracing, at least in name, some of the very programs whose elimination he had repeatedly promised in his campaign.

Pat Moynihan's remarkable success in achieving so large a continuity between the Democratic and Republican administrations was but part of a much broader success. In his struggle for influence with Arthur Burns, Moynihan was coming off the clear winner. He was picking his shots carefully and scoring with most of them: the continuity of the Great Society programs, a Presidential policy of hands-off-the-campus, new programs of aid to higher education, a landmark welfare-reform program.*

By contrast, 1969 was a dismal year in the distinguished career of Arthur Burns. Attempting to counsel the President on a much broader range of subjects than Moynihan, Burns was suffering one rebuff after another. Almost everything proposed by Moynihan was opposed—generally without success—by Burns. Beyond that were other failures: inability to restrain federal spending nearly as much as he wanted; inability to stop continued federal sponsorship of the supersonic transport (SST); inability to block Nixon's advocacy of textile quotas (promised during the 1968 campaign); inability to save the investment tax credit from repeal.

As the only White House aide with Cabinet rank at the beginning, Burns clearly felt himself in a senior position with some supervisory responsibilities. On two separate occasions he called Moynihan to his office and lectured him for leaking to the press. At the start, Burns scheduled a daily 5:30 P.M. meeting, at which the senior staff would report to him on how their day had gone and what had been accomplished. After a few days, however, the senior assistants began sending deputies, then their second- and third-ranking aides, and, finally, anybody who happened to be around the office. Burns' 5:30 meeting died an unmourned death.

*The inception of the welfare-reform proposal is discussed in Chapter VIII.

Burns' failure to assert control derived from the perception of other senior staffers that his influence with the President was waning. While Moynihan was one of the few White House assistants with access to Nixon for frequent and protracted discussions, Burns was sputtering in White House corridors about occasional delays in getting past the President's appointments secretary. By late summer, 1969, Burns was marking time in expectation of that happy day when he would move to the independence and power of the Federal Reserve Board.

But why? Why should Nixon favor Moynihan, a stranger whose background, ideology and party affiliation were foreign to his own, over tried-and-true Arthur Burns, conservative and Republican, his faithful ally for so many years beginning with their bold challenge to the Eisenhower administration's restrictive economic policies? The answer reveals something about Richard Nixon.

"Never underestimate the importance of proximity," Moynihan told a friend in mid-1969. As a seasoned veteran of the bureaucratic wars, Moynihan made certain that he and his Urban Affairs Council staff had their offices in the West Wing of the White House, only a step from the President's. Burns and his staff were assigned next door in the Executive Office Building (the old State Department Building), and Burns never protested, expressing satisfaction that he was away from the hurly-burly of the White House itself.

Beyond proximity was fascination. In both conversation and writing (he was a master in the bureaucratic art of memo-writing), Moynihan was a delight and a fascination for the President. Nixon would react happily upon finding a sprightly Moynihan memo mixed in with all the dreary government prose. But Burns had become pedantic and ponderous for the President. His advice, which in more than one instance would have saved Nixon from errors he long would regret, was ignored partly because it was just plain boring to listen to. And partly because it was negative. In Nixon, Moynihan found a fertile field for novel approaches and new ideas. Burns, presenting the conservative viewpoint as to why something should *not* be done, found an unreceptive President.

But Moynihan's triumphs of 1969 were limited and impermanent. His advice covered social-welfare questions and not much more, barely touching on economics, foreign trade, governmental reorganization or most aspects of Congressional relations. The Urban Affairs Council never did become the fulcrum for domestic policy that Moynihan had hoped it would. Nor could it have, considering the un-Republican and unconservative nature of its staff and Moynihan's own disinclination for administrative details.

In truth, *neither* Dr. Burns nor Dr. Moynihan was suitable for handling the broad sweep of domestic policy, though both had been thought of for the job by Nixon in his fuzzy conceptions of White House staffing just after the election. In the meantime, little was heard of Nixon's desire that policy be made by Cabinet members collectively and individually to permit a much smaller White House staff. Once planted in the fertile bureaucratic soil of Washington, the White House staff began growing at a frantic pace while the proposed rejuvenation of the Cabinet was never pursued with much seriousness. Thus, *somebody* at the White House had to coordinate domestic policy for the government. That bureaucratic vacuum was soon filled by two men, utterly unknown nationally as Nixon took office but whose presence and power would be felt long after Pat Moynihan and Arthur Burns had left the White House: an advertising executive from Los Angeles named Harry R. Haldeman and a zoning lawyer from Seattle named John Ehrlichman.

Haldeman and Ehrlichman, "The Germans," as they came to be known, were almost wholly ignorant of major national issues, the federal government, and politics in its broadest sense. Their principal involvement in national public life had been as "advance men," campaign technicians who handle the myriad details on a campaign trip. That positions of such power and responsibility should be filled by men of such slight experience in public affairs is the single most extraordinary aspect of the early Nixon White House.

"Haldeman was inevitable; Ehrlichman was evolutionary," said a one-time aide in seeking to explain their remarkable ascendancy.

Based merely on his background with Nixon, however, there would seem to be nothing inevitable about the rise of H.R. (Bob) Haldeman. Deeply conservative, he joined the Los Angeles office of the J. Walter Thompson advertising agency in 1949 after graduation (with a B.S. in Business Management) from UCLA, and soon thereafter became a volunteer for Richard Nixon. An advance man in his 1956 campaign for Vice President, he was chief advance man in the 1960 campaign for President and managed the disastrous 1962 campaign for governor that had seemed to end Nixon's career. In 1966 he politely declined a request to help out in the arrangements for Nixon's midterm campaigning, the invaluable prelude to his 1968 campaign. Even in 1968, Haldeman did not leave J. Walter Thompson to take over as Nixon's chief of staff until May 1968, by which time Nixon had become a comfortable front runner.

This record of involvement with past Nixon defeats and obvious reluctance to abandon all earthly pursuits to rush to Nixon's side at campaign time would ordinarily be sufficient to demote a Nixon lieutenant to inferior status. But not Bob Haldeman. With scarcely anyone appreciating it, the Nixon-Haldeman tie had grown unbreakably strong over the years. Haldeman shared Nixon's belief that hard work, long hours and unflagging industry were the key to success. Even more than Nixon, he was hostile to the press; the President could be absolutely certain that no press leaks would come from Haldeman.* And once he did leave private life to join Nixon, Haldeman could be counted on to sublimate his private life to unending hours in the service of his chief. On top of this, Haldeman's expertise as a super advance man complemented Nixon's own constricted view of politics. What Nixon really enjoyed and excelled in was not grand political strategy but the minutiae of campaign politics: what to say in what town; what town to go to; how to schedule a candidate. It was natural for Nixon to ignore Haldeman's inexperience in broad political strategy.

But the true key to the inevitability of Haldeman may be best explained in the personality *differences* between him and the President. Haldeman, crew-cut and unsmiling, had a most un-Nixonian ability to demolish an aide, a colleague or an outsider with harsh word and icy stare. In memo or head-to-head conversation, Haldeman was a master of blunt, insulting prose. As with John Mitchell,

---

*An incident on the President's trip to Spain on October 3, 1970, vividly pointed up Haldeman's attitude toward the press. As he did on all Presidential travels, foreign and domestic, Haldeman was furiously taking motion pictures of the procession through Madrid with a hand camera he had purchased in Bonn on the President's first European trip in 1969. The wire-service correspondents in the auto behind Haldeman's complained to Press Secretary Ronald Ziegler that Haldeman, leaning out of his car window, was obstructing their view. When Ziegler relayed the complaint by radio, Haldeman replied coldly, "Ask the wires [wire-service correspondents] to keep their car back so I can photograph the event, please."

Nixon seemed to draw from Haldeman intangible qualities that he himself lacked. Nixon had always wanted to give the impression of the tough, hard-boiled politician, whereas in truth he flinched from unpleasant confrontation and abjured the impolite deprecation to the face of friend or foe. Haldeman *was* that tough politician in being, and his toughness became a tangible asset for Nixon in providing the isolation and looseness of schedule he craved.

If there was any doubt of the inevitability of Haldeman, it was erased even before the inauguration at the first staff meeting in the Sapphire Room of the Pierre Hotel. Haldeman read aloud the words of Louis Brownlow, an aide to President Franklin D. Roosevelt in 1936–37, commending White House assistants with "a passion for anonymity"—a willingness to submerge their own destinies in the service of their chief. It showed what kind of aide Haldeman would be, what kind of colleagues he wanted and, most important, who was setting the tone at the Nixon White House.

It was easy enough for other staffers to err in minimizing Haldeman's stature and importance. He seemed to be playing the role of flunky, carrying in a cup of coffee for the President (as Arthur Burns or Pat Moynihan would never dream of doing). He and his young assistants, short-haired and bright-faced in Haldeman's image, brought to Washington by him from J. Walter Thompson's, rushed about with such Boy Scout enthusiasm and determination that they were given the lasting designation of "the Beaver Patrol" by more sophisticated colleagues. Early in 1969, Haldeman ordered all White House male personnel to wear ties and jackets at *all* times while at work—an edict producing concealed hilarity and massive disobedience; the order was quietly forgotten. Following the Brownlow formula, Haldeman put out the word that he was merely an office manager with no power over the substantive questions.*

The truth was otherwise. As the modern Presidency has grown

*This resulted in early press assessments downgrading Haldeman's importance. Even John Osborne, doing trenchant analyses of the Nixon White House in *The New Republic*, was misled. "Bob Haldeman and his seven assistants are efficient functionaries, no more," he wrote. "For what really matters at the Nixon White House, the wise inquirer will turn . . . to such advisors in the actual stream of power as Henry Kissinger and Counsellor Burns." Before 1969 was over, however, Osborne had reassessed the situation with a recognition of Haldeman's power; some journalists were still being misled into 1971.

more overburdened with duties, the keeper of the gates has become a Presidential assistant of increasing power. By determining who would and would not see the President, Kenneth P. O'Donnell under Kennedy and W. Marvin Watson, Jr., under Johnson exerted indisputable power. Bob Haldeman in that same role exerted vastly more power because of the peculiarities of the President he served.

The new President was fearful of being smothered by visitors, so monopolizing his time that the long periods alone he cherished for reading, writing and just plain thinking would be gone. Although the real danger of the Presidency is isolation, Nixon's fears ran in exactly the opposite direction, and he granted Haldeman unprecedented latitude in regulating the flow of visitors, with specific instructions to keep the number as low as possible. Nor, as in the case of Kenny O'Donnell and Marvin Watson, was there any real appeal from a Haldeman decision. The politician or government official whose request to see the President had been denied had the right of appeal, but that appeal traveled a closed circuit that reached Haldeman at its terminus.

Further enhancing Haldeman's power was Nixon's dislike for frequent contact with his own aides, particularly aides below the very top level. Whereas Lyndon Johnson enjoyed nothing better than sitting around the Oval Office with his staff and talking politics (usually LBJ diatribes against political enemies), Nixon deplored such unstructured bull sessions. His contacts with his senior staff were surprisingly infrequent, with his junior staff spasmodic, with middle-level Presidential appointees almost nonexistent. A full year after he had entered the White House, an aide with middle-level rank of Deputy Assistant to the President doubted that Nixon knew his first name. An assistant secretary in a major department had to be introduced to the President in a White House reception line after two years on the job. When a White House or departmental official did obtain a rare audience with the President, Haldeman was invariably present. In the absence of frequent and easy contact with his own staff and departmental officials, Nixon relied on Haldeman.

Nixon also made it clear early that he did not care for structured meetings any more than unstructured meetings. He wanted written rather than oral communications, much preferring a thorough reading of reams of memoranda to face-to-face contact with his advisers. Here again, it was Haldeman who selected which memoranda should reach the President's desk as their final destination.

Bob Haldeman was suddenly thrust upon the national scene with few recorded ideological leanings, though he had first been attracted to politics and Richard Nixon by an ideological cause: support for Nixon's anti-Communist investigations on the House Committee on Un-American Activities in the late 1940s while Haldeman was a student at UCLA. Although Haldeman continued at the White House to keep his views out of public print, his new colleagues there soon found him to be a conservative of a thoroughly conventional Republican variety—markedly more conservative and more conventional than Nixon and lacking his taste for the innovative.

Haldeman took no position on disputes over issues in either meetings or through formally circulated memoranda (though he may well have been asked his opinion on such questions, and given it, during his daily meetings alone with the President). Rather, the conservative influence that Haldeman exerted over Nixon was more a conservative life-style than a conservative ideology. Haldeman's suspicion and distrust of the press, blacks and students reinforced just such deeply embedded tendencies in Nixon. Haldeman's own tendency toward reclusiveness (he seldom entertained or dined out save with his very closest associates) reinforced similar habits in Nixon. Moreover, soon after Nixon took office, Haldeman was to have a direct and intimate link with the policy-making machinery in the person of John Ehrlichman.

If Ehrlichman's rise was evolutionary, it was also derivative of his relationship with Haldeman. Indeed, the fact that Ehrlichman was playing any role at all in the great world of politics stemmed from his association with Haldeman, his classmate and close friend at UCLA, fellow Eagle Scout, fellow Christian Scientist and fellow abstainer from liquor and tobacco. Ehrlichman had joined the Nixon campaign for President in 1960 at Haldeman's urging and, again at his friend's request, came down from Seattle to work in the 1962 campaign for governor of California. Like Haldeman, he sat out Nixon's 1966 travels. Like Haldeman, he was a late arrival for the 1968 Presidential campaign—turning up at the Miami Beach convention. At the reorganization of the campaign at Mission Bay, Calif., following the convention, he was given the important post of "tour director," a ticklish administrative job of pulling together all the detailed planning for a campaign stop—from getting there to releasing the proper number of balloons when Nixon entered the hall. Ehrlichman did the job well but played no part in either issue-formation or campaign strategy. He was no Nixon intimate on Election Day.

Entering the White House in January 1969, in the Counsel's office Ehrlichman was handed legal and not terribly important assignments, but that did not last long. Through Haldeman's subtle sponsorship, the evolution of John Ehrlichman was rapid indeed. At the same time that Arthur Burns was finding it difficult to penetrate Haldeman's Oval Office guard (also known as the Berlin Wall) to see the President, Ehrlichman—on the formal table of organization many levels below Dr. Burns—was quickly ushered in to give carefully prepared presentations. Nixon was becoming impressed by him, and as the inadequacy of both Burns and Moynihan to fill the role of chief of the domestic-policy staff became obvious, Ehrlichman stepped into the vacuum.

By early spring, Ehrlichman on the President's orders was building a new policy staff structure that would dwarf the modest six- or seven-member staffs of Burns and Moynihan.* When an outraged Arthur Burns complained that Pat Moynihan was publicly issuing policy statements that had the approval of nobody, the telephone call went to Ehrlichman.

To the outside world, Haldeman and Ehrlichman looked indistinguishable from each other, Rosenkrantz and Guildenstern, Tweedledee and Tweedledum. But there were differences. Ehrlichman's mind was more open, more receptive to new ideas. He was more accessible to outsiders, to politicians and even to the press. Scandalously uninformed at first about national issues—considering the magnitude of his assignment—Ehrlichman displayed not only a keen intelligence but a surprising liberalism on most issues as he immersed himself in national policy. If Haldeman was a step to the right of the President, Ehrlichman was a step to his left.

Yet, the Haldeman-Ehrlichman team was, on balance, danger-

*On April 2, 1969, our column reported that "an obscure aide named John Ehrlichman [was] purposefully assuming direction of domestic policy in a manner not approached during the new Administration's first three months," However, we shared the general underestimation of Haldeman, assuming incorrectly—as did several White House aides—that Ehrlichman's rapidly growing power might come at the expense of Haldeman and his Beaver Patrol.

ously distant from the constituencies that a President must take into
serious account: Congress, his political party's leaders, the press.
Haldeman and, to a lesser extent, Ehrlichman, busily developing a
Teutonic staff mechanism in the White House, had no time for these
bothersome outsiders, and were in no small part responsible for the
collective White House face of arrogance and indifference that was
turned to Congress, the Republican Party and the press in 1969 with
results so ruinous that they were to affect the entire Presidency of
Richard Nixon. The Haldeman-Ehrlichman team, in short, exaggerated Nixon's own introverted tendency to rely on hard work and
devotion to duty while ignoring the outer world. And the face that
the White House staff was presenting to the outside world on domestic policy was all the more important because, from the very beginning, the Cabinet was secondary to it.

The notion of the Cabinet serving as a policy-making body ran
counter to the post-World War II evolution of the federal government. It was probably impossible to put into effect no matter how
hard President Nixon might have tried and no matter how distinguished his Cabinet might have been.

In fact, however, he did not try very hard, and the Cabinet was
perhaps the least distinguished in the postwar era. Nixon was far too
preoccupied with foreign affairs to worry about governmental organization at that stage, and the meetings of the full Cabinet tended to
bore and irritate him, evoking unwelcome memories of lugubrious
sessions of the Eisenhower Cabinet. The Cabinet proved to be precisely the ill-assorted, themeless band that it had seemed at the time
of its haphazard selection.

Most of the Cabinet members in the older, traditionally powerful seats wielded little influence beyond their own departments. Melvin Laird had hoped to delegate much of the workaday operations
of the Pentagon to his lieutenants and roam widely to deal with
questions that had concerned him every bit as much as national
defense during his heady days as a party leader in the House: health,
education, welfare, intergovernmental relations, fiscal reform and, of
course, his first love—politics. But the burden of devising strategy for
winding down participation in the Vietnam war, piled on top of the
normal Pentagon managerial headache, proved too much, and Laird
spent most of his time on the other side of the Potomac. Nixon had

hoped to have William Rogers in the Cabinet for his wise and shrewd counsel on nondiplomatic questions, but Rogers was involved in a frantic cram course in international affairs. Although the Secretary of the Treasury in Republican administrations during this century— Andrew Mellon, Ogden Mills, George Humphrey, Robert Anderson —had tended to dominate the Cabinet in domestic affairs, this was not to be true of David Kennedy. Indeed, he scarcely dominated the Treasury. After naming an outstanding team at the Treasury, he then settled back to bankers' hours and let his subordinates do the work. But what worked beautifully at Continental Illinois Bank was unacceptable for the Secretary of Treasury.

Nor was Kennedy the only disappointment in the Cabinet. From the beginning, Nixon was displeased with the three state governors who had resigned their elective offices to join the Cabinet: George Romney of Michigan at Housing and Urban Development; Walter Hickel of Alaska at Interior; John Volpe of Massachusetts at Transportation. Each was an extroverted self-made millionaire businessman who had entered politics late in life, was unaccustomed to taking orders and was absolutely certain of the rightness of his convictions. Each was to be embroiled in quarrels with "The Germans" at the White House. Proud men, they insisted on penetrating Haldeman's Berlin Wall to talk directly to the President himself, thereby robbing Nixon of his two most prized treasures: his time and his solitude. When one high government official stopped by the Oval Office for a farewell visit after a particularly undistinguished stint in Washington, Nixon praised him for never having pressed himself on the President's time—not like John Volpe. The President told how the voluble ex-building contractor from Boston had once sought and gained an audience in the Oval Office to waste twenty-five minutes trying to convince Nixon to assign a certain Roman Catholic priest from Massachusetts, a close friend of Volpe's, to preside over a Sunday worship service at the White House. Nothing was more irritating to the President than the style used by Romney, Hickel and Volpe: evangelistic and self-righteous, long on fury and short on facts, high-decibel arguments augmented by not a little fist-pounding. The President would look on silently, without reproach, a grin frozen to his face. But this was not the way to impress Richard Nixon.

Hickel was to fall in an incident bitter for the Nixon Presidency.

Romney was to linger on, an outsider who was in but not of the Nixon administration. But Volpe, curiously, was a success. His effusive, glad-handing style was not to Nixon's liking, but by sheer force of energy he showed how effective a hard-working politician could be in an administration woefully short of experienced politicians. Unique among Nixon's Cabinet officers, Volpe roamed the halls of Capitol Hill to win friends and supporters. Also, by his shrewd understanding of how to sell his projects to the President, he was often able to win the day—and sometimes for projects that were politically questionable.

Volpe had arrived in Washington with no special background in aviation and little knowledge of the proposed supersonic transport (SST), a new high-speed concept in commercial aviation being built by Boeing Co. under heavy federal subsidy. Volpe was quickly won over by aviation-oriented aides at the Transportation Department. But as an SST supporter he was alone in the upper reaches of the administration, and for good reason. Arguments against the SST were multiple: the government could not afford it; it might not be financially feasible; it might damage the environment. Arthur Burns was particularly vehement in telling Nixon that this was a potential white elephant that ought not be imposed on the American taxpayer. Besides, it was Lyndon Johnson's project. Its quiet burial would do no political damage.

But Volpe, single-handedly, sold the President and did so by employing, instinctively, the one argument that would move Richard Nixon—not economic, nor ecological, nor concerned with the international balance of payments, but a plea to national pride, what Nixon himself called a "sense of nation." Could Nixon bear to see America fall behind for the first time in aeronautical development, to see a Soviet-built SST or even the Concorde being developed jointly by the British and French preempt the international market? "Mr. President," asked Volpe, "how would you like to go to Dulles Airport and see Americans traveling to Europe on an SST with the words *fabriqué en France* stamped on it?" That appeal would not have lifted John Mitchell's eyebrow. But to Richard Nixon, it was deeply convincing. He ordered a go-ahead on the SST.

Later Volpe used the same appeal to evoke the desired response from Nixon when he sent forward a Transportation Department proposal called "Railpax," a plan to save the nation's dying intercity passenger railroads through selective subsidies. John Ehrlichman and the rest of the White House staff were adamantly opposed on grounds that there were projects—even transportation projects—with far higher priority than Railpax. Besides, they said, the plan would put the President in the uncomfortable political position of arbitrarily deciding which cities should have rail service and which should not. Once again, Volpe swept aside all substantive arguments with a question that went to the core of Richard Nixon's sentimental view of nation: What would America be without its passenger trains? It was a devastating question for the man who had often talked and written about the poor boy lying in his bed at night in Yorba Linda, Calif., listening to strange locomotives in the darkness. After much infighting between Ehrlichman and Volpe, Volpe once again was the winner.*

Successful though he was, however, Volpe's style was not best suited to impress Richard Nixon. He preferred the soft-spoken, well-organized presentation, low on oratory and high on facts, lawyerlike in organization, not overly zealous toward a single point of view—just the kind of presentation that Nixon himself might make.

Surprisingly, in 1969, Secretary of Commerce Maurice Stans occasionally made such presentations. Having swallowed his disappointment at not getting the Treasury portfolio, Stans tried to swell the importance of a department that had grown increasingly less significant since the heyday of Herbert Hoover in 1921–29, but his voice was never truly influential. Postmaster General Winton Blount, a millionaire contractor from Montgomery, Ala., was another pleasant surprise in Cabinet meetings, but his jurisdiction was so restricted that his influence, too, was circumscribed. The one important pleasant surprise to emerge out of the Cabinet was George Shultz, a stranger to Nixon and to politics, scholarly to the point of pedantry and, as Secretary of Labor, in a post of no great importance in Republican administrations. But his quiet, well-organized style, summarizing and synthesizing arguments, was precisely

---

*A thoughtful conservative aide in the White House was asked, after two years, which Nixon's most mistaken domestic projects were. His reply was, first, the Family Assistance Payments scheme in the welfare-reform bill; second, the SST; and third, Railpax (whose name was changed to Amtrak in 1971). Two of the three, he noted grimly, were of John Volpe's doing.

what would most impress the President. In fact, it was somewhat the same style that Richard Nixon had used years before at Eisenhower Cabinet sessions. In an administration high on pomp and ritual, Shultz was the tweedy, informal college professor. Dr. Jean Mayer, a Harvard nutritionist on duty as Nixon's consultant on hunger, bumped into Shultz one morning and called out, "Good morning, Mr. Secretary." "Oh, come on," Shultz shot back, "knock off that 'Mr. Secretary' stuff." He was a first-rate man in an administration short on first-rate men and, soon, was given assignments beyond the scope of the Labor Department—such as chairmanship of the task force studying the touchy oil-import question—with bigger things yet to come.

And at those early Cabinet sessions were two members who very seldom said anything: John Mitchell and Robert Finch. Mitchell: staring somberly from behind his pipe, his trembling hands (caused, he said, by a shrapnel wound suffered as a World War II PT boat commander) hidden from view. Finch: fidgeting, chain-smoking, his eyes darting nervously about the room. These were the two Cabinet members boasting special relationships with the President, and the way those relationships evolved—one growing stronger and the other growing weaker—revealed much about the direction of the Nixon administration.

During 1969 a prominent academician on the White House payroll as a part-time consultant visited the Oval Office on three occasions for meetings with the President. On two of these, he noticed John Mitchell waiting in an antechamber outside the President's office. "He didn't seem to have an appointment," the professor recalled later. "He just seemed to be waiting, like a chauffeur, in case the President wanted him for something that might turn up. I was puzzled. I said to myself: 'Why is he here? Why isn't he back in his office running the Justice Department?'"

Nixon's chauffeur, Mitchell never was. Whenever he waited outside the Oval Office, one could be certain there was important business. Still, through much of 1969, it often seemed that the Attorney General was spending more time at the White House than the Department of Justice. He would generally visit with Nixon once each day and talk to him on the telephone several times more (at night from his apartment in the luxurious new Watergate, where his telephone was connected to the White House switchboard). "I think he hears my views on most important questions, and I think he values my judgment," Mitchell said in 1969.

Those "most important questions" ran from Vietnam to oil-import quotas, but there was one specific function he played that cut across all issues. Richard Nixon was vulnerable to a convincing argument eloquently put to him for a project that might not fit his overall political purposes and, on the contrary, might hurt him politically. He was easy prey for a Pat Moynihan advocating Family Assistance Payments, a John Volpe boosting Railpax, a George Shultz pressing plans to bring Negro workmen into the segregated construction trades. The antidote to them was John Mitchell, whose advice on issues was rigidly chained to this grand strategy: those who voted for Nixon and for George Wallace in 1968 compose Nixon's present constituency and his potential majority for 1972; to ensure their vote for 1972, the decisions and policies of the government must help them.

"These are very nice people," Pat Moynihan told a friend in early 1969 in describing his new Republican colleagues, "with a perfectly dreadful constituency." It was those "dreadful" people— 1968 supporters of Nixon and George Wallace—whom John Mitchell was representing before the President, not out of love but because he felt they must be served if Richard Nixon was to be reelected. That meant governmental actions designed to please, or at least to not displease, the South, textile manufacturers, oil producers, law-and-order advocates and whoever else had opposed Hubert Humphrey. It was a static theory of politics, militating against the expansion of the Republican Party and bearing within it inherent seeds of national disunity.

All this ran counter to Moynihan's subtle, low-keyed efforts to establish continuity between past and present administrations and cool the national rancor. Mutual personal dislike between Pat Moynihan and John Mitchell was manifest, surfacing in fights over such questions as the "no-knock" provision—permitting forcible surprise entry by police once a bench warrant had been issued—in the District of Columbia anti-crime bill. Moynihan opposed it inside the White House on civil libertarian grounds, but also because it was, he felt, bad politics; it would cast Nixon in the role of the repressor with faintly anti-Negro overtones. Nonsense, said Mitchell. The peo-

ple who voted for Richard Nixon were promised a return to law and
order, and they are entitled to law and order. Neither civil libertari-
ans nor blacks—and certainly not the black criminal element in the
District of Columbia—voted for Nixon. On this, as on most everything else, Mitchell prevailed.

His influence with Nixon unmatched, his agents spread through
the administration and into the White House itself; Mitchell became
the President's troubleshooter, doing what had to be done for the
1968 constituency. Because those things often were not pleasant, the
Attorney General more often than not worked behind the scenes in
1969.

Early in the year, Mitchell turned up at a closed meeting of
House Republican leaders to urge that they not repeat their opposition of the previous year to a rider offered by Representative Jamie
Whitten, a segregationist Democrat from Mississippi, to the educational appropriations bill barring the use of any federal funds for
school desegregation. That certainly was not official administration
policy, but Mitchell did not want Congressional Republicans to take
an anti-Southern stance that might alienate part of that 1968 constituency. The House leaders agreed.

In September, when the inexorable workings of the seniority
system threatened to give Senator Charles Goodell of New York a
Republican vacancy on the Senate Judiciary Committee, Mitchell
paid a secret visit to the office of Senator Robert Griffin of Michigan,
a loyal administration supporter soon to be elected Minority Whip
of the Senate. Goodell, who had been moving left at a furious pace
since his appointment in 1968 to the Senate seat left vacant by the
assassination of Robert F. Kennedy, would be most embarrassing to
Nixon on the Judiciary Committee. He could be counted on not only
to oppose the administration's anti-crime proposals but to vote
against the then pending nomination of Judge Clement F. Haynsworth for the Supreme Court. Hence, Mitchell asked Griffin to use
his seniority and take the committee vacancy in Goodell's place.
Griffin agreed.

Both these Mitchell operations on Capitol Hill could be broadly
viewed as within the confines of an Attorney General's duties
(though his intervention in the Senate's own system of committee
selection was rare indeed, if not unprecedented). Inside the administration, however, Mitchell was by no means limited by the perimeter

of an Attorney General's duties, as when he intervened in the functioning of George Shultz's task force on oil imports.

Big Oil had been growing progressively more nervous through the summer of 1969 as the Shultz task force seemed ready to recommend a drastic scaling down in protection of the industry, replacing the import quotas with a tariff that would sharply reduce costs to the American consumer and force a general reorganization of the oil production industry which would drive small, uneconomic producers out of business. That was scarcely what Big Oil had expected when it generously supported Richard Nixon for President in 1968, and it had made clear to Mitchell that it might well look elsewhere in 1972 if Shultz were permitted to have his way.

Thus, the members and staff of the task force sensed that John Mitchell was making no mere courtesy call when he turned up at a meeting in December. The Justice Department did not have a seat on the task force, though it had been represented there by Richard McLaren, Assistant Attorney General for Antitrust, sitting in as observer. McLaren, a Republican trust buster in the Teddy Roosevelt tradition, had enthusiastically applauded proposals to whittle down the domestic industry's monopolistic advantage. But his boss, the Attorney General, had other views. Speaking briefly and laconically, Mitchell urged the task force to practice extreme caution. "Don't put the President in the box," he said. No further explanation was needed. He was gently instructing the task force to forget its long months of economic computations rather than embarrass the President with his allies in Big Oil. After Mitchell's intervention, the task force markedly scaled down the scope of its recommendations.*

Mitchell's surprise visit to the Shultz task force epitomized both his style and his political strategy. Although he neither ordered the task force around nor invoked the President's name, there was no doubt that he was speaking for Richard Nixon. Inherent in that visit was the Mitchell doctrine that keeping a few sure old friends is far more important than gaining many potential new friends. The prospect of lower consumer prices resulting from increased oil imports

---

*Even those scaled-down recommendations incurred dissents from two pro-oil task force members, Stans and Hickel, and were ultimately rejected by Nixon. Although Shultz was later to rise to the top in the White House, the President never again solicited his view on oil imports.

opened vistas of new Republican converts among the Democratic-voting consumers of the Northeast. Mitchell preferred to consolidate the President's oil industry support, and Richard Nixon agreed.

In the early months of 1969, Robert Finch was scarcely less a special member of the Cabinet than John Mitchell. He seemed in those days to be balancing a hundred balls, dashing in and out of Cabinet meetings, preoccupied with many details. He had been Richard Nixon's first choice for Vice President at Miami Beach, but had tearfully declined on grounds that for the nominee to pick his protégé was too close to nepotism. Nevertheless, the future seemed unbounded. In his 1966 election as lieutenant governor of California, his margin had surpassed even Ronald Reagan's landslide for governor. Now he was a Cabinet member at age forty-four, handsome, articulate, the President's favorite. Did the White House beckon in 1976?

However, progressively harsh difficulties began to close in on Finch. Whereas Mitchell could attend the President while his lieutenants ran the Department of Justice, Finch could not keep the Department of Health, Education and Welfare under control without devoting full time to the job, if then. He had badly underestimated the difficulties posed by HEW's sprawling, uncoordinated operations, its rebellious bureaucracy, its politically explosive problems. His plans to provide Nixon with advice on a variety of issues, and, hopefully, influence him, were smashed from the beginning.

But the simultaneous rise of Mitchell and decline of Finch were perhaps caused by factors more subtle than Finch's preoccupation with HEW. If Mitchell was the man Nixon wanted to be, Finch was all too much the man he always had been. "The President's problem is indecision," said a friend, "and Bob Finch is indecision squared."

On top of this, Finch in 1969 was promoting a political strategy directly antithetical to Mitchell's 1968 victory strategy and what Mitchell had convinced Nixon would be necessary for reelection in 1972. "This is the last election that will be won by the un-black, the un-poor and the un-young," Finch told newsmen as the 1968 campaign neared an end. In other words, Mitchell could run 1968 with the Old Politics, but the future belonged to the New Politics and Bob Finch.

In this frame of mind, Finch began staffing HEW with officials whose policies would be designed to attract the black, the poor and the young to the banner of the Republican Party. Feasible or not in theory, it could scarcely be successful in practice: the Department of Health, Education and Welfare following Finch's strategy while the rest of the administration—the White House and indeed the President himself—was going Mitchell's way.

Just how out of touch Nixon was with what Finch was doing became obvious from the early sub-Cabinet-level appointments at HEW—particularly Dr. James Allen. Having gained nationwide prestige during sixteen years as State Commissioner of Education in New York, Allen had changed his party registration from Democratic to Republican as a result of his deep admiration for Governor Nelson Rockefeller, but was essentially a nonparty liberal. He had rejected an offer from President Kennedy to be U.S. Commissioner of Education on grounds that the federal role in elementary and secondary schooling was not then sufficiently important. Later he brushed aside a feeler for the same job in the Johnson administration. But when Allen, vacationing in Florida, received a telephone call from Finch the weekend of January 18–19, he was ready to move from Albany to Washington to wear two hats: Commissioner of Education and Assistant Secretary for Education. The fact that Dr. Allen, famed nationally as an advocate of busing children for the purpose of achieving racial balance in the schools, was being appointed by a President unequivocal in his opposition to busing, did not, strangely, seem to bother Allen, Finch or Nixon.*

But for Allen, second thoughts started setting in early. Visiting the new President soon after accepting Finch's offer, Allen listed for Nixon his goals in American education, particularly education in the inner city. Nixon listened attentively, then replied, "I hope, Dr. Allen, that you can do something to improve discipline in the schools." Allen was struck dumb. When in later meetings the President stressed the responsibility of the parent and the family in education, Allen came to feel that Nixon was oblivious to modern educational problems and wanted to return to Elm Street. The more accurate answer was that Richard Nixon was then deeply immersed

---

*It did bother Senator Strom Thurmond of South Carolina, Nixon's most important Southern supporter, who led an unsuccessful Senate floor fight against Allen's confirmation.

in questions of foreign policy and would react to domestic problems intelligently only when challenged by someone as entertaining as Pat Moynihan.

Out of place though he was in the administration, Allen had many a kindred soul at HEW. John G. Veneman, a peach rancher and state assemblyman from Modesto, Calif., who had been Finch's campaign chairman in 1966 and Governor Reagan's liberal Republican hairshirt in the Legislature the next two years, was brought in as Under Secretary over Reagan's objections. James Farmer, a leading civil rights activist during the 1960s as head of the Congress of Racial Equality (CORE) and a registered Liberal from New York who had supported Hubert Humphrey for President, was named an Assistant Secretary. In this setting, Finch's selection of Dr. John Knowles as Assistant Secretary for Health, the government's chief health officer, scarcely seemed unusual. In fact, it was to prove a catastrophe for Finch, for the administration and for the President.

In checking through names before the inauguration, Finch and his lieutenants were overjoyed to find a qualified health administrator (head of Massachusetts General Hospital in Boston) with progressive, innovative views who was not only a Republican but had actively supported Nixon for President in 1968. Summoned to Washington on January 15, Knowles so impressed Finch with his verve and dynamism that, less than ten minutes into the interview, he was offered the job by Finch. He promptly accepted. In the preinaugural confusion, however, Knowles' name was not transmitted to the White House for the Presidential nomination.

A few days later Finch received a routine delegation from the American Medical Association, the highly conservative national organization of physicians, which submitted a short list of names they preferred for Assistant Secretary for Health. Knowles was not on the list. Would Knowles be acceptable? No, he would not, the AMA replied. But neither Finch nor his Under Secretary, Veneman, was unduly worried.

They underestimated and miscalculated what was at stake for the AMA. Alarmed by its political weakness after the passage of Medicare against its wishes in 1965, the AMA had set up a political arm—the American Medical Political Action Committee (AMPAC) —mainly for the purpose of distributing campaign funds to candidates friendly to organized medicine. In 1968 alone, AMPAC disbursed $681,965 from contributions of individual doctors. How could the AMA justify such expenditures, mainly for Republican candidates, if the Republican President were to name as his chief health officer John Knowles, who had testified before Congress: "I do believe in comprehensive prepaid health insurance for all Americans on a public and private basis—if the private basis will not do it, then I think the federal government has got to do it." To Dr. Phillip Thomsen, president of the Illinois Medical Society, this was testimony "that all medicine ought to be socialized . . ." With considerable political logic, the AMA felt it should have the same veto power over the Assistant Secretary for Health in a Republican administration that the AFL-CIO had over the Secretary of Labor in a Democratic administration.

After learning about Knowles from Finch, the AMA immediately went to its many powerful Republican friends, the most formidable of whom was Senator Everett McKinley Dirksen of Illinois, Minority Leader of the Senate. Dirksen and the other Republican leaders immediately descended upon Finch and the White House, which became nervous at the thought of alienating both a powerful lobby and a group of prominent Republican members of Congress. With Dirksen vowing to filibuster the Knowles appointment in the Senate, Finch called Boston to tell John Knowles that his appointment had been delayed for the time being: the formal request for the President to make the appointment had been held up. On January 30 the *Washington Post* reported that Knowles had been selected, but the announcement had been delayed by AMA opposition, thereby beginning five months of Kafkaesque indecision and intrigue that was to sear permanently everyone it touched.

Heartened by the delay, the AMA intensified its campaign against Knowles (while not taking a public stand against him).* The President told Finch that the decision was his to make. However, if we're going to recommend Knowles, Nixon advised Finch, he should

*The nature of the opposition came out through such AMA friends in Congress as Representative Bob Wilson of California, who as chairman of the Republican Congressional Campaign Committee was intimately involved with AMPAC contributions. Said Wilson, "Every time we get together with politically minded doctors, they say: 'We certainly hope Nixon doesn't appoint Dr. Knowles.' " Their objection, according to Wilson, was that "Dr. Knowles has no history of backing or support for organized medicine."

try to overcome the opposition of Dirksen and other Republican senators. In any event, said the President, he would name whomever Finch recommended.

It was now that Bob Finch showed he was "indecision squared." His self-confidence shaken by his bruising struggle with John Mitchell over school desegregation* and his frustrating attempts to master the bureaucratic machinery at HEW, Finch procrastinated as week followed week. He was not, as many public reports indicated, trying to talk the President into sending Knowles' name to the Congress. The subject scarcely ever came up between them. Rather, Finch was devoting long, unhappy hours to personal conversations with Dirksen and other Congressional Republicans, trying to convince them that Knowles should have the job. It was fruitless.

"We've lost Knowles," Finch finally concluded to Veneman at luncheon one day late that winter. Veneman argued that "we're in too deep" to quit now, and talked Finch into pursuing the nomination (a decision that Veneman, in retrospect, regretted). On several occasions, John Ehrlichman urged Finch to send Knowles' name to the White House. But Finch was now deep in the agonies of indecision; his repeated public promises that a decision would be made were invariably followed by more weeks of indecision. By late June, the President was growing impatient. In his news conference of June 19, he said publicly what he had told Finch privately back in January: "When [Finch] makes a recommendation, after he has made every effort to clear it with the senators involved, *I will support that recommendation.*"

That was enough for Finch. He finally sent the recommendation to the White House, and the newspapers of June 25 predicted Knowles' imminent nomination. Dirksen threw in the towel that day, telling reporters: "When Napoleon sent Marshal Ney to Russia, he told him he would have plenty of time to discuss with him how he conquered that country and no time to discuss how he lost the battle. And I have not time to discuss Dr. Knowles."

But not only did the AMA not give up, it kept on urging Republican politicians not to give up. Representative Rogers Morton of Maryland, the new Republican National Chairman, made a final appeal to Finch, pointing out how disastrous to the Republican Party

*The Mitchell-Finch civil rights showdown is discussed in Chapter VI.

would be the loss of organized medicine's support. June 25 passed without a White House announcement of Knowles' appointment, and now Finch and his men at HEW were worried. The next day, June 26, Finch spent much of the afternoon at the White House. "They're trying to change Bob's mind," liberal Republican Senator Jacob Javits of New York told reporters, "and I don't think he's going to change."

It was not quite that way. Nixon left it up to Finch, as he had for five months past. He still would nominate Knowles if Finch insisted. But at the White House, Finch was again warned of the possibility of greatly decreased contributions to Republican Congressional candidates from AMPAC in 1970 and the problems that that would mean for the administration with angry Republicans on Capitol Hill. Returning to his office late that afternoon, Finch told his staff, "It's just not worth it." On the next morning, Finch announced, "I have reluctantly and regretfully decided . . . that the protracted and distorted discussion regarding [Knowles'] appointment . . . has resulted in a situation in which he would not be able to function effectively in this critical position."

On June 26, when Finch notified the White House he was withdrawing his sponsorship of Knowles, the President had handed him an ultimatum. Finch earlier in the week had publicly promised an appointment would be made by Saturday, June 28. If Finch had no new name, said the President, *he* would make the selection himself. Thus, Finch was now being given forty-eight hours to make a recommendation that he had agonized over for five months. Moving quickly to make sure that he would not be totally emasculated, Finch selected Dr. Roger Egeberg, Dean of the University of Southern California Medical School. Egeberg, just as liberal as Knowles and a registered Democrat besides, was not on the AMA's approved list either, but it was too late for organized medicine to launch a campaign of opposition. Egeberg was nominated by Nixon on June 28.*

---

*If Finch had not come up with Egeberg, the President was ready with his own choice: Dr. Louis M. Rousselot, Deputy Assistant Secretary of Defense for Health, a conservative Republican who would have been totally acceptable to the AMA. Rousselot met with Nixon, Finch and Ehrlichman, thought he had the job and was awaiting a phone call to confirm it. Typically, he learned of Egeberg's selection over the radio.

The bitter end of the Knowles affair produced torrents of criticism from the liberal press and liberal politicians. Senator Javits was unusually vitriolic about his own party's President: Nixon "hasn't made up his mind who he is . . . He yields to outside influences." An embittered Knowles, declaring Nixon to be "in the grip of the archconservatives," said he would not support him for President again. The attacks, invariably, were directed against Nixon, not Finch.

But Finch suffered far more than Nixon from the Knowles affair. His self-assurance, worn thin by the abrasive pounding from Mitchell in the school desegregation dispute, was now disappearing altogether. Disappearing with it was confidence in Finch from the outside world, the HEW bureaucracy, the White House and the President himself. Finch was to linger at Health, Education and Welfare for nearly another full year, increasingly tormented and ineffective. But the day he reached the end of the line as an effective force for the shaping of broad policy and strategy inside the administration was that June evening when he told his staff, "It's just not worth it."

Much of the damage was self-inflicted. At any point during those five months, Finch could have pounded the table and said, I *insist* that Knowles be nominated. The President would have complied. But the absurd and embarrassing prolongation of the Knowles affair is no less attributable to Nixon. Although he realized that his dear friend and protégé suffered from the same affliction of indecision that he had so often experienced, the President offered no helping hand. At any point during those five months, Nixon could have told Finch to name Knowles or not to name Knowles, and it would have been all over. That he did neither contributed substantially to Finch's ultimate downfall. Richard Nixon was deeply distressed and saddened by the failure of Finch at HEW, but, however unwittingly, he played no small part in that failure.

The fall of Robert Finch had far more than mere personal significance. Poignantly personal, yes, but the Knowles affair also removed the man who was potentially the most important counterweight to Mitchell in the entire administration. The fact that the one member of the Cabinet enjoying access to and relationship with the President to argue for expanded boundaries of the Republican Party was now, for all practical purposes, silenced poses this unanswerable question: What would have been the impact on Nixon and his administration had the course Finch wanted to travel been promoted with the decisiveness and purposefulness of John Mitchell?

In one of the first Cabinet meetings of 1969, Richard Nixon discussed federal patronage without sufficient preparation and put forth guidelines he would long regret that would have a profound effect on the nature of his administration. Still imbued with hopes for a revitalized Cabinet, Nixon impulsively delegated primary responsibility for filling some twenty-five hundred noncareer political positions (out of a total of three million federal jobs) to the separate Cabinet officers. Furthermore, the President said, these political jobs would be filled on the basis of, first, ability, and second, loyalty.

As he left the Cabinet Room, the new President turned to an aide and said softly, "I just made a big mistake." Indeed he had. By dispersing patronage powers throughout his administration instead of holding them in the White House as John F. Kennedy had done in 1961, and by placing ability above loyalty, he crippled any chance of fulfilling one of his original Presidential goals: to take over the federal bureaucracy as General Eisenhower had failed to do in 1953. The dreams nurtured those past sixteen years by the Republican Party faithful were now to be completely crushed. The Cabinet officers, good Republicans though they were for the most part, were more concerned with the efficient operation of their departments or appeasement of powerful Democratic committee chairmen in Congress. Only the President himself could successfully seize political control of the governmental apparatus, and, for all he had said about it during his years out of power, this simply was not on Nixon's mind in early 1969.

Harry Flemming, the twenty-eight-year-old politician-businessman assigned by John Mitchell to the chief patronage task, was off to a late start anyway, and Nixon's dispersal of power made his job impossible. When Flemming would demand that a Cabinet official name a politically reliable Republican to an appointive position, the Cabinet member would invariably reply: The President told me when I signed on that I could run my own shop. Tension between the departments and Flemming's patronage office in the White House grew to ugly levels, but Flemming was fighting a losing battle. In department after department, holdover partisan Democrats were running things. Baffled by the intricacies of government, the Cabinet officer would turn day-to-day operations over to the administrators inherited from the Johnson administration.

Typical was the case of Joseph Robertson, an active member of Minnesota's Democratic Farmer Labor Party who had been state tax commissioner under Governor Orville Freeman and was brought to Washington in 1961, as Assistant Secretary for Administration, when Freeman became John Kennedy's Secretary of Agriculture. Robertson was still there in 1969 when Freeman was replaced by Clifford M. Hardin, Chancellor of the University of Nebraska, in the new Nixon Cabinet. Equally unfamiliar with politics and the Agriculture Department, Hardin kept Robertson on temporarily to smooth over the transition. Hardin soon grew dependent on Robertson, and Joe Robertson was running the Agriculture Department as before—much to the horror of farm-belt Republican Congressmen and Harry Flemming.

Arguments that Robertson had actively supported Hubert Humphrey for President in 1968 and charges that he was favoring Democratic holdovers inside the department made no impression at all on nonpolitician Hardin. What did make an impression was a visit to Hardin in the late summer of 1969 by Clark Mollenhoff, the prize-winning investigative reporter, who had been added to the President's staff as a house detective. Mollenhoff submitted evidence to Hardin showing that, during the Kennedy administration, Robertson had recommended putting Texas manipulator Billie Sol Estes on the government's cotton advisory committee long after Robertson had been informed of Estes' scandalous cotton deals. Grudgingly Hardin was getting ready to ease Robertson out when syndicated columnist Richard Wilson reported that fact, adding that Hardin was bowing to White House pressure. "I will not be bullied," an outraged Hardin told Flemming, and Robertson stayed.* Nixon wanted Robertson out but said nothing to Hardin.

An even more outrageous patronage case was that of Randolph Thrower, Commissioner of Internal Revenue. Unlike Hardin, Thrower had partisan experience as Republican county chairman

---

*Flemming was convinced that Wilson's story was leaked by Mollenhoff, who had worked with Wilson in the Washington bureau of the *Des Moines Register and Tribune*.

back home in Atlanta. But to administer the massive Internal Revenue Service he depended wholly on holdovers, particularly Deputy Commissioner William Henry Smith, a career bureaucrat of twenty-five years' standing. Viewed by the White House as a partisan Democrat, Smith was running the IRS with Republican Thrower as a figurehead. In October, Flemming telephoned Thrower to tell him he *must* clean the Democrats out of the IRS, especially Smith. Nothing happened. Flemming next went to the White House senior staff with his problem. Peter Flanigan (another Mitchell man and Flemming's immediate superior), Haldeman and Ehrlichman all agreed in principle that Thrower must clean out IRS but said the order to do so would have to come from his chief, Secretary of the Treasury Kennedy. Flemming next talked to both Kennedy and Under Secretary Walker, but they had troubles more important to them than political control of the IRS, and gave Flemming only vague promises. The question never got to Nixon's desk, and Smith stayed.

Even when a Cabinet member *was* able to cooperate in patronage matters, he sometimes ran head-on into the Democratic feudal barons of Capitol Hill. Trouble between Flemming and Finch was severe, but Finch did agree to replace Robert Ball, thirty years a bureaucrat and for ten years head of the Social Security Administration, and thereby gain political control over a substantial segment of the huge department. But the powerful Representative Wilbur D. Mills of Arkansas, whose House Ways and Means Committee handled social security legislation, was furious when he heard of the impending change. Privately referring to Finch as a "cheap politician," Mills vowed there would be trouble if Ball was fired. Ball stayed, and, secure in his power, was impossible for Flemming to deal with. When Flemming asked Ball to name a man recommended by Vice President Spiro T. Agnew to an $18,531-a-year post in the Baltimore office of IRS, Ball replied contemptuously that if Agnew wanted a job for his buddy, Agnew ought to call him up personally—exposing the absurd spectacle of the Vice President coming on bended knee to a career bureaucrat. Agnew's man was not appointed.

The problem extended down to middle-level appointments around the country, such as U.S. district attorneys, appointments that John Sears, the political aide in the White House, had planned to use as cement for building a stronger, broader Republican Party. But such appointments had long fueled the personal political organizations of Democratic Congressional committee chairmen, and they were not going to surrender them.

A case in point was Senator James O. Eastland, Chairman of the Senate Judiciary Committee and reigning political power in the State of Mississippi. After Attorney General Mitchell finished testifying before the Judiciary Committee one morning early in 1969, Eastland approached him with a few idle comments about the court reform bill to establish several new judgeships then being drafted by the administration. He next brought up the fact that all the new federal judges to be named by Nixon would go before his committee. Warming up, Eastland then got to the nub of the matter: a "good old boy" —that is, an Eastland Democrat—down in Mississippi was about to lose his job as U.S. attorney in Jackson. Could President Nixon reappoint him? If not, Eastland made clear, he might just stick some of those judgeship appointments in his coat pocket and never get around to bringing them before the Judiciary Committee for confirmation. As for that court reform bill—"Well," said Eastland, "I just don't know."*

What followed was one of the last of the tense, knock-down battles between Mitchell and Sears.† Mitchell could see nothing wrong with making a trivial appointment to please Eastland if to do otherwise would endanger judgeship confirmations, the court reform bill and possibly even Eastland's vote for the antiballistic missile (a point sharply disputed by Sears). Sears had a fundamentally different view. In states such as Mississippi where the Republican Party was so weak, he said, it was essential that federal patronage be preserved for the Republican faithful. Accordingly, he argued, Eastland's wrath must be braved or else a dangerous precedent would be set. Mitchell, of course, won out, and the dangerous precedent was set.

Ultimately, however, the task of Republicanizing the administration was the President's. On two occasions in 1969, Flemming relayed a request to the President through Flanigan and Haldeman that Nixon appeal to the Cabinet. On both occasions the President complied, urging Cabinet members to crack down on Democrats

*It was no idle threat. Eastland held up President Eisenhower's bill for extra federal judgeships for years. Only when Democrat Kennedy was elected did Eastland permit additional judgeships.

†Typically, Sears was not fired. But given nothing to do as the year wore on, he quit in October 1969.

holding strategic positions in their departments. But his tone was polite, discreet. What was needed was a table-pounding declamation by the President that the Cabinet members *must* make this a genuinely Republican administration. Such face-to-face pressuring of lieutenants was the Presidential style of Lyndon Johnson, not Richard Nixon. And patronage was far from the front of Nixon's mind in 1969.

That, in fact, was the core of the Nixon patronage failure: his failure to pay it enough heed. That failure was no result of any genteel nineteenth-century ideal of civil service reform or abhorrence of the spoils system, but of a lack of hard attention that characterized so much that was done in domestic affairs at the White House in 1969. In turn, the continued presence of non-Republicans in policy-making positions—Joe Robertson at Agriculture, William Henry Smith at IRS, Bob Ball at Social Security—dramatized the absence of theme in Richard Nixon's domestic policy.*

Thanks to the botched performance at the Pierre Hotel during the interregnum, Richard Nixon entered the White House with a man he did not want, Ray C. Bliss, hanging on as Republican National Chairman. Nixon still wanted Bliss removed as soon as possible, and complicating that desire was a secret commitment that had been made to Murray Chotiner.

Murray Chotiner is a name that pops in and out of any political biography of Richard Nixon: his early political tutor, responsible for strategy—including the memorable Red-baiting—in his 1950 campaign for the Senate; his closest political counselor in 1952, who with William Rogers devised the strategy for keeping Nixon on the ticket after his slush-fund scandal; then, long banishment from Nixon's presence after being hauled before a Senate investigating committee on influence-peddling charges; his absence during the 1960 Presidential campaign, running his own horribly unsuccessful campaign for Congress from the Beverley Hills, Calif., district; his return in 1962 as a key strategist in Nixon's campaign for governor; his disappear-

---

*Smith finally left the IRS for private law practice on January 16, 1971, and Robertson was eased out of Agriculture and transferred over to the Civil Serivce Commission on March 5, 1971. However, Ball was still running the Social Security Administration in mid-1971.

ance until 1968, then his sudden reappearance at Nixon-for-President headquarters in New York as coordinator for the key Midwestern states. Chotiner was in many ways the most interesting personality in Nixon's political camp: aggressive, egocentric, a professional among amateurs, brilliant, overbearing, ruthless, engaging, habitually guilty of overkill, constantly enlarging his area of operation. Painted in sinister colors by the press, he was both a public relations problem for Nixon and an invaluable campaign strategist.*

On the day after Nixon's election in 1968, Chotiner and the rest of the top campaign staff were engaged in a wandering discussion with the President-elect. Nixon asked his old friend Murray Chotiner what he would like to do. Chotiner, hardly one to downgrade himself, replied he would like to replace Bliss as Republican National Chairman. Taken aback, Nixon said that, of course, was impossible, and the matter was dropped. Within the next two weeks, Mitchell and Haldeman agreed that Chotiner should be given a post at the National Committee—such as deputy chairman or executive director—where he would in fact run things while a figurehead National Chairman as Bliss' successor would be the front man, giving speeches around the country. From the standpoint of Mitchell and Haldeman, this tactic would sidetrack Chotiner, a potential rival for influence, away from the mainline of Washington power. Worried about Chotiner's reputation as a hatchet man, Nixon was less than enthusiastic about his running the party's national headquarters, but finally agreed. Haldeman and Mitchell then made a flat promise of the job to Chotiner—a promise, not idle talk. When Chotiner informed them that he was selling his home and dissolving his law practice in Los Angeles, they said, Go ahead, the job is yours.

So, late in November 1968, Chotiner was given a desk at Republican National Headquarters in downtown Washington, ostensibly for the purpose of doling out inauguration tickets to deserving politicians. When Bliss' aides, somewhat disturbed, asked what Chotiner was doing there, they were informed by the White House that he would be on his way out on January 21, the day after the inaugura-

---

*There are thoughtful veterans of the 1968 campaign who feel Chotiner really had more to do with plotting grand strategy than did Mitchell. But this is a distinctly minority view.

tion. In truth, Chotiner was ready to take over as soon as Bliss was forced out and a figurehead selected to replace him as National Chairman. The figurehead was to be personable, attractive and articulate. Representative Donald Rumsfeld and Charles (Bud) Wilkinson, the former Oklahoma football coach who was now Republican national committeeman from Oklahoma, were considered. But Nixon picked Representative Rogers C. B. Morton of Maryland, a handsome, engaging, six-foot–seven millionaire, whom Nixon had originally wanted for Secretary of the Interior (an appointment blocked by Western senators). Asked by the White House to become National Chairman, Morton said yes, as soon as Bliss resigned. Nobody bothered to tell Morton about the secret promise to Chotiner.

Then came the January 10 meeting at the Pierre in which Nixon could not bring himself to fire Ray Bliss, who went about the party's business secure in the knowledge that he would not have to leave until June or July, if then.* That made Chotiner's position untenable. January 21 came and went, and he stayed at the National Committee, with absolutely nothing to do while Bliss and his staff cast suspicious glances at him, wondering why he was there. Nixon, Mitchell and Haldeman, preoccupied elsewhere, did *absolutely nothing* to resolve that situation as the weeks sped by.

Fully one month had passed since the inauguration when late one afternoon Chotiner walked down to Bliss' office and took matters in his own hands. Blunt as always, Chotiner propositioned Bliss in words to this effect: Ray, I've been promised by the White House that I will run the National Committee as No. 2 man here, and I have got to get going. I've promised jobs here to people, and they're pressing me. Now, Ray, you can stay on as National Chairman if you want, but I can't wait a minute more to take over the machinery.

Deeply shaken, Bliss telephoned Haldeman at the White House to arrange a meeting. Yes, Haldeman told Bliss at that meeting, it was all too true. Chotiner was taking over. In that case, Bliss said, he would resign then and there. On February 18, when most Republican politicians thought the Bliss problem had been safely resolved for at least several more months, Bliss sent a letter to

*See pp. 32–33.

Nixon saying that after "much thought" he had decided to resign and "return to my private business" (insurance in Canton, Ohio). "In our party's six score years," replied an effusive Nixon, "we have never had a Chairman more dedicated than you have been, more professionally competent, or with a record of greater achievement than yours."

Bliss' angry aides told the press that he had quit when Chotiner was forced upon him, and David Broder of the *Washington Post* contacted Chotiner, whose ego and garrulousness betrayed him now as it had in the past. "Chotiner says that whoever becomes Chairman," wrote Broder in the February 19 *Post,* "will concentrate on speechmaking and 'meeting the public' while he runs the headquarters as 'deputy chairman or associate chairman or executive director or whatever they choose to call it.' "

Whether Rog Morton would have accepted Murray Chotiner as his deputy under any conditions is doubtful. But Chotiner's statements to Broder erased the possibility. Securing a meeting with the President, Morton told Nixon he would not take the National Chairmanship with anything less than complete authority. Chotiner imposed on him from above would significantly erode that authority. So, said Morton, No hard feelings, Mr. President, but I can't be your Chairman. But I need you, Nixon replied, and if that is your position, there is no need for you to take Chotiner or anybody else. Neither Nixon nor Haldeman, sitting at his side, made the slightest effort to talk Morton into accepting Chotiner, even as a clear subordinate, in order to honor their commitment.

Morton reported the President's decision to the press on February 25. An astounded Chotiner tried frantically to get in touch with Mitchell, but his calls went unanswered. At length, neither Mitchell nor Haldeman—who had made the commitment—but John Sears was dispatched to Chotiner to give him the bad news. Well, replied Murray, he had been kicked before. In fact, he added, his estranged wife had predicted that "Nixon is going to screw me."

Bryce Harlow made one last effort to honor the pledge to Chotiner. Sears was sent to inform Morton for the first time of the secret pledge to Chotiner and the fact that, assured by Haldeman and Mitchell, he had liquidated his affairs in Los Angeles to move East. Surely, Sears told Morton, Chotiner hadn't meant the things he had said to Broder. Rogers Morton definitely would be in charge even if

Chotiner were around. So why not give him a job as a clear subordinate? No, said Morton, it was too late for that. Acceptance of Chotiner, he told Sears, after all the publicity would dilute Morton's authority.*

So, the simple act of replacing Ray Bliss with Rogers Morton had been accomplished, but only after three months of intrigue, errors, confusion and personal anguish. The scars would endure. When he won the contest of wills with Richard Nixon and demanded the National Chairmanship on his terms or not at all, Morton received a black mark in that invisible ledger kept by the President. Not a critical word was said to Morton, however. Similarly, Nixon was unhappy when, upon taking over at the National Committee on April 16, Morton kept on most of the permanent staff there—regarded as incompetent by Nixon and his aides—instead of firing the whole lot. Again, not a word was mentioned to Morton. The gap between White House and National Committee was widening, with implications for the 1970 midterm elections.

Approximately one month after Morton became Chairman, Bob Haldeman told fellow Presidential aides that the National Committee was not going to amount to anything, ever, and that they would please take note of that fact. The fears of state party leaders that Richard Nixon, party man *par excellence,* was about to ignore the party, which were set off by the November rumors that Bliss would be fired, were now confirmed in May.

It was a shaky, uncertain beginning—the staff, the Cabinet, the programs and the policy lacking any discernible theme. But after all, the President was wholly immersed in his concentration on foreign affairs. And there could be found a theme, a purpose and not a little accomplishment as the Nixon administration began.

---

*With Chotiner having pulled up his roots in Los Angeles, a place still had to be found for him in Washington. That was no easy task, with Haldeman having vetoed him for a White House spot and the Senate likely to reject him for any post requiring its confirmation. At length, he was given an obscure post in the bureaucracy (general counsel to the Office of the Special Trade Representative), stayed there for a year and then quietly slipped into the White House as a political aide, where he played a major role in shaping the disastrous campaign of 1970.

IV

A Very Personal Diplomacy

Peace does not come through wishing for it. There is no substitute for days and even years of patient and prolonged diplomacy.

—Richard M. Nixon, in his
Inaugural Address, January 20, 1969

It was Melvin Robert Laird, pragmatist and realist, who in the new Nixon administration perceived the realities in Vietnam. Laird, as Secretary of Defense, approached the delicate, difficult problem of getting American soldiers out of Vietnam like a ferocious bulldog gnawing on a bone; he couldn't let it alone. It consumed his energies, stretched his imagination and made him something of a terror to the nonpolitical advisers on foreign policy whom Nixon had surrounded himself with—principally Harvard history professor and long-time adviser to Presidents, Henry M. Kissinger.

"Mel?" Kissinger mused long months later when asked about Laird. "Mel is a rascal, but a good rascal."

Laird had carefully started to build his case for a rapid U.S. pullout long before he dreamed he would go to the Pentagon, long before the election, long before even the Republican National Convention at Miami Beach. As the powerful chairman of the House Republican Caucus, his politically sensitive antenna was sending out quiet vibrations as early as February 1966, when Senator Robert F. Kennedy infuriated President Lyndon Johnson, Vice President Hubert Humphrey and the entire foreign and military policy team then in power with his proposal for a coalition government in Saigon.

Laird took pains immediately to warn fellow Republicans not to knock Kennedy, as Humphrey and other Johnson satellites were doing. Instead, Laird counseled House Republican leaders to stay mute in the face of Kennedy's challenge to Johnson. "We may be endorsing the same proposal if we win the 1968 election," Mel Laird said. In short: Don't close the negotiating door.

At the Miami Beach convention, it was Laird who spelled out his "de-Americanization" policy during the platform hearings. It was Laird who told the press, while riding with candidate Nixon from Bismarck, N.D., to Boise, Ida., in October 1968, that up to ninety thousand American troops could be pulled out of Vietnam in the next twelve months (and was sharply rebuffed by Johnson's Secretary of Defense, Clark Clifford, who noted that the troop level was still going up in Vietnam).

As the brainiest politician in the Nixon circle of advisers during the campaign, Laird took it upon himself to educate Nixon on the absolute imperative of moving out of Vietnam immediately, not all at once, of course, but to set wheels in motion that would calm the antiwar passions beginning to spread beyond the peace bloc. He never lost a chance to try to proselytize Republican politicians, campaign advisers and candidate Richard Nixon himself.

Such missionary work was absolutely necessary. Nixon's entire public record had been that of a hard-line anti-Communist, eager to halt Red aggression all over the world—including Vietnam. After the Republican election debacle of 1964, Nixon assumed, incorrectly, that Johnson would be sparing in help for the beleaguered Saigon regime, and therefore proposed that the divided Republicans unify in 1965 around the issue of stopping Communist aggression in Southeast Asia, just as they had unified a century before on the issue of no more slave states. In the 1966 midterm election, he criticized the details of the Johnson intervention but defended fighting the war itself: "We believe this is a war that has to be fought to prevent World War III." Nixon was then an unequivocal hawk in Vietnam, favoring a military victory. By 1968, however, he was being advised that military victory was impossible. That, and the unpopularity of the war, watered down the militancy in his speeches. By the time the campaign for President opened in New Hampshire in February, Nixon was pledging to "end the war," implying he had a tidy plan to be unveiled in due time. It was not dovish and not hawkish but very Delphic, susceptible to favorable interpretation by ~ ~~ and hawk alike.

Laird cautioned Nixon not to say "end the war." The phrase was not accurate, Laird explained, because the war might go on long after Nixon had completed his first term. The proper pledge was "end American participation in the war"—get American troops out and transfer the burden of combat to the South Vietnamese.

Nixon did not follow the advice and decided to keep things murky throughout the 1968 campaign. He never did spell out a detailed policy to fulfill his pledge to end the war. Indeed, Nixon's election found him uncertain on detailed planning of any kind for foreign policy, including the war in Southeast Asia. He possessed a strong, well-defined global strategy but few of the tactics to pursue it. Certain that he would win the election from the day the Democrats ended their bloody convention on the Chicago battlefield, Nixon saw no political need to get specific in a bid for votes. Although he was beginning to intellectualize a U.S. strategy that became the Nixon Doctrine, his specific plans for getting Americans out of Vietnam—throughout the campaign and right up to the inauguration—scarcely advanced beyond this broad-brush campaign pledge (stated by Nixon behind closed doors to Southern delegates at the Miami convention): "We need a massive training program so that the South Vietnamese can be trained to take over the fighting, that they can be phased in while we phase out."

But what about a negotiated settlement? What were the chances for cease-fire? Would Hanoi settle for a fair distribution of power in South Vietnam, based on a genuinely free election? Or did "coalition government" doom South Vietnam to eventual Communist domination? These questions had not been considered by Richard Nixon, either as candidate or as President-elect.

The President-elect's first order to Henry Kissinger was succinct: Tell me where the United States stands today in Europe, Southeast Asia, the Middle East and lesser geographic regions, how to organize the National Security Council setup in the White House, what my immediate crises will be, how I should proceed with the Strategic Arms Limitation Talks, and on and on. The order to Kissinger was designed to produce a complete inventory of the entire range of U.S. foreign policy, upon which the new President would then construct the details of his own policy—details he had conspicuously avoided setting forth during the campaign.

Kissinger's first step was to call in half a dozen experts in national security affairs; several were to become bitter critics of Nixon foreign policy—such as Morton Halperin, who stayed with Kissinger in the White House until the Cambodian intervention in 1970, and Dan Ellsberg, a brilliant RAND Corporation analyst and a strong Vietnam dove.

Consulting frequently with Laird, Kissinger and his staff holed up at the Pierre Hotel and prepared five options for Nixon on how to deal with the war that had driven his predecessor out of the Presidency. The options, one or a combination of which would establish the Nixon war policy, were these: Option I—Immediate escalation, with full-scale bombing in the North including the supply port of Haiphong and industrial areas around Hanoi, aimed at quick military victory (or, if the North Vietnamese chose, a negotiated settlement in Paris); Option II—Vigorous military prosecution of the war, with steadily increasing U.S. pressure on the ground, but no escalation, also aimed at outright military victory. Options III, IV, and V all embraced the troop-withdrawal concept, with No. V calling for an immediate end to the U.S. combat role and total reliance on the Paris peace negotiations.

Kissinger was operating at the Pierre under a Nixon timetable that set Vietnam as the principal topic for discussion at the first National Security Council meeting, which the President-elect had scheduled for January 25, five days after the inauguration. Nixon wanted the options presented then.

Next, Kissinger turned to the mechanism that would soon be playing the vital role in the development and carrying out of U.S. policy: the National Security Council. Both he and Nixon wanted that mechanism to be more supple than the old NSC structure (with its Planning Board and Operations Coordination Board) under Eisenhower, but more precise in its procedures than the informal, conversational method which Lyndon Johnson employed to make high national policy at his famous Tuesday luncheons. Kissinger's assignment was to strike a balance, and as it turned out, he chose a form closer to John F. Kennedy's than either Eisenhower's or Johnson's.

On December 30 he took his completed memorandum on the new NSC system to Florida ("I apologize for the length," read a notation), and Nixon approved it on the spot. Kissinger's memorandum discussed the Johnson system briefly, pointedly criticizing the Tuesday policy-making luncheon for "the frequent uncertainty about precisely what was decided." As for the Eisenhower system, Kissinger told Nixon that "its very formality tended to demand too much of the participants' time and insufficient priority to issues of primary presidential concern."

Nixon's approval of the memorandum established the NSC as the only forum for top-level review and policy-making, and gave power over the agenda to a Review Group headed by Kissinger, with the State and Defense departments and the Central Intelligence Agency having one seat each—a division of power strongly advocated by Laird. It also proposed for the first time that the President, using the NSC staff, make an annual State of the World report to Congress to "permit a more extended discussion of the President's view of the international situation than is possible in the State of the Union message."* Thus, the great advantages that Kissinger brought into the White House in becoming Nixon's preeminent foreign policy adviser—his expertise against Secretary of State William Rogers' utter unfamiliarity with foreign affairs—were reinforced institutionally from the beginning.

Richard Nixon and Henry Kissinger, it quickly became happily clear to both, thought much alike on U.S. global strategy. At heart, Nixon perceives the world in classical balance-of-power terms and is totally unwilling to cede U.S. influence in any part of the world where it exists. But the United States, given the vast drain of the ten-year war in Vietnam and having lost the nuclear superiority that so well served Eisenhower (in Korea) and Kennedy (in Cuba), now had to define a strategy that would explain military withdrawal from Vietnam in terms other than the virtual surrender demanded by more and more war-weary Americans.

At that first NSC meeting called by Nixon to discuss Vietnam,

---

*The timing of that proposal, and its immediate acceptance by Nixon, clearly demonstrate how wrong certain critics were when, one year later, Kissinger was accused of deliberately undercutting Rogers and the State Department by persuading Nixon to shelve Rogers' own State of the World Report in favor of the Nixon-Kissinger report. In fact, the Nixon-Kissinger report had been in the planning stage for slightly more than one year.

a tentative decision was made to adopt a mix of options III, IV and V in Kissinger's five-choice scenario—a withdrawal keyed to the ability of South Vietnamese forces to take over the U.S. combat role. The strongest voice at the table for this option was Laird's, in keeping with his long-held views. He wanted the fastest withdrawal possible *within* the outer limits of what the President's military advisers, the Joint Chiefs of Staff, would accept (and Laird well knew that to get the Pentagon brass to accept *anything* in the way of meaningful withdrawals was going to demand all the President's and his own powers of persuasion).

Rogers spoke quietly for an even faster withdrawal. Unencumbered by military advisers, and by profession an expert negotiator and mediator (like all good lawyers), Rogers was convinced that the faster the pace of withdrawals, the more chance there was for a breakthrough at the Paris peace talks.

Kissinger, in those early NSC meetings that determined the course of the United States in Vietnam, was most skeptical about the South Vietnamese ever becoming the kind of fighting force that could assume a primary combat role against the legions from Hanoi, or even their Vietcong guerrilla allies in the South. To Kissinger, a far harder military posture—forcing North Vietnam to choose between devastation or genuine negotiation—seemed the best of a series of hideously bad alternatives. In those days, the generals and the admirals would rather have had Kissinger at the Pentagon than Laird.

But while Laird pressed for withdrawals as quickly as possible, Kissinger was scrupulously neutral, tossing in questions and making comments in a way calculated to conceal any preference of his own, and to define the choices available to Nixon in the clearest possible terms. ("I will never give advice unless you order me to," he told the President privately when he agreed to take the job. "But I will do my best to see that all options are fully exposed.")

On January 25, then, Nixon made the first and most difficult of his foreign policy decisions. He would withdraw, gradually but unilaterally. But like his Secretary of State, he had set far too high a probability on a breakthrough at the Paris peace talks. He had erred —and the months ahead would prove it—as Lyndon Johnson had erred, time and time again, by judging the actions of the tough and hardened Communists in Hanoi by Western standards of rationality.

In his very first press conference, on January 27, Nixon gave a revealing clue to his inner hopes for a negotiated settlement: "I believe that as we look at what is happening in the negotiations in Paris, as far as the American side is concerned, we are off to a good start . . . we have laid down those things which we believe the other side should agree to and can agree to"—mutual withdrawal of forces, exchange of prisoners and, although not yet spelled out, free elections. In Paris, Nixon's newly appointed chief Vietnam negotiator, Henry Cabot Lodge, was also optimistic. The optimism did not last long.

With or without success at Paris, Nixon's plan for withdrawal from Vietnam served as the centerpiece of the Nixon Doctrine, the President's still-developing scheme for a global American strategy in the era of nuclear parity. In essence, the doctrine was half a cover for getting U.S. troops out of Vietnam and half a challenge to U.S. allies elsewhere to do more in the common cause of resisting Communist aggressions. If Paris failed as a source for bringing the war to a negotiated end, Nixon had to have an explanation for Asian countries on the rim of Communist China as the troop-withdrawal process went on. He had to convince them, or at least make a valiant effort to convince them, that the United States was not turning its back and retiring across the Pacific. The Nixon Doctrine and its ramifications were to be a recurring theme in his Presidency.

First, however, there was an essential follow-up to the January 25 NSC decision. On March 6, Nixon sent Laird to Saigon to get the approval of General Creighton Abrams, the U.S. Field Commander in Vietnam, for the withdrawal concept. No figures were mentioned and the timing was left vague. Under those conditions Abrams acquiesced, but he did not attempt to conceal what he regarded as an overwhelming risk in the concept itself. Laird returned to Washington on March 10, reported to Nixon, and working through a Pentagon task force headed by Admiral William Lemos, began charting a withdrawal schedule under the imposing title "Conceptual Overview."

Kept in a locked cabinet in his own office, the Conceptual Overview of Laird and his Vietnam task force became the master chart that would determine the pace and size of U.S. troop withdrawals: which units would come out first, what balance should be kept between combat and logistical backup troops, and which geographic areas of combat should be gradually turned over to the South Vietnamese. It became the road map of Nixon's withdrawal journey.

Only one major decision now remained: the date and circumstances for announcing the withdrawal of the first contingent. Nixon wanted maximum publicity for this occasion. He decided to meet President Nguyen Van Thieu of South Vietnam on June 8 at Midway Island, the halfway point between the United States and Saigon. But a note of high drama awaited the President when, en route to his meeting with Thieu, he put down at Hickam Field in Honolulu on June 7 for a face-to-face consultation with General Abrams. The source of that drama was Abrams himself.

Ever since Nixon had chosen the troop-withdrawal option, the military high command had been seething, fighting the idea of spending scarce defense dollars to build up Saigon's military power. The principle of troop withdrawal—pulling out of a war in which forty thousand Americans had already given their lives—went squarely against their military training and strong convictions not to yield to Communist aggression. They also bitterly resented the President's decision to withdraw *combat* troops first and not backup support troops. They had offered their own troop-withdrawal schedule, based on quick pullback of up to seventy-five thousand supply troops. But to disengage the cream of Army and Marine Corps combat forces on some, to them, vague hope that Saigon's own army could take up the slack seemed the height of stupidity. During the four and one-half months preceding Nixon's trip to Honolulu and Midway, General Earle G. Wheeler, Chairman of the Joint Chiefs of Staff, and General William Westmoreland, Army Chief of Staff, had led an internal struggle to reverse or at least modify the President's plan.

But Nixon's tactic of withdrawing combat, not support, troops was grounded in concrete because it had become fundamental to his larger strategy to make the Paris peace talks come alive. What Nixon counted on was the impact that withdrawing combat troops would have on Hanoi. Once Ho Chi Minh, the North Vietnamese leader, perceived that the new President was in fact reducing U.S. warmaking capability in South Vietnam, surely he would become less intransigent at the Paris peace talks. On the other hand, withdrawal of strictly noncombat troops would never be taken as evidence in

Hanoi that Nixon was really moving toward winding down the war.
To the contrary, Hanoi would sneer at it as sham, a maneuver to
make negotiating points. All this was carefully spelled out to the
American generals, but they resisted every step of the way.

The full force of this resistance did not strike Nixon until his
meeting with Abrams in Honolulu. Abrams, as judged by one participant there, "oozed with distaste" when Nixon revealed the formal
orders he was about to give that twenty-five thousand combat troops
would be withdrawn as the first contingent. In tight-lipped polite-
ness, Abrams raised hard questions: Was the U.S. risking the substance of four years of war? Would the withdrawal plan be
interpreted as a sellout by the South Vietnamese, no matter what
Thieu said publicly? Was not the U.S. taking a fantastic gamble? The
opposition was so remorseless that the high civilian officials there
"knew we had done something hard to do when we got through with
the brass and made that first announcement."

And so President Nixon, in the hardest and most significant
decision of his new Presidency, set an immutable course in Vietnam
that reversed the long build-up of the previous decade, a build-up
that had taken U.S. military strength from a handful of advisers to
543,400 troops. He desperately hoped that this evidence of good faith
would persuade Ho Chi Minh to begin serious negotiating in Paris,
but in this he would be disappointed (as Laird always suspected he
would be). He desperately prayed that his policy reversal would cool
domestic passions, but the political effect at home was neither dramatic nor permanent. He desperately trusted in the growing ability
of Thieu's own army to fill the gaps left by the departing Americans
—a trust yet to be entirely fulfilled. But the meeting with Thieu on
Midway Island was set in circumstances inherited by Nixon at their
most desperate stage. Given his commitment to withdraw from Vietnam with "honor," not surrender, the formula he devised was probably the best if not the only one available.

On March 21, Melvin Laird testified before the Disarmament
Subcommittee of the Senate Foreign Relations Committee and, for
the first time, faced the full force of antiwar passion from the committee's chairman, Senator J. W. Fulbright of Arkansas. "You've got
to do something radical to change this war," Fulbright lectured
Laird, "or we're going down the drain. Soon it will be Nixon's war,

and then there will be little chance to bring it to an end. It is time to de-escalate and settle it."

Thus, with Richard Nixon barely two months in office, antiwar politicians were breaking their silence, feeling that Nixon was moving down the same path that sucked in Lyndon B. Johnson. One reason the political lid was lifting was the post-Tet offensive by Communist troops and a counteroffensive by the Americans and South Vietnamese. The other, more important reason was statements of administration officials. On March 14 at his televised news conference in the White House, Nixon was asked by Charles W. Bailey II of the *Minneapolis Tribune* whether he saw "any prospect for withdrawing American troops in any numbers soon." The President's reply set the official line that would have serious implications far into the future:

> Mr. Bailey, in view of the current offensive on the part of the North Vietnamese and the Vietcong, *there is no prospect for a reduction of American forces* in the foreseeable future. [Emphasis added.]
>
> When we are able to reduce forces as a result of a combination of circumstances—the ability of the South Vietnamese to defend themselves in areas where we now are defending them, the progress of the talks in Paris, or the level of enemy activity—when that occurs, I will make an announcement. But at this time there is no foreseeable prospect in that field.

Nixon administration spokesmen took up the line. On March 19, Laird told the Senate Armed Services Committee that the United States was planning no troop pullout "at the present time." When published reports appeared that indeed such a pullout was inevitable,* administration spokesmen denied it. Confusion proliferated. John Gardner, the liberal Republican who had quit as President Johnson's Secretary of Health, Education and Welfare mainly over the war, talked privately with Nixon that spring of 1969 and was delighted to learn of the pullout, passing the good news on to his friends. Gardner and his friends were subsequently mystified and distraught by the official disclaimers of any withdrawal.

The logic behind this goes to the heart of the political strategy being practiced in 1969 by Richard Nixon and John Mitchell, and

---

*Our column of March 24 predicted "significant withdrawals of U.S. forces from Vietnam within six months."

enunciated by Mitchell, in connection with civil rights. "Watch what we do instead of what we say," said Mitchell. The Nixon–Mitchell strategy was predicated on the fear of alienating the dominant conservative majority that voted for Nixon and Wallace in 1968. To prevent that alienation, progressive policies must be masked in conservative rhetoric. In the case of Vietnam, that meant *denying* reports of the decisions for a troop withdrawal that had already been made and were being relentlessly pursued against opposition from the uniformed military.

The self-inflicted damage stemming from this was incalculable. Had the withdrawal policy been clearly enunciated when first decided upon, the period of grace from Fulbright and the Senate doves would have been significantly lengthened. But, as it was, Fulbright and his allies were pulled prematurely into a posture of opposition from which it was difficult to withdraw. More important, Nixon's harsh rhetoric and soft policy built doubts within the intellectual and student peace bloc that he was really serious about taking troops out. Living in the world of rhetoric, students and intellectuals *believed* Nixon's rhetoric (which was misleading) and *doubted* his actions (which were genuine). Far into the future, doubt that Nixon really was pulling out of Vietnam would haunt the campuses.

Even after his June announcement of the first troop withdrawal, Nixon continued to talk a hard line. With one giant antiwar demonstration having taken place nationwide on October 15 and a massive march on Washington planned by more extreme leftist groups for November 15, Nixon had a golden opportunity in his speech to the nation of November 3 to soften dissent by simply emphasizing the extent of troop withdrawals, now and into the future. In this he failed to consult Laird and, instead, took an opposite course. In contrast to the preparation of his speech in May stating the U.S. negotiating position, before the first troop withdrawal was announced, foreign policy experts had no hand in preliminary drafts for this speech. It was written by one hand alone: Richard Nixon's. In a conscious imitation of Winston Churchill speaking without notes during the dark days of the Battle of Britain, the President memorized the speech for television.

Thus, the November 3 speech, embodying the political tactics of John Mitchell and the unmistakable political prose of Richard Nixon, appealed to those Americans who would *not* be demonstrating in the streets of Washington on November 15: the Silent Majority, so designated for the first time. Asking "you, the great Silent Majority of my fellow Americans" for support, the President declared, "I would be untrue to my oath of office if I allowed the policy of this nation to be dictated by the minority who . . . try to impose [their view] on the nation by mounting demonstrations in the streets." Instead of emphasizing the irreversibility of his withdrawal policy, the President stressed his willingness to re-escalate if need be: "If I conclude that increased enemy action jeopardizes our remaining forces in Vietnam, I shall not hesitate to take strong and effective measures to deal with that situation."

The explicit threat in those words was, of course, partly aimed at Hanoi in the hope that the prospect of escalation would loosen the adamant negotiating posture of the Communist mission in Paris. The impact there, however, was zero. At home, it was immediate and politically dangerous.

Liberals of both parties, infatuated with rhetoric, were dismayed by the November 3 speech. But all polls and other political barometers indicated it was a smash hit with that Silent Majority for which it was intended. Nixon and his aides were well satisfied, not realizing they had lost another opportunity to defuse antiwar sentiment by matching words to deeds.

Vietnam was Nixon's most acute problem, but his and the world's most dangerous situation was halfway across the globe in the Middle East. Within weeks of entering the White House, a distinctively Nixon plan to defuse the Arab-Israeli mini-war had been drawn up—not by Kissinger in this case, but by professional diplomats in the State Department.

The single foreign problem from which, in those early days, Kissinger kept arm's length was the Middle East. That was partly because, as a Jew, he wanted no charges of divided loyalty aimed at the Nixon White House, as they had been aimed at Jewish assistants to Johnson and Kennedy. But it was also because, as he made no effort to conceal, in all his writings about foreign policy there was no mention of the Middle East. Kissinger was not a student of the rancid politics of oil, the Suez Canal and the modern-day hatreds between Jew and Arab that had led to two Israeli sweeps across the Sinai Peninsula to the East Bank of the Canal. Eisenhower had forced Israel back home after the first invasion, in 1956. Now they were there again, and a new element—Soviet arms and advisers in enormous quantities on Egyptian soil—threatened to escalate Egypt's war of attrition to recover the Sinai into war between the United States and Russia.

The President's first signal of intent to play a far more positive diplomatic role in the Middle East than his predecessors was the dispatch of William W. Scranton, his first choice for Secretary of State, on a fact-finding mission before the inauguration. Scranton made headlines with a statement midway in his trip that the new President favored an "even-handed" policy for the United States. That statement set Israeli nerves on edge and had precisely the same political effect in the large and powerful American-Jewish community. Nixon immediately became suspect. He had, after all, been elected with only marginal help from American Jews, who traditionally backed Democratic Presidential candidates with both votes and lavish campaign contributions. What the American-Jewish community suspected was that Nixon, unencumbered by political obligations, would impose a settlement on the Israelis that would force them off the vast lands they had captured in the 1967 six-day war without guaranteed security, just as Eisenhower had done.

Nixon saw it quite differently. The Middle East would become the first major test of his pledge to move from an era of confrontation into an era of negotiation, and he quickly gave an extraordinarily free hand to Rogers and his Assistant Secretary of State for Near Eastern Affairs, a brilliant, imaginative and abrasive career officer named Joseph J. Sisco.

Sisco had been the Assistant Secretary of State who handled international organizations during Rogers' brief tour as a delegate to the United Nations in 1965, and Rogers came to know him well. Accordingly, one of Rogers' first decisions after being named Secretary of State was to have a long cozy lunch with Joe Sisco in late December. Sisco briefed him on some of the department's top foreign service officers (strongly recommending, for example, that Rogers put Marshall Green and William Sullivan in charge of the Far Eastern Bureau, advice that was followed). Before Rogers left Sisco that day, he asked him to be Assistant Secretary for Near Eastern Affairs and to draft some position papers for what Rogers knew was in the immediate offing: a highly activist Nixon policy to put out the Arab-Israeli fires and stabilize Middle Eastern politics.

Despite his reputation as being slightly pro-Israeli (gained in his days at the UN), Sisco in fact was as objective as any diplomat could be, within the context of the special relationship between the United States and Israel. He had studied the Middle East at a distance (having never set foot in the area) and was convinced that the only way to stop the alarming growth of Soviet influence in Egypt and lesser Arab states was to obtain a genuine settlement, thus eliminating Arab dependence on Soviet military help. He took as his guideline for this settlement the policy carried over from the Johnson administration—that, with only "insubstantial" border alterations, Israel would have to withdraw from the territories she seized in 1967.

Within two weeks after Rogers gave Sisco the Middle East portfolio, Sisco had finished work on a series of secret position papers containing the general outlines of the policy that Nixon, with dogged persistence, would pursue the next two years. Having prepared his long-range plan, working at night and in complete secrecy, Sisco turned it over to Rogers, who in turn took it to the President.

Using the Sisco briefs as the foundation stone, Nixon called an all-day session of the National Security Council on February 1 and discovered a surprising administration consensus, led by the Rogers–Sisco team, and shared by Under Secretary of State Elliot Richardson (Kissinger's most intimate contact in the State Department), Laird and Richard C. Helms, Director of the Central Intelligence Agency. The basic Rogers–Sisco format was approved and a clear understanding reached that despite Israel's specially favored position within past Democratic administrations, the United States would construct its diplomatic case with strictest objectivity. As one key participant privately remarked, "It is high time that the United States stopped acting as Israel's attorney in the Middle East."

But Nixon's decision to embrace Sisco's activist policy carried high risks. It depended, first, on that most elusive and mercurial element—cooperation from the Russians, an ingredient conspicuously lacking in the post-World War II experience of every American President. Nixon's plan was to develop agreement with the Russians, working through Soviet Ambassador Anatoly F. Dobrynin in Washington and the Soviet UN delegation in New York, based on an Israeli withdrawal from the Sinai Peninsula, from a large part of Israel's captured holdings on the Syrian Golan Heights, all of Gaza and most of the Jordanian West Bank. The questions of Jerusalem and the Palestinian refugees, now numbering over two million, would be worked out later.

If the Egyptians could be persuaded to sign a peace agreement with Israel and guarantee Israeli passage through the still-closed Suez Canal and the Strait of Tiran, leading to the Israeli port of Eilat, Nixon and the Rogers-Sisco team believed their settlement plan might work. And on just such an overall settlement rested the administration's anxious hope for halting the dangerous rise in Soviet influence and military power within the Arab world. If an acceptable settlement could be made, the Arabs would no longer need Soviet help. Most important, Nixon believed that long-term security for Israel would lie only in a settlement that was genuinely acceptable to the Arabs.

As for the Soviets, they had become a major Mediterranean sea power since the 1967 war, a fact that the United States could complain about but not undo. They had thriving military-aid programs going in Egypt, Syria and Iraq which opened the door wide to political and economic influence. These Soviet assets were also permanent. But if a settlement between Israel and the Arabs could be arranged, a ceiling would be imposed on the further expansion of Soviet influence, and the Egyptians, who for a hundred years had been a Westward-looking people, would look toward the West once more.

Nixon was acutely conscious, during his early discussions on the Middle East, of how shabbily the Eisenhower administration had treated the Egyptians and how the growth of Soviet power could be directly traced to inexcusable mistakes made by Secretary of State John Foster Dulles. Moreover, Nixon was also conscious of rising discontent among the Mediterranean European powers, particularly Italy and France, which blamed the U.S.-Israeli intimacy for the sudden appearance of Soviet power in the Mediterranean as an ally of the embattled Arab world.

As for domestic politics, the President conspicuously stayed in the shadows as Rogers, Richardson and Sisco conducted the most active and aggressive foreign policy ever witnessed in Washington on the Middle East. From Jerusalem came ominous warnings that Nixon was preparing, in concert with the Russians, British and French, to "impose" a settlement to Israel's disadvantage. At home, the American-Jewish community played a low-keyed opposition role along the same lines, with pressure groups making frequent trips to the State Department to badger Rogers and Sisco. This campaign was kept low-key for fear that Richard Nixon, who owed so little to the pro-Israeli lobby, might react with anger and close off the lifeline that, filled with arms and credits, ran from the Pentagon to Israeli defense headquarters in Tel Aviv.

But the heart of the Rogers-Sisco plan depended on Soviet cooperation. In early meetings with Dobrynin, Rogers outlined the overall settlement strategy: a joint Washington-Moscow agreement on general guidelines, including borders, which would be endorsed by the Big Four, then handed to the special United Nations Mideast envoy, Gunnar Jarring of Sweden. Jarring in turn would then "sell" the plan, backed by the world's mightiest powers, to the Egyptians, the Jordanians and the Israelis.

The Soviet reputation for mean and tough bargaining quickly proved itself. Thus, the first still-secret draft of the U.S. plan for new borders between Egypt and Israel stated that "the former international boundary [before the 1967 war] is not necessarily excluded" —language that left a clear implication that Israel might wind up with a piece of the Sinai. As attorneys for President Nasser, the Russians rejected that bit of doubt. The final draft accepted by Rogers in October 1969 was precise: the Sinai border would be the same as before the six-day war. In a phrase, no annexation of territory.

Nixon kept close personal touch with Sisco, on whom the burden of these tough negotiations with the Russians fell, with telephone calls and Oval Office chats. Not only did the President believe that territory should not be acquired as a "right of conquest," but he was willing to accept any Soviet bargaining position in the interest of a settlement so long as it did not sell out Israel's existence. More important, this long, agonizing negotiation with the Soviet Union was, so the President thought, breaking new ground every day and setting a negotiating precedent that might point the way toward an eventual arms control agreement. What Rogers and Sisco were doing was testing the Russians in perhaps the most difficult negotiation in the twenty-five years of confrontation since World War II. A generous U.S. bargaining position on the Middle East, if paralleled by the Russians, would be useful in gaining other agreements with the

Russians to end other major confrontations; failure here would hurt elsewhere.

But there was also the higher objective of stopping the dangerous rise of Soviet influence in the eastern Mediterranean, which in Nixon's opinion demanded that the United States supply hard proof to the Arabs that the old days of Washington playing the role of Israel's attorney had ended.

In Israel, hawks and doves alike bitterly disagreed with this Nixon scenario. There was only one way to deal with the Russians, proclaimed Israeli politicians, and that was to possess such overwhelming power—and the will to use it—that they would be frightened out of the Arab world rather than risk World War III. To make that show of strength, Israel asked for substantial shipments of late-model U.S. military equipment, from the F-4 Phantom, by far the best aircraft in the Middle East, to highly sophisticated electronics systems that could frustrate the Soviet surface-to-air missiles on the West Bank of the Suez Canal that Egypt was using, in vain, to stop Israeli air attacks.

In pressing Nixon hard for this policy of strength, the Israelis conveniently ignored Nixon's determination to reestablish friendly relations with the Arabs. The position-of-strength policy might have been fine for containing the Russians, but its collateral effect would be worsened relations between the United States and the Arabs. It would reinforce—in full view of the Arabs—the strong ties between Washington and Jerusalem. Nixon, convinced that the road to peace led through Cairo, would have none of it. The force of his conviction on that central dispute with Israel came through time and again as the Russians put up one roadblock after another and Nixon moved his negotiating position to accommodate them—but never at the expense of Israel's security.

When, in October 1969, Rogers sent Moscow his final "formulation" on Israeli withdrawal from Sinai, for presumed acceptance by the Soviet government, the Russians rejected it. It would by no means be the last disappointment experienced by Nixon in seeking cooperation from the Kremlin to bring peace to the Mideast.

Richard Nixon came into office with few specifics clear in his mind on the large foreign policy problems he would confront. But on the general directions he would take, there was never any doubt.

He knew what he wanted. He had a *theme,* born of long study, fascination with the subject and almost continuous world travel since the time twenty-two years before when he took his seat in the House of Representatives. If anything distinguished the President's conduct and habit in foreign as contrasted to domestic policy, that was it; in one he had a theme, in the other he did not.

One central part of the foreign policy theme Nixon had been composing for several years before he entered the White House was the need to reverse the gradual deterioration in the old intimacy between the United States and Western Europe, particularly between Washington and Paris. Nixon had been a member of the famed Herter Committee of the House of Representatives which studied the postwar industrial and social devastation in Europe.* He watched it grow and thrive on the Marshall Plan. Those had been glorious days for the United States—when, in the words of one of Nixon's principal foreign policy aides, "We did not need a foreign policy. The West looked to us to save them from the Russians. With our comfortable superiority in nuclear bombs, we could do anything we wanted any way we wanted."

Thus, long before his inauguration, Nixon resolved—and so informed newly appointed Henry Kissinger—that he wanted to take a trip to Europe early in his first year for what he regarded as an overdue mission: strengthening and invigorating the Atlantic Alliance. He wanted, in short, to polish what he called the "blue chip" of American foreign policy: Western Europe. To prepare himself for this all-important first exposure beyond his own country, Nixon enthusiastically turned himself over to the career diplomats in the State Department for unprecedented face-to-face briefings in the Oval Office. This was, for the State Department, exhilarating and surprising, for Nixon had always had a deeply skeptical and some-what scornful attitude toward the State Department bureaucracy— a skepticism that sooner or later had overtaken every new President since Herbert Hoover. But Kissinger's White House operation was

---

*The Herter Committee, headed by Republican Representative Christian A. Herter of Massachusetts (later President Eisenhower's Secretary of State), was appointed in the postwar Republican Eightieth Congress (1947–48), in which Nixon was a freshman Congressman, to study war-torn Europe and recommend ways in which U.S. aid could rebuild European commerce and industry. Its recommenda-tions became a central feature of the Marshall Plan.

scarcely functioning, Nixon had been President for less than a month, and the need for speed overcame scruples. The briefings, at the low-echelon level of country desk officers for each of the five countries to be visited, were not only a success, but they lifted morale inside the State Department to an unaccustomed high (a condition that was not to last long). The professionals who were summoned to brief the new President found not only a spongelike mind that sopped up their briefings with surprising ease but a student of foreign affairs who displayed precise and intimate knowledge of the subject.

Nixon regarded the lofty Charles de Gaulle, President of France, as by far his most important target when he left Washington on February 23, and it was to De Gaulle that the major thrust of the trip was directed. Stymied in his long travail to dominate Europe and lead the way toward rapprochement with the Communist East as the West's best friend of the Soviet Union, De Gaulle now seemed ready to reverse directions a bit and recognize the inevitable: the United States would indeed remain a powerful factor to reckon with in Europe for a good while longer, and West Germany's steadily rising economic power posed a serious threat to De Gaulle's quixotic vision of European dominance. Nixon knew De Gaulle was undergoing just such a subtle change of heart, and he wanted to encourage it early in his administration and then build on it to foster faster European integration, the admission of Great Britain into the Common Market and a more meaningful European partnership with the United States. Moreover, there was in Nixon a vague identification with De Gaulle, founded on De Gaulle's humiliation after his postwar term of power and his glorious comeback in the midst of the Algerian crisis. Nixon, too, had suffered humiliation and turned it into a miraculous rebirth of personal power.

But beyond De Gaulle, Nixon was determined to explain his dream of a healthier relationship between America and Europe in which burdens of responsibility were to be more equally shared, with the United States ending what Nixon regarded as its patronizing way of dealing with European allies. He phrased it carefully and rather well on arriving on February 28 at Paris' Orly Airport, the most important stop on his trip. Decrying "unilateral decisions on the part of one great power," he said what is needed is "the very best wisdom that we can find in finding the policies that will save freedom and maintain peace in the world."

That was the heart of Nixon's European policy: a new partnership in which Europe would make larger contributions to common Western policy, and the United States would stop pressing so hard to mold events to its own special taste. For France, the publication *La Politique Ce Matin* summed it up this way: "Now that the United States itself no longer intends to play the role of Director in Europe, the roots of the conflict disappear. . . ."

There was another high purpose in the President's mind. With Washington and Moscow about to start their talks on Strategic Arms Limitation (SALT), Nixon wanted to remove any doubt in Western Europe that the United States was making private deals with the Russians that might damage its allies in Europe. Suspicion is usual among partners, and Nixon feared the SALT talks could corrode the alliance.* Consequently, Nixon promised full and speedy consultation with each of the heads of government of the countries visited: De Gaulle, Wilson of England, Kiesinger of West Germany, Rumor of Italy and Eyskens of Belgium.

With De Gaulle, who was unexpectedly to yield office a few months later, Nixon was an unmixed success. De Gaulle's aides said that the arrogant old statesman at an Elysée Palace state dinner on February 28 gave Nixon the longest and warmest toast he had ever accorded any visiting head of state. That, of course, was a mere detail, but on just such details is the success of meetings between heads of state often judged. Nixon's poise throughout that first European trip amazed the career diplomats who watched him in action. They also learned two other things about Nixon: he responded to cheering crowds in the streets of foreign capitals with even more self-satisfaction than Lyndon Johnson (who used to have precise crowd estimates telephoned to *Air Force One* before landing in a foreign capital); and he loved talking political business over coffee after dinner, but detested ceremonial functions.

The real achievement of the European junket was Nixon's abil-

*Kissinger had sounded precisely that warning long before when President Eisenhower was preparing to receive Soviet Premier Nikita Khrushchev in 1959. "We face a delicate task in the forthcoming meetings," Kissinger wrote in the *New York Times Magazine*. "If we negotiate about specific settlements we may disrupt the Western alliance by giving our allies the impression that major decisions are being taken in their absence." If the warning was worthwhile then, it was triply so in 1969, at a time when overall European industrial and economic strength had reached a level far above that of 1959.

ity to impress the men who ran Europe as a substantial and serious figure, attributes they could not be sure of from reading about Nixon, Republican politician, in the American press. Sophisticated European politicians had respected Eisenhower, the savior of Europe, and gloried in Kennedy, whom they regarded as a "European" American, but Johnson had both puzzled and somewhat frightened them, with his protean personality and what they took to be his inability to look or think beyond the agony of Vietnam. Europe had been on the back-burner during five Johnson years, and Nixon's purpose was to put it back in its proper place. To each of his hosts, he confided in general terms his plan for liquidation of the Vietnam war. From each he asked help in working with neutralist states and the Soviet Union to prod Hanoi into a serious negotiation at the Paris peace talks. All this was reassuring.

He scattered small but significant victories all over Europe, the most revealing of which came during his visit to London, where the government of Prime Minister Harold Wilson was in a minor diplomatic crisis over the delicate matter of John Freeman.

Freeman had been appointed British ambassador to the United States in March 1968 under a unique political arrangement with the Conservative Party which delayed his taking up the post until the spring of 1969. Had the Labor government known that Nixon would be nominated and elected President, Freeman would never have been named, for the simple reason he had said too many nasty things about Richard Nixon. Thus, during his editorship of the liberal weekly *The New Statesman,* Freeman had called Nixon's defeat in the 1962 California gubernatorial election "a victory for decency in public life." When Nixon was elected President, British newspapers strongly criticized the government for not substituting someone for Freeman as the new ambassador. But Wilson held firm. With Nixon coming to London, however, the problem became acute. Should Freeman be present at Wilson's stag dinner for Nixon at 10 Downing Street? The somewhat nervous answer by the British government was yes, he should.

Freeman arrived to shake Nixon's hand in an agitated state, uncomfortable and perspiring. As dinner ended, Nixon rose to make the inevitable toast. There had always been a special relationship between Britain and the United States, he said, and recently, a very special relationship between British ambassadors and American officials. (At this, tension increased around the table.) It was time, he said, to "clear the air." He was aware of many of the things that John Freeman had written in the past as editor of *The New Statesman* and they were no worse than much that had been written about him by many American commentators. But that was water over the dam. It should in no way affect his effectiveness as the new British ambassador to the United States. He turned directly to Freeman with this concluding line: "After all, he's the new diplomat and I'm the new statesman."

Sitting on one side of Freeman, U.S. Ambassador David Bruce saw Freeman's eyes glisten with emotion. Sitting on the other side was Assistant Secretary of State Martin Hillenbrand, to whom Freeman murmured, "That was a splendid thing the President just did."

Around the table, there was much table-thumping and foot-stamping and "hear, hear"s. Wilson turned over his menu card and wrote the President a note. "That was one of the kindest and most generous acts I have known in a quarter of a century in politics," he scribbled. "Just proves my point. You can't guarantee being born a lord. It is possible—you've shown it—to be born a gentleman." Signing his note "H," Wilson passed it to the President.

The incident, in itself a small thing, was symbolic of the overall success that marked Nixon's first excursion as President into the treacherous paths of international diplomacy. He had managed to display a *style,* distinctive and reassuring to the harassed European statesman who had worried that America seemed to be going slightly mad. In sum, Nixon performed in Europe as he had never quite been able to perform at home. People liked him.

The transfer of foreign-policy-making power from the austere bureaucracy of the State Department to the cluttered White House basement office of Henry Kissinger started from the moment Nixon tapped Kissinger as his National Security assistant, and gave him carte blanche to assemble whatever staff he wanted. Kissinger needed no encouragement. Swiftly he began to populate the cramped quarters in the White House basement with cerebral experts from the State and Defense Departments and from such foreign policy think-tanks as the New York-based Council on Foreign Relations. Within weeks, a listing of the Kissinger staff read like a *Who's Who* of some of the brightest, most innovative geopolitical thinkers in the country (many of whom would later leave Kissinger, either out of disillusion with Nixon's Vietnam policy or because of their feeling of isolation from Kissinger himself, who ran a one-man shop with infrequent staff meetings or direct contacts with his high-pressure assistants).

At the top of the Kissinger-staff list was Helmut Sonnenfeldt, snatched from his job as chief of the division of Soviet Research and Analysis for the State Department's Bureau of Intelligence and Research. Then came Morton Halperin, Deputy Assistant Secretary of Defense for International Security Affairs; Viron Vaky, Acting Assistant Secretary of State for Latin American Affairs; Lawrence Lynn, Deputy Assistant Secretary of Defense for Systems Analysis (one of the famous "whiz kids" of Robert McNamara days, whose influence over military policy Nixon had promised to end); Robert Osgood, Director of the Washington Center of Foreign Policy Research, a unit of Johns Hopkins University; Daniel Davidson, Averell Harriman's top aide at the Paris Vietnam peace talks; and Richard Sneider, Country Director of Japan in the State Department. The Kissinger staff was an imposing group. Under his direction, its influence on policy almost immediately became pervasive, a shift away from the State Department that was much aided by Secretary Rogers' own sparse background in foreign affairs. Rogers perforce was taking on-the-job training; Kissinger's convictions had been forged in years of study.

Thus, policy at the Presidential level became centered in the White House basement, and the surest sign of how quickly this process started came in late June when desk officers on the State Department Rumanian desk learned, about one hour before it was announced, about Nixon's intention to break all precedent and become the first President of the United States to visit a Communist country.

Unlike his earlier trip to Western Europe, no junior careerists were invited into the Oval Office for cozy chats between June 28, the day the trip to Rumania was announced, and July 23, the day Nixon left Washington for San Francisco, the Far East (including a brief stop in Saigon), India, Pakistan—and, finally, on August 2, Bucharest. Briefing papers, yes; direct contact, no.

With the exception of Secretary of State Rogers, the Rumanian visit was tightly held in the White House, where it had been plotted, planned and programmed by Nixon and Kissinger. Of all Presidential missions in this century, Nixon's trip to Rumania was one of the most fascinating.

The story of the visit started in Bucharest, where President Nicolae Ceausescu dropped a conversational nugget at a reception. Wouldn't it be wonderful, he said with a smile to Richard H. Davis, the U.S. ambassador, if President Nixon could visit Rumania and see his old friends there again? Nixon's last visit had been as a private citizen in 1967, when he, a political has-been who was going nowhere, visited Eastern Europe and Moscow. In Czechoslovakia he was brutally, unbelievably snubbed—to the point that the Czech foreign minister ordered a foreign office boycott of a reception at the Pakistani embassy to which U.S. Ambassador Jacob Beam had arranged to take Nixon.* Accordingly, when Nixon arrived in Bucharest he was dumbfounded with pleasure at being received by Ceausescu as though he were a head of state. Ceausescu had already moved away from the Soviet orbit and was desperately looking for ways to make his apostasy more comfortable. One such way was to pay special attention to Americans, even political has-beens. It was risky, to be sure, but Ceausescu was a brave man accustomed to risks. He had shown his bravery by taking an independent foreign policy line, the heart of which was a relationship with Communist China that infuriated the Soviet Union. Then, only three months before Nixon's election, Ceausescu braved Soviet wrath again, along with Yugoslavia's Marshal Tito, in publicly chastising the Russians for invading Czechoslovakia and smashing the liberal regime of Alexander Dubcek. And when Richard Nixon became President in such an unlikely comeback a year later, Ceausescu saw a golden opportunity to resume an old friendship while singeing the spires of the Kremlin.

Ceausescu was packed with political *machismo,* and when he whispered his offhand invitation into Ambassador Davis' ear, he meant it. Davis dutifully cabled his report to Washington, where it was first greeted in the State Department with disbelief, then brushed off as a joke. But in the White House, it was anything but a joke. Did Ceausescu really mean it? Was he sounding Nixon out? Should Nixon accept? The answer to the last question was an immediate yes,

*Bad as his Czech experience was, it did not match Poland, which refused to grant him an entry visa.

but it couldn't be given on the strength of an offhand remark. The White House could do nothing but wait for a proper diplomatic invitation.

It came a few weeks later, when the Rumanian foreign minister called Davis to his office. Within hours after Davis' cable arrived at the White House, the Nixon-Kissinger team sprang into action. Kissinger, not Secretary of State Rogers, invited the Rumanian ambassador, Corneliu Bogdan, to the White House. The invitation was confirmed and quickly accepted.

It was the announcement of that acceptance on June 28 that caught the State Department bureaucracy by surprise. So unique was the invitation, so contrary to all established policy, that foreign service officers could scarcely believe it. Cautious by nature, the foreign service immediately counted half a dozen reasons why the invitation should be handled with circumspection, studied and researched, and then, possibly, rejected. One reason: a Communist state in Eastern Europe *never* invited a foreign head of state until the Russians had first crack. That was the way the satellite system worked, both before and after the Brezhnev Doctrine laid down the rule of Soviet hegemony over Eastern Europe. A second reason: even if Ceausescu was foolish enough to try to break the rule, perhaps the American President should save the Rumanian President from so great a risk. Surely the Soviet Union would bitterly resent Nixon's going to Bucharest. Surely, too, Moscow would read into the visit not only a snub to the Russians via Bucharest, but a warning to the Russians that Nixon, using Rumania as a foil, was ready to warm up to Communist China, Russia's bitter enemy but Rumania's friend.

These potential hazards gripped the State Department, but the objections never found their way into the White House. Nixon's acceptance had already been made public, and he was obviously anxious to go. Nothing better dramatized the relative weight of influence on the President, as between the State Department in Foggy Bottom and the Kissinger Department in the basement of the White House, than the President's handling of this invitation. And nothing so well distinguished the adventurous quality of the Nixon-Kissinger team from the conservative and traditionalist qualities of diplomacy inside the State Department.

Nixon left Washington on July 23 for Guam, where he spelled

out the Nixon Doctrine for the first time, then flew on to Manila, Djakarta and Bangkok, thence to New Delhi and Lahore, finally landing on August 2 in Bucharest, where an immense turnout of the populace greeted the first American President ever to set foot on Communist soil. The mass emotional outpouring was an obvious surprise to Ceausescu, who had never before witnessed anything like it in size and spirit. The significance of that demonstration could not be lost in any capital of Eastern Europe. It proved that despite the long war in Vietnam, the magic of America was still bright in the Communist world of the Brezhnev Doctrine—an asset with potentially enormous political power.

For precisely that reason, Nixon's decision to make the Rumanian visit was a gamble in his larger game of negotiating with the Soviet Union, and it did indeed infuriate and frighten Moscow. Fully a year later, the Soviet foreign office was still pinning American visitors to the wall with resentful questions about Nixon's trip to Rumania, which the Kremlin viewed as an affront not only because of Rumania's independent brand of Communism but also, and what struck the Kremlin as being even more insidious, as an effort to build up Communist China at Moscow's expense. The Russians went further. They tried to make the case that the Nixon-Ceausescu love affair proved that Nixon was not serious about negotiating with Russia on arms control and hinted that they had delayed the start of those talks to show their anger.

This argument did not impress Nixon or Kissinger (although some Kremlinologists including Llewelyn Thompson, former ambassador to Russia and a senior diplomat in the State Department, had privately warned that the Russians would indeed be genuinely angry). Nixon and Kissinger saw it differently, a difference that goes to the heart of Nixon's theme of how a great power should conduct itself. The President wanted very much to send a signal to Peking that the new administration was prepared to open a dialogue. He wanted to show Moscow that his foreign policy would be activist, often unpredictable and calculated to get the United States off the defensive in relations with the Communist world. More important signs of this activism would appear in more dramatic fashion later on. Nor was the President greatly impressed by the hint from Moscow that the Rumanian visit would hurt SALT, the negotiations in which Nixon, Kissinger and Rogers put such great faith. Nixon had long ago concluded that the Russians negotiate when the objective circumstances surrounding the negotiations appear to them to be favorable. They do not, in Nixon's view, allow extraneous events to distract them. The Rumanian visit could by no stretch of the imagination be said to lower or heighten the danger of world suicide in a nuclear war.

These early moves by the new President established a dramatic style and an extraordinarily fast pace in global affairs. Nixon had moved decisively to start winding down the war in Vietnam, encourage a settlement in the Middle East, reassure Europe. He had displayed flexibility, showing restraint when an American plane was brutually shot down by North Koreans in international airspace, positiveness in dealing with Rumania, and imagination in devising the Nixon Doctrine as a mechanism for reducing U.S. vulnerability in future small wars. In a country perilously close to neo-isolationism, it was a good start that fit into an overall theme. Unhappily for Nixon, the good start abroad was not being matched at home—particularly in his troubled dealings with a Democratic Congress.

V

Nixon and Congress

. . . save in times like the extraordinary Hundred Days of 1933—times virtually ruled out by definition at mid-century—a President will often be unable to obtain Congressional action on his terms or even to halt action he opposes. The reverse is equally accepted: Congress is often frustrated by the President.
—Richard E. Neustadt, in
Presidential Power

I have watched the Congress from either the inside or the outside, man and boy, for more than 40 years, and I've never seen a Congress that didn't eventually take the measure of the President it was dealing with.
—Lyndon B. Johnson, in impromptu remarks to
departmental lobbyists, January 1965

When Bryce Harlow walked into his room at the Pierre Hotel after the 1968 election, the telephone was ringing. With one hand he tipped the bellboy, with the other he picked up the phone. His briefcase and suitcase sat on the floor. They were to stay there for the next several hours as Harlow—a trim little man with upright military bearing and huge, luminous eyes—was chained to the telephone, making one call after another, talking slowly in his soft Oklahoma drawl. With no secretary, he filled a menu lying on his bedside table with scrawled notes from his hours on the telephone.

That introduction to the just-forming Nixon administration told Harlow two very important things: first, except for himself and, of

course, the President-elect, no one in the inner Nixon circle was
known to anyone *outside* that circle. This meant that Republicans
based in Washington on the fringe of active politics—officers of trade
associations, lawyers and lobbyists—had only one entrée into the
new administration. That was Harlow, whose eight years in the
Eisenhower administration and ten years before that in the Pentagon
(as a staff officer) and on Capitol Hill (as a committee aide) had made
him one of the most familiar and respected figures in Washington.
The second meaning of all those telephone calls was more important,
and more ominous, to Harlow: members of Congress were just as
helpless as the lawyers and lobbyists in their efforts to penetrate the
inner Nixon circle. They, too, had only one place to go: Harlow.

Not for decades had an incoming White House staff appeared
so much a mystery to Congress or been populated with so many
unknowns as Richard Nixon's in that early winter of 1968–69. When
General Eisenhower came to town in 1952, he put men in top White
House jobs who were well known to Congress. Most of John Kennedy's top aides had worked in Washington for years and had intimate political connections both on Capitol Hill and around the
country. Lyndon Johnson had no problem because he retained the
men he found in the White House after Kennedy's assassination. But
now there was Nixon with his advertising account executives, public
relations experts, nonpolitical lawyers—and Bryce Harlow. Reluctantly taking leave from his high-priced job as chief Washington
representative for Procter and Gamble, Harlow had joined the Nixon
campaign as a full-time senior adviser in the summer of 1968, and
again staying on reluctantly, was Nixon's first White House appointment as President-elect. He would be in charge of Congressional
liaison, the same job he held at the end of the Eisenhower administration. But the job would be far more difficult than it had been
nearly a decade earlier under Eisenhower. It would also be far less
fun.

For Harlow, that endlessly ringing telephone at the Pierre was
an inauspicious beginning. It absolutely assured a crisis of communications, and from just such a crisis, Harlow well knew, could flow
an ocean of petty grievances and hurt feelings on the part of Congressmen who wanted to talk to nobody at the White House other
than Bryce Harlow and who couldn't get through on the telephone
or whose calls were not answered. When two hundred calls from
Congressmen came in for Harlow on a single day, as occasionally

would happen, there was no physical way of answering all or even most of them.

Harlow was inundated. The inundation would last throughout his twelve months in day-to-day charge of Nixon's lobbying on Capitol Hill and would frustrate his work with Congress. A typical example occurred in January. A new portrait of Richard Nixon was being installed with some ceremony at the new municipal airport at Houston, and the President was invited to attend or at least send a letter of acknowledgment. But when Representative George Bush of Houston tried to arrange it, he found to his dismay that his letters and, later, his telephone calls went unanswered. Bush was a loyal Republican and a Nixon man who would cause no trouble and hold no grudges, but others would and did.

Part of the trouble with Congress was of Harlow's own making. In the eight Kennedy-Johnson years, Congressional liaison operations at the White House had mushroomed in size and function well beyond the Spartan limits of Eisenhower days. What had been formed then as merely a lobbying organization to promote administration legislation (there had been no such formal office previously inside the White House) had been transformed in the Kennedy-Johnson era into a service agency devoted to the care and feeding of Congressmen—arranging White House tours for constituents, helping to handle constituent problems with governmental agencies, providing Congressmen with autographed photos of the President. Harking back to the good old days, Harlow intended to return the office, much reduced in manpower, to its original functions. "We're going to wean the Congress off the White House teat," commented one of Harlow's aides in January 1969, reflecting Harlow's own sentiment. The weaning succeeded only in irritating Congressmen not willing to forgo such favors. As the months went on, Harlow's office gradually returned in function and size to Kennedy-Johnson proportions.

And then there was Congress itself. Not since Whig Zachary Taylor and a Democratic Congress were elected in 1848 had a President in office for the first time confronted a Congress of the opposite party. Nixon faced a Congress controlled by the Democrats 57 to 43 in the Senate and 242 to 190 (with three vacancies) in the House. In Nixon's inner circle, only Harlow truly perceived how difficult this would make it for the President—any President, but particularly Richard Nixon.

Despite his own four years in the House of Representatives, two in the Senate and eight as the Senate's presiding officer, Nixon knew remarkably little about the workings of Congress and cared less. He had always had an inferiority complex about the Senate, which had not taken him into its mysterious inner club. During his four years in the House he had been uninterested in the team play of passing bills, concentrating instead on the investigation of Communism that made his rise so rapid.

Harlow and his first staff appointment, William Timmons (a conservative, broad-gauged Tennessee Republican with long staff experience on Capitol Hill), did not have a single serious talk with Nixon on legislative strategy during all those days of planning at the Pierre. That omission betrayed a cardinal fact about Richard Nixon that again and again would emerge to haunt him: his lack of interest in Congress, leading to his tendency to use it as a whipping boy.

At the Kentucky Derby on May 1, 1969, the President spoke confidentially to Senator John Sherman Cooper of Kentucky, a liberal Republican and a gentleman of the old school who was fond of Nixon. Is there any Democratic senator, Nixon asked, whom I can really trust and who will help me in the Senate? Surprised at this question from a politician who had known most of the Democratic senators personally for many years, Cooper replied yes, there surely was. He would strongly recommend Mike Mansfield of Montana, Democratic leader ever since 1961. But, said Cooper, if the President wanted to establish a bona-fide relationship with Mansfield, he would have to see him *alone* and frequently, and of course he would have to handle the relationship with complete confidentiality. Nixon took that advice, and started a series of cozy White House breakfasts with Mansfield.* But the Nixon-Mansfield entente never approached in

---

*However, some of Nixon's advisers recommended that he not trust Mansfield because of his close relationship with Senator Edward M. Kennedy, then Majority Whip (No. 2, after Mansfield, in the hierarchy), and front runner to oppose Nixon in 1972. These advisers told Nixon that Mansfield was so committed to Kennedy for President that he would let Kennedy call the tune on legislative strategy, as indeed seemed to be the case on some issues where the course taken by Senate Democrats was considerably more partisan than it would have been had Mansfield been left to his own devices. However, the problem was erased on July 18, 1969, when Miss Mary Jo Kopechne drowned at Chappaquiddick Island, Mass., after a car driven by Kennedy went off a bridge. That pulled Kennedy out of the Presidential picture, for the time being at least, and greatly circumscribed his activities in the Senate, finally resulting in his defeat for reelection as Majority Whip in 1971.

effectiveness either the comradely partnership President Eisenhower enjoyed with the Democratic leaders of Congress, Senator Lyndon B. Johnson and Speaker Sam Rayburn, or the conspiratorial, nearly collusive alliance between President Johnson and the Republican leader of the Senate, Everett Dirksen. The Nixon-Mansfield breakfasts were sterile as a source of Nixon power or even influence in the Senate. There just was not that much that Mansfield could or would do. An ascetic former professor of Oriental history, he had served as Majority Leader of the Senate longer than anybody else in history by establishing an unequaled record of permissiveness that let senators do pretty much as they pleased. In the spring and summer of 1970, he permitted endless, unproductive debate on the Cooper-Church amendment to restrict future U.S. military operations in Indochina, thereby tying up Nixon's entire legislative program. For his part, Nixon would not think of pressuring Mansfield or even asking so normal a favor as to get the word-loving senators moving during the impasse over Cooper-Church.

Indeed, Nixon had no more stomach for face-to-face confrontations with members of Congress than for those with anyone else. When he did invite a member into the Oval Office to ask his help, the personal Nixon pressure was mild indeed—the antithesis of the insistent Johnson treatment. "I know you have your problems with this," the President would say, "and I will completely understand if you can't come with me, but if you can I'd appreciate it."

Thus, although no contest with Congress engaged Nixon so viscerally as his humiliating failure in the spring of 1970 to win Senate confirmation of Judge G. Harrold Carswell to the Supreme Court, he never personally demanded or pleaded for any senator's vote.* When Senator Charles McC. Mathias, a liberal Republican from Maryland, informed the President in a personal meeting that he would vote against Carswell, Nixon replied that he understood Mathias' problems perfectly and that there would be no hard feelings —a sentiment expressed with more conviction than Nixon felt. When Senator Edward Brooke, a liberal Republican from Massachusetts, gave him the same bad news, Nixon replied, "That's all right, Ed. We can still make a lot of good medicine together."

In the relative privacy of discussion with close aides, however, Nixon's reaction was neither so conciliatory nor so simple. In truth,

---

*The Haynsworth and Carswell nomination fights are discussed in Chapter VI.

he placed Mathias and Brooke in two different categories of liberal Republicans. He felt that Brooke, John Sherman Cooper, Senator George Aiken of Vermont and Senator Jacob Javits of New York were genuine in their liberalism and opposed him when they did only out of conviction and never out of malice. Mathias was another matter. Nixon ranked him with Senators Charles Percy of Illinois, Charles Goodell of New York, Mark Hatfield of Oregon and, most of the time, Hugh Scott of Pennsylvania, as Republicans who took liberal positions and attacked him personally only for personal political gain. While the President was unfailingly and blandly courteous to their faces, these "phony liberals" were reviled by Nixon in blunt terms in the privacy of the White House official family. Only his critics in the communications media were targets of harsher denunciation by Nixon in private. "I was amazed," said one aide who had never been in close contact with the President before, "at the intensity of his feeling against the liberal Republicans."

That intensity of feeling was communicated to members of the White House staff, and many of them—principally those not on Harlow's Congressional liaison team—responded with harsh action on Capitol Hill. For instance, when the *Chicago Tribune* printed unfavorable stories about Percy's opposing Nixon's antiballistic missile, the senator attributed them to news plants from Herb Klein, the administration's chief of public relations, and deeply resented them. The combination of the President's courteous supersoft sell and the discourteous superhard sell from many of his staff further spoiled relations between Capitol Hill and the White House.

So did the rivalry, present from those first days at the Pierre, between Harlow's liaison staff (here called the Hill Staff) and certain senior assistants to the President who concerned themselves with legislative strategy—principally Haldeman, Ehrlichman and Peter Flanigan (whom, for purposes of easy identification, we shall call the Downtown Staff). Flanigan had no more experience with Washington or Congress than did Haldeman or Ehrlichman. A brainy, millionaire socialite from Manhattan who had been working hard in Nixon campaigns since the 1950s, Flanigan could turn on the charm when he wanted, but that charm was frequently suffocated by arrogance. On one occasion early in 1969, Flanigan refused a telephone call from a Republican senator, Henry Bellmon of Oklahoma (who had been Nixon's Presidential campaign manager briefly in 1967).

Flanigan's secretary instructed Bellmon to put in writing whatever it was he had to say.

The basic problem was that Haldeman, Ehrlichman and Flanigan saw Congress as an awkward and obnoxious obstacle, a hostile foreign power. From this starting point, the Downtown Staff oscillated between two extremes. One was that Congress was not to be negotiated with on equal terms but was meant to be ordered around. Haldeman, in particular, favored a take-it-or-leave-it, the-hell-with-them attitude in dealing with Congress. The other extreme was the conviction, later dimmed by events, that the way to get Congress to do the President's bidding was precisely the same as the way to get gullible housewives to buy soap—in other words, by using every public-relations and ad-man technique, to go out and *sell*. Housewives found this technique irresistible; so would Congress. At least, that was the thought of the Downtown Staff and they continued to think so, long after Harlow, with the wisdom of experience, had tried to disabuse them of the idea.

Harlow knew there was no magical way of getting Congress to give Nixon or any President exactly what he wanted. To manage Congress required mostly hard work that would reveal a Congressman's Achilles heel, discover a Congressman's most influential supporters back home, disclose a Congressman's hidden aspirations and thereby offer the raw material of a bargain. But as Harlow once advised Lawrence F. O'Brien, when O'Brien succeeded him as chief White House lobbyist under Kennedy in 1961, "There are no tricks that haven't been tried over and over—stilettos, swords, pistols, poison, rifles, shotguns, cajolery, wheeler-dealing, private meetings, public meetings, secret meetings—all of it has been tried repeatedly by every President. If you think you have a new fix on this deal, Larry, you're nuts!"

In 1969, Harlow's basic strategy was to maximize a Republican majority on each issue that came before Congress, then pick up enough Democratic support from the left or the right, depending on the ideological cut of the issue, and hope to put it across.

On top of this disagreement between the Hill and Downtown Staffs on how to manage Congress, there was a curious element of jealousy. With Harlow so much the center of attention from Congress and much of the rest of the outside world, and therefore quite indispensable to the President in the early days, he became an object of some suspicion, even hostility in the eyes of the Downtown Staff, so new and uneasy on the Washington scene. As long as he was in the White House, Harlow's wise counsel would be sought out by Nixon. But, imperceptibly, as the months went on, he began to be sidetracked and subtly undermined by the Downtown Staff.

Harlow suffered one setback during the interregnum at the Pierre Hotel. Mel Laird had led a fight with Harlow's support, for the new President to submit a full program to the Ninety-first Congress and to deliver a State of the Union Message to Congress close on the heels of the lame-duck message delivered by President Johnson on January 14. Nixon decided otherwise, spelling out clearly that Congress was not high on his list of priorities as his new administration began.

Despite the absence of a full-fledged Nixon program, there was one legislative imperative early in 1969 on which the President was staking not only an early test of his ability to handle Congress, but also his hopes for a nuclear arms control agreement with the Soviet Union. That was to win Congressional approval of the new-style Safeguard antimissile missile—or antiballistic missile (ABM)—to defend against a possible Soviet strike. This defense system had to pass the Democratic Congress in the President's larger plot to negotiate with the Russians on nuclear arms control from a position of strength. All his early efforts on Capitol Hill were turned to that end.

On March 14, after six weeks of frantic study at the Pentagon and White House, Nixon announced in his fourth press conference that he had decided the ABM program, renamed Safeguard, was "vital for the security and defense of the United States." Few issues had such a sharp emotional and ideological fault-line. Long before making his announcement, Nixon knew that the battle in Congress over the ABM would be by far his toughest battle of the year and, he was convinced, his most important. Thus, several weeks before his March 14 press conference, he had already approved a proposal by Harlow to put one of his newly appointed deputies—Colonel Kenneth BeLieu, a Korean War hero who had been Assistant Secretary of the Navy in the Kennedy administration—in overall command of the ABM fight. Taciturn, laconic and with ramrod military bearing despite the loss of his left leg in Korea, BeLieu had tucked under his belt valuable experience in Congressional relations as a staffer on the Senate Preparedness Subcommittee under Chairman Lyndon B. Johnson.

So concerned was Nixon about the ferociously mounting opposition to the ABM in the Senate that he ordered BeLieu to report directly to him. He also gave BeLieu a Presidential mandate to coordinate the administration's entire lobbying effort, including the Pentagon's, under his personal control. Considering BeLieu's personal contacts in the Pentagon, this was a natural, but it showed the extent of the President's understandable worry on his first major battle with Congress. He wanted a successful, administration-wide drive, spearheaded by the White House, and that is what he got— with a notable and ironic exception: repeated bungling and inexcusable interferences with Harlow and BeLieu by the Downtown Staff, and an occasional inexplicable blooper by Nixon himself, induced by that same Downtown Staff.

Keeping Nixon informed on all his key moves, BeLieu's first order of business was a visit to the office of Senator Richard Brevard Russell of Georgia, a powerful Presidential ally on the ABM and the grandest of the Senate Democratic grandees. Together, he and Russell went over the Senate roll call and compared it with the 46-to-27 Senate margin that President Johnson had gained in June 1968 for his much larger Sentinel ABM program, which had been designed as a protector of cities—not, as Safeguard was, a protector of offensive-missile sites. They prophetically concluded that, when the issue came to a vote, probably six months later, Nixon would defeat weakening amendments either on a tie 50–50 vote, or by a 51-to-49 margin. With a Republican in the White House, Democratic senators who had supported Sentinel would not back Safeguard. Besides, peace lobbyists had drummed up anti-ABM sentiment since then.

Nixon, fearful of losing his first major Senate test and thereby much of his bargaining power at the forthcoming Strategic Arms Limitation Talks (SALT) with the Russians, moved early and fast to shore up his position. One of his first targets was the touchy and unpredictable Margaret Chase Smith of Maine, who, although never unfriendly to Nixon, was chary about favors for Presidents—any President. Maggie Smith was tough, independent and snappish when it came to her vote and she guarded it for her constituents as she guarded her life. Senator Smith and Senator Howard Cannon, a

Nevada Democrat, were the only two senators whom Dick Russell put in the wrong column in late February when he and BeLieu studied the likely Senate roll-call result.* Mrs. Smith had voted for an amendment to gut Sentinel in 1968, and they assumed, only half correctly, that she would vote against Safeguard in 1969. With Cannon, their reasoning was just the reverse: he had supported Sentinel and would, they thought, therefore support Safeguard. To woo and win Mrs. Smith now became the President's high purpose. He and the Downtown Staff, despite repeated and pointed warnings by Harlow and BeLieu, enthusiastically began stalking Mrs. Smith.

Difficult, indeed oppressive for the Hill Staff, trained in the care and feeding of Congressional prima donnas, was the tendency of the Downtown Staff to strike out in all directions without ever asking guidance from the Hill Staff or, all too often, without even informing the Hill Staff what it was up to. Thus, Senator George Aiken, the liberal Republican from Vermont, who was absolutely opposed to the ABM, was quietly asked to "talk to" Mrs. Smith and try to persuade her to support the President. Aiken, a good soldier, did as he was asked, but he must have wondered at the strategy of sending a committed anti-ABM activist to persuade another anti-ABM senator to vote *for* the ABM. The visit boomeranged. Instead of selling Mrs. Smith on the ABM, Aiken's effort simply strengthened her resolve to introduce her own amendments to cripple the bill, just as Harlow knew it would.

That was the way it went as the Downtown Staff, pushing both itself and the President into avoidable blunders, usurped the Hill Staff's functions time and again without having the understanding of Congress essential to making its lobbying effective. Thus, when the Hill Staff suggested that a private visit between Nixon and Representative Mendel Rivers of South Carolina, powerful Chairman of the House Armed Services Committee, would be useful, Haldeman put the appointment on the official calling list of the President, and so made it automatically available to the press. That was just what

---

*The White House was extremely worried about two other senators who did not tip their hand until very late in the game. But Russell forecast that both—Republican John Williams of Delaware and Democrat Clinton Anderson of New Mexico, one of Nixon's few real Democratic friends in the Senate—would vote for the ABM. They did.

the Hill Staff did not want. They had visualized the President's using Rivers clandestinely to help sell the ABM in the Senate. With the visit publicly known, Rivers was sure to be asked embarrassing questions on his way out of the White House.

Beyond that, the President's Downtown Staff had the quaint notion that a senator could be proselytized simply by being asked, and that Congress as a whole could be programmed and computerized as a precise mechanism. Nixon himself knew better, but he never did catch on that a dispute of serious dimensions was building up between Haldeman's and Harlow's men.

One afternoon at a staff meeting in the White House several weeks before the ABM issue was coming to a head, Haldeman turned to BeLieu and said sharply, "You shouldn't be sitting here, you ought to be up in the Senate telling Hugh Scott how to vote." "Telling" Scott, at that time the Senate Republican Whip and by conviction opposed to Safeguard, "how to vote" would have been one likely way of ensuring his opposition.*

Harlow and his aides got earfuls of complaints from senators and congressmen. But when the Hill Staff suggested to a senior Republican senator that a quiet chat with the President would reveal these errors by the Downtown Staff and end them, the senator flatly refused. Nixon, he said, had served in both House and Senate and therefore considered himself an expert in the arts of Congressional relations. For the senator to suggest otherwise would be a mortal affront.

As the ABM vote neared in the Senate, pressure from the White House grew ever more intense, creating a mood of hostility that would sour Congressional feelings about the Nixon administration far into the future. Publicly, administration lobbying on the ABM had probably surpassed anything ever seen in high-pressure tactics for handling Congress. But it was the invisible lobbying, strongly felt but difficult to prove, that infuriated Congressional targets such as Senator James Pearson of Kansas, a moderately liberal, independent-minded Republican opposed to the ABM. Pearson was told by a

---

*As it turned out, Scott reversed his position of 1968, when he supported anti-Sentinel amendments and voted against amendments aimed at gutting Safeguard. His vote, absolutely essential, was based primarily on considerations of party loyalty stemming from being Senate Minority Whip.

home-state plane manufacturer at a crucial point in the debate that an Army general had informed him a Pentagon contract might not be forthcoming if the ABM failed in the Senate. Then, in a continuing sequence, Pearson learned from the Agriculture Department that a rural job-development bill Pearson was backing, which the department had told him privately it was also backing, would unfortunately not get the department's public support. Finally, a small but revealing incident occurred in Pearson's political life. When the White House made a decision in his favor not to move a regional federal office from Kansas City to Denver, it failed to tell him before the decision was announced—a routine political courtesy somehow "overlooked," with the vote on the ABM approaching and Pearson opposed to it.

None of that pressure, felt in similar ways by many anti-ABM senators, changed Jim Pearson's mind on the ABM. But it may have changed the mind of many senators about Richard Nixon because the ABM pressures from the White House were so unusually intense. Furthermore, Nixon's passion to achieve Senate passage of the ABM led him to applying pressures on his own lieutenants at the Department of Health, Education and Welfare, who found themselves forced by the White House to make some outrageous concessions on school desegregation in order to pacify Senator John Stennis of Mississippi, Chairman of the Senate Armed Services Committee and leader of the pro-ABM Senate bloc.* When the vote was finally taken on August 6 after a month of emotional debate, crippling amendments were beaten by the narrowest margins—a 50–50 tie vote (which defeats an amendment) on one, 49–51 on another.†

---

*The effect of Southern political pressures on the administration's school desegregation plans is discussed in Chapter VI.

†On a 50–50 tie vote in which Vice President Agnew needlessly cast his own vote against (making the official vote 51 to 50 against), the Senate rejected Mrs. Smith's amendment to block the spending of any funds at all on Safeguard. Then it rejected, 51 to 49, the key anti-ABM amendment, authored by Senators John Sherman Cooper, Kentucky Republican, and Philip Hart, Michigan Democrat, to restrict ABM funds to research and development, not deployment. The unpredictable Mrs. Smith voted *against* the Cooper-Hart amendment because, she said, "it is a partial approval of the Safeguard ABM . . . I do not approve of such a compromise." It was little wonder that Senator Russell, way back in February, was wrong in predicting how Mrs. Smith would vote.

When, three months later, the House overwhelmingly approved Safeguard, Nixon gained his first great triumph in the Democratic Congress, but at high cost. He gained it with the expert help of his Hill Staff and *despite* bungling interference, based on lack of political experience, and an infuriating hauteur on the part of his Downtown Staff.

Having accepted the Moynihan Doctrine, President Nixon duly recommended a one-year extension of the antipoverty program, although he acted without much enthusiasm and with major parts of this ambitious Great Society program stripped out of the Office of Economic Opportunity and dispatched to old-line Cabinet-level departments.* When, in April, Donald Rumsfeld left Congress and became the new director of OEO, the first thing he did was to persuade Nixon to give OEO a new two-year lease. Confirmed by the Senate on May 23, Rumsfeld was testifying ten days later before the House Education and Labor Committee for a two-year extension of OEO on grounds not "simply to continue present programs" but rather as a means to find out "what works and what does not." For Rumsfeld it was a bold gamble. Inside the White House, the poverty program had few friends other than Pat Moynihan. To get Nixon's approval for the two-year extension he wanted, Rumsfeld worked directly with the President.

But what was to prove even bolder was Rumsfeld's early determination to oppose any move in Congress to give state governors an absolute veto over individual poverty projects, a veto that a coalition of conservative Republicans (including Congressman Rumsfeld) and Democrats had been vainly trying to pass in the last days of the Johnson administration. Once removed from Capitol Hill to the OEO offices in midtown Washington, Rumsfeld understood that an absolute governors' veto would virtually end the poverty program by emasculating central direction of policy. Thus, Rumsfeld determined to preserve the existing law, which provided that a governor's veto of any project could be overridden by a simple act of the President (who, in practice, delegated the authority to the director of OEO). That determination of Rumsfeld was not only to pose a severe test to the overall legislative strategy of Bryce Harlow but to expose the

*See pp. 41–42.

ambiguity and apathy with which Richard Nixon often approached domestic questions.

The Democratic-controlled Education and Labor Committee, under the chairmanship of Representative Carl Perkins of Kentucky, sat on the bill for four months after hearings ended while Perkins, fearful that it would be gutted when it got to the floor of the House, tried vainly for unanimous agreement within the committee that no major amendments would be offered on the floor. Then, on December 3, with the bill scheduled for debate the following day, Democratic leaders abruptly postponed all action indefinitely. They were frightened by a bipartisan amendment co-sponsored by two of the Labor Committee's most formidable figures: Representative Albert Quie of Minnesota, one of the most impressive of the new breed of Republican moderates, and Representative Edith Green of Oregon, a strong-willed liberal Democrat inclining to conservative positions on such social questions. Backed by conservatives of both parties, the Quie-Green amendment would turn the poverty program over to state governors, giving them an opportunity to run state programs themselves with an absolute veto power.

The ideological affinity inside the White House for the Quie-Green amendment was to be expected. It embodied precisely those good Republican principles that Nixon himself had so long enunciated: decentralizing authority over federal programs, transferring to the states some of the power accumulated in Washington during the preceding eight years of Democratic rule. More vital to Harlow, the top Republican leadership in the House was for Quie-Green. Representative Gerald Ford of Michigan, Minority Leader; Representative Les Arends of Illinois, Minority Whip, and Representative John Rhodes of Arizona, Policy Committee Chairman, all favored dispersing the program to the governors.

This went to the heart of Harlow's basic doctrine of how a Republican President should handle a Democratic Congress. On November 4, 1969, Harlow had been removed from the job of day-to-day supervision of Congressional liaison and given the Cabinet grade of Counsellor so that the mountain of unanswered telephone calls and letters could be trimmed and he would have more time to advise the President. William Timmons, who had been in charge of House lobbying, was promoted on February 4, 1970, to head the whole Hill

Staff.* But Harlow never got away from the perpetual problem of Congressional relations—giving constant guidance to the Hill Staff —and in any event, Timmons fully shared his strategic doctrine. Harlow's firm conviction was that the center of Nixon's power must be a Republican center—not Democratic—moving left or right to pick up needed Democratic votes. When there was any issue on which Nixon could lose Gerry Ford, his top lieutenants and most Republicans, that strategy was undermined. Moreover, on this one issue, the Hill Staff and the Downtown Staff were of one mind. Harlow, Timmons, Ehrlichman and Haldeman all wanted to reshape the antipoverty bill to assure the support of Ford and a majority of House Republicans, and wanted Nixon to so instruct Rumsfeld. That that course would have wrenched the antipoverty program out of shape was not important. What *was* important was keeping a Republican hard core intact for later, more important votes.

For his part, Rumsfeld's disagreements with Harlow on the Quie-Green amendment transcended the poverty issue. As the only ex-Congressman then on the White House staff, he had from his first day there basically objected to the Harlow strategy on grounds that it irrevocably linked the President's policy to the fraction of conservative Republicans in the House who would always be reelected from safe districts no matter what calamity befell the party nationally.

His hands full with the poverty program, Rumsfeld had little impact on overall legislative strategy.† But now with his own bill up in the House, he had a chance to make some broader points. To tame an overwhelmingly Democratic Congress, Rumsfeld believed, Nixon

---

*At one point, Harry Dent, White House political aide and former Republican State Chairman of South Carolina, had been in line to succeed Harlow. However, Dent was scuttled by ferocious protests from Senator Hugh Scott, who—perhaps mistakenly—believed Dent had opposed his election for Senate Minority Leader on September 24, 1969, against Senator Howard Baker of Tennessee following the death of Everett McKinley Dirksen. The White House was supposed to be scrupulously neutral, but Senator Ralph T. Smith of Illinois told Scott he had been asked by Dent to vote for Baker and did so.

†The Hill Staff felt Rumsfeld had little impact in the House Republican cloakroom, where senior members still regarded him as an impertinent upstart. Those senior members had not forgotten the night that Rumsfeld and other junior Republican Congressmen (calling themselves Rumsfeld's Raiders) held the House in session around-the-clock in an unsuccessful effort to force procedural reform, and had not forgiven them.

should not always shape policy to extract maximum votes from the Republican side of the aisle, but rather make policy on its merits and then deal with the entire bipartisan membership of Congress. Depending on the issue, that majority might be liberal or conservative. In effect, Rumsfeld envisioned a floating majority. On the Quie-Green amendment Rumsfeld saw this floating majority consisting of an overwhelming Democratic vote, together with Republican moderates and liberals. The fact that most Republicans would vote against the President bothered Rumsfeld not a bit.

Hastening to Capitol Hill late in November, Rumsfeld took a careful head count of the House membership. It showed that the two-year bill should hold on the floor without change, with the Quie-Green amendment defeated, despite the loss of Ford, Arends, Rhodes and perhaps one hundred other Republicans.* Only two members of the Republican leadership would oppose Quie-Green: Robert Taft, Jr., of Ohio, Chairman of the Research Committee, and John Anderson of Illinois, Chairman of the Caucus.†

Rumsfeld experienced nothing but trouble from other Presidential assistants. When he met with the House Republican leadership on Capitol Hill on November 29 and in the White House on December 2, White House staffers sided with Ford and against Rumsfeld. Armed with his poll, Rumsfeld then went to the President and vehemently argued that the administration must oppose Quie-Green.

Nixon agreed, not insisting—as Harlow and Ehrlichman had recommended—that Rumsfeld capitulate and accept a crippling compromise. But why? Did Rumsfeld's triumph mean that Nixon was choosing Rumsfeld's overall legislative strategy in preference to Harlow's? Surely not. Such discussions of grand Congressional strategy interested him not at all. Did he feel ideologically committed to saving OEO from the extreme decentralizing tendencies of Quie-Green? The contrary was probably true. Rather, Nixon seemed to be taking the position that this was essentially Don Rumsfeld's busi-

*Les Arends, House Republican Whip since 1943, was furious that Rumsfeld conducted the head count without consulting him. He was making whip checks, Arends stormed in the cloakroom, when Rumsfeld was "still in diapers."
†Ironically, in January 1969 Taft had defeated Rumsfeld by a one-vote margin for Chairman of the Research Committee and a place in the leadership. Had Rumsfeld won that election in the Republican caucus, he would never have accepted Nixon's plea to join the administration.

ness, not his. Busy with other things, he was willing to let Rumsfeld have his own way.

The passivity of the President's approach became obvious as Perkins finally let the bill out of his committee and the vote on the House floor approached. Nixon sent no letter to the House Republican leadership calling for defeat of the Quie-Green amendment. His regular lobbying team, headed by Harlow, lifted not a finger against it. On the contrary, some whispered to Republican Congressmen that Rumsfeld was not *really* reflecting the wishes of the President, who in his heart *favored* Quie-Green. The spectacle of Presidential lobbyists working against a stand taken by a President would have been utterly unimaginable under Kennedy or Johnson. But all this paled in comparison with Nixon's performance at his press conference of December 8, four days before the House vote. Asked his position on the Quie-Green amendment, the President replied:

> I support the Director of OEO. He has asked for a two-year extension. He has pledged to reform the OEO, and I think he should be given the chance to reform it.
>
> I hope he is able to work out with the leadership in the House, most of whom are Republicans in this instance, who want the changes, and some Democrats—will be able to work out some kind of accommodation with them. But, of course, I support my Director that I have appointed.

Working out "some kind of accommodation" was precisely what Rumsfeld had been opposing and Harlow demanding. Now Nixon seemed to be reversing his earlier decision on Rumsfeld's side. Universally, friend and foe alike, everybody in Washington interpreted Nixon's remarks in this way: Of course, I appointed Don Rumsfeld and I have to live with him. And if he insists on being pigheaded, I'll go along with him on Quie-Green. But I sure wish he wouldn't be so pigheaded but would sit down with Gerry Ford and work things out, just like Bryce Harlow wants him to.

Rumsfeld's Republican allies in the House were crestfallen, disgusted at what they considered Nixon's vacillation. "I think Rummy ought to pack it in—quit right now and go back to Illinois to run for Congress," said one of them.

On December 9, Nixon summoned Rumsfeld to the Oval Office. Genuinely perturbed by press reports that he had undercut and humiliated Rumsfeld, he protested he had no such intention.* He really supported him on Quie-Green and was just expressing a forlorn hope that something could be worked out. Rumsfeld replied that *he* had never doubted the President's intentions. But it was all quite vague and it was not followed by a public declaration by the President that might have helped Rumsfeld in the House. Passage of the Quie-Green amendment seemed a certainty.

But Rumsfeld's head count proved quite accurate. The Quie-Green amendment was defeated on a close teller vote, 183 to 167.† On the key roll-call vote on a motion to recommit the bill to committee and bring it back with the Quie-Green amendment, only 63 Republicans stayed with Nixon-Rumsfeld, as opposed to 103 Republicans against. Voting for the Nixon-Rumsfeld position in the 231-to-163 vote were 168 Democrats, while only 60 Democrats opposed. Rumsfeld had not only saved the poverty program but shown how a floating majority obviated any need to gear Presidential policy to Congressional Republican leadership. But Harlow was not convinced. His theory required continual collaboration with the Congressional Republican leaders, and many more such "victories" as Rumsfeld's would badly damage that relationship and, in his view, Nixon's overall prospects in Congress. Nor are there any signs that Nixon was aware of long-range implications in the poverty vote. As administered by Timmons, the Harlow strategy remained in effect.

Apart from Nixon's curious ambiguity regarding the Quie-Green amendment, his attitude toward the poverty bill in the House provided a startling contrast to his handling of the ABM issue in the Senate. With the ABM in danger of defeat, Nixon applied every last ounce of pressure available to the executive branch. But

*Nixon certainly felt some obligation to Rumsfeld for having talked him into surrendering his safe seat from Illinois in Congress. When he first announced Rumsfeld's appointment, Nixon noted the fact that at the same age, thirty-six, he also had surrendered a safe Congressional seat (from Southern California) to run a chancy race for the U.S. Senate.

†The House of Representatives resolves itself into a Committee of the Whole to perfect a bill. No roll-call votes are conducted in the Committee of the Whole; instead, Congressmen vote by walking down the center aisle, where they are counted by tellers. There was no record of how individual Congressmen voted on teller votes, the most important votes taken by the House, until a reform was adopted by the House in 1971.

when the poverty bill was in danger of being gutted in the House, the President stayed on the sidelines, besieged by opposing arguments within the White House staff, keeping himself out of the battle. Richard Nixon probably felt in his political heart a far greater attraction for the Harlow approach than Rumsfeld's, but Rumsfeld was too persistent to ignore. Nixon also felt a far greater kinship for foreign policy issues, such as the ABM and its role in SALT, than for such domestic issues as the antipoverty program. His militancy in pushing one through the Senate and his aloofness in dealing with the other in the House measured the President's inner convictions.

There was still one other lesson to be learned from the antipoverty legislation: the significance to the President of Democratic control of Congress. That bill sat in the House Labor Committee for four months after hearings were finished and after it was ready to be reported. Nixon himself had no more voice in influencing that timing than the lowliest member of the House. That was one of the many hidden aspects of divided government that made Richard Nixon's role as President far more difficult than it would have been if he had had a Republican Congress to work with.

These disabilities were seldom manifest in dramatic headlines or on the evening television news shows, but they were constantly at work in the background, undercutting Presidential prerogatives taken for granted when Congress is under the control of the President's own party. Thus, a President normally has great influence over the scheduling of witnesses before a Congressional committee on highly controversial issues, and that scheduling can materially affect public support or opposition. Nixon did not have this power. Likewise, a President normally can influence when and what measures are to be taken up on the floor of the Senate or the House, but not Nixon—as in the case of the Cooper-Church amendment.

During the interregnum at the Pierre Hotel, some of those telephone calls that inundated Harlow came from Democratic chairmen of powerful Congressional committees. "Bryce, let me give you just a little wise counsel, my boy, the President had better be very careful about this"—or that or the other thing—"because remember that I'm not at his beck and call, I'm a Democrat."

Nixon and Harlow spent hours in secret evaluation of the Democrats who were in charge of the Congress, trying to work out costly little political deals—such as giving Senator Mansfield a patronage appointment for a federal job in Montana—and watching their freedom of action corroding a little bit here, a little bit there. This was a pervasive, compelling process that perforce reduced Nixon's maneuverability far more than it would have been if his own men had been running Capitol Hill.

The real-life political exposure for the White House staff came every morning in the 7:30 meeting conducted by Ehrlichman, a free-for-all discussion which gave the Hill Staff its best chance to portray the outside world of politics as it really was, not as the highly insulated Downtown Staff thought it was.* These meetings became the closest thing there was to serious political talk in the White House or, indeed, in the entire administration. And in early January 1970 the talk turned for the first time to what the President and his senior advisers were beginning to see as the central political issue for the 1970 campaign: Democratic big spending, generating inflation.

With a very low unemployment rate for 1970 being forecast by Nixon's economic experts at just over 4 percent, the political issue for the fall campaign looked far more like inflation than unemployment and recession. Thus, to paint the Democratic majority in Congress as big spenders seemed an obvious way to get the jump on the inflation issue. And one way to so paint the Democrats was to veto a couple of big-spending bills, and to stage the veto with the highest drama possible. The bill at hand in January 1970 was the appropriations measure for the departments of Labor and Health, Education and Welfare for the year ending June 30, 1970, which went to the President from Congress with an extra $1.1 billion that he had not requested and did not want. At issue here was not just the 1970 campaign (although to those pushing the veto strategy that was reason enough). The President was more and more concerned that if he did not take drastic action against the Democratic Congress he might soon find that he had lost all control—that, in the words of an assistant, he would have a "runaway" Congress on his hands.

The President, then, was extremely receptive to staff advice that he must veto the Labor-HEW money bill, and do it with a very loud

---

*After George Shultz came to the White House as Director of the Office of Management and Budget in July 1970, he took over the 7:30 meeting from Ehrlichman.

noise indeed. The only caveat came from Harlow, a traditionalist who would not have recommended a veto unless he felt the President could prevent Congress from overriding it. And neither Harlow nor Timmons and the Hill Staff could say for sure.

Harlow had presided over the most successful veto binge in modern American political history when, during the last two years of Eisenhower's second term, the general decided to expend some of his vast popularity and prestige, hoarded all those years, and dominate the Democratic-controlled Congress with what he called his "veto pistol." It was Harlow's advice that persuaded Eisenhower that he could, in fact, sustain his vetoes even though he was then a lame duck. But Harlow knew that Nixon, elected with 43 percent of the vote, was no Ike. And Harlow agonized over whether Congress would override. To Harlow, besides being a tactical defeat for Nixon, that would be strategically harmful to the office of the Presidency. Whatever it might gain for Nixon in political issue-making for the fall campaign, it would lose far more in making him appear a lesser figure than the Congress, unable to control his administration's destiny and at the mercy of the Congressional Democrats. Harlow gave his approval, however, because the odds looked better than even on sustaining the veto, and because the President himself was raring to go down the veto trail. But still, Harlow worried. The last thing he wanted at that time was a series of *political* vetoes, or issue-making vetoes, that would not be sustained in Congress. In the long run, that could be catastrophic for President Nixon.

The Labor-HEW appropriations bill was clearly way out of line, and therefore vulnerable to Presidential attack, because much of the extra funds would be spent in "federally impacted areas"—that is, areas with large federal installations that reduce taxable real estate, the tax base for the public school system—many of them, in fact, affluent areas with little need for federal aid. Over the years, federal spending on the impacted areas' school program had soared to scandalous heights.

Now firming up his desire to veto, Nixon ordered his Hill Staff to estimate the result of the inevitable attempt to override. That estimate was favorable, and so on January 26 Nixon went on television and for the first time in history a bill was vetoed in view of millions. With his eye on the equation of inflation and politics, Nixon said that the bill would force Americans "to pay far more in the rise of the cost of living than they will receive from the increased spending provided for in this bill." That was the first step in trying to attach the "big spender" label on the Democratic Congress.

The House handily sustained the President, then rewrote the bill and sent it back to Nixon for signing at a level about half a billion dollars under the vetoed amount (with a number of little deals between the administration and certain powerful Congressmen guaranteeing that despite the cutback in impacted-area school funds, they wouldn't be hurt politically back home).* But even then, there were worries both among the President's leaders on Capitol Hill and in the White House about the veto strategy. In the first place, Congressional cuts in military appropriations would almost surely equal or exceed the total of all the increases to be voted in social-welfare programs, which meant a problem for Nixon in blaming the Democrats for sending his budget into orbit. But more important was the problem of individual Republican Congressmen risking, under Nixon's veto strategy, going on record against programs that were extremely popular back home, such as education. That first veto of Labor-HEW funds was sustained, but when, in early June 1970, the President began quietly talking about a veto of the Hill-Burton Hospital Construction program, his Hill Staff began to get nervous. Here was one of the most popular programs of them all back home, and it had an equally strong constituency in the Congress. Moreover, the Hill-Burton bill was not even an appropriation but an authorization of $2.79 billion over the next three years (so that the money could not be spent until a later appropriation).

Nervous Republican leaders in Congress had somewhat reluctantly agreed to go along with the Nixon veto policy in the interest of creating a 1970 Congressional campaign issue, but were not entirely happy with it. Both Senator Hugh Scott of Pennsylvania and Senator Robert Griffin of Michigan, Republican Majority Leader and Whip in the Senate, had strongly advised the President to limit his vetoes to appropriations bills. When it came to Hill-Burton, Nixon did not have to ask them for their judgment; he knew they would be against a veto.

---

*It was the virtuoso performance in the House by Timmons that clinched him the job as Harlow's successor in charge of the Hill Staff. He was named the next month.

In the White House, the Hill Staff was also nervous about the prospect of a Hill-Burton veto. Harlow, Timmons, BeLieu and two former Congressional aides who had been added to the staff—Richard Cook, who worked the House side, and Eugene Cowen, who helped BeLieu in the Senate—were unanimously opposed. Moreover, they predicted that a Hill-Burton veto would be overridden by Congress, a slap at a President that had not occurred even once in the last ten years (and had occurred against veto-prone Eisenhower only once during his entire eight years in the White House).

But the nonpoliticians in the White House, including George Shultz, who had just left the Labor Department and moved into the White House as head of the new Office of Management and Budget, did not see it that way. The Downtown Staff argued with Nixon that he must be consistent in his veto policy, that the budget really was beginning to look like a runaway and that only by a series of Presidential vetoes could Nixon command the national attention they wanted him to have on the spending issue. So the President decided to veto Hill-Burton.

For the Hill Staff, that portended a crisis. Harlow knew how savage the reaction in Congress would be, how certain the veto was to be overridden and how impossible it would be to soften the political split that the veto would open up between the President and his own leadership in Congress. The Democrats, on the other hand, had nothing to fear. They would gain by the veto: first, because they would override and thus irreparably erode the President's authority; and second, because most voters would react against Nixon and for the Democrats on this issue. So the President's Hill Staff resorted to a rare policy decision: they would not consult the Republican leaders in Congress on the veto, but simply inform them. That would give the leaders a way of saving face—they could honestly say they had not been consulted. Even if they had been consulted, their protests would have accomplished nothing. Nixon had decided, and his mind was beyond changing. But the well-intentioned attempt to let Republican Congressional leaders off the hook failed. When John Anderson took the House floor to urge that the veto be sustained, Democrats twitted him with the undeniable fact that he had not been asked his opinion in advance. Gerry Ford was furious at being kept in the dark, and took pains not to hide his wrath from the Hill Staff.

Nobody else was let in on the President's little veto secret—

including his own top officials in HEW. Elliot Richardson, who had just resigned as Under Secretary of State to replace the harassed Robert Finch as Secretary of HEW, was flabbergasted and angry when he learned of the veto not from the White House but from a news ticker. He did what Bob Finch never would have done—he placed a call to John Ehrlichman to protest.

Reaction in Congress was swift and remorseless: the House knocked down the veto with a huge 279-to-98 vote, far more than the required two-thirds, and the Senate followed with a 76-to-19 vote.

The Hill-Burton veto told much about Nixon. Mesmerized by what he believed to be the immense political power of the spending issue (despite the fact that not since World War II had a President been able to saddle Congress with the charge of high spending), Nixon swept away the feelings of his own leaders in Congress, disregarded the advice of his Congressional lobbyists inside the White House, failed to inform his lieutenants in HEW and rushed to veto a nonspending bill authorizing funds for one of the federal government's most popular programs. In the sad outcome, his strategy drew a candid response from Timmons' staff: a warning to Nixon that the veto angered Congress without being able to bring the sharp point of the spending issue against the Democrats (less than one-half the Senate Republicans voted to sustain the President), and a warning to Nixon that to drift into a full-scale veto war could be politically dangerous for the President and the Republican Party—could, in short, be not only futile but counterproductive.

That wise counsel confronted the advice Nixon was getting from other senior advisers, particularly Shultz and his chief deputy, Caspar Weinberger, who for purely budgetary reasons continued to pressure the President to veto bills they deemed inflationary. Barely six weeks later, this internal struggle boiled up once again when two bloated appropriations bills—one for the Office of Education and the other for the Housing and Urban Affairs Department—were sent to the President for his signature. Both were far out of line with his budget requests, the Office of Education bill exceeding his spending guidelines by about as much as the education portion of the HEW bill he vetoed in January. But so angry had been the Republican Congressional reaction to the veto of the Hill-Burton Hospital Construction Act that the President was now being strongly advised not to veto the educational funds (for the fiscal year that started July 1, 1970). Although Shultz and Weinberger argued that consistency demanded *two* new vetoes, Harlow's men told the President that it would be disastrous for him if he vetoed both Education and HUD (which included some well-publicized money for veterans) and both vetoes were then overridden by Congress. That would subject both the President and his office to a cataclysmic loss of prestige.

A confidential note to the President was written by Representative Albert Quie of Minnesota, who advised Nixon that although he had voted to sustain the January veto of the Labor-HEW money, he could not support a veto now of the Education money bill. Backing up Quie, Ford and other party leaders told the President flatly that he could not sustain a second education veto. Thus, the prospect was high that Nixon would be slapped down for the second straight time —first Hill-Burton, then the Office of Education. "Don't veto" came through loud and clear from the Republican cloakrooms in Congress.

But from the OMB office of Shultz and Weinberger came option papers strongly advising a second Education-funds veto, as well as a veto of the HUD money bill. Political advisers at the White House were pushing the President that way, too, conjuring up happy visions of the Democrats pinned against the wall with many Presidential vetoes, advertising their inflation-promoting spending. Nixon hedged. Then, in close cooperation with his Hill leaders and Richardson at HEW, so blithely ignored in late June, he decided to split the difference: veto HUD but let the education bill become law, with a Presidential statement that the overage of about half a billion dollars would be recouped by cutting social-welfare spending in other areas.

But, as had happened so many times before, the inner ambivalence of the White House took over, and Nixon at the last instant changed that plan. Meeting with his leaders from the House and Senate early on the morning of August 11, he found the session dominated by the Republican National Chairman, Representative Rogers Morton of Maryland. Morton strongly counseled that *both* bills be vetoed, pounding home his theory that Nixon would look weak and inconsistent if he vetoed the housing bill but let education become law. Moreover, splitting the difference would have a second disadvantage; it would infuriate the mayors if Nixon set a different

standard for cities (benefiting from the HUD bill) than for education.
Finally, said Morton, the spending issue simply could not be ex-
ploited politically against the Democrats for the fall campaign unless
Nixon was consistent and dramatic with his vetoes. A half-and-half
strategy was neither consistent nor dramatic.

When Ford, Scott and other Congressional leaders said nothing
to counter Morton's strong appeal, Nixon decided on a great gamble:
veto both bills even though he had already been assured that one of
them would positively be enacted over his veto. If he lost both vetoes,
the political result would of course be catastrophic, but Nixon had
been told by Ford that a veto of the HUD bill would, by Ford's
preliminary count in the House, be sustained by a close vote. That
was enough for the President. On the same day Morton made his
strong pitch at the White House, Nixon vetoed both bills. Two days
later, the measure carrying funds for the Office of Education was
passed by a two-thirds vote over the President's veto, but the HUD
veto was sustained. It was, then, an indecisive result. Considering all
the planning, agonizing and hard Congressional lobbying that had
gone into the veto strategy for the 1970 election and considering how
the relationship between Nixon and the Democratic Congress had
been rubbed raw by that veto strategy, it accomplished far less than
Nixon had hoped it would. The political issue that would dominate
the 1970 campaign was, it would soon turn out, not inflation and
government spending but unemployment and recession. Even his
successful vetoes of the Labor-HEW money bill in January and the
HUD-veterans spending bill in June were neutralized by the override
of the second Education-funds veto and of the Hill-Burton Hospital
construction authorization. In fact, the damage to Presidential prestige from one override far surpassed any bolstering of it from one
sustained veto. The issue was therefore fuzzy, as the President's Hill
Staff had always felt it would be, and added nothing to the campaign
of 1970.

But the internal battle in the White House over whether to veto
this or that bill revealed something more ominous about the President's legislative pursuits. It revealed a lack of consensus by those
who were closest to the situation and to the President. Divisions in
the White House staff were due to differing parochial interests within
different parts of the staff and there was no consistent legislative
philosophy to override those parochial interests: there was, in short,

no legislative theme, but instead an essentially negative political drive—to make the Democrats look bad as big spenders.

Those vetoes by Richard Nixon in 1970 had far more to do with political than fiscal concerns. All the more remarkable, then, was the fate of another Congressional measure having nothing to do with fiscal responsibility but everything to do with politics. Clearing the House and Senate after a vicious battle between the two branches of Congress, it went to the White House for what, politically, should have been a certain Presidential veto. But instead of a veto, that bill —the Voting Rights Act of 1970, extending the 1965 Act that gave the vote to roughly one million Southern Negroes—was signed into law in June over ardent protests of the President's top political adviser, Attorney General John Mitchell, and the entire White House Congressional liaison staff.

What activated Harlow and the Hill Staff was not the extension of voting rights but the addition to the bill of a provision granting the vote to eighteen-year-olds, starting with the 1972 Presidential election. Nothing better illustrated the lack of political homogeneity within the White House, which had so dogged the President during the internal disputes over the money-bill vetoes, than the President's surprising decision to sign the Voting Rights extension with the eighteen-year-old vote attached.

Originally, the administration plan for the bill was to fulfill a pledge to the South and strip it of its regionalism by applying it beyond the Deep South. To make good on his pledge to bring the South back into the Union and pursue his grand political strategy of welding together the Nixon and Wallace votes of 1968, Attorney General Mitchell succeeded in getting the House to weaken enforcement provisions of the 1965 Act as of August 1970. But in the Senate, the 1965 Act was extended virtually intact over the administration's protest. Hugh Scott and other Republicans running for reelection in the North and West were fearful that if the House version of the bill —that is, the Nixon-Mitchell version—became law, they would suffer in November as the black vote went to the Democrats in even heavier percentages than usual. Scott pleaded with Nixon to make this pledge to him: that if Congress ended up passing the Senate version of the bill, which retained the sanctions of the 1965 Act, he would sign it. The President, although torn, finally gave Scott his pledge, but most reluctantly. Scott, triumphant, spread the word all over the Senate, thus giving moderate and liberal Republicans the assurance they wanted before voting to keep the 1965 Act intact, without risking a Presidential veto.

But then in a surprise move, on March 12 the Senate approved an amendment sponsored by Mansfield to give the vote to eighteen-year-olds, attaching that basically unrelated provision to the Voting Rights Act. Now Nixon was in a dilemma. He had promised Scott he could accept extension of the 1965 Act, but he had never promised to sign into law a bill extending the right to vote to eighteen-year-olds.

In the White House, Nixon confronted civil war. Leonard Garment, out of Nixon's own New York law firm and now handling minority problems for the President from the White House, insisted that a veto would be sinful. With youth in the country threatening violence and revolution, he argued, a Presidential veto would simply prove what militant youth had been parroting—that the system itself was beyond reform and therefore should be scrapped. But the politicians, with an eye on the 1972 election, saw the issue perhaps more clearly. There was not the slightest doubt among them that the eighteen-, nineteen- and twenty-year-olds would vote Democratic en masse. The constitutional issue, they told Nixon, had been made both by him (he had called the Mansfield amendment "an unconstitutional assertion of Congressional authority") and by recognized legal authorities.* He should veto the bill without hesitation and make clear in his veto message that he hoped Congress would quickly reenact the bill as passed, but without the provision giving eighteen-year-olds the vote. Just before the President's decision, Timmons delivered a tightly reasoned memorandum to the President spelling out in the most forceful way possible why the entire Hill Staff felt a veto was essential. Harlow made the same points personally, and so did Mitchell. All had the same reason: the youth vote would go hell-bent for the Democratic Presidential nominee in 1972, and that,

---

*For example, six distinguished members of the Yale law faculty (including Alexander Bickel and Eugene V. Rostow) issued a statement saying that "it surpasses belief" that the Constitution would permit Congress to lower the voting age by statute. In fact, the Supreme Court ruled in 1970 that the statute was constitutional for federal elections, unconstitutional for state and local elections.

all by itself, could defeat Nixon's second-term bid. Mitchell, in fact, privately informed Representative William Colmer of Mississippi, Chairman of the House Rules Committee, not only that he was planning to recommend that Nixon veto the bill but that he thought Nixon would veto it. Instead, on June 22, 1970, five days after final passage by the House, the President signed it into law.

The emotion that surrounded this behind-the-scenes debate inside the White House was intense. After the President decided not to risk public obloquy and sign the bill, accepting whatever its impact might be in the 1972 election, one White House aide said he regarded the decision as "one that will go down as Richard Nixon's major political blunder." Others agreed. Why, then, did the President not take the advice of his political and legislative managers, starting with his own gray eminence, John Mitchell? One answer could be that his fear of an anti-Nixon youth rebellion erupting as soon as he vetoed the bill would have even worse political repercussions on his 1972 chances than giving the vote to the potential 11.5-million extra-young voters. Another, perhaps more plausible possibility was that Richard Nixon, eying his role in history, did not want to be the President who blocked the young from voting.* Or, he might have taken to heart Len Garment's warning of fire in the streets should a Negro voting bill be vetoed if only as a temporary expedient.

Veto strategy dominated Nixon's relationship with Congress for his first two years in office, eclipsing efforts to get his own bills passed. But while his veto battles with the Democratic Congress overshadowed their relationship, important bills did pass Congress: notably postal reform (a courageous Presidential initiative), a lottery system as part of draft reform, a tax reform bill. The list was slim, and its slimness caused two important side effects.

First, John Mitchell, the man with the President's ear, blamed it—unfairly in large part—on the incompetence of the Hill Staff

---

*Concern over his role in history may also have been the reason why, acting against the advice of his political aides, Nixon in early 1969 endorsed a Constitutional amendment to abolish the Electoral College and substitute direct election for President, even though it would demonstrably hurt him and the Republican Party. Fortunately for Nixon, a filibuster in the Senate killed the amendment after it had passed the House by a large margin.

generally and Bill Timmons in particular, making them scapegoats
for failures whose true sources were manifold. Politically naïve about
Congress, Mitchell and a surprising number of other Presidential
advisers had the childish notion that if a bill Nixon wanted did not
pass Congress, or if a bill Nixon did not want did pass Congress, the
Hill Staff was automatically culpable. The Hill Staff, accordingly,
was viewed as ancient kings viewed the messengers who brought
them ill tidings; the bad news was blamed on the messengers and
their heads came off, just as the bad news from Capitol Hill was often
blamed on the Hill Staff, not on the underlying political realities.

The second side effect was that the Downtown Staff convinced
the President—contrary to the wishes of the Hill Staff—that he
should campaign in 1970 against a do-nothing Democratic Ninety-
first Congress, which ought to be replaced by a do-everything Republican Ninety-second Congress. That tactic was no more profitable
than trying to paste the big-spender label on the Congress.

Besides the slimness of the accomplishments, there were two
crushing defeats for Nixon during those two years that soured his
relationship with the Senate as no President's had been since Woodrow Wilson lost his fight for Senate ratification of the League of
Nations. Those two defeats were the rejection of two Southern judges
nominated by the President to the Supreme Court. The reason for
their nominations—and the explanation of their rejection by the
Senate—was only one part of a larger story, by all odds the most
engrossing and in some ways the most discreditable story of the early
Nixon Presidency: his consuming desire to pay off his debt to the
South for what the South did to get him nominated and elected
President.

VI

The Politics
of Civil Rights

*It is particularly gratifying that at a dinner honoring
Lincoln's birthday we can point to more progress in
the field of civil rights in this Administration than in
any since Lincoln's. . . . the struggle for civil rights
. . . involves the whole of our struggle for world peace.
Nothing is more damaging to the United States in the
battle of ideas and ideals . . . than our failures and
our shortcomings in this area.*

—Vice President Richard M. Nixon, in a speech at
Milwaukee, Wisconsin, on February 8, 1960

*It seems to me that there are two extreme groups.
There are those who want instant integration and
those who want segregation forever. I believe that we
need to have a middle course between those two extremes.*

—President Richard M. Nixon, in his
press conference of September 26, 1969

Negro leaders had always been apprehensive about Richard Nixon's
position on race relations, and his successful campaign of 1968 did
nothing to lessen that apprehension.* Having monitored everything

*An example of the reasons for the Negro leaders' unhappiness with Nixon prior
to the 1968 campaign was his failure specifically to endorse the 1964 Kennedy-
Johnson civil rights bill during its passage through Congress. He did so only after
it became law.

he said during the campaign, they were fearful that the momentum of Negro progress—started during the Eisenhower administration, given a powerful thrust forward late in the Kennedy administration and continued with new fervor under Lyndon Johnson—was about to be halted in the Nixon Presidency. To them, the Southern strategy had an ominous ring. Even before the inauguration, six black leaders, ranging in their politics from John Johnson, publisher of the middle-class-oriented *Ebony* and *Jet,* to the Reverend Ralph Abernathy, Martin Luther King's successor, were granted an audience by the President-elect to discuss general civil rights and racial problems.* During that meeting Nixon was quoted by those present as pledging "to do more for the underprivileged and more for the Negro than any President has ever done."

Less than three weeks after the inauguration, the NAACP's Roy Wilkins, the most influential moderate black leader, met with Nixon in the White House. Emerging, Wilkins predicted that the President fully intended to "rectify" the problem of Negro disaffection from him. And nearly two years later, on December 7, 1970, Nixon told James Farmer, at the time of his resignation as Assistant Secretary of Health, Education and Welfare (one of the few high posts in the Nixon administration held by a black), that he wanted to do "what's right" for the Negro. "I care," the President told Farmer. "I just hope people will believe that I *do* care."

Undeniably, Richard Nixon's self-image in these conversations over two years was certainly not that of a racist bigot, or certainly not of an expedient politician prepared to sell out the Negro minority, but of a man prepared to do all *practically* possible for the blacks. He had always perceived himself as a civil rights advocate, and unquestionably always would.

But Roy Wilkins was to regret his optimistic comments on the front stoop of the White House within days after he made them. With lightning speed, Nixon was on his way to becoming the President

---

*Others who came to talk to Nixon that day were Hobson Reynolds, grand exalted ruler of the Improved and Benevolent Order of Elks (the Negro Elks); John Murphy, president of the National Newspaper Publishers' Association; Sandy Ray, first vice president of the National Baptist Convention; and Dr. Nathan Wright, chairman of the Black Power Conference. Also attending were Robert J. Brown, Nixon's black White House aide, and Pat Moynihan.

most disliked and distrusted by Negroes since the rise of black political power following World War II. Their feeling was bluntly conveyed to him in language he seldom experienced firsthand during a meeting with the thirty-five highest-ranking Negro officials in the federal government in April 1970. James Farmer informed him of "a growing spirit of [Negro] hopelessness that the Administration is not on their side."*

That feeling was the direct outgrowth of a public posture taken by Nixon in the White House that seemed overtly anti-Negro, anti-integrationist. How, then, could this be reconciled with Nixon's self-image as civil rights advocate?

Part of it stemmed from his uncomfortable shyness and unwillingness to deal with outsiders, applicable to everybody but very pronounced with Negroes. In the few meetings he had with Negroes as President, Nixon seemed tense and ill at ease. For the most part, he employed brokers to deal with them: Daniel Patrick Moynihan and Leonard Garment, the house liberal and Democrat in Nixon's Wall Street law firm who joined the White House staff early in 1969. Although James Farmer was a famous civil rights leader with incomparable contacts in the black community, he was *never* summoned from his office in HEW to advise Nixon in the White House.

Added to this aloofness was the failure to follow up the one proposal of his 1968 campaign intended to appeal to the Negroes: black enterprise, a scheme of government subsidies and loans for Negro businessmen. The program withered in embryo—a victim of bureaucratic infighting and, more important, a lack of federal money caused by Nixon's campaign to fight inflation through austerity in federal spending. Nor did the President show much interest in promoting black capitalism once he entered the White House.

But basically, Nixon's problems with the Negro could be directly traced to grand questions of party politics. For one thing, Nixon had never quite shaken off the bitter memory of his poor

*A bizarre outgrowth of that meeting was the use of the official White House photograph of the President seated with the black officials used as the cover of a Republican National Committee campaign pamphlet for the 1970 election titled "The Black Silent Majority"—an attempt to indicate that most Negroes were conservative and on Nixon's side. Farmer, who had never been "silent" during a long career of articulate struggle for civil rights, laughed out loud when he saw the pamphlet.

showing—unfairly poor, he felt—among black voters in his 1960 campaign for President. Expecting to expand on the gains among the blacks made by General Eisenhower in 1952 and 1956, Nixon instead was held to a lower percentage of Negro voters than any Republican in history. The principal and perhaps the only explanation, he felt, was John F. Kennedy's public intervention after the sentencing of Dr. Martin Luther King, Jr., to four months in jail for his part in an Atlanta restaurant sit-in, while Nixon, deeming it improper to tamper with the judicial process even though he felt King was getting a "bum rap," had kept silent. Writing two years later, he revealed his resentment over what he saw as the fickle nature of Negro voters:

> . . . I had been one of the most consistent and effective proponents of civil rights legislation in the Administration. I had made several key rulings in the Senate which were essential in getting such legislation to the floor for debate. As Chairman of the President's Committee on Government Contracts, I had helped develop an effective program, among companies with government contracts, which resulted in providing job and promotion opportunities for thousands of Negroes in Northern and Southern states alike. As far as Martin Luther King himself was concerned, I had met him in Ghana and respected him for his advocacy of nonviolence in working for equal rights for his people. But this one unfortunate incident in the heat of a campaign served to dissipate much of the support I had among Negro voters because of my record.*

The experience of 1960 left Richard Nixon with the unbreakable conviction that no matter how hard he tried, no Republican could make significant inroads in the black vote. The converse of this axiom—that passionate courting of the black vote would hurt Nixon with the white vote, particularly the Southern white vote—was always felt by Nixon, and that feeling hardened into an article of faith as the 1968 election neared. With all the big Northern states, except Illinois and New Jersey, controlled by Republican governors who were resolved to keep their delegates away from Nixon, he was

*That interpretation is widely accepted by many Democratic analysts as well. However, a nationwide survey of Negro voters conducted by the *Wall Street Journal* well before the King incident showed Nixon would lose most of the gains among Negroes made by Eisenhower in 1956.

forced to go South, where Republican delegations were under far less control. Here was the birth of the Southern strategy, conceived in necessity but gradually taking on the trappings of grand political doctrine under the guidance of John Mitchell. He decreed that anything the South might perceive as faintly hostile was forbidden.

Indeed, anything that seemed faintly favorable to blacks was also forbidden. Nixon was actually advised not to attend the slain Martin Luther King's funeral in Atlanta on April 9, 1968, and went despite the advice. His political advisers flinched on April 25, 1968, when he first proposed his program of federal aid for black enterprise. Following his advisers this time, Nixon said almost nothing about the subject for the rest of the campaign. Rejecting first the pleas and then the angry demands of Republican leaders in states with a heavy Negro population and following Mitchell's advice, Nixon visited only one Negro ghetto (in Philadelphia) throughout the 1968 campaign.

The pattern carried over after the election. Roy Innis of the Congress of Racial Equality had been the only major black leader to say a good word for Nixon during the 1968 campaign and had worked covertly with Nixon aides in preparing the black enterprise program. After the election, Innis clearly wanted to work out a deal with Nixon to be the President's man in the ghetto. But Mitchell, fearing reaction among whites—particularly Southern whites—to Innis' militant black separatism, advised the President to shun Innis. He did. Innis' letters and telephone calls went unanswered; his requests for an interview with the President were ignored. Naturally, he soon became as critical of Nixon as the next black leader.

Far more important was the political frame of mind in the Nixon White House as his Presidency began. The pivotal element in John Mitchell's grand strategy of combining the 1968 Nixon and Wallace votes for a Republican majority in 1972 was the South. Mitchell's absolutely correct view, largely shared by the President, was that an immense debt was owed to the Republican South for both the nomination and the election. And by no single man was that debt more clearly collectible than Senator Strom Thurmond of South Carolina, Dixiecrat candidate for President in 1948, convert to Goldwater Republicanism in 1964 and Richard Nixon's great Southern vassal in 1968. That debt and how it would be paid became the guiding compass for Richard Nixon's civil rights policy and his dealings with the Negro minority for the next two years.

Even before his inauguration, Nixon began to feel the political heat from his Southern friends. The pressure, gently at first, came from Republican state chairmen, led by charming, aggressive Chairman Clarke Reed of Mississippi, and from Republican officeholders, led by Senator Thurmond, partly funneled through Thurmond's former chief political lieutenant, Harry Dent, who signed on to the Nixon White House staff as political aide during the Pierre Hotel interregnum. Their objective was nothing less than total suspension of the hated "guidelines" established in 1966 by the Department of Health, Education and Welfare as a yardstick to enforce school desegregation under the 1964 Civil Rights Act. By 1968, these guidelines were calling for "terminal desegregation" in many Southern school districts. Those districts that failed to show progress in ending de jure, or legally countenanced, segregation called for by the guidelines lost their federal education funds under the Primary and Secondary Education Act of 1965.

Thus, Thurmond appealed to Nixon to halt the fund-cutoff process immediately and "take a long look" at the entire school desegregation process. Thurmond and other powerful Southerners of both parties really wanted, first, a complete end to cutting off funds and, second, a lifting of the "terminal desegregation" deadlines, which in most cases set a 1969–70 deadline for starting desegregation.

What Thurmond wanted, in short, was nothing less than a sudden halt to federally imposed school desegregation begun when the Supreme Court under Chief Justice Earl Warren (once referred to by Nixon as "that great Republican Chief Justice") had launched it in the landmark case of *Brown vs. Board of Education* in 1954. The way to signal the halt was to suspend the guidelines, now the despised symbol of educational race-mixing in the schools all through the South. Once the guidelines were suspended, Thurmond privately counseled Nixon, any number of ways could be found to delay fund cutoffs until new legislation had been devised that would sanction a "voluntary" approach to integration favored not only by the South but by President Nixon himself.

Or if that could not be done, Thurmond thought, the Presidential power over judicial appointments could be used to place "strict constructionists" not only on the Supreme Court but on lower federal courts throughout the South. School desegregation could then be turned over to the courts and taken away from the social planners of HEW.

Thurmond well knew that in talking to Nixon he had a most receptive audience. Nixon had campaigned across the country in 1968 strongly recommending the freedom-of-choice route to school desegregation, which left the choice of a school up to the parents and children. The trouble with freedom of choice was that except in rare instances of courageous Negro parents, frightened black families left their children in segregated black schools. Put bluntly, freedom-of-choice plans of the kind envisaged by Thurmond were seldom more than a subterfuge for maintaining the status quo.

Nixon himself, in his labored political discussions of freedom of choice as the way out of the race-mixing dilemma, was well aware of this and sought to distinguish between "good" freedom-of-choice plans and "bad" ones. But if he could dramatize his own position inside the South as a freedom-of-choice man, with its corollaries of supporting neighborhood schools and opposing pupil busing, then his great hope of capturing the Wallace segregationist vote and adding it to the Nixon Republican vote for the 1972 election would be well advanced. There was one crippling problem. The Supreme Court in a decision handed down on May 27, 1968, specifically dealt with the freedom-of-choice question, and in a way distinctly hostile to Nixon's plan for using it as an escape hatch out of the nasty political dilemma involving Southern school desegregation.* That decision stated flatly that "the general experience under 'freedom of choice' to date has been such as to indicate its ineffectiveness as a tool of desegregation."

Despite that clear finding by the Supreme Court, candidate Nixon plugged freedom of choice hard during his Presidential campaign. His classic response on the question came in a long interview over television station WBTV in Charlotte, N.C., on September 11, when he was asked by Charles Whitehurst, news director of WFMY-TV in Greensboro, N.C.: "We have had in this area several communities threatened with the withholding of federal funds because the freedom-of-choice plan has been held not valid and not sufficient.

* *Green vs. (New Kent) County School Board,* 391 U.S. 430.

Do you have a position on this?" In view of how it was to influence the first year of his Presidency, Nixon's response is worth recording in some detail:

> Well, the freedom of choice plan is one as you know [that] has been extremely controversial, not only in HEW, not only in the states in the South in which it has been applied, but within the two great parties. . . . My view generally speaking is that there has been too much of a tendency for both our courts and for our Federal agencies to use the whole program of the—of what we could call school integration for purposes which have very little to do with education and which as a matter of fact, I do not—I do not believe serve a very useful purpose in so far as the long range desire that we all have to bring up the educational level of all people within the South and other parts of the country.
>
> Uh, with regard to freedom of choice, I would have to look at each one of the states involved to see whether actually it was a true freedom of choice. If it were, I would tend to favor that. I tend to look with, I would say, great concern, uh, whenever I see Federal agencies or whenever I see the courts attempting to become in effect, local school boards. I think the decision in the local areas should be made primarily by people who are more familiar with those problems. Now, if you come to a school district or to a state where freedom of choice is simply used as a device to perpetuate segregation, that's something else again.

Whitehurst then asked whether the withholding of funds under the HEW guidelines was a "valid weapon," and Nixon replied:

> I think that the use of that power on the part of the Federal Government to force the local community to carry out what a Federal administrator or bureaucrat may, what he may think is best for that local community, I think that is a doctrine that is a very dangerous one. It is one that I generally would not approve. You understand now, I want to make it very clear simply because I am speaking here in North Carolina where there's great interest in this, I want to make it clear that I supported the actions of the Eisenhower Administration in this field, I believe that the Supreme Court decision was a correct decision, the *Brown vs. Board of Education,* but on the other hand, while that decision dealt with segregation and said that we would not have segregation, when you go beyond that and say that it is the responsibility of the Federal Government and the Federal courts to, in effect, act as local school districts in determining how we carry that out, then to use the power of the Federal Treasury to withhold funds in order to carry

it out, then I think we are going too far. In my view, that kind of activity should be very scrupulously examined and in many cases should be rescinded.*

Despite the miasmic confusion wrought by candidate Nixon's effort to identify himself with a desegregation doctrine virtually ruled out by the Supreme Court, he left the solid impression with Thurmond, Dent, Reed and other potent Republicans throughout the South that as soon as he took the oath of office, President Nixon would fix everything. No one knew exactly how, but the conviction was rampant that by fiat, by new legislation or by packing the courts with strict constructionists, Nixon would make the South whole.

Richard Nixon had scarcely entered the White House before the administration was in the middle of its first major school crisis, resulting from a time bomb left him by the Johnson administration. Like so many that were to follow, it was caught up in conflicting passions that confronted Finch's dedicated civil rights stalwarts at HEW in total warfare against Southern-oriented White House politicians, led by Dent, with the powerful presence of John Mitchell locked in similar hostilities only slightly more genteel with the ambivalent and insecure Robert Finch.

Those hostilities would continue into the fall of 1970 on fundamental questions of school desegregation until a formula was found that enabled the President to pull off a political feat of great difficulty: achieving a breakthrough in the most difficult black-majority Southern school districts without impairing his own political standing in the South. In the interim, however, the President's successive retreats on the school issue, heavily cloaked in legal and political ambiguities, took their toll—including the messy firing of HEW's chief civil rights official; a mass revolt by lawyers in the Justice

---

*A week later, at a press conference in Anaheim, Calif., Nixon's emphasis was slightly different. He was told by a reporter that in his Charlotte, N.C., television interview he had "seemed to be open to the interpretation that if you were elected President you would ask Congress to rescind Title VI of the 1964 Civil Rights Act [the title containing authority to cut off school funds]." The reporter then asked, "Would you ask Congress to rescind that authority?" Nixon replied, "Certainly not," and went on to say, "I said that where a freedom-of-choice plan was subterfuge for segregation, then, of course, that violates not only *Brown vs. Board of Education* but it also violates the mandate of Congress and funds should be withheld."

Department's Civil Rights Division; and public accusations of sellout by the U.S. Civil Rights Commission, headed by Father Theodore Hesburgh, president of the University of Notre Dame.
Moreover, until peace of sorts was reached in 1970, the administration was in a constant state of turmoil over the race question.

Shortly after Nixon's inauguration, Finch informed his liberal
new Assistant Secretary for Education, Dr. James Allen, "We're
going to be hard. We're going to stick to the guidelines." Assistant
Secretary James Farmer was convinced then—and remained convinced long after both had left HEW—that Finch was absolutely
sincere in his conviction. Finch had two highly placed allies: Moynihan and Garment. As part of the overall Moynihan Doctrine of
establishing the legitimacy of government by not tampering with the
liberal actions of the past administration, Moynihan argued with the
President that it would be folly to draw back on school desegregation.* To press his point, Moynihan brought one of the nation's most
respected students of the pros and cons of school desegregation,
Professor James Coleman of Johns Hopkins University, to the White
House for a long interview with Nixon.

But this pro-integrationist clique in the administration was
scarcely a match for the iron resolve of John Mitchell and his over-
powering influence on the President. As part of his strategy, Mitchell
wanted the onus of school desegregation shifted from the federal
bureaucracy (controllable by Nixon) to the federal courts (not controllable by Nixon), so that Nixon could tell the South: It's not my
fault. This clearly meant an increasingly minor role for HEW in
enforcing desegregation. Considering Mitchell's determination and
Finch's irresoluteness, Mitchell's rising star and Finch's falling star
in regard to Nixon, this was never truly a battle. Mitchell was fated
to win. But as he entered HEW, Finch was totally unaware of the
inevitability of his defeat or that Mitchell—and Nixon—wanted a
lesser HEW role in enforcing desegregation. Nobody told him that.
Nor did anybody tell him how to handle that first time bomb left him
by the Democrats.

The time bomb that exploded almost at the same time that
Nixon took office had been deposited on Finch's desk by his Democratic predecessor, the artful Wilbur Cohen, crafty in the ways of

*See p. 41.

both the Washington bureaucracy and national politics. Cohen had ruled that five school districts—two in Thurmond's South Carolina, two in Mississippi, and the other in Martin County, N.C.—must lose federal school funds as of January 29 for failure to submit desegregation plans meeting HEW's guidelines. Here it was, the very thing that Nixon had spoken out so strongly against during the campaign. During confirmation hearings before the Senate Finance Committee, even Finch allowed himself to attack the concept of fund cutoffs ("Each community is a different slice of America. Each area has a chemistry all its own. You don't just come in with a meat-ax and bludgeon somebody into compliance").

But Finch also promised the Senate he would "keep the pressure up, and it must be constant pressure." Thus, besides *private* pressure from Mitchell and the White House, Finch had to operate under the outright contradiction of the Nixon administration's *public* approach to school desegregation: pressure, yes; bludgeon, no. And yet, as the next few months would clearly tell, the two often had to go together.

Faced with a predetermined January 29 cutoff date for the five districts, Finch had three options: let Wilbur Cohen's order stand; reverse it completely; find a middle ground. Pressures from Congress were mounting, the complainants were citing candidate Nixon's Charlotte statement promising no arbitrary fund cutoffs—in fact, perhaps no fund cutoffs at all—under his administration. The first complainant was a veteran Southern Republican Congressman, Representative Charles Jonas of North Carolina, a state in which no school district had yet lost its federal education money because of failure to desegregate. Jonas called White House lobbyist William Timmons and politely demanded that Cohen's order be reversed by Finch. Timmons then placed calls to three very different Californians in HEW to convey to them Jonas' strong feelings.

The first was Finch, who believed in desegregation but never put it above his loyalty to Nixon and the administration. The second was Leon Panetta, a thirty-year-old liberal Republican lawyer who had worked for the just-defeated Senator Thomas Kuchel of California and had been appointed by Finch to run the Office of Civil Rights in HEW. Though a loyal Republican, Panetta tended to put his deep conviction in the need to follow the letter of the law on school desegregation over his interest in Nixon's political progress. The third was Robert Mardian, a Goldwater Republican who had been named general counsel of HEW by Nixon at Mitchell's urging relayed through the White House. A go-slow advocate on school desegregation, Mardian drove to work each day with Deputy Attorney General Richard Kleindienst and was the eyes and ears of the Justice Department and John Mitchell inside HEW.

The pressure from Jonas was more than matched by Thurmond, who worked through Dent, who went to Harlow, who talked to Finch. Before making up his mind, Finch consulted with the President himself, who, at that early period, was far more deeply involved in foreign policy than racial issues. Nixon repeated to Finch his well-known campaign pledges and his personal feeling about fund cutoffs. He wanted the order stayed. Finch then called Timmons with this news: a sixty-day stay would be granted.

With that good news, Timmons immediately telephoned Jonas, who quickly issued a press release rejoicing—and well aware that he would be blessed with political credit for making the good news known to the public—in the first major desegregation, or nondesegregation, decision made by the new President.

On that same evening, January 24, Finch and his Under Secretary, John Veneman, a hard-boiled liberal California Republican, were riding back from the office to their temporary residence at the Statler-Hilton Hotel when Finch suddenly turned to Veneman and said he had "lost" on the fund cutoff. That was the first Veneman heard of Finch's decision, and he was thunderstruck. Did Finch comprehend the significance of the stay? Did he realize that the new administration's whole posture on the race issue, badly tarnished by the Nixon campaign, would be judged by this first fundamental decision? Finch said yes, but the President had made up his mind and wanted the fund cutoff stayed for sixty days.

Veneman kept pressing. A far more committed liberal than Finch, Veneman knew that such a dramatic and rapid surrender to Southern pressure on so basic a school desegregation matter could do irreparable harm to the new administration. He also knew it could cause revolt within HEW itself, where, under Lyndon Johnson, Southern resistance to school desegregation had been given short shrift. Finally, he convinced Finch that another effort to persuade the President had to be made. Between them, then, they came up with an alternative plan: the five districts would be cut off from their

federal funds effective January 29, but if they came up with acceptable desegregation plans in the next sixty days, they could get it all
back (and, indeed, two of the five districts did produce plans that
HEW later found acceptable, recovering all their funds).*

When Nixon accepted that compromise and Finch announced
it, no one was happy. Unhappiest of all was Republican Jonas, whose
press release proclaiming there would be no fund cutoff had been
based on information that originated with Finch himself. Now the
White House had changed its mind, leaving Jonas looking silly. It
would not be the last time that an administration split down the
middle on the race issue would be unable to make up its mind
without an extraordinary and unseemly number of political and
ideological contortions.

Richard Nixon moved into the White House with Harry Dent
carrying the title of Deputy Counsel but actually performing the very
special assignment of keeping a wide-open Southern eye on every
single action the administration was to take. About a year later the
President issued an unprecedented order to H. R. Haldeman: Establish and enforce a policy in this administration that no statements are
to be made by any official that might alienate the South. Haldeman
issued the directive and assigned Edward Morgan, a deputy counsel
to the President, to enforce it. The President not only wanted his
Southern allies protected from hostile statements within the administration, but he also ordered that from that point on every aspect of
school desegregation should be handled sotto voce. When Stanley
Pottinger replaced Panetta in February 1970, he received an amazing
order from the White House. Before issuing any statement that in
any remote way might be interpreted as hostile to the South, he was
to check it with Morgan.

Considering what had happened during the year preceding that

---

*One of the two was Martin County, N.C., which voted soon after Finch's
decision to desegregate its sixteen public schools. Expressing the disappointment of
many Southerners that Nixon had not canceled the fund cutoff, School Board
Chairman Leroy Harrison said, "A portion of the people in this country thought
the new Administration would lighten up." On the other side, Roy Wilkins and the
Leadership Conference on Civil Rights, composed of leading civil rights organizations, saw the Nixon-Finch action as "bound to stimulate new violations of a law
overwhelmingly passed by Congress."

directive culminating in the departure of Panetta, this Presidential order was understandable. Certainly, it fit the Nixon-Mitchell grand strategy: to achieve that Nixon-Wallace majority in the 1972 election. The South had expected favored treatment from the very start, but that first year had not run consistently to form. The problem started in earnest one day before the inauguration when the Southern Republican chairmen, under the leadership of Clarke Reed, arrived in Washington and asked for an appointment with Finch. Instead of seeing them in his new office at HEW's headquarters on Independence Avenue, Finch met the Southern chairmen surreptitiously in the Statler-Hilton Hotel and asked that the meeting be kept secret, out of the hands of the press. That was the first shock to the Southerners. As their reward for having been instrumental in nominating and electing Richard Nixon, his best friend in the Cabinet was refusing to be seen with them in public.

The second shock was far more serious: the discovery that despite their conquest of the Presidency, there was simply no chance, no chance at all, that the "instant change" they expected in school desegregation policy could be made to happen. The fault was not in the new policies of President Nixon, but in the cut and force of the law, a fact of which they had been woefully ignorant. For eight years, with Kennedy and Johnson in the White House, most of these Southern Republican leaders ignored the finer points of the law and simply issued one press release after another attacking the Democratic administration. That was easy. But when they arrived in Washington in 1969, they discovered that what they had been led to believe would be an easy, immediate and dramatic rollback of school desegregation was absolutely out of the question because *the law would not allow it.*

As one of these Southern Republican leaders said of their second trip to Washington, in early February, "We came to Washington and asked, do we get freedom of choice? They took us to Justice and Joe Rogers [a Republican lawyer who later became U.S. Attorney in South Carolina] explained the *Green* case to us. We were just dumb. We had won the election, we wanted big changes in everything—and we couldn't even get freedom of choice!"

Panetta would remember somewhat differently that Southern chairmen's second trip to Washington two weeks after the inauguration. Held at the Sheraton Carlton Hotel in a second-floor room called the Cabinet Room, the meeting oozed hostility when he was summoned to the platform to tell about HEW's plans on school desegregation. He gave a quick, concise rundown on the law since the 1954 *Brown* decision, ending with a description of the *Green* case virtually outlawing freedom of choice. When he finished, the party chairmen from South Carolina, Mississippi, Alabama, Texas and Louisiana started in on him, one by one. The theme was unpaid obligations that quickly turned into genuine anger: we stuck our necks out for Nixon and all you Northern Republicans, we want freedom of choice for our schools; that's what Nixon said he was for; you just can't *not* change the old Democratic policy.

Panetta listened. The next attack came on Finch's appointment of James Farmer. Reed, a handsome young millionaire industrialist and planter from Mississippi, who had just been elected chairman of the Southern Republican Chairmen's Association, was furious at the symbolism of Farmer's appointment. Another Southern chairman facetiously suggested assigning quotas to administration officials invited to speak to future sessions of the Southern State Chairmen's Association. "We'll give Farmer a zero quota," he laughed.

When Panetta left the Carlton that day, his first exposure to the Southerners, he went directly to Finch's office at HEW. "They were talking to me," he said, "in Wallace-ite terms."

Wallace-ite or not, the hard fact was that there was not a great deal that the administration could do, whatever pledges Nixon had made during the campaign. The President could not repeal the *Green* decision; he could not repeal the 1964 Civil Rights Act, with its specific sanctions against de jure segregation and its specific mechanism for HEW guidelines and the cutoff of federal school aid; he could not extend the doctrine of desegregation to the North, thus taking some of the heat off the South, even though the North had more housing patterns that led to de facto school segregation— segregation that is not *legally countenanced* and, therefore, not illegal.

But there was one step Nixon could take, if the courts would let him get away with it: suspend the fall 1969 deadline for most of the remaining still-segregated Southern school districts and move it back to the fall of 1970; do the same for the bulk of the black-majority school districts, the hardest nuts of all to crack, which were due for desegregation in the fall of 1970, and make that deadline the fall of 1971. That became the prime objective of the political managers of civil rights in the Nixon administration: Mitchell, Dent, Mardian, Jerris Leonard (a conservative Republican state legislator from

Wisconsin named the Assistant Attorney General for Civil Rights) and the powerful Southern Republican contingent in Congress. To Veneman, Panetta, Dr. James Allen, and the Northern liberal wing of the President's party, this retreat was unacceptable. They set out first to win the allegiance of well-meaning Bob Finch, who was being slowly squeezed into line by Mitchell and the White House and, second, to dilute the planned new slowdown as much as possible.

Finch in his heart was solidly on the liberal side as a series of painful meetings between him and his staff, on one side, and Mitchell and his staff, on the other, were held to draft the new administration policy. But Finch could never quite be counted on. He was peculiarly vulnerable to White House pressure, partly because he felt it unfair to put the overburdened President on the spot (a reluctance clearly evident in his unsuccessful battle for Dr. John Knowles), partly because he was extremely sensitive toward pressure on himself from White House aides.* For example, even after Veneman persuaded Finch not to capitulate on the January 29 fund-cutoff dispute, Finch accepted without a quibble some highly significant language from the White House in the statement that he wrote announcing his decision. That language declared that it would be Finch's intent "to reassess all of the Department's procedures to develop policies which will encourage negotiations, provide flexibility and fairness, and assure enforcement of the law consistent with the interpretation the President repeatedly expressed in the campaign."

"The trouble was that no one really understood what Nixon had said or promised during the campaign, and his statements were shrouded in ambiguity and controversy," Panetta wrote later. "What was clear was that the campaign statements and the actions by the White House on this statement foretold that something would have to change, something would have to give, and that pressures would continue until that something happened."†

The "something" was now, in the late spring of 1969, being

*See pp. 61 ff.

†Despite all the furor, the South still had nothing solid on which to base any genuine claim of a breakthrough under Nixon. So when Finch gave an interview to the *U.S. News and World Report* on March 10, 1969, and used all the catch slogans dear to the Southern heart, inveighing against the Feds for trying to "come in and impose your will with a meat ax," Clarke Reed ordered thousands of copies distributed all over the South as an example of desegregation thinking in the Nixon administration. They had nothing more solid to distribute.

hammered out in contentious meetings between HEW and Justice, with Justice pushing a balky HEW to consent, under heavy White House and Congressional political pressures, to remove the autumn 1969 desegregation deadline and give those Southern districts one more year of grace. When the statement was finally issued on July 3, it was a masterpiece of equivocation, a hollow egg laid after a long and noisy incubation period. It did not, as the South and White House politicians had hoped, do gross violence to the 1969–70 terminal desegregation deadlines set by the Johnson administration for white-majority school districts. Instead, it allowed only a small chink of hope that "there may be sound reasons for some limited delay." That language was narrow enough to permit Panetta and Veneman, who (with Justice's Jerris Leonard) had issued the July 3 statement in the names of Mitchell and Finch, to claim that it changed nothing at all—absolutely nothing. The statement also put the freedom-of-choice question into its best perspective ever since Nixon began talking about it during the campaign. It said that freedom-of-choice desegregation plans proposed by school districts in compliance with the fall 1969 deadline would be considered only if the plan as a whole "genuinely promises to achieve a complete end to racial discrimination at the earliest practicable date."

But so successful was the White House in making the July 3 statement *seem* like a massive retreat from the old days, and a bountiful gift to the South, that there were instant, ugly repercussions from civil rights leaders. Roy Wilkins, who with the entire leadership of the NAACP was attending the NAACP convention at Jackson, Miss., actually accused the administration of "breaking the law." Said the normally even-tempered Wilkins, "It's almost enough to make you vomit. This is not a matter of too little, too late. Rather it's a matter of nothing at all."*

Wilkins and other liberals whose voices were raised against the July 3 statement did not know it, but the statement as finally issued

---

*Among the more vigorous critics of the July 3 statement was M. Hayes Mizell, who resigned as a member of the South Carolina Advisory Committee to the U.S. Commission on Civil Rights, calling the statement a retreat that was "racist"-inspired. A respected white liberal who was still on the Columbia, S.C., school board in the spring of 1971, Mizell wrote Nixon a letter of protest that the retreat represented "lawlessness and disorder just as much as any violent and bloody crime in our streets" and subjected blacks to a feeling "that their rights are subject to the whims and manipulations of your Administration."

was almost unrecognizable from earlier drafts written by Mardian and White House politicians, including the ubiquitous Harry Dent. As late as June 20, these politicians with a Southern exposure hoped that the final statement would routinely lift the 1969 deadline for any district that simply said it needed more time. Furthermore, a proviso stating that "community resistance" would be a permissible reason for putting off desegregation was also to be included in the statement —an open invitation to massive delay and procrastination. So scandalous a retreat was prevented by a combination of strong resistance at HEW (particularly Veneman and Panetta bucking up Finch); by Len Garment, a liberal voice then newly arrived at the White House; by Jack Landau, a liberal lawyer-journalist who was Mitchell's press secretary; and, to a markedly lesser extent, by Jerris Leonard. The July 3 statement was not all that the liberals inside the administration desired, and far from the desires of those outside, but it was at least as much as, if not more than, the maximum they thought they would get. It was, indeed, their high-water mark.

One reason commonly given for the relative success of the Finch-Veneman-Panetta effort to hold most of the line in the July 3 statement was Finch's bitter defeat in the Knowles affair. A second defeat could have been the *coup de grâce* for the President's old protégé, and he fought harder than usual to prevent it. But it was a momentary triumph of very limited scope in a losing war. Other things done quietly behind the scenes within the administration revealed much about the backward thrust of civil rights as pursued by the Nixon administration, in school desegregation and elsewhere.

In April, Clifford L. Alexander, Jr., a Democrat and a Negro, resigned as chairman of the Equal Employment Opportunity Commission because of a "crippling lack of administration support." In April, the President requested Congress to reduce the enforcement program for fair housing by $4 million. A few weeks later the U.S. Civil Rights Commission charged that the Nixon administration was subsidizing racial discrimination by cooperating with private firms that defied the ban on job bias written into the 1964 Civil Rights Act. In June came by far the most ominous break with civil rights that the administration had yet attempted: the Justice Department came out against extension of the Voting Rights Act of 1965, offering a substitute that would end the special sanctions against the South—

sanctions that had added almost one million black voters to the rolls.* That administration decision, in the works since the 1968 campaign and on which Nixon had pledged action to his insatiable Southern allies, profoundly shocked the bipartisan civil rights bloc in and out of Congress. The NAACP attacked the plan as "a sophisticated but nonetheless deadly way of thwarting the progress we have made." Then, in June, Philip Pruitt, head of the Small Business Administration's minority entrepreneurship program, resigned with a blast at the administration for failing to give financial support to its overballyhooed program of aid to black business. "There's been lots of rhetoric in government about helping blacks but no money has been forthcoming," he said.†

On July 6, explaining the administration's July 3 statement by Mitchell and Finch on the future course of school desegregation, the President's press aide, Ronald Ziegler, told reporters at Key Biscayne, Fla.: "The American people as a whole will judge the Administration on our performance." Six weeks later the performance the American people watched from a ringside seat shocked even sympathetic pro-Nixon partisans outside the South. What they saw was the unedifying spectacle of the executive branch of government entering a federal appeals court not for an order on *behalf* of school desegregation but to petition the court to *postpone* school desegregation already ordered—and this despite the clear mandate of the Supreme Court in the 1968 *Green* case, more than one year earlier, demanding that school desegregation proceed forthwith, *now*.

This set up the climax of almost one full year of Nixon promises, starting after the Miami convention in 1968, with very little that was solid yet delivered which the South could get its hands on as evidence that what it had done for Nixon had really slowed the course of desegregation. There were a few minor triumphs, however. Thurmond and Dent had managed to get HEW to water down desegrega-

---

*The administration bill would have deleted the pre-clearance provision of Section 5 of the 1965 Act, thus returning to Southern states their power to obstruct Negro voting by discriminatory laws and regulations. The 1965 Act required the U.S. Attorney General to approve every change in state voting law. It was this sanction that opened the polling booths to unprecedented Negro voting.

†Although Pruitt's charges were well taken, liberal critics of the SBA felt that he was unqualified to perform his duties and was thereby part of the problem he was attacking.

tion plans for twenty-one school districts in South Carolina. In the 8th Congressional District of Tennessee a special election brought blatant pressure on HEW from the White House and the state's two most important Republicans, Senator Howard Baker and Representative William Brock, to postpone a fund cutoff involving one school district on grounds that the cutoff would hurt the Republican candidate. After a proper amount of agonizing, Finch went along with the White House and agreed to appease the politicians.* But none of this constituted the turning back of the clock that so many Southern Republicans in their unawareness of the law had been expecting. Then the Mississippi case suddenly burst onto the scene against a backdrop that seemed quite unexceptional.

The U.S. Court of Appeals for the Fifth Circuit, at the request of the Justice Department, had ordered thirty-three school districts in Mississippi desegregated for the school year beginning in the fall of 1969, not later than September 11, with desegregation plans for twenty-nine of them aimed at total desegregation during the 1969–70 school year. Final plans for this heavy load of desegregation had been ordered to be given to the appeals court on August 11.

On August 1 Finch summoned his top school aides to his office, including Veneman, Allen, Panetta and the technical experts in charge of drawing up desegregation plans. Although they did not know it that day, Finch was just then beginning to feel the pressure of politics on the Mississippi desegregation cases, a pressure that emanated not from some obscure Congressman but from that courtly patrician, Senator John Stennis of Mississippi, who, as Chairman of the Senate Armed Services Committee, was floor manager of the President's top legislative issue of 1969, the antiballistic missile program.† The ABM was only one part of the huge military authorization bill, which was nearing a vote in the Senate under the capable management of John Stennis, the Phi Beta Kappa who had spent seven years as a state circuit judge before getting elected to the U.S.

---

*The argument pushed by Baker, Brock and the White House was that if the fund cutoff was allowed to take place, the candidate in the special election of George Wallace's American Independent Party would win the segregationist West Tennessee district. If the cutoff was delayed, the Republican candidate would have a good chance. The cutoff was postponed, and the Democratic candidate, Ed Jones, won in a landslide, followed by the Wallace candidate, second, and then by the Republican, third.

†See p. 114.

Senate and who was now, on the eve of his sixty-eighth birthday, one of the reigning princes of the Senate. Stennis was angry about the sweeping desegregation about to engulf his state and he conveyed his anger to no less a person than Richard M. Nixon. He had already conveyed it to Melvin Laird, John Mitchell and Robert Finch, but nothing positive had happened. Stennis, a gentleman of the old school, was not one to wave empty threats. He simply made clear an incontrovertible fact: that the school desegregation being planned for Mississippi might well result in public unrest and that as a result he, John Stennis, might have to spend a few days or even more back home in Mississippi.

Stennis used no intermediaries and no sign language to convey that fact to the President. He wrote a letter to Nixon and had it hand-delivered at the White House in mid-August. The senator's letter was teletyped from the White House to the President at the Western White House, at San Clemente, where Nixon had gone on August 9. It had precisely the effect Stennis calculated: consternation, tinged with panic. If Stennis left Washington, the military authorization bill would fall into the hostile hands of Senator Stuart Symington of Missouri, second-ranking Democrat on the Armed Services Committee. A former Secretary of the Air Force, Symington in his early Senate days was strong for military preparedness and took Soviet weapons development with deadly seriousness. Now, however, Symington had become a dove on the war in Vietnam and deeply skeptical about the arms race. In his hands, the military authorization bill, already in some trouble in a Senate moving toward a form of neo-isolationism, would have been in real danger.

Thus, the danger that Stennis might walk out on him in the Senate galvanized Nixon into action. He made a stab at bargaining with the senator, but Stennis was adamant. Nixon then took the easy way out: he ordered Finch to delay the big desegregation attack on Mississippi. It was a shocking decision by Nixon, but politically it would assure two things: keep Stennis on the Senate floor (actually, some of Nixon's wisest political friends never really thought he would leave, no matter what the provocation in Mississippi); and for the first time since he became President, show the South that the Nixon administration was willing to bring down on its head the wrath of every civil rights group in the nation in order to salve the wounds and ease the path of the South.

Here, in brief, was a heaven-sent opportunity to endear himself to the South after seven months of flabby back-and-forth on school desegregation. There could be no more dramatic way to prove himself than to send his Justice Department attorneys into the Court of Appeals to argue not for but *against* desegregation. The President left the details to Mitchell and Finch, who quickly decided that the only possible grounds for reversing the earlier decision, which had asked for desegregation plans to be presented to the court on August 11, was to beg for more time on grounds that reliable and workable plans could not be drawn up in so short a time. The fact that the technical experts in the Office of Education had already drafted complete plans for the Mississippi districts was a detail to be brushed aside. Finch would handle that in a letter to Chief Judge John R. Brown, and his letter minced no words. To attempt implementing the new desegregation plans on such short notice, he wrote Judge Brown on August 19, "must surely, in my judgment, produce chaos, confusion and a catastrophic educational setback to the 135,700 children, black and white alike, who must look to the 222 schools of these Mississippi districts for their only available educational opportunities." Finch's proposal: postpone the business until December 1, when a new set of terminal desegregation plans would be presented to the court.

The desegregation plans already approved by Finch's own educational experts belied what Finch had written Judge Brown. These experts, moreover, were not even told about Finch's letter until after it had been written. When they read in his letter to Judge Brown that "the time allowed for the development of these terminal plans has been much too short for the educators of the Office of Education to develop . . . plans which can be implemented this year," they felt betrayed.

The decision to delay had come from the very top, from Nixon himself, and Finch never hesitated in carrying it out. Now, however, he and Jerris Leonard had to dig up expert witnesses to testify in federal court that the original desegregation plans could not work— in other words, to support the claim made in Finch's letter. Leonard arrived at HEW on Saturday, August 23, to meet with Finch, Veneman, Panetta and Dr. Gregory Anrig, chief of the technical experts in the Office of Education. Tension was high because Dr. Anrig had already written his formal opinion to the Court of Appeals before Stennis intervened, asserting that "each of the enclosed plans is educationally and administratively sound, both in terms of substance and in terms of timing." Tension was high, too, because Leonard had brought a court stenographer with him to the meeting. This looked to the HEW experts to be official pressure with the implication of a threat.

When Leonard asked Dr. Anrig about the educational soundness of the old plans, he stood on his letter, thus flatly repudiating Finch's position that the plans would "produce chaos, confusion and a catastrophic educational setback." Anrig clearly was not a candidate for one of Leonard's witnesses. In fact, it was becoming apparent to Finch and Leonard that getting educational experts to back up Finch and validate the grounds on which the Nixon administration had asked for the delay would be extremely difficult. At one point, Finch offered himself for that role, but his top aide, Patrick Gray, immediately ruled him out. Finally, two HEW regional officers were found by Leonard in Atlanta and Charlottesville, Va., who agreed to be his expert witnesses and tell the court that the plans could not be implemented. The circuit court heard the arguments, agreed to the Stennis-Nixon-Finch request and postponed the effective date of the desegregation until the winter. But the cost, both politically and from the standpoint of encouraging other school districts to sue for the same kind of relief, was staggering.

For the first time since the 1954 *Brown vs. Board of Education* decision, the NAACP Legal Defense and Educational Fund, Inc., headed by Jack Greenberg, entered a major civil rights case against the federal government. As soon as the appeals court handed down its ruling in the Mississippi case, Greenberg appealed to the Supreme Court (where Leonard himself, who at heart had been a reluctant participant in the whole Mississippi proceeding, felt confident that the circuit court would be overturned and the Nixon administration sharply reprimanded). He was right. With Nixon's newly appointed Chief Justice, Warren Burger, joining in a unanimous decision, the Court held on October 29 that "the obligations of every school district is to terminate dual school systems at once and to operate now and hereafter only unitary schools."*

The Supreme Court's October 29 order for desegregation "at

*Mitchell confided to friends that he was stunned by the 8-to-0 decision. The Attorney General had been confident that Berger would support the President.

once" directly contradicted Nixon's public position set forth just a
month earlier. At his September 26 press conference, Nixon made his
famous formulation that "there are those who want instant integration and those who want segregation forever. I believe that we need
to have a middle course between those two extremes." But politically
he had enhanced himself tremendously in the South. His current
position was typified by this exchange at the President's press conference of December 8:

> *Question:* Before the Supreme Court ordered immediate school inte-
> gration [the ruling of October 29], you said you preferred a middle road
> policy, that is between segregation forever and instant integration.
> What is your policy now?
> *The President:* To carry out what the Supreme Court has laid down.
> I believe in carrying out the law even though I may have disagreed as
> I did in this instance with the decree that the Supreme Court eventually
> came down with. But we will carry out the law.

Now Richard Nixon, more than ten months as President, had
fulfilled John Mitchell's formula. By reversing his own HEW and
Justice Department officials, the President had been reversed by the
Supreme Court and so had dramatized his Southern credentials. He
had become the first President to publicly "disagree" with a Supreme
Court ruling for desegregation. The responsibility for the forced
desegregation, he made clear on December 8, was the Court's, not
his.

As a way of conducting the U.S. government, it left much to be
desired. But as a way of ingratiating himself with the South—of
taking one more step toward the ultimate goal of joining the 1968
Wallace voters to the Nixon voters—it was not bad politics.

The Supreme Court decision in the Mississippi case was a shock
to the White House aides, particularly those who, like chief lobbyist
Bryce Harlow, were forever being pressured by Southern Congressmen. Harlow had never really understood the complexities of the law
on school desegregation, either by statute or in rulings by the courts.
Nor did Ehrlichman, though a lawyer, have a solid grounding in civil
rights law. Even Attorney General Mitchell had trouble understanding the distinction in legal approach to de jure and de facto segregation. On those few occasions that Mitchell addressed himself
specifically to the school issue, he would reveal his ignorance of the

law in little ways—for example, by talking up enforcement in the Northern cities (where de facto segregation was beyond existing legal remedy). In the White House, Harlow often voiced the same futile hope—that the North should be forced to catch up with the South on desegregation before any more pressure was placed on the South.

Those who *did* comprehend the law, such as Jerris Leonard and Leon Panetta, knew how far out of line the administration had gotten in the Mississippi case, but their influence was insignificant in competing with Nixon's Southern strategy. Leonard would occasionally lose his temper over the outlandish efforts his boss and the President were making to woo the South. "The South . . . the South, I'm so goddamn tired of hearing about the South," he said once. "When is somebody going to start worrying about the North? That's where the votes are, to begin with. Instead, we're fighting over the law in order to give something to a bunch of racists."

But Leonard did not often permit himself to engage in such emotional outbreaks, and, on the surface at least, was a team player.* Panetta was another matter. All during that first year Panetta had not only rubbed the White House staff the wrong way by throwing embarrassing questions and raising awkward issues, but had also gotten in Mitchell's hair and in the bad graces of Deputy Attorney General Richard Kleindienst. On their morning ride to work each day, Bob Mardian filled Kleindienst's ear with anti-Panetta gossip.

The White House staff decided in the fall of 1969 that Panetta had to go. He was too outspoken, he was a "zealot" (because he kept adverting to the law), he was a troublemaker. But how to persuade Finch to fire him? The first effort failed, when Panetta's most important supporter in HEW, Under Secretary Veneman, flatly warned Finch that if Panetta was fired he himself would quit on the spot and take some of HEW's best men with him.

That only delayed the White House campaign to get Panetta out of the administration. The second effort came early in 1970 after Panetta had made clear that, on the strength of the Supreme Court decision in the Mississippi case, he would move quickly against *all* segregated school districts in the South, including those with black

---

*Leonard's loyalty was rewarded in 1971, when he was named to one of the most coveted posts in the Justice Department: Director of the new Law Enforcement Assistance Agency.

majorities. Panetta assumed that the Supreme Court decision had opened some eyes in the White House and that the White House staff would now see the futility, not to mention the political danger, of continuing a policy of appeasing the South. But Panetta seriously misjudged the politics of the White House. After the October 29 decision on the Mississippi case, Harlow, for one, actually talked of the possibility of Nixon issuing a statement castigating the Supreme Court and saying, in effect, its decision could not be enforced.

At HEW, Mardian counseled Finch to reply to the Mississippi decision with a mealy-mouthed statement that, despite the Court's edict, HEW would continue to examine each case as it came up without any across-the-board policy (as Panetta was insisting on pursuing). Finch flatly rejected Mardian's counsel, but that didn't make it any easier for Panetta. *Human Events,* the right-wing journal, had for months been predicting the sacking of Panetta, a message received from conservative Congressmen with ties to Harry Dent and other White House aides.

Finch tried one delaying tactic after another to protect Panetta, but he never once used his great and warm friendship with the President to ask that Panetta be retained. In conversations at the White House, Finch did contrast Panetta's control over his liberal civil rights staff at HEW with Leonard's lack of control over his liberal staff of Justice Department civil rights attorneys. When Nixon ordered the switch in the Mississippi case in August, the Justice Department lawyer already on the scene to argue, so he thought, for the original plan of immediate desegregation was so outraged by the abrupt change of plans that he rose in court and publicly disagreed with the administration. He was fired on the spot. The capitulation to Stennis also provoked an unprecedented revolt among Leonard's staff of civil rights lawyers, sixty-five of whom signed a stiff protest petition to Mitchell with a copy for Leonard, held a series of well-publicized "secret" meetings and generally embarrassed the administration. At Panetta's office, Finch kept telling his White House friends, there was nothing like that.

To no avail. Dent and other anti-Panetta White House assistants collected evidence against Panetta from legislative assistants on Capitol Hill who had heard him speak out critically about the administration's Southern strategy. That information went into a dossier, which was read to Finch over the telephone (but which was never directly shown to Finch, nor, of course, to Panetta). When the *Washington Daily News* appeared on the streets on February 17, 1970, with a headline saying, "Nixon Seeks to Fire HEW's Rights Chief for Liberal Views," the story under the headline, leaked by an anti-Panetta Congressman, confirmed Finch's premonition: Panetta had indeed been fired in the time-honored way—his unwritten "resignation" had been accepted.

The ouster of Panetta, a lifelong Republican, for adhering too closely to the law on school desegregation was the clearest possible signal that Richard Nixon was following John Mitchell's grand strategy. The President's handling of a vacancy on the Supreme Court was an even clearer signal of the depth of Nixon's commitment to that strategy.

The list on John Mitchell's desk had grown to more than a hundred and seventy names, many of them federal judges, some state judges, some prominent attorneys. From that list, President Nixon selected the name of Clement F. Haynsworth, Jr., of Greenville, S.C., fifty-seven years old, a graduate of the Harvard Law School and now Chief Judge of the Fourth Circuit Court of Appeals. He was nominated on August 18, 1969, to the seat that Justice Abe Fortas had vacated on May 14 under threat of impeachment for having accepted and kept for eleven months a $20,000 check from a foundation set up by financier Louis Wolfson.* This had become known as the Jewish seat since the appointment of Louis Brandeis to it in 1916. Brandeis was the first of a succession of brilliant lawyers appointed to the seat: Felix Frankfurter, Arthur Goldberg, Abe Fortas. But Richard Nixon, hearing other political trumpets, was to break the Jewish succession, which had lasted for fifty-three years. His requirement was: a white Southern conservative federal judge under age sixty (so he would have a long-range impact on the Court). Not many of Mitchell's more than a hundred and seventy names could satisfy the prerequisites, but Clement Haynsworth did, perfectly.

Haynsworth's nomination was in fulfillment of Nixon's repeated campaign pledges to place proven strict constructionists on the Supreme Court—and, as he put it during the Miami Beach

---

*In September 1966, eight months after Fortas accepted the $20,000, Wolfson was indicted for illegal stock manipulations. He was later imprisoned.

convention, "men who are for civil rights, but who recognize that the first civil right of every American [is] to be free from domestic violence." That was his recognition of the deep-seated resentment in the land, especially strong in the South, against decisions for civil rights and civil liberties by the Supreme Court during seventeen precedent-shattering years under Chief Justice Earl Warren. Thus, when Nixon promised to fill vacancies on the Court with judges who would make a strict, or literal, construction of the Constitution, he was appealing to both the South and the law-and-order vote. The first strict constructionist he chose was Warren Burger, Chief Judge of the U.S. Court of Appeals for the District of Columbia. He was nominated on May 21 to be Chief Justice in place of the retiring Warren. Nineteen days later, the Senate confirmed him with three negative votes, all Democrats. That indicated no trouble ahead for Judge Haynsworth, a distinguished Southerner who had followed his father and grandfather into Greenville's most prestigious law firm before accepting President Eisenhower's appointment to the Circuit Court of Appeals in 1957. Born and reared a Democrat, Haynsworth revealed a glimpse of his personal ideology when he switched to the Republican Party in 1964, the year Barry Goldwater carried the Republican Presidential banner. That was scarcely grounds for the U.S. Senate to deny confirmation. But there were two moods then vaguely drifting through the U.S. Senate that were to change Clement Haynsworth's life and deeply affect Richard Nixon's Presidency.

In the week preceding Fortas' letter of resignation to President Nixon, Senator Robert Griffin of Michigan, who had led the successful battle in 1968 against President Johnson's effort to elevate Fortas to Chief Justice, had introduced a bill requiring for the first time full financial disclosure by all federal judges, including Justices of the Supreme Court.* Griffin reflected a Congress which had been sickened by the revelations involving Fortas—a mood that was still at a high pitch when Nixon, three months later, chose Haynsworth. The financial affairs of nominees to the Supreme Court would henceforth be given the closest scrutiny.

The second and darker mood, not far below the surface among

---

*Griffin's bill died at the end of the Ninety-first Congress without action by the Senate.

the Senate's Democratic majority, was one of revenge for what had been done to Abe Fortas, imprudent though he had been. Griffin and other Republicans had, correctly, interpreted President Johnson's nomination in the summer of 1968 of Fortas to be Chief Justice as born of pure politics. At age fifty-eight, Fortas, one of Johnson's oldest and closest advisers, could be counted on to give the Court Democratic leadership far into the future, even if the Republicans regained the Presidency in 1968, as then seemed likely. The Republicans were determined to stop Johnson's ploy and responded with an investigation of Fortas' affairs without precedent in its thoroughness. That led to the blocking of his nomination for Chief Justice and, finally, to his resignation from the Court. Bitterly, Democratic senators resolved that any Nixon nominee to the Court with the slightest blemish would be accorded the same treatment.

Coinciding with this mood of the Senate was the deepening anxiety of the civil rights bloc about Nixon in August 1969. That was the month Nixon ordered government lawyers into court to argue for delay in the Mississippi desegregation cases. At the climax of that proceeding, Nixon sent Haynsworth's name to the U.S. Senate. The reaction was immediate, although low-key. Civil rights groups charged that the Fourth Circuit under Chief Judge Haynsworth had dragged its heels over school desegregation, particularly during the long vitriolic dispute over school desegregation in Prince Edward County, Va. When the Fourth Circuit ruled against the county and ordered desegregation, Haynsworth voted against the majority. When the Fourth Circuit ruled that hospitals receiving federal funds could not maintain segregated facilities, Haynsworth again voted against the majority. Haynsworth was philosophical about such dissents, noting that some of the cases for which he was being criticized went back to 1958 "when none of us was thinking or writing as we are today," as he told the *New York Times* on August 12.

By the time the Senate Judiciary Committee began its hearings on the nomination on September 16, a rather benign suspicion was becoming outright hostility. Haynsworth's civil rights record on the bench partly explained that change in mood, but a more important factor was his role as judge in a 1963 labor dispute involving the Textile Workers Union and the Darlington Manufacturing Co., a textile giant embroiled with the union in one of the longest, bitterest labor-management wars in the nation's history.

Bitter litigation stemming from that labor dispute was before Haynsworth on the appeals court in 1961 and 1963. But Haynsworth, it soon developed, had owned stock in and served on the board of the Carolina Vend-A-Matic Co., which held contracts to supply vending machines in some Deering Milliken plants.* This whole matter had been thrashed out in early 1964, with Haynsworth officially exonerated of any conflict of interest.†

Nevertheless, the AFL-CIO now threw the influence of organized labor hard against Haynsworth. Not only was Haynsworth anti-labor, said AFL-CIO President George Meany, he was indifferent to the "legitimate aspirations of Negroes." After inordinately long hearings, running from September 16 to October 9, the Judiciary Committee approved the nomination by a 10-to-7 margin, raising for the first time the real possibility that Haynsworth might fail Senate confirmation—something that had not happened since 1930 with the defeat of John J. Parker of North Carolina, appointed by Herbert Hoover.

As the storm rose, President Nixon betrayed no inner tensions. On September 26 he confirmed his confidence in Haynsworth. So did Mitchell, who joked dryly that "if we'd put up one of the twelve Apostles it would have been the same." Three weeks later, just after the 10–7 committee vote, the President said that nothing would lead him to withdraw the nomination, a course now being pressed on him by his two top Republican leaders in the Senate, Hugh Scott and Robert Griffin. Again, on October 20, Nixon held an impromptu press conference in his office and announced that he would not withdraw the nomination even if Haynsworth himself requested it. He denounced the judge's detractors as perpetrators of "a vicious character assassination."

But behind the scenes, the situation was growing worse, and the

*Haynsworth resigned from the board of Carolina Vend-A-Matic in the fall of 1963 after the Judicial Conference of the United States adopted a resolution stating that "no Justice or Judge of the United States shall serve in the capacity of an officer, director or employee of a corporation for profit."

†In early 1964, Simon E. Sobeloff, then Chief Judge of the Fourth Circuit Court of Appeals, wrote a letter to the Textile Workers Union saying that Haynsworth "had no active participation in the affairs of Carolina Vend-A-Matic, had never sought business for it or discussed procurement of locations for it with the officials or employees of any other company."

White House and Justice Department were failing to respond with sufficient imagination and force. One problem was that Hayns-worth's principal sponsor—Senator Ernest F. Hollings, a South Carolina Democrat—was scarcely on speaking terms with Harry Dent because of their political battles in South Carolina; those two should have been working in tandem to pull Haynsworth through the Senate. The Republican leader in the House, Representative Gerald Ford, hurt Haynsworth's cause when he threatened on November 7 to bring impeachment proceedings against Justice Wil-liam O. Douglas if the Senate rejected Haynsworth on ethical grounds; the attempted pressure on the liberal Democrats in the Senate boomeranged.

On November 21 the Senate rejected Judge Haynsworth by a vote of 55 to 45. No fewer than seventeen Republicans opposed the President's choice—itself a shocking show of lack of confidence—and among them were Minority Leader Scott, Assistant Minority Leader Griffin, Senator Margaret Chase Smith of Maine, Chairman of the Senate Republican Caucus, and Senator John J. Williams of Delaware, Chairman of the Committee on Committees.

Richard Nixon was outraged. Aides who had not seen him raise his voice in anger during ten months in the White House, facing both blunders by aides and attacks from enemies with a bland equa-nimity, were amazed at the emotion that Haynsworth's rejection aroused in him. In the privacy of the White House, Nixon inveighed against the liberal press which had built the opposition to Hayns-worth, against organized labor for its vendetta against the judge, and most of all against those Republican senators who had betrayed their President.

The President made clear this would not stop him. He most definitely would *not*, he made clear, sound retreat by naming a non-Southerner. Nor would he name a Southern Republican judge with a liberal record on the bench, such as John Minor Wisdom of Louisiana or Frank Johnson of Alabama. He listed the same prerequisites that dictated his choice of Haynsworth: white, South-ern, strict constructionist, experience on the federal bench, under age sixty. "You know," one surprised White House aide told another, "the President really *believes* in that Southern strategy—more than he believes in anything else."

A suggestion for a nominee fitting those specifications came from Senator Spessard Holland of Florida, a conservative Democrat about to retire from public life. He passed the name to Colonel Ken BeLieu, White House lobbyist for the Senate. BeLieu passed it to John Mitchell. The name was that of Judge G. Harrold Carswell of Tallahassee, Fla., a member of the Fifth Circuit Court of Appeals. Just five months before the Senate rejected Haynsworth, Nixon's nomination of Carswell (then a U.S. district judge) to the appeals court had been routinely confirmed by the Senate. Now Mitchell quickly recommended Carswell to Nixon. After all, he had just won Senate confirmation without a shadow of opposition. Nixon sent Carswell's name to the Senate on January 19, 1970.

Months later, those in the administration most intimately involved in the selection of Harrold Carswell admitted privately that they had acted too quickly after Haynsworth's defeat, that Carswell simply did not possess the quality required for a Supreme Court Justice and that, from the standpoint of the President and the nation, the eventual rejection of Carswell by the Senate was a blessing. Yet, this unbelievable blunder was the act that finally enshrined Richard Nixon in the South.

Nixon, Mitchell and everybody else in Washington were certain that the Senate would consent to Carswell's nomination after Haynsworth's defeat. One rejection was a serious blot on any President's record; two rejections would be out of the question, an insult beyond the limits of political hostility to any President, an unimaginable humiliation. The post-Fortas lust for revenge among Democratic senators had been spent. When Carswell's name went to the Senate, then, his confirmation was all but preordained. And, indeed, if Carswell's name had been Haynsworth and the precedence of their appointments had been reversed, there is no slightest doubt that he would have been confirmed. But Carswell was by no means the equal of Haynsworth.* He was not a first-class judge or, as the Senate became convinced after full study of the record, even a first-class man. Everything about Carswell was a little less than first class: his clear deception of the Judiciary Committee during his confirmation

*Senator Hollings of South Carolina, who had led the fight for Haynsworth's confirmation, said of Carswell that he "was not qualified to carry Judge Haynsworth's law books," but voted for Carswell's confirmation.

hearings;* a speech he made in 1948, when he ran a losing race for
the Georgia Legislature (before moving permanently to Florida),
stating his belief in the doctrine of white supremacy; the fact that
seven of the eighteen judges in the Fifth Judicial Circuit refused to
sign a telegram to Nixon on March 28 endorsing the nomination
(including the respected Judge Elbert P. Tuttle and Chief Judge John
R. Brown).

Before Carswell's name was sent to the Senate, Mitchell briefed
Republican senators on the Senate Judiciary Committee and described the prospective new nominee as a "middle-of-the-roader"
who met all qualifications for a seat on the Supreme Court. He then
asked the Republican senators to give Carswell their support, and
Senator Hugh Scott replied, "If you are right about him, you can
count on me."

As the story unfolded before the committee, however, not only
did Scott decide that Mitchell had not given him an accurate reading
of Judge Carswell, but Mitchell himself, well before the Senate vote
that rejected him, came to realize that he had been wrong about
Carswell. If Mitchell had known in the beginning all he knew in the
end about Carswell, the nomination would never have been sent to
the Senate. Yet, there was no single, overwhelmingly obvious blemish in the Carswell record that persuaded the Senate to vote against
him. The case that Democratic liberals made against him was replete
with secondary items, not wholly convincing in themselves—such as
his hostile attitude toward Negro plaintiffs and attorneys in civil
rights cases—but which, when added together, offered the compelling portrait of a less than first-rate jurist who had no business in the
seat of Louis Brandeis and Felix Frankfurter.

When the nomination came out of committee by a vote of 13

*The issue here was Carswell's role as an incorporator in the purchase by a private
group of white citizens of a public golf course in 1956 in Tallahassee. The previously
all-white public golf course was ordered to desegregate. To avoid doing so, the
purchase group converted it into a private white-only club called the Capital City
Country Club. When Carswell was asked about this transaction at his confirmation
hearings, he said the details were vague but that he had not been an incorporator.
That statement was given to the Senate Judiciary Committee one day after the
circumstances of the golf-course transaction had been forcefully recalled to Carswell
by a group of Washington attorneys acting on their own, who showed him the
papers of incorporation.

to 4, Mitchell was still confident that confirmation, though sure to be close, was probable.* But Nixon began to smell what was coming in mid-March and moved with a typically heavy-handed overkill to set things right in a letter to Senator William Saxbe of Ohio, a Republican moderate who was backing the nomination but who often strayed from the Nixon pasture. What was "centrally at issue" in the Carswell nomination, said Nixon, was "the Constitutional responsibility of the President to appoint members of the Court—and whether this responsibility can be frustrated by those who wish to substitute their own philosophy or their own subjective judgment for that of the one person entrusted by the Constitution with the power of appointment." Then, with another typical Nixonian touch —the note of self-pity—the President said the question boiled down to whether "I, as President of the United States, shall be accorded the same right of choice . . . which has been freely accorded to my predecessors of both parties."†

The letter boomeranged, as indeed it had to. The Constitution, far from giving the President a "right" to name any federal judge, specifically limits that authority to the *nomination* of judges, with the Senate empowered to advise and consent, including the power to advise and dissent. Several wavering senators of both parties were affronted by the first direct Presidential effort to lobby Carswell through to confirmation. If they thought the April 1 letter was unduly presumptuous, the course of the downfall of Judge Carswell would soon lead to a far greater Presidential attack on Congress.

During the last three weeks of debate, with the nomination

---

*Voting against the nomination were Birch Bayh of Indiana, Philip Hart of Michigan, Joseph Tydings of Maryland, Edward M. Kennedy of Massachusetts, all Democrats. Senator Charles Mathias of Maryland, a liberal Republican, voted to send the nomination to the floor, but his eventual decision to vote against the nomination was clearly presaged during the debate. Scott wanted to vote against, but his obligation to the President, particularly after his vote against Haynsworth, finally persuaded him to vote for confirmation. Griffin also voted for confirmation.

†The letter was drafted by Charles W. Colson, special Presidential counsel, and signed by the President without full clearance with the White House Hill Staff. Two years before, when the Senate was refusing to confirm President Johnson's nomination of Abe Fortas to be Chief Justice, Nixon's view of the prerogatives of the Senate differed considerably. He told a caucus of Southern delegates to the Republican National Convention in Miami Beach on August 6, 1968: "It is up to the Senate, and I hope the Senate will examine very carefully the qualifications of Mr. Fortas, as I'm sure they will, and whatever the Senate does, I, of course, will abide by."

sitting in the Senate and ample time for opposition to roll in, Mitchell was ordered by his doctor to take two weeks off, after months of nonstop twelve-hour days. Mitchell had been carrying all the pressures and responsibilities of the Carswell campaign. When he left town, Nixon summoned Deputy Attorney General Kleindienst to the Oval Office and asked him to take over the growing burden of confirmation. From then on, every morning at nine o'clock Kleindienst and Harlow met in the White House to plot strategy and keep the dike from breaking. It was a depressing task. The legal community was mobilized against Carswell, as it had not been against Haynsworth.*

The two key Republicans that Kleindienst and Harlow knew they must have were Senator Marlow Cook of Kentucky, a moderate with a strong streak of independence, and Senator Margaret Chase Smith, who, once again, was keeping her options open and standing aloof. Although Cook had been a strong supporter of Haynsworth, he had made little secret of his leanings *away* from Carswell, a sentiment that administration officials were quite sure was deeply affected by Cook's running battle with the Justice Department over a judicial appointment in Kentucky. For months Cook had been badgering Mitchell to send the Senate the name of Bemis Lawrence for U.S. district judge, and Mitchell aides had probably spent more time on that one judgeship than all other put together. But Lawrence, in their opinion, did not measure up; the Kentucky bar would not approve him. Then, on April 7, Cook went to the White House as the President's guest at a posthumous Medal of Honor ceremony for several Americans who had lost their lives in Vietnam. The following day, Cook voted against confirmation of Carswell, and afterward said, "The thing that really convinced me" was that White House ceremony. He added, "Those were men who did their best and lost their lives and all of a sudden I thought that we're going to vote for someone who did not fulfill the degree of excellence in the legal

---

*The opposition to the unfortunate Carswell had been unprecedented. Anti-Carswell committees went on record from Notre Dame, Villanova, Chicago, Harvard, and Washington and Lee, among scores of other law schools. Nine of fifteen law professors at the University of Florida, in Carswell's home state, wrote Nixon a letter opposing him. More than two hundred former law clerks to Supreme Court Justices, including former Secretary of State Dean G. Acheson and the deans of the Georgetown, Chicago, Michigan, Stanford and Yale law schools, wrote a joint letter to every senator.

field that I thought these men deserved." So Cook's vote was lost, but no one in the White House could have known until it was actually cast.

Mrs. Smith's defection was even more dramatic. Bryce Harlow had been told, erroneously, that she had decided to vote for Carswell. Cook, to all appearances, was still on the fence, along with Senator Winston Prouty, a Vermont Republican facing an apparently difficult fight for reelection. Leaving those two in the undecided column, Harlow's count just before the April 8 vote was 48 against and 46 for Carswell, counting Mrs. Smith's vote as pro-Carswell. Harlow immediately saw that he needed only two more votes to bring about a tie, which Vice President Agnew would then break in favor of Carswell. So, armed with what he thought was accurate information about Mrs. Smith, he quietly went to Cook and Prouty, told them about Mrs. Smith and bid for the final two votes he needed. Quickly the word got back to Maggie Smith. In a rage—for, in fact, she had *not* yet made up her mind—she telephoned Harlow and blistered him with words that literally reddened his ears. She also informed the mild-mannered Harlow that he had impugned her honor and that she would under no condition vote for Carswell. The altercation broke into headlines and sealed off whatever slim chance Carswell might have had. The final vote was 45 to 51 against him. President Nixon had now been twice defeated, and twice in a row, in his effort to put a strict constructionist Southern judge on the Supreme Court —the first time since Grover Cleveland that a President had suffered such indignity.

The immediate repercussions were expectable. Mitchell and the Justice Department were blamed, both for treating the Senate cavalierly and for doing their homework badly (the Federal Bureau of Investigation had failed to turn up the offensive vote-losing Carswell speech in 1948 praising white supremacy).* Republican leaders im-

---

*One example of cavalier treatment: Senator Mathias asked the Justice Department to permit him to have a face-to-face conversation with Carswell, but did not even have the courtesy of a reply until the night before the vote. He was told Carswell would be flown up to Washington to see him in a postmidnight meeting in a motel room. By then Mathias had made up his mind and turned down the opportunity. After the vote, high administration officials conceded that they did not want Carswell interviewed by fence-sitting senators. All such personal contacts, they felt, would damage Carswell's chance for confirmation.

mediately claimed the vote was a partisan Democratic exercise to embarrass the President. Underneath it all, however, and notwithstanding the humiliation to President Nixon, most of the administration men who had worked so hard for Carswell's confirmation were secretly pleased that he was denied a seat on the Supreme Court. They had come to know him, and in knowing him had come to realize that he did not belong there. Even Arthur Burns, now in residence in the marble palace of the Federal Reserve Board and not known as a student of judicial appointments, had been unhappily moved by the President's appointment of Carswell. "He may deserve some place," Dr. Burns remarked cryptically to a close friend before the Senate vote, "but mind what I say—it's going to be trouble."

From the White House there was only silence immediately after the April 8 vote. That night, Mitchell, who had returned from his vacation in Florida on April 5, was invited by the President to go down the Potomac River on the Presidential yacht *Sequoia*. The other guest was H.R. Haldeman, Nixon's constant attendant and a man who oftentimes had revealed an attitude toward Congress that bordered on arrogance.

The three had dinner and talked: about Haynsworth and Carswell; about the South and their political aspirations to bring it into the Republican Party; about the liberals, both Democrats and Republicans, who seemed (in their eyes) to have gone so far off the normal paths to tear down the President's two Supreme Court nominees. They agreed tentatively that Nixon should make a statement the following day, setting forth his ideas about Presidential prerogatives in the appointive process, about the right of the South to be represented on the highest court and about his deep disappointment over the outcome.

And in the background lurked an obvious political thought: that even though Haynsworth and Carswell would never sit on the Supreme Court, President Nixon had gone that last mile to try to get them there. He had put his reputation squarely on the line, had been smashed, fully as much as Haynsworth and Carswell had been smashed, fully as much, indeed, as the South had been smashed. *That* was something worth talking about. In the fall of 1969 the Supreme Court had administered a spanking to the Nixon administration for its delays and equivocation on school desegregation. In the spring of

1970 the Senate had administered another spanking, not on desegregation but on the Supreme Court. Both were hard blows for
any President to accept, but at the same time both were powerful evidence of the President's intentions toward the South and a
powerful thrust forward for the President's deeper objective—the
capture of the South in the 1972 Presidential election. With
dinner on the *Sequoia* ended, the President returned to the White
House, resolved that on the morrow he would have something
to say.

In the early afternoon of April 9 Nixon had scheduled a two-
hour meeting with his chief conservationists. He was agitated, his
mind seemingly off the subject, and several times he digressed to
make slighting remarks about the eastern part of the United States
and about the intellectuals. The only decent places left in the United
States, he said, were the South and the West. When the formal part
of that session ended, he reverted to his feelings about the East,
mentioned the vote in the Senate the preceding day on Carswell.
John Ehrlichman, on leaving that meeting, turned to another White
House aide, who had remarked that Nixon seemed pretty worked up,
and said yes, he surely was. Just then the President, alone now in his
office with Mitchell, sent for Harry Dent. Dent hurried into the Oval
Office and the President handed him a couple of sheets of paper and
asked him to take a look at what had been written there. Dent read
a very sharp statement attacking the Senate, and the more he read
the more he liked it. He turned to Nixon and said, "Gosh, Mr.
President, this is terrific stuff. Do you think we could get anyone to
say it?" At that moment, Ron Ziegler entered the Oval Office and
said, "They're ready, Mr. President." In a flash, Dent got the point:
not only would the statement be given, *it would be given by the
President himself.* Dent hurried after Mitchell and Nixon, who by
now was standing at the podium in the press room. He and Mitchell
watched as the President, with scarcely a glance at the statement in
his hand, delivered it almost verbatim, leaving out a couple of sen-
tences near the end.

> I have reluctantly concluded, with the Senate presently con-
> stituted, I cannot successfully nominate to the Supreme Court any
> federal appellate judge from the South who believes as I do in the strict
> construction of the Constitution.

Judges Carswell and Haynsworth have endured with admirable dignity vicious assaults on their intelligence, their honesty and their character. They have been falsely charged with being racist. But when all the hypocrisy is stripped away, the real issue was their philosophy of strict construction of the Constitution, a philosophy that I share—and the fact that they had the misfortune of being born in the South. After the rejection of Judge Carswell and Judge Haynsworth, this conclusion is inescapable.

Nixon went on to elaborate, saying that he had set three criteria for both appointments: strict construction of the Constitution to help restore the balance on the Supreme Court; experienced jurists to be chosen only from the Court of Appeals; and "men of the South." More than one-fourth of the people of the United States, he said, live in the South and "they deserve representation on the Court." He continued:

With yesterday's action, the Senate has said that no Southern federal appellate judge who believes in a strict interpretation of the Constitution can be elevated to the Supreme Court. As long as the Senate is constituted the way it is today, I will not nominate another Southerner and let him be subjected to the kind of malicious character assassination accorded both Judges Haynsworth and Carswell.

The next nominee would come from "outside the South," said Nixon, adding:

I understand the bitter feeling of millions of Americans who live in the South about the act of regional discrimination that took place in the Senate yesterday. They have my assurance that the day will come when men like Judges Carswell and Haynsworth can and will sit on the high Court.*

Just before Nixon had departed the Oval Office for the White House press room an urgent telephone call had been placed at his command to Bryce Harlow, who was located making a speech at the International Inn, about ten minutes from the White House by car. But when the message got to Harlow, he was not told that it was the President himself calling. Nearly through with his speech, he said he

*On April 14 Nixon named Judge Harry Blackmun of the Eighth Circuit Court of Appeals to the still-vacant seat. Like Burger, Blackmun was a Minnesota Republican and a strict constructionist. Like Burger, he was confirmed by the Senate without difficulty.

would call back in ten minutes. By that time it was too late. If Harlow, the senior staff expert on Congressional affairs, had known in advance the kind of statement Nixon wanted to make, he would have tried to stop it. Harlow was concerned more about Congress than he was about the South, and he knew the President's statement, which depicted the Senate as having been on a lynching bee against Haynsworth and Carswell, would badly hurt the President on Capitol Hill.

But whether Harlow could actually have stopped the statement is doubtful. Because if Harlow thought first of Congress, then of the South, the President was thinking first of the South, then of Congress —if he thought of Congress at all. It was also apparent that, quite apart from objective politics, the two defeats for his Supreme Court nominees had rubbed him raw inside. In many other defeats Nixon had taken his medicine philosophically, seldom allowing a flicker of internal sentiment to show, if indeed he felt any. On April 9 he seemed consciously to throw off all restraint to confront his enemies deliberately with powerful and vengeful rhetoric and to portray himself as the victim of malicious enemies who were out to punish not only him but the entire South.

It infuriated the Senate, but the South loved it. Richard Nixon, first by being reversed by the Supreme Court on the Mississippi desegregation case and then by being humiliated by the Senate on the two judgeships, had identified himself with the Lost Cause mentality of the South. Had either Haynsworth or Carswell been confirmed, or had Nixon after Carswell's rejection named any of the many moderate Southern judges who *could* have been confirmed by the Senate, his standing with the South would not have been cemented with the emotionalism of defeat.

On March 24, 1970, Nixon delivered the most tightly reasoned statement on school desegregation ever uttered by a President. His administration under attack for months on this issue, he came down hard and foursquare with a pledge: "We are not backing away. The Constitutional mandate will be enforced." Nixon chose a middle way in this statement of principles by strongly upholding what had been national policy based on Supreme Court doctrine for sixteen years, and strongly opposing new departures—such as busing—not insisted upon (as yet) by the Court.* But there was not a word in this statement to support the thrust of his 1968 campaign to save freedom of choice. That, it appeared, was now tacitly admitted to be impossible. Even Clarke Reed and the other Southern Republican state chairmen were now aware of that fact. But after all that had happened, climaxed by the Carswell affair, it was no longer politically necessary. Richard Nixon had proved himself to be the friend of the South.

Accordingly, as 1970 progressed, Nixon finally was able to put forth a desegregation strategy without constant political sniping from the South or potential damage within the South. Just as John Mitchell had planned it all the time, the burden for promoting desegregation was passed from the White House and the administration to the federal courts. To ease the process, Nixon talked not of cutting off funds under HEW guidelines but of giving extra funds to school districts to help them desegregate. On May 21, 1970, the President asked Congress for $1.5 billion in such funds.†

Southern politicians, however, kept the pressure on. Its climax was a minor revolt in the summer of 1970 centering on the question of tax exemption for the private white academies popping up around the South as a way to avoid desegregated public schools. Civil rights groups had gone to court to challenge the Internal Revenue Service ruling permitting donors to these schools to claim their contributions as a tax deduction—a ruling vital to the life of any private school. As part of his consistent attitude toward such matters, Mitchell had ordered the Justice Department lawyers to defend the IRS ruling. But on July 10 Randolph Thrower, Commissioner of Internal Revenue, exploded a bombshell in the face of the South. Thrower, a liberal Republican from Atlanta, revoked the tax exemption for the lily-white academies. Clarke Reed and the other Southern Republican chairmen reacted with wrath. At a long-scheduled reception for government officials given by the Southern chairmen at the Mayflower Hotel in Washington on July 15, Reed and the other Southerners descended on Thrower. "Why don't you go over to HEW with the rest of the revolutionaries?" Reed asked

---

*By a 9-to-0 vote (including Burger and Blackmun), the Supreme Court in April 1971 approved busing.

†The bill passed the House but not the Senate.

Thrower. An angry Strom Thurmond showed up at the reception, claiming he had been promised by Nixon back in February that the tax exemption would not be rescinded. On the morning of July 17 Thurmond became angrier still when he read a *Washington Post* account (based on an interview with Jerris Leonard) of one hundred Justice Department lawyers ready to go South that fall to police desegregation. Taking the Senate floor that day, Thurmond sounded as though he were about to break with Nixon. Warning that the administration's present school policies would lead to the President's defeat in 1972, Thurmond declared, "I can only conclude that a group of liberal advisers around the President are misleading him and that their advice will bring disruption to the nation."

In a press conference on July 20, Nixon promised he had "no intention . . . of sending vigilante squads, in effect, of Justice Department lawyers in to coerce Southern districts to integrate." Mitchell repudiated the story Leonard had given the *Post.* At the White House, Peter Flanigan promised Southerners that Thrower's ruling would be reconsidered. All this rhetoric appeased Thurmond, Reed and the rest of the Southerners. But it was no more than rhetoric. In fact, the Justice Department lawyers *were* dispatched to the South; Thrower's IRS ruling *stayed* in effect; Southern demands that Thrower be fired were finessed.* Having secured his Southern base, Nixon in 1970 could act more responsibly on the school desegregation question than he had before.

Gradually the level of public controversy about school desegregation subsided. At a White House meeting of the Cabinet Committee on School Desegregation in the summer of 1970 (not attended by the President), James Farmer suggested a televised address to the nation by Nixon urging calm and restraint in connection with desegregation ordered in the South's black-majority districts by federal courts for September. But Harry Dent advised Farmer that he doubted the President would do any such thing. Dent was quite right. Shortly thereafter, word came out of the Oval Office that

---

*Thrower did resign in January 1971, but was still in the job in late spring at Nixon's personal urging. White House unhappiness with him had less to do with civil rights than with his handling of federal patronage. See pp. 67–68.

Nixon would keep a very low profile on what might happen that fall.*

The tactic worked. In September 1970, peacefully and without violence, black-majority districts of the Deep South, where the white power structure had shouted "Never!" a few years before, were integrating. What's more, they were integrating by court order, not Richard Nixon's. The Mitchell plan had worked.

On balance, Richard Nixon could scarcely be called a civil rights President. He never forgot Mitchell's grand strategy or his real constituency. Efforts at the Department of Housing and Urban Development by George Romney to push for desegregation of all-white suburban housing patterns were slowed down by the White House. Nixon avoided taking a strong stand until the very last minute on Southern-sponsored anti-desegregation amendments in Congress. Undoubtedly, a Lyndon Johnson or a Hubert Humphrey in the White House in 1969 and 1970 would have integrated Southern schools more rapidly than Nixon.

Nevertheless, his administration felt that Nixon was not properly credited for what he had done for the Negro. There was scant applause from civil rights groups for his removal of the tax exemption for private academies. Nor did they vigorously applaud his one major innovation, the Philadelphia Plan.

The Philadelphia Plan, a bold design to bring blacks into traditionally lily-white construction unions, was the brainchild of George Shultz as Secretary of Labor. It set up a quota system to compel half a dozen hard-hat construction unions to train black youth as apprentices, with full union membership at the end of their training program, on federal construction programs. The unions flexed their political muscle, and legislation outlawing the Plan was pushed

---

*Despite the low profile, Nixon went to New Orleans on August 14 against the recommendations of some of his staff to confer with biracial desegregation advisory committees from seven states which had been set up by the Cabinet Committee. That meeting was extremely successful in establishing the right psychological climate for the big desegregation push that fall. The President followed up the closed-door session with a public promise to uphold Supreme Court desegregation decisions "not in a punitive way . . . but treating this part of the country with the respect that it deserves."

through the Senate in December 1969. At the peak of the legislative battle, Shultz defended the Philadelphia Plan on the White House steps with full backing of the President and persuaded the House to reject the legal ban passed by the Senate. In April the Third Circuit Court of Appeals upheld the Philadelphia Plan in a suit against it by a group of Pennsylvania contractors.

In addition to the private academies and the Philadelphia Plan, the Nixon men could also argue that the area of greatest criticism —school desegregation in the South—was by no means the focal point of the black crisis in America. By the time Nixon was inaugurated, younger black leaders had been turning away from integration as a high priority item and were far more interested in various forms of separatism and faster economic development. Anyway, despite all the struggles of 1969, desegregation was under way in the worst of Deep South districts by September 1970.

All this being true, why, then, was Richard Nixon the most unpopular of postwar Presidents with the black minority and far more popular in the South than any other part of the country? The answer is that his style, his rhetoric and his tone were more important than specific actions. Neither his unsuccessful Mississippi appeal nor the Carswell affair had long-lasting substantive meaning. But the symbolism was unmistakable. He was on the side of the South, the white majority and the status quo. The blacks read it this way, and so did the South. He had, thereby, buttressed his Southern base for the 1972 campaign, but at a high cost: further racial division, disillusionment of civil rights advocates of both races and ceaseless uproar within his administration and in its relations with Congress.

VII

Nixonomics

Nixonomics means that all the things that should go up—the stock market, corporate profits, real spendable income, productivity—go down, and all the things that should go down—unemployment, prices, interest rates—go up.

—Lawrence F. O'Brien, Chairman
of the Democratic National Committee,
May 21, 1970.

In early April 1969 Richard Nixon called Representative Wilbur D. Mills of Arkansas, Chairman of the House Ways and Means Committee, to the White House to reveal his plans for fiscal austerity. He had managed to cut some $4 billion, the new President informed Mills, from Lyndon Johnson's last and "uncuttable" budget. No member of Congress was more disturbed than Mills by the way federal spending had gone out of control under Johnson, and he was pleased by the reduction. But he wanted more—say, another $4 billion?

"Oh, no! We can't do that," said Nixon. "We can't cut so deep that we start a recession."

Mills was puzzled. As he understood it, Nixon's economic strategy—or "game plan" as it was called, in deference to the football-loving President—called for slowing down inflation in 1969 at the lamentable expense of some temporary unemployment. Thus Nixon seemed to be saying that he was willing to slow down the economy enough to cause some unemployment but not enough to cause a recession. To Mills, it made no sense.

What puzzled Mills was the ambivalence that confused the new President's thinking on this, as on so many other questions, as he entered office. On the question of how much to slow down the economy, the ambivalence was deeply ingrained, born not of mere intellectual agnosticism but of two deeply embedded, conflicting impulses that Nixon carried with him into the White House.

The first impulse was graphically discussed early in 1968 by General Dwight D. Eisenhower before the series of heart attacks that were to end his life a year later. "I think Dick's going to be elected President," he told one of Nixon's political advisers, "but I think he's going to be a one-term President. I think he's really going to fight inflation, and that will kill him politically." To Eisenhower, as well as to most orthodox Republicans, that would be the worthy sacrifice of a courageous political martyr. For the old general, there was no higher imperative for a new Republican President than to curb the torrent of inflation that had been loosed on the economy since full U.S. intervention in the Vietnam war in 1965. At stake was nothing less than the value of the dollar, the role of the United States as a great power and the very quality of life in this country.

To save all this entailed sacrifice. Attempting a reduction in the rate of inflation (considerably less virulent than the 1971 siege) from 1953 through 1960, President Eisenhower's economic policy induced three recessions, with disastrous consequences for the Republican Party: first, the Democratic landslide in the midterm elections of 1958, which ended the previous postwar pattern of a virtually even balance between the parties in Congress and established huge Democratic majorities (which persisted even when Nixon was elected President a decade later); second, the election of Democrat John F. Kennedy for President in 1960; finally, and perhaps worst of all, reinforcement in the voter's mind of the Republican image—formed in the days of Herbert Hoover—as the party of bad times. Now, eight years later, blessed with not a fraction of Eisenhower's unlimited popularity, Nixon would have to take far more unpopular actions to fight a worse inflation. The resulting unemployment, business slowdown and stock market decline almost surely would prevent his reelection in 1972, Eisenhower speculated. But considering the good deeds he would be performing in the service of his nation, Eisenhower felt that the sacrifice not only would be worthwhile but would assure Nixon a place in history.

Nixon, too, regarded inflation as something more than merely a campaign issue handy for attacking the Democrats. Some two weeks before the election of 1968 in a paid address over the CBS radio network, Nixon declared, "Inflation penalizes thrift and encourages speculation. Because it is a national and perverse force—dramatically affecting individuals but beyond their power to influence—inflation is a source of frustration for all who lack great economic powers." That is, in Nixon's diagnosis, inflation was a virus affecting the health not just of the economy but of the frame of mind of the entire country. He fully agreed with the assessment by Theodore White as the Nixon administration took office that "inflation, in the past four years of American life, has ravaged our standards of behavior."* There was, then, reason to suspect that General Eisenhower's assessment was correct.

There was also, however, a conflicting impulse in Nixon. During that difficult decade since his defeat in 1960, aides and close friends had heard Nixon privately insist time after time that had President Eisenhower only taken his and Arthur Burns' advice early in 1960 and moved rapidly toward stimulating the economy, he—not Jack Kennedy—would have been elected President. The implication was that Richard Nixon, if he had the power, would never again go into a Presidential election with the economy in a state of deflation.

The closest Nixon came to putting this view on the public record was in a passage from *Six Crises,* his autobiographical work published in 1962. Thus did Nixonologists in the world of business cite that passage to their colleagues as the true test of what they could expect in the next few years. After telling of Burns' failure to per-

*In an eloquent passage in *The Making of the President 1968*, White gave his own views of inflation that surely also represented Nixon's: "As in other inflations I have lived through, notably those in China during the war, and Germany and France after the war, the beginning ravages are almost unnoticeable, indeed, pleasant. As inflation continues, however, it changes moralities, it destroys reason itself. Prosperity opens opportunities; inflation urges haste in using them. Not saving, but shrewd spending becomes the mark of wisdom in planning; the 'operators,' not the creators, thrive. It divides those who can manipulate from those locked into fixed incomes who see their resources dwindling and their savings shrinking, who are helpless to recapture their share of rising well-being. Above all, it victimizes the poor, the old and those who have planned ahead. Inflation is, at the beginning, a technical problem of public finance—and in the end raises problems of morality, of the disciplining of indulgences artifically incubated by the disappearance of values."

suade Eisenhower to act, Nixon, unable fully to restrain his bitterness, writes this memorable assessment of the 1960 election:

> Unfortunately, Arthur Burns turned out to be a good prophet. The bottom of the 1960 dip did come in October and the economy started to move up again in November—after it was too late to affect the election returns. In October, usually a month of rising employment, the jobless rolls increased by 452,000. All the speeches, television broadcasts, and precinct work in the world could not counteract that one hard fact.

To many, those words carried promise that Nixon as President would never permit the economy to sink low enough to be the controlling factor in an election, particularly a Presidential election.

Here, then, was the source of the ambivalence perceived by Wilbur Mills in April 1969. Should he be the self-abnegating statesman sacrificing his personal future to save the republic from inner rot or the pragmatic politician finally removing from the Republican Party the curse of Herbert Hoover? Whether or not this ambivalence was appreciated by Richard Nixon in his inner thoughts, it never surfaced in the early meetings on the economy in his new administration.

Those meetings were concerned almost exclusively with the problem of inflation, which had dropped the value of the 1957–59 dollar to 81.1 cents as Nixon took office. Presiding occasionally at meetings of the Cabinet Committee on Economic Policy, and of the Quadriad and the Troika, Nixon made obvious his deep commitment to curbing inflation.* Nixon as President could engage his full attention on only three or four large items at one time, and inflation was the only domestic issue that had that level of Presidential attention as his administration began. In private conversations with his staff, Nixon asserted he must deal rapidly and decisively with two principal crises: the Vietnam war and inflation. Furthermore, those few members of his economic team who also had served President Eisen-

---

*The Quadriad consisted of the four top economic officials of the government: the Chairman of the Federal Reserve Board, the Secretary of the Treasury, the Director of the Bureau of the Budget and the Chairman of the President's Council of Economic Advisers. The Troika consisted of the three top economic officials of the administration: the Quadriad less the Chairman of the Federal Reserve Board, an independent official serving a fixed term and not a member of the administration.

hower noted with satisfaction that Nixon had an incomparably more sophisticated grasp of economics than did the general.

But that scarcely qualified Nixon as an economist. "This is not his long suit," "This is not his cup of tea," "This is not his background" are the remarkably similar assessments of Nixon the economist by three separate members of his economic team. More serious than lack of technical competence, however, was Nixon's lack of emotional commitment. Though he intellectually understood the seriousness of inflation, the Dismal Science did not capture his imagination as did the Vietnam war, détente with the Soviets or rehabilitation of the Western alliance.

Given these deficiences in both his knowledge of and interest in economics, his first-string economic team—the Quadriad—was of peculiar importance. For the first year of Nixon's Presidency this was the Quadriad:

William McChesney Martin, sixty-two, Chairman of the Federal Reserve Board, now completing his eighteenth and last year in charge of the nation's central bank. Martin (a nominal Democrat) had not for some years been the dynamic proponent of economic conservatism that he was during the Eisenhower and Kennedy administrations and was now a somewhat dispirited lame duck. He had no personal relationship with Nixon and did not develop one.

David Kennedy, sixty-three, Secretary of the Treasury. Named on the recommendation of banking interests and Wall Street, this distinguished Chicago banker, unskilled in macro-economics, conceived of himself more as manager than policy-maker. His relations with Nixon were scarcely any more intimate the day he left the Treasury than the day he entered it.*

Robert Mayo, fifty-two, Director of the Bureau of the Budget. After nineteen years as a career government economist at the Treasury, he joined the banking business as a subordinate to Kennedy, who recommended him to Nixon for the Budget Bureau. In the government, too, Mayo seemed more Kennedy's subordinate than Nixon's.† Not in recent memory had a Budget Director been more distant from the President.

Paul McCracken, fifty-three, Chairman of the President's

*See p. 26.
†See p. 26.

Council of Economic Advisers. This cool, unflappable, unfailingly gracious economics professor from the University of Michigan had been a member of the council in Eisenhower's second term and was so well regarded professionally that, despite his conservatism, his appointment was hailed by liberal economists. Recommended for the post by Arthur Burns, he was to be the principal author of Nixon's economic Game Plan and the dominant member of the Quadriad through 1969. But he, too, would never achieve an intimate relationship with the President. McCracken was the essence of the pedagogue, his presentations to the President having the bloodless quality of professorial lectures in Economics 100. As McCracken unfolded historical background and explored every conceivable side of the subject, Nixon's eyes would glaze over. McCracken bored him stiff.

In contrast to the rest of Nixon's domestic policy team, the Quadriad was older, more professionally qualified, better known to the outside world and more distinguished generally. But it was also less dynamic and less able to penetrate the Haldeman-Ehrlichman Berlin Wall. There was in the Quadriad no John Mitchell, Mel Laird, Pat Moynihan, George Shultz or John Volpe who, for one reason or another, could enchant, pester or talk the President into accepting his point of view or, at least, actively engage Nixon's interest.

Present at the White House as Counsellor, of course, was an economist who *was* an old Nixon intimate: Arthur Burns (who did sometimes sit with the economic team as "the Quadriad Plus One"). But Burns was reluctant to be looking over the shoulder of Paul McCracken, the man he had recommended, and felt his post as Counsellor required as much devotion to noneconomic as economic questions in the domestic area.

Thus did Nixon begin his Presidency with a built-in ambivalence over whether to practice self-immolation in fighting inflation or to take only those steps that would ensure his reelection. He knew that inflation was a crisis ripping at the innards of America but he lacked consuming interest in the subject, and his economic team neither stimulated nor influenced him. What nobody could realize in January 1969 was that this issue would prove to be Nixon's most intractable (far worse than Vietnam), that it would lead to wrenching Republican disappointments in the 1970 midterm elections, and by 1971 would make General Eisenhower's prediction of a one-term Presidency seem very real indeed.

. . .

In 1942, just four years before he was to run for Congress and
only ten years before he was elected Vice President of the United
States, Richard Nixon spent ten months in wartime Washington as
a lawyer for the Office of Price Administration. It was an experience
forever seared on his soul, as he revealed early in his Presidency, on
February 14, 1969, while attempting to give an inspirational address
to personnel at the Treasury. Speaking without a text, Nixon wanted
to establish empathy with the bureaucrats by recalling the days when
he himself was one of them. What came out, however, was more
melancholy reminiscence than nostalgia:

> I was once a P-3 when they had that. Some of you will remember
> that. A P-3 lawyer in the OPA in 1942 was a very low form of life, I
> can assure you.
> I remember then the task that I had of preparing form letters and
> also preparing Congressional mail to be signed by the President of the
> United States on tire rationing.
> It seemed to me to be a very boring job at times.*

Dick Nixon, P-3 lawyer, was then twenty-nine, working in a
dead-end bureaucratic job in Tempo D, a dreary wooden shack left
over from World War I—without money, without family connections, without much in the way of prospects and certainly without
political ambition. His own unhappy condition might be the reason
he carried from OPA such an uncharacteristically dogmatic opposition to wage and price controls of any kind. Although the wartime
OPA in retrospect has been given generally high grades for its performance of a difficult and onerous but necessary task, Nixon's personal
recollection—perhaps influenced by the then unpromising state of
his personal career—was otherwise. In private conversations over
the years, he talked of the corruption, the cheating by the public and
the unhappy consequences when a government seeks to control the
private economic decisions of private citizens. His ideological view
shaped by unforgettable personal experience, Nixon the supreme

*Nixon then went on to make a little moral point to the Treasury employees.
Boring though his work was as a P-3 lawyer, he said, "what really made it mean
something to us was that we felt that we were part of a bigger cause . . ." So, the
President implied, today's bureaucrats should feel the same way. The February 14
visit to the Treasury was one of a series of pep talks Nixon gave at each of the large
departments and agencies early in his administration.

pragmatist was utterly inflexible about economic controls. However much his interest might flag in discussion of other economic questions, his enthusiastic advocacy on this point was constant.

Nor did Nixon's inflexibility terminate with outright government controls. He was equally determined against a return of the policy instituted by President Kennedy in 1961: voluntary guideposts issued by the government to limit wage and price increases—what is called an "incomes policy" in Great Britain and Canada. The guideposts had been plowed over and abandoned in the inflationary surge of 1966 following President Johnson's full-scale intervention in Vietnam. But late in 1968, Johnson's Cabinet Committee on Price Stability recommended a return to official guideposts (based on a maximum 5 percent wage increase in 1969), and Hubert Humphrey almost surely would have followed the recommendation had he been elected. But a guidepost policy would work, Nixon believed, only if the government used muscle to enforce it—as when John F. Kennedy forced the steel industry to roll back a price increase in 1962. That, to Nixon, was nothing more than mandatory wage-price controls without statutory sanction. Finally, Nixon ruled out even those admonitions by a President and other federal officials called "jawboning," used by Kennedy-Johnson officials both in conjunction with a guideposts policy and after the guideposts had been abandoned.

Fatefully, Nixon's prejudices happened to coincide perfectly with the expert opinion of his advisers. The entire Quadriad plus Burns agreed with Nixon's opposition to controls, to an incomes policy, to jawboning. This further coincided with the prevalent opinion in the business community, which had so rapturously given its support to Nixon against Humphrey. Following the eight prosperous years of the Kennedy-Johnson era uninterrupted by a genuine recession, business was riding high in January 1969. With its goal of quick profits and an ever-expanding economy, business wanted nothing more than to be left alone by the government.* That was precisely what Nixon's campaign promised business, and to be let alone meant

*This euphoric mood created by high incomes and quick profits made it difficult for Nixon's talent scouts to lure young business executives to middle-level government jobs after the 1968 election. "The money tree is running in New York, and the young fellows want to tap it rather than come down to Washington," said one such talent scout.

not only easing federal control of regulated industries (including the stock exchange) but also a moratorium on nagging about higher wages and higher prices.

Consequently there had been no previous great debate either inside or outside the new administration when Nixon told his first press conference on the morning of January 27:

> I do not go along with the suggestion that inflation can be effectively controlled by exhorting labor and management and industry to follow certain guidelines. I think that is a very laudable objective for labor and management to follow. But I think I am aware of the fact that the leaders of labor and the leaders of management, much as they might personally want to do what is in the best interests of the nation, have to be guided by the interests of the organization they represent.
>
> So the primary responsibility for controlling inflation rests with the national administration and its handling of fiscal and monetary affairs.

With these comments, the new President was reflecting a view widely held not only by his own advisers but by economists generally: the inflation roaring wildly in January 1969 was essentially caused by the federal government. The record of the Federal Reserve Board in controlling the nation's money supply in the second half of the 1960s was a sorry one. Having choked off the money supply as an anti-inflation device in 1966 so tightly that it produced a serious slump in housing and construction (called by some a "mini-recession"), the central bank started pouring out money too quickly and too generously in 1967 and thereby spoon-fed a new inflation. The Federal Reserve's culpability, however, did not approach Lyndon B. Johnson's. Refusing to ask Congress for a tax increase to finance the Vietnam war when he intervened in 1965, President Johnson piled up huge inflationary budget deficits climaxed by $28.4 billion in red ink for the year ending July 1, 1968. To compensate for these governmental excesses, the Nixon Game Plan was to hold down the money supply (monetary policy) and achieve a budget surplus (fiscal policy).

But the business community interpreted Nixon's comments of January 27 in slightly different fashion. What it thought Nixon was saying was this: Fighting inflation is *our* business, not yours; you fellows have no responsibility to do *anything* in the way of self-restraint. In the wake of Nixon's January 27 press conference, businessmen were being alerted that Washington was now laissez faire on prices. Dr. Pierre Rinfret, an influential economic consultant in New York City and an adviser to Nixon during the 1968 campaign, was telling his clients to raise their prices and raise them *now;* because everything else was going up, they would get no backlash from Washington and, besides, the responsibility for fighting inflation was the government's, not theirs. So, unwittingly, Nixon's abandonment of jawboning helped to generate the inflationary psychology he was trying to control and imposed a still greater burden on the government's monetary and fiscal policies.

Monetary policy was no immediate problem. William McChesney Martin and the rest of the Federal Reserve Board had instituted a tight-money regime in 1968 and were keeping the screws tightened down.

Fiscal policy was another matter. Almost unbelievable in retrospect, as Nixon entered the White House he was undecided even about proposing an extension of the 10 percent income-tax surcharge proposed by President Johnson in 1967 and finally passed by Congress in 1968. Burns and the Quadriad were unanimous in advising Nixon that letting the surtax lapse (along with its $10 billion a year in revenue) was sheer madness. But Nixon had his doubts. He was on record with a somewhat wishy-washy commitment during the 1968 campaign to repeal the surtax, and a great many Republican candidates for Congress had made a far less equivocal commitment. Besides, Nixon was not happy about the LBJ label on the surtax.* But in the end, he reluctantly agreed to propose reenactment.

There still remained the far more difficult, far more basic problem of putting a rein on federal expenditures, terribly bloated by the Vietnam war. The results were disclosed by the President in a message to Congress on April 12. The expenditure estimate of $195.3 billion contained in Johnson's final budget (for the fiscal year ending July 1, 1970) was spurious, the Nixon men found. The more realistic figure was $196.9 billion. The President then reduced this by $4 billion, to give him a projected surplus of $5.8 billion, which Nixon

---

*Although generally passive during the transition period, Johnson tried his hardest to get Nixon behind surtax extension in the fear that refusal to do so would bring the inflation to catastrophic heights. Joseph Califano, Johnson's chief domestic aide, was in close touch with the Nixon staff on this question. Johnson even talked his old friend and comrade Senate Republican Leader Everett McKinley Dirksen into recommending surtax extension to the new President.

quickly labeled the largest surplus in eighteen years and the fourth largest in history.* Seemingly, Nixon had moved quickly and masterfully to bring the budget under control—an indispensable asset in his fight against inflation.

In truth, however, the budget balancers in the administration were defeated. Arthur Burns, in particular, felt that Nixon had lost the golden opportunity to check federal spending. He realized that the highly publicized budget cuts were largely cosmetic, without seriously drawing back long-range spending programs. As Budget Director, Mayo tried manfully to bring the budget into line but failed. Part of the trouble stemmed from the inability of the gentlemanly ex-Treasury bureaucrat to force deep cuts in expenditures on Nixon's department and agency heads, who now were championing the causes of their new bureaucratic constituencies. But the blame cannot be placed solely on Mayo. Many of his most important initiatives to cut expenditures were not backed up by the President. The reduction of $1.1 billion for the Pentagon would have been still larger had Nixon sided with Mayo instead of Laird. Nor was the space-exploration program cut to Mayo's specifications. Nixon overruled Mayo's attempt to eliminate the costly supersonic transport (SST) subsidy program. And he lost his argument with the President that the proposed new program of income maintenance for the poor, whatever its long-range savings, was fiscally irresponsible in the short range.†

Mayo's failure is traceable in part to the peculiarities of the Nixon Presidency. A stolid fellow lacking the ability to entrance Nixon, Mayo had no standing in the White House. He could not compete with a Pat Moynihan persuading the President to support income maintenance or a John Volpe drumming home arguments for the SST. His only budget cutting ally in the White House was Arthur Burns, who was having his own trouble influencing the President. Indeed, before long Mayo lost all physical contact with Nixon. By late 1969, he was getting his instructions from the President via John

---

*Actually, the size of the surplus was exaggerated by a new accounting method (recommended by a citizens' commission headed by David Kennedy) that had taken effect on January 1, 1968, and for the first time counted Social Security trust funds as part of the budgetary picture. For example, Johnson's calamitous $28.1 billion deficit would have been $25.1 billion under the new system.

†The struggle over income maintenance in the welfare reform is discussed in Chapter VIII.

Ehrlichman and relaying his proposals to the President via John Ehrlichman—an unprecedented ignominy for a Budget Director that he should not have tolerated.

Beyond personalities, however, there was also Nixon's fear, as expressed to Wilbur Mills, that too great a budget reduction would induce a whopper of a recession. The result was a policy enunciated by Dr. McCracken as "gradualism," the gradual reduction of inflationary pressures by moderate, not precipitate, pruning of federal spending. That McCracken and just about every other Nixon adviser (with the conspicuous exception of Burns) agreed that gradualism was the proper antidote shows how badly they underestimated the stamina of inflation.

McCracken's concept of the power of gradualism was succinctly described by Hobart Rowen in his column in the *Washington Post* on March 22:

> At some point . . . , probably suddenly and without advance notice, big and little people are going to decide that prices (including the price of money) are too high.
>
> At that point (and Mr. Nixon's people hope it will arrive soon), plant expansion projections will ease off, consumers will start to save a little more and spend a little less, and the exaggerated pace of the economy will settle back to earth.

On March 22, 1969, Richard Nixon seemed to have put all his own faith in the Game Plan of gradualism. Four months later the chilling doubts set in.

Pierre Rinfret, a flamboyant Canadian-born economist, had been an early Nixon-for-President enthusiast and was on the team of advisers at Mission Bay, Calif., in the summer of 1968 making campaign strategy following Nixon's nomination for President. After the election, a Nixon aide sounded out Rinfret on the possibility of his becoming a member of the President's Council of Economic Advisers; Rinfret replied he would not give up his lucrative New York-based consulting firm, Rinfret-Boston Associates, Inc., for any federal post. Thereafter, although McCracken and the other Council members tended to look down their noses at his professional credentials, Rinfret remained in close and amiable contact with several figures in the administration, including Arthur Burns.

But by July 3, Rinfret had become so disaffected that he distributed to clients of his firm a two-page confidential memorandum titled "We Accuse," which said, "We accuse this Administration of incompetence." In attempting to curb inflation, charged Rinfret, the administration (in collaboration with the Federal Reserve Board) was promoting "the current mood of economic and financial terror." In Pierre Rinfret's view, the administration had started badly and was steadily getting worse. "We accuse the Administration of totally miscalculating the need for advance economic planning before it got into office and for being totally unprepared once it did. It went into office with slogans and little else." Most of all, it erred in thinking "that inflation could easily be turned off" and therefore did not sufficiently cut federal spending. Instead, it was risking a financial panic by relying on the Federal Reserve Board's tight-money policy as the first line in the war against inflation. This administration was "fostering, abetting and creating inflation while it has advocated deflation" because "the first thing it did was to announce the abandonment of the wage and price guidelines, which created 'open sesame' on prices and wages."

Rinfret's harsh language typified the startlingly rapid turn of sentiment against Richard Nixon in the business community during those first five months. On July 3 the President's ratings in the polls were still high, the peace movement had not stirred and the Democrats had scarcely pinked him. But his friends in the world of business had turned against him with the ferocity of a friend betrayed. Under the man they had supported for President, the idyllic business climate was becoming a bad dream: stock market down and falling; interest rates up and rising; money so tight that some businessmen were unable to operate; a recession on the horizon; and finally that immeasurably precious commodity—business confidence—failing. And yet, all this had not brought an end to inflation. On June 11, David Kennedy, using language more candid than other members of the Quadriad, told a meeting of the Advertising Council in Washington that the nation was on the brink "of a runaway inflation."*

---

*In the same speech, Kennedy warned that wage and price controls might be used as the ultimate weapon to curb inflation if all else failed. Since Nixon had unequivocally ruled out all such controls, the White House was not pleased with Kennedy's attempt to dramatize the administration's concern with the situation.

Kennedy's candor was unusual. According to the Nixon party line, the Game Plan was working and everybody should be patient. But by the time of Pierre Rinfret's broadside, Nixon's economic team —though probably not Nixon himself—knew it had badly underestimated inflation and that inflation so far had not been controlled. The further cold reality was that present policies would produce a moderate recession in 1970, whether or not they stopped inflation. The Nixon administration faced the nightmare world of *both* inflation and recession for the first time in modern economic history.

At the White House, Arthur Burns was clearly less than pleased with McCracken, the man he had chosen to be Nixon's chief economic adviser. He confided to friends that McCracken was talking too much publicly about stopping inflation and not talking hard enough privately about cutting back on federal spending. Burns doggedly fought for greater budget austerity and in August came up with a notable success. He won Nixon's approval for an immediate cutback of 75 percent in all federal construction, including the massive interstate-highway program. To Burns, the shock value of this move might just jolt the inflationary psychology still gripping the nation. One political obstacle, however, was the predictable outrage of the state governors, now overwhelmingly Republican. To deal gently with the governors, announcement of Nixon's move was delayed until the first week in September when they would all be together at their annual national conference in Colorado Springs, Colo. Burns would be there to do the explaining.

What followed was one of those strange attacks of indecisiveness, compounded by failure of communication, that sometimes undermined the best domestic intentions of Richard Nixon.

Nixon arrived in Colorado Springs on the afternoon of September 1 from his beach house at San Clemente, Calif., where he was spending much of the summer. Scheduled to address the governors' black-tie banquet at the Broadmoor Hotel that night, the President might have taken the opportunity to slip the governors the bad news about the construction cutback and urge them to keep a stiff upper lip for the good of the republic. Instead, Nixon delivered a conventional jeremiad against social-welfare spending under Johnson the past five years ($250 billion that had "reaped a harvest of dissatisfaction, frustration and bitter division"), without revealing his new plans for austerity, and returned to San Clemente that night.

The reason he left without mentioning the cutbacks was a counterattack by politically conscious advisers still worried about the adverse impact on the governors. Vice President Spiro T. Agnew, only seven months away from being governor of Maryland and now playing a liaison role with the governors, told the President the governors were far more worried about recession than inflation and would rise up in wrath against a flat-out cutback. He was backed by Volpe, who as governor of Massachusetts had led a delegation to the White House in 1967 to protest a highway-construction freeze imposed by Lyndon Johnson. Agnew's alternative: delay the cutback on Federal grants to the states for six months, until April, giving them a chance to inventory federally financed projects and to select the ones to cut back.

With *Air Force One* shuttling the President back and forth between California and Colorado, with key officials of the government scattered across the continent between Washington, San Clemente and Colorado Springs, the difficulty in communications at top levels of the administration was compounded. Agnew thought he had Nixon's agreement to the six-month delay. The White House thought no such thing. On the afternoon of September 2, Agnew privately briefed the governors about the impending cutback plans, adding that there would be a six-month reprieve on federal-state projects. In Colorado Springs, when Arthur Burns learned about Agnew's retreat, he was furious. Now, having promised the governors a six-month reprieve, there could be no immediate cutback, the essential shock value had disappeared, and worst of all, both the press and the politicians would believe that Nixon simply did not have the stomach to deal courageously with inflation. That bothered Burns the most.*

Two days later at San Clemente, Nixon issued a statement ordering an immediate 75 percent cutback in new federal construction. In view of Agnew's intervention, he temporized about federal grants to states, urging state and local governments "to follow the example of the Federal Government by cutting back temporarily on

---

*The six-month reprieve scarcely blunted the fury of the governors at Colorado Springs. Typical was the reaction of Governor Tom McCall of Oregon, a Republican who said he was "horrified" by the cutback, then added, "It would stop inflation, but it might also stop the economy in its tracks."

their own construction plans." He warned that he himself would reduce federal grants by an undetermined amount "if the response proves insufficient," but even in that event, said the President, "the states and localities will, of course, be given due notice, so that they can adjust their affairs properly." Predictably, the states and municipalities did not heed the President's admonition; predictably, the President did not make good on his threat, even with the Agnew formula included. So ended still another effort by Arthur Burns for a drastic slowdown in federal spending.

Even before that defeat, however, Burns had concluded that this administration was not going to curb federal spending enough to hold down inflationary pressures. By August, he had come to believe something else was necessary, and that something else was an incomes policy—a return to wage-price guideposts rejected by Nixon on January 27. Throughout his career as an economist, Burns, like most conservatives, had opposed the concept of an incomes policy. He firmly believed that mandatory government controls on wages and prices were incompatible with a free society and that an incomes policy was but a way station to controls. In the late summer of 1969, however, Burns was changing his mind. He noted that an incomes policy had been instituted in Canada, the Netherlands and the United States (the Kennedy era guideposts) and had been followed not by the controls but by a return to no government intervention at all. For Burns, at age sixty-four considered one of the most dogmatic figures in the administration, to abandon this position reflects the depth of his anxiety. Burns allied with himself a good part of the Cabinet concerned with economic policy: Kennedy, Romney, Volpe, Postmaster General Blount. But not McCracken or the rest of the Council of Economic Advisers. And, most important, certainly not the President.*

In an October 17 radio address to the nation on inflation, the President rejected an incomes policy, rejected any substantial change in his economic Game Plan and rejected any suggestion of failure. "We are not going to change our game plan at the end of the first quarter of the game, particularly at a time that we feel we are ahead,"

---

*At about the same time, Burns was lining up most of the Cabinet against Moynihan's welfare reform but, here as well, failed to get the President's approval. The details are in Chapter VIII.

he said. Recalling yet again his experience with the OPA in World War II ("rationing, black markets, regimentation"), he rejected not only direct controls but the guideposts that Burns had been urging on him, describing guideposts as "putting the Government into the business of telling the workingman how much he should charge for his services or how much the businessman should charge for his goods." The President's dogmatism on the wage-price question had not been diluted by nine months of failure. He even reiterated his objection to jawboning: "Instead of relying on our jawbone, we have put some backbone in Government's determination to hold the line for the consumer." In fact, however, he did engage in a very benign form of jawboning. Pledging that the government would stick to a strict anti-inflationary policy, Nixon asserted that "by responding to the changed conditions," labor and management "will be following their self-interest and helping the national interest as well." This was a perceptible departure from his January 27 implication that labor and management had no stake in the national welfare, but far from what Burns wanted.

Even that minimum of jawboning was forgotten little more than a month later. On November 27 the administration assembled some 1,600 top-rank American business leaders to hear Nixon and his economic team give an off-the-record briefing at Washington's Sheraton Park Hotel. Not a word urging price restraint came from the President or anybody else. It was the same old line: The government means business about curbing inflation. "Those who bet on inflation will lose their bets, but those who bet on a cooling off will win, because we're committed," said the President.

There was one attempted change in the Game Plan in the closing months of 1969. In August, just when Burns was changing his mind about an incomes policy, a one-man campaign against the tight-money policy of the Federal Reserve Board was being waged by an influential Republican economist outside the government: Professor Milton Friedman of the University of Chicago. In his column in *Newsweek,* in discussions with key figures in the administration and even in one telephone conversation with William McChesney Martin, Friedman argued that the Federal Reserve had now kept the money supply choked off for so long that further restrictions threatened a severe recession. Friedman's arguments made no impact on Martin or other members of the Quadriad, but he did pick up one influential disciple, George Shultz, Friedman's former colleague at Chicago and now a rising figure in the administration, who took the view that Friedman had studied the money supply with greater care and perception than anybody in the administration had and deserved to be listened to. After taking this line in private conversations through the early autumn, Shultz surfaced with it in Nixon's presence at a mid-October meeting of the Cabinet Committee on Economic Policy.

There was no immediate support for Shultz at that meeting, but it was not long in coming. By November, McCracken believed the tight-money policy must be ended (though, for public consumption, he denied it, lest he give the impression the administration was backing away from the fight against inflation). In a meeting of the Quadriad, McCracken asked William McChesney Martin what the prospects were for loosening the money screws. Martin, scheduled to be replaced on January 31 by Burns, was unresponsive. But the Federal Reserve did switch to a less restrictive policy late in the year —far too late in the opinion of many economists.

Thus 1969 ended with the President's economic Game Plan disintegrating, his advisers split and the economy failing. By year's end, the value of the 1957–59 dollar had slipped from 81.1 cents when Nixon took power to 76.7 cents. And although inflation was not curbed, unemployment was rising fast and a recession loomed. Yet, there was no sense of crisis in the Oval Office. Buoyed by his continued high popularity, by his successes abroad and by scattered off-year Republican election victories, Richard Nixon could not focus on the black specter of economic crisis confronting him. Economic policy continued to be made in a casual manner with little regard for consequences. The tax bill he signed to end the year on December 30 was proof enough of that.

When Nixon early in 1969 bowed to the swelling demand for tax reform, there was little thought of economic consequences.* Tax reform concerned equity; it was not part of the fight against inflation. Yet, in pursuing tax reform, the administration could not avoid making vitally important economic decisions. But instead of approaching the task judiciously, it made these decisions in slapdash fashion, with rueful consequences.

*The reform aspects of the bill are discussed in Chapter VIII.

During a discussion of tax reform proposals with a group of Congressional leaders in March 1969, the President began considering a step profoundly important to the economy: repeal of the investment credit. Adopted by Congress in 1962 to stimulate the economy, the investment credit provided substantial federal tax relief for businessmen investing in new plant and equipment. It was extremely popular with business, but Democrats had begun to look on it as an unneeded windfall for business.

So at that March meeting in the White House, Senator Russell B. Long of Louisiana, the voluble Chairman of the Senate Finance Committee, concluded a monologue on tax reform with this admonition: "And you ought to repeal that goddamn investment credit!"

"Oh?" said the President, turning to Representative John Byrnes of Wisconsin, senior Republican on the House Ways and Means Committee. "What do you think, Johnny?"

"I agree," said Byrnes.

After the meeting, Nixon chatted briefly with Byrnes and Dr. Charls Walker, Under Secretary of the Treasury (substituting for David Kennedy, then on an official mission in Australia). The President had given the matter no thought at all and wanted to know what Byrnes and Walker thought of repeal. He was told that business would apply heavy pressure to prevent repeal but that the Democrats would repeal it anyway. After Byrnes and Walker attended a meeting of the Republicans on Ways and Means and found them solidly against the investment credit, Walker returned to the White House to recommend repeal.

At the ensuing Cabinet-level meeting, Walker argued that Presidential support of investment-credit repeal must lessen Democratic resistance to extension of the surcharge. Dr. Herbert Stein, a member of the Council of Economic Advisers, supported repeal on grounds that the credit was inflationary. But Arthur Burns hit the roof. The investment credit was not inflationary, he said, but should be preserved to combat a possible future recession. Suspend it if necessary, but do not repeal it, he argued.* The President decided against Burns, the first of many decisions Burns would lose. But Burns was prophetic. Combined with the strange unfolding of the tax reform

---

*In his July 3 "We Accuse" memorandum, written after Nixon had proposed repealing the investment credit, Pierre Rinfret made much the same point. "You lick inflation by increasing capacity, and not by holding it back," he contended.

bill, the investment-credit repeal would cast a long economic shadow.

With repeal alone recovering $3 billion in revenue, the tax reform bill being shaped by the House Ways and Means Committee over five arduous months now showed a net revenue gain of $7 billion. But Wilbur Mills, the committee chairman, did not conceive of tax reform as a device to increase revenue. His idea was that by ending special tax advantages, tax rates for run-of-the-mill taxpayers could be lowered. So, on the morning of August 1, Mills appeared in the committee room with a proposed tax-rate table providing $7 billion in tax relief for individual taxpayers. Not only did the Treasury not object; its experts had helped Mills prepare the table. In order that the House could pass the bill before beginning its summer recess, the committee had to act on Mills' table that very morning, and it did so, the administration choosing to play a passive role. After laboring five months to raise the $7 billion, the committee decided how to spend it in less than two hours.

But what the committee did not realize was that Mills' new rate table was so constructed that it would discourage middle-income taxpayers from itemizing their tax deductions, a step toward Mills' long-range goal of simplifying the tax structure. Nor did they realize that this had the effect of depriving those middle-income taxpayers ($8,000–$13,000-a-year salary bracket) of almost any benefit from the $7 billion of tax reductions. This anomaly was spotted by a sharp-eyed economist at AFL-CIO headquarters, who passed the information on to Democratic liberals in the House. The liberals immediately threatened Mills with a rewritten bill providing an equal share of relief for the neglected bracket. Mills, instead of challenging the liberals or accepting their version in a humiliating surrender, chose a third course that was to have fateful consequences: he rewrote the bill to provide an *additional* $2.4 billion in tax relief especially for the $8,000–$13,000 bracket. The liberals had no choice but to accept, and the Treasury, caught by surprise, said not a word, though the bill was now $2.4 billion in the red.

The instinctive reaction at the Treasury was to try bringing the revenue aspects of the bill back to balance in the Senate with the implicit threat of a veto, and Dr. Walker said as much in a nationally televised interview. But for the first time, the economists began to look at the large impact of the tax reform bill on the troubled economy. Dr. Stein analyzed the substantial $9.4 billion of tax relief for consumers along with the $7 billion of substantially higher taxation for certain areas of business ($3 billion of it from the repeal of the investment credit that Stein advocated earlier in the year), and came to this conclusion: the bill was not only out of balance in revenue but was downright bad for investment. Besides tending to be inflationary, Stein concluded, it could inhibit long-term economic growth. The suggested antidote came from Arthur Burns: replace some of the reductions in personal income taxes with a cut in the corporate rate. The Treasury's response was to propose slicing off just enough of the personal income tax cuts passed by the House to offset a one-percentage-point decrease in the corporate rate and still maintain a balance in revenue for the bill. Not enough, replied Stein and the other economists. To remove the dangerous anti-investment bias from the bill, it would be necessary to lower the corporate rate by *two* percentage points—even if the bill wound up with a net deficit. The Treasury resisted, objecting to any deficit at all.

A Presidential decision was clearly needed. Accordingly, in that unreal summer of 1969, when euphoria infected the President and his inner staff, and the decision-making process required incessant intercontinental travel, the Nixon economic team hurried to San Clemente the last week of August to see the President—the Council of Economic Advisers and Burns favoring a two-percentage-point decrease in the corporate rate, the Treasury opposing it.

Arriving in San Clemente, they huddled to try to resolve their differences. Secretary Kennedy began backing down. When it was pointed out that the revised bill would lose only $1.3 billion a year even with the two-percentage-point reduction, Kennedy said, "Well, that's not much of an imbalance." That left only Under Secretary Walker in opposition. But Paul McCracken then made the argument that the corporate rate was too high for healthy long-term growth and that, historically, Congress never lowered corporate rates unless it was also lowering personal rates. Therefore, here was a rare chance not to be wasted. That argument effectively cooled off Walker's opposition.

At the next day's meeting with the President, effective opposition to corporate rate reduction no longer existed on his economic team. After hearing only perfunctory debate, Nixon agreed to cut back the personal rate reductions approved by the House in return for the two percentage points of corporate rate reduction.

It is not surprising that the Treasury officials and economists at

San Clemente, with not a party politician among them, did not perceive the political folly of what they were doing. Haldeman and Ehrlichman, sitting by the President's side, were also too new to the world of grand political strategy to understand it. But why not Richard Nixon? Should not that battered veteran of partisan intrigue have bristled immediately at the mere thought of a Republican President proposing that tax relief be transferred from the overtaxed average citizens to the overfed captains of industry? But precisely such political grand strategy was where Nixon was often at his weakest, particularly on economic questions.

That is not all that was overlooked at San Clemente. By agreeing to sponsor a bill $1.3 billion in the red, Nixon had lost all moral authority in his battle with Congress to bring out a balanced bill. "It was like being a little bit pregnant," one of the participants in that meeting said later.

In truth, however, the talk of corporate rate reduction amid the gentle breezes of the Pacific had no basis in reality. The Senate Finance Committee, though one of the Senate's most conservative committees, gave the proposal no serious attention. The committee's Republican members, though business-oriented to the man, showed more political sensitivity than the President and would not promote any cut in corporate rates. But the mere fact that Nixon had made the proposal, only to have it so rudely ignored by the Senate, further undercut his prestige, and therefore his power to control the bill when it reached the Senate floor in December.

The biggest threat there came from Senator Albert Gore of Tennessee, a veteran populistic liberal Democrat fighting what was to prove an unsuccessful battle for his political life against the rising tide of conservative Republicanism in Tennessee. To rehabilitate himself at home, Gore was polishing an old chestnut that had been a favorite proposal of Democrats for a generation: an increase in the $600 personal exemption allowed each taxpayer. That would unbalance the bill still more, both losing revenue and tilting the bill's economic bias toward the consumer and away from investment. Although Gore was badly beaten in the Finance Committee, his proposal was endorsed by the Senate Democratic Policy Committee and had overwhelming support from the Senate's Democratic majority. Dr. Walker, managing the tax reform bill for the administration, misread Senate sentiment and decided Gore could be defeated. Senator Scott, the Minority Leader, disagreed. He argued that the Gore amendment would carry unless the Republicans could devise a substitute of their own to increase the personal exemption.

Next came another misunderstanding of the kind endemic to the Nixon administration. When the Treasury offered technical assistance to Republican senators in drafting the substitute Scott wanted, some Republicans naturally assumed it implied endorsement of an increase in the personal exemption. Further leading to this assumption by the Republicans was the interference of John Ehrlichman, operating wholly independently of the Treasury. Ehrlichman took upon himself the function of talking to Scott in a way that reinforced Scott's feeling that the administration was indeed backing a Republican alternative on personal exemptions. That ad hoc intrusion by Ehrlichman was typical of the growing confusion and lack of meaningful communication on the tax bill. It was no wonder, then, that many Republicans felt betrayed when, on December 2, Nixon sent letters to Mansfield and Scott threatening a veto if the additional tax relief was voted. As expected, the Republican substitute (for a more gradual increase in the personal exemption than Gore wanted) was roundly rejected and the Gore amendment overwhelmingly adopted. Scott and other Republicans stormed that the administration had witlessly given the Democrats full credit for tax relief when a bipartisan measure might have been possible. Enraged, Scott took to the Senate floor with this denunciation aimed at Walker: "I do hope that responsible officials in the Treasury of my own administration will listen when next time we advise them we understand more about strategy than they do."

On the next day, December 4, when the President met with his legislative leaders, Nixon pledged he would veto any fiscally irresponsible bill. But that pledge in privacy was scant preparation for Nixon's public declaration at his press conference four days later.

> *Question:* Sir, if the final version of the tax reform bill now pending in Congress includes the Senate-adopted $800 exemption provision and the 15 per cent Social Security increase, can you sign it?*
> *The President:* No.

*Gore had begun by proposing a $1,250 personal exemption, later reduced it to $1,000 and finally settled on $800, reached in gradual stages.

So terse and unequivocal a reply was not Richard Nixon's style. His patience with Congress in turning a tax reform bill into a tax relief bill was clearly running out. But now it was too late. Earlier, the President had rejected a suggestion by Dr. Walker that he go on television to use his then ascendant popularity to try to fight the Congressional tax-cutting schemes. "No," replied Nixon. "You can't explain economics to the American people." Nixon also turned aside requests that he lobby members of Congress. Now on the night of December 8 his threat of veto—over prime-time television—came too late. With the bill to be passed by the Senate four days later, the only chance of reducing its loss of revenue was in the House-Senate conference, and even there the best that could be hoped for was a split between the $2.4-billion revenue loss in the House bill and the eventual $4.7-billion loss of the Senate bill. It was inconceivable that the President would end up vetoing the bill that preoccupied Congress all year long. By making a threat he would never fulfill, Nixon had committed an egregious error in the delicate art of husbanding Presidential strength with Congress.

Reluctantly, at the Treasury's request, Nixon called the two top tax men in the House, Wilbur Mills and John Byrnes, to the White House to press them to reduce the losses in the conference. They did so, cutting back Gore's $800 exemption to $750 and otherwise making up revenue, so that the net loss of the bill was $2.5 billion. Although even this final version (containing the $750 exemption and the 15 percent Social Security increase) fully met Nixon's specifications for a veto, he signed it, as everybody knew he would, on December 30, complaining that its "effect on the budget and on the cost of living is bad." The President's sour comments on the bill contained more censure than approbation, as well they might have.

Thus, at a time when Nixon was trying his best to fight inflation and avoid recession, he had signed a bill that was both inflationary (through its deficit spending) and recessionary (through its anti-investment bias). This had happened because the President's economic team concentrated on the economic aspects of tax reform only belatedly, and then in a haphazard manner that proved totally ineffective. Throughout the late summer and autumn, when tax reform was being transformed into tax relief, the President was remote from the struggle—his ineffectiveness and irresolution culminating in his unfulfilled threat to veto an out-of-balance tax bill. By allowing his bluff to be called, the President had suffered a loss of prestige almost as great as he would have if Congress had overridden an actual veto.

On the evening of January 30, 1970, Richard Nixon's first press conference of the new year was opened by Douglas B. Cornell, of the Associated Press, whose question graphically revealed how much the economic outlook had changed in the month since the President had signed the tax reform bill.

> Mr. President, for several days I have been collecting some headlines that sort of point up the question I would like to put to you . . . "Big firms' 1969 profits down." "Dow average hits new low for three years." "GNP rise halted." "Ford joins GM and Chrysler in work cutbacks." "Wholesale prices show sharp rise." "U.S. Steel will raise sheet prices February 1."
> The question is: how, sir, do you assess the possibility that we may be in for perhaps the worst possible sort of economic conditions—inflation and a recession?

Indeed, the nightmare world of simultaneous recession and inflation was fast becoming a reality. Key economic indicators—industrial production, personal income, business sales, real Gross National Product—were down. So was the badly slumping stock market. Unemployment was on the rise. But at the same time, interest rates and prices continued to climb. Dr. Walter Heller, Chairman of the Council of Economic Advisers in Kennedy-Johnson days, had a name for this unholy combination of bad economic news never before experienced in America: Nixonomics.*

McCracken, Stein, Kennedy and Walker, who had spent 1969 promising that an end to inflation was just around the corner, now not only reiterated those promises but pledged there would be no recession either—their credibility being undermined by every un-

---

*Heller coined "Nixonomics" in an off-the-record speech to the Bohemian Club Summer Encampment in San Francisco on July 16, 1969. He first mentioned it publicly in a speech addressing the National American Wholesale Grocers Executive Conference in Honolulu on September 27, 1969. Ironically, a Nixon speech writer, William Safire, early in the administration had toyed with using "Nixonomics" to describe the administration's Game Plan but had been dissuaded on grounds that it sounded too contrived.

fulfilled promise. Nixon himself joined the parade of sunshine talkers. In answer to Cornell's press-conference question, he said:

> Our policies have been planned to avoid a recession. I do expect that the present rate of inflation, which was less in the second half of 1969 than in the first half, will continue to decline and that we will be able to control inflation without recession.

Specifically, the President promised that three days later he would offer a bare-bones budget for the fiscal year ending July 1, 1971. The new budget, he promised, "will be a major blow in stopping the inflation psychology." That budget, in fact, was a much more serious attempt at austerity than his first one a year earlier, and it represented a major, though temporary, victory for Arthur Burns.

Late in December, Mayo had reported to the President at San Clemente that there was no possible way to cut expenditures deeply enough to balance the new budget. But there simply had to be a balanced budget. Everybody in the administration now agreed with Milton Friedman that the Federal Reserve Board's tight-money policy must be loosened or the economy would strangle. But Dr. Burns, who would replace William McChesney Martin as chairman at the Federal Reserve on January 31, had made clear he could not countenance an easier monetary policy unless *fiscal* policy were tight —which meant, at the bare minimum, a balanced budget. With Mayo pleading inability to cut expenditures enough, new revenue would be needed for a balance. The Treasury came up with a $4.5 billion painless tax package: a speedup in estate and gift tax collections and higher excises on liquor, tobacco and gasoline. Nixon promptly bought the package.

But not Arthur Burns. To make fiscal policy properly tight enough was a matter of not only a balanced budget but a *properly* balanced budget, he told the President, not a budget balanced through some patchwork tax gimmicks. The implication was clear. There would be no easing of policy at the Federal Reserve unless the last drop of blood was squeezed out of expenditures. Nixon had already made up his mind to go the Burns route when he returned to Washington from San Clemente in time for a January 13 meeting of the Cabinet. Although it lasted three and one-half hours, it was a *pro forma* affair. Mayo, supported by Kennedy, pleaded that the budget was uncuttable. Burns' position was voiced with great passion by his usual acolyte, George Romney, who exhorted his colleagues to cut even deeper into their own budgets and capped his plea by an astonishing sermon calling on all members of the Cabinet, *and* the President, to take a 25 percent pay cut! "This is going to make me as popular as a skunk at a Sunday school picnic," he said, and he was right.* Soon after the meeting, Nixon ordered anguished department heads to make still greater cuts to achieve a Burns-style balance. When the budget was sent to Congress on February 2, it called for a $1.3 billion surplus.

Arthur Burns had demonstrated that, blessed with the massive power of the Federal Reserve System, he now had leverage with the President that he never had as Counsellor. But the victory was one year too late. Nixon, Burns and everybody else sitting around the Cabinet table on January 13 refused to face the grim reality that there was no possible way to balance the budget—neither the Mayo-Kennedy way nor the Burns-Romney way. The economic rot of recession was at so advanced a stage that tax receipts were already falling precipitately, which explained why the fat $5.6 billion budget surplus projected by Nixon in his first budget for the year ending July 1, 1970, had disappeared and would end up as a $2.8 billion deficit. As for the 1971 budget, the $1.3 billion surplus bullied through by Burns never had a chance. The recession-induced loss of revenue would, instead, create a deficit to rival Lyndon Johnson's worst.

The President would not admit it, but the Game Plan was dead. Even before Burns formally replaced Martin, the tight-money policy at the Federal Reserve was quietly abandoned; Burns in charge made sure that the badly needed money kept flowing into the banking system. By early spring, it was obvious that a massive budget deficit —eventually to exceed $23 billion—was in the works (though administration officials still piously denied it). If a recession loomed and neither the Federal Reserve nor the budget was now being used to fight inflation, what could be done? More and more, Nixon's economic team was doing what would have been inconceivable a year earlier: looking hard at an incomes policy.

. . .

*Romney voluntarily took the 25 percent pay reduction, although no other Cabinet member followed his example. On May 20, his wife, Lenore, told the press in Detroit that it had resulted in some penny-pinching: "We don't take vacations, we don't have a maid and George helps me with the dishes."

At his January 30, 1970, press conference, Richard Nixon once again was asked about incomes policy (or, as his questioner put it, "jawboning"). Once again, he categorically rejected any change in the Game Plan. Denouncing any interference with the pricing decisions of private industry, Nixon called jawboning a "basically unfair" policy and balanced budgets the "only effective way" to fight inflation. "We are going to continue on our present course," he said. "We believe it is the right course."

Nixon believed what he said, but doubts were spreading through his administration. Moving to the Federal Reserve Board had not stopped Burns from continuing to lobby for an incomes policy, vigorously supported by Romney. By May, the combination of rising unemployment and rising inflation led to a desperate attempt to change the Game Plan toward adopting a modest incomes policy. The President had decided to deliver an address to the nation on the economy in mid-June, and this could be the vehicle for a major turn in policy.

Arthur Burns led off the campaign on May 19 with a major policy speech to the American Bankers Association Monetary Conference in Hot Springs, Va., urging a form of voluntary controls as the only way to fight inflation without risking "a very serious business recession." Second- and third-level officials of the Treasury and the Budget Bureau, meeting with their counterparts from the Council of Economic Advisers (in groups called Troika II and Troika III), began pressing for an incomes policy. On May 28 Dr. Walker went on NBC's *Today* show to say he saw "merit" in a bill introduced by Senator Jacob Javits of New York that would instruct the Council of Economic Advisers to analyze and publicize wage and price decisions to spotlight inflationary increases—the rudimentary start of an incomes policy.

On June 5, Maurice Mann, a professional economist and political independent who had been recruited by Mayo from the Federal Reserve Bank of Cleveland to become Assistant Budget Director, addressed a Washington meeting of the Rural Electric Cooperative Association and brought out what was happening inside the administration. Speaking without notes, Mann described the government economists as being divided into two camps: one camp for continued tight fiscal and monetary policy, the other camp for attacking inflation with an incomes policy because the present policy was "an abysmal failure." Mann left no doubt he was in the second group.

Not until he had finished speaking did he realize that a reporter, Murray Seeger of the *Los Angeles Times*, was present.

Hobart Rowen, business and financial editor of the *Washington Post*, read Seeger's story on the *Los Angeles Times* news wire and cornered Mann two days later at the District of Columbia Bankers Association annual convention in Hot Springs, Va. Mann then clearly told Rowen what no administration official had dared admit up to that point: the Nixon Game Plan had slowed down the economy without stopping inflation, and "an additional step"—that is, a moderate incomes policy—would be helpful.

To the outside world, all this sound and fury surely was a preliminary barrage preparing everyone for a radical shift, to be revealed in the mid-June speech. But the outside world little knew how the Nixon administration functioned. In fact, most of the agitation for an incomes policy came from second-echelon officials at the Treasury and Budget Bureau operating without the sanction of their bosses. Walker had gone on the *Today* show to endorse the Javits bill without telling Kennedy; Mann had not had Mayo's backing when he publicly endorsed an incomes policy (in fact, he was later reprimanded in a telephone call from White House aide Peter Flanigan for undercutting the party line).

Among officials with direct access to the President, only Burns favored an incomes policy, and he made no progress in early May when he again proposed voluntary controls to the President. Kennedy and Mayo were passive and seemingly uninterested in the entire debate. Paul McCracken publicly denounced Burns' initiative, privately admitted it might have merit, but vigorously protested that the council was not equipped to oversee wage-price decisions as envisioned in the Javits bill. If Nixon needed any further justification for opposing Burns, it came from George Shultz. By the spring of 1970, his unsmiling, slightly intimidating manner had made him a force to reckon with. Now the Secretary of Labor turned his new influence with the President against an incomes policy. It would not work, he argued, but besides that, it would lead to shameful abandonment of the Game Plan by tending to justify a reckless binge of deficit spending. Indeed, Shultz told Nixon, the Hot Springs speech by Burns advocating an incomes policy was inflationary in itself. It would impel businessmen to raise prices quickly *before* an incomes policy was instituted.

With that line-up, the final draft of the speech handed Nixon for

his final editing and rewriting did not contain anything that even
went so far in the direction of an incomes policy as the very mild
Javits bill. The tiny step taken was the announcement of periodic
Inflation Alerts (the wording was speech writer William Safire's) to
be issued by the Council of Economic Advisers "to call attention to
outstanding cases of price or wage increase"—in other words, jawboning *after* the fact.* It was only a slight departure from total
laissez faire on wages and prices, and a bitter disappointment for
many who had hoped for a major change. In his speech to the
nation over nationwide radio and television at noon on June 17,
the President once again indulged his deeply felt bias against
government interference in wage-price decisions in prose unmistakably his own.

> Now, I realize that there are some people who get satisfaction out
> of seeing an individual businessman or labor leader called on the carpet
> and browbeaten by Government officials. But we cannot protect the
> value of the dollar by passing the buck. That sort of grandstanding
> distracts attention from the real cause of inflation and it can be a
> dangerous misuse of the power of Government.

It was as if the past eighteen months of deepening failure had
not occurred, as if Arthur Burns had not made serious proposals that
had nothing to do with "browbeating" anybody or "grandstanding,"
as if serious economists in his own administration were not turning
toward an incomes policy.† Never did the failure of communication
between the President and the experts in his own administration
come through more clearly.

A few days before that speech, the President took a step that
further militated against an incomes policy in the foreseeable future.

In December 1969, Nixon had briefed Robert Mayo on the
details of a major reorganization of the Executive Office of the Presi-

*McCracken issued the first Inflation Alert on August 8, 1970, a 123-page docu-
ment describing wage increases in the trucking and construction industries and price
increases for cigarettes, rubber and electric power as contributing to the cost of
living. Its impact on public opinion was invisible.

†Besides the Inflation Alert, the June 17 speech revealed two other anti-inflation
measures. One was appointment of a National Productivity Commission to seek
ways of combating the recent slump in productivity, which had contributed to
inflation. The other was appointment of a board to study federal purchasing regulations and determine whether they tend to drive up wages and prices. Little was heard
from either in subsequent months.

dent, not to be publicly disclosed until the next spring, that would transform the Bureau of the Budget into a new Office of Management and Budget (OMB), with greatly enhanced authority for managing the entire federal government.* In one of those countless misunderstandings, derived from Nixon's often oblique manner of conversation, Mayo got the idea that the job would be his. In fact, however, the President had no intention of giving a post of such vast and pervasive power to a man with whom he had little rapport and in whom he had no great confidence. But he said nothing of this to Mayo. Mayo did not learn the President's real frame of mind until he received a telephone call from a White House aide on June 8, 1970. The aide bluntly informed Mayo that the President on June 10 would name George Shultz as Director of OMB, with Mayo shunted off with the title of Counsellor (retaining Cabinet rank),† obviously a way station while he sought other employment. There was no telephone call from Nixon himself.

Quite a different story was given the public when the President announced the change at the White House Rose Garden on the afternoon of June 10. Nixon claimed that Mayo had recommended Shultz for OMB and further implied he had not wanted the job for himself. As in the sacking of Ray C. Bliss as Republican National Chairman, Nixon never did fire Mayo in a face-to-face confrontation and tried to cover up the humiliation with fulsome praise (telling the Rose Garden audience that Mayo had made "one of the most distinguished records, one of the best records as Budget Director that this Government has ever had").

The humiliation of Robert Mayo was transcended by the elevation of George Shultz. Having managed to impress the President and shape his policies while operating from the bureaucratic backwater of the Labor Department, he now had unlimited possibilities functioning from the White House as general manager for the entire federal government. Replacing Mayo on the Quadriad, Shultz would become the dominant force whose influence would far eclipse that of McCracken, Kennedy and Burns. Behind his back, some of the

---

*This important reorganization is discussed in Chapter VIII.

†This now made four Cabinet-rank Counsellors at the White House with no duties or responsibilities: Harlow, Moynihan, Finch and Mayo. However, on July 18, Mayo announced he was resigning to become president of the Federal Reserve Bank of Chicago.

government's top economists belittled Shultz's academic background as being limited to wage structuring and not centered on macro-economics. They questioned his competence to be the President's most influential adviser on what had become his most terrifying domestic problem. But the fact that Shultz *was* his most influential economic adviser could be denied by nobody. In terms of mid-1970, that meant an end to any immediate hopes for a meaningful incomes policy, because Shultz's doctrinaire opposition would only reinforce Nixon's emotional bias. Maurice Mann, one of the most forceful advocates of an incomes policy, quickly perceived the incompatibility of his own economic views and Shultz's and quietly left the Budget Bureau and the government. Walker and other Treasury officials pushing for an incomes policy went underground. At the Federal Reserve, Arthur Burns bided his time.

Lawrence F. O'Brien, Chairman of the Democratic National Committee, in a luncheon speech to the Women's National Democratic Club in Washington on May 21, 1970, sounded his party's new theme for that year's midterm campaign. O'Brien talked of "the President's very special brand of economic double jeopardy: the paradoxical and unprecedented spectacle of inflation continuing to accelerate in the face of a rapidly mounting recession." To describe this, O'Brien appropriated Walter Heller's term "Nixonomics." Henceforth the publication of the Democratic National Committee would have a regular section called Nixonomics.

O'Brien was on the right political track. Through that summer and autumn of 1970, inflation and recession worsened together to stunt hopes for significant Republican gains in November.* By mid-year, nothing could be done in time for the election about either inflation or recession.

In all fairness to Nixon and his economic advisers, they had inherited from Lyndon Johnson a raging inflation that might have persisted against any proposed remedy, including an incomes policy. Nor was the intensity of the recession wholly attributable to the Nixon Game Plan: the United Auto Workers struck the General Motors Corporation on September 14, closing plants for the rest of the year and deepening economic distress.

*The 1970 campaign is discussed in Chapter XI.

Yet, pervading the period of all the bad luck was a certain thoughtless separation between dream and reality that was given another graphic exhibition on July 1, 1970, after the Nixon administration had been in office for more than seventeen months. Shultz became Director of OMB on that date, with Caspar (Cappy) Weinberger, a San Francisco lawyer long politically allied with Nixon, as his Deputy Director. A former state party chairman, Weinberger had served as Governor Ronald Reagan's chief budget officer before coming to Washington in 1969 as Chairman of the Federal Trade Commission. Nixon decided Weinberger could handle the budgetary functions at OMB while Shultz concentrated on the larger management functions.*

A little more than two weeks after taking over his new post, Weinberger met with a group of newspaper correspondents over breakfast at the National Press Club and betrayed a brand of economics seldom seen in Washington since Herbert Hoover's day. Describing himself as a "fiscal puritan," he called for consistently balanced budgets—in good times *and* bad. "I don't think a deficit benefits anyone," said Weinberger. "It may work for a year or two, but in three or four or five years, you really pay the piper." Each year, he said, the federal government ought to try to spend less money than the last. At OMB, career economists scarcely knew whether to weep or laugh when they read their new chief's comments in the morning newspaper and realized how oblivious he was to reality: a federal budget climbing so steeply that even controlling its *rate* of increase would be difficult; back-to-back budget deficits a certainty, with the present budget to reach a horrendous deficit of $20 billion plus; a recession that would grow if the budget—by some miracle—were balanced.

A man of intelligence and ability, Cappy Weinberger would soon grasp these realities. But that he should have been named to a key economic post with so little preparation or qualification was part

---

*Actually, this arrangement was never consummated. Shultz realized that the greatest part of his power still derived from budgetary questions, and he quickly established himself as Weinberger's clear superior in both budgetary and management questions. With Weinberger having been selected directly by Nixon instead of at Shultz's recommendation, his relationship with Shultz was strained from the beginning.

of the President's limp approach to his most pressing domestic crisis. Weinberger's breakfast with the press on July 16, 1970, was a climax of sorts for the Nixon economic team's naïveté in believing that the unruly economy would quickly and promptly respond to simple remedies. It was a naïveté that extended to Richard Nixon himself.

VIII
The Reformer

The social measures passed in 1874–80 did something to make the lot of the urban masses less unhappy, less precarious and less unhealthy. Disraeli was at the head of the Administration that brought this about, and he encouraged the policy even if he did not concern himself with its details.

—Robert Blake, in *Disraeli*

Mr. Nixon is reported to be explaining himself to himself and to his inner circle as a sort of latter-day Disraeli . . . As Disraeli could do things the Liberals couldn't, so Mr. Nixon can do things Humphrey couldn't.

—Kenneth Crawford, in *Newsweek,*
September 1, 1969

At no time during his campaign for President in 1968 did Richard Nixon even faintly suggest the possibility of reforming the Internal Revenue Code, that tangled mass of special advantages which governed the great income-taxing system of the republic. What little Nixon did say about taxes during the 1968 campaign went in a direction opposite from that of basic tax reform, a concept that would strip away the accumulated deductions, credits and exemptions in the tax law, so that one man would pay income taxes at the same rate as the next, no matter how the money was made. To the contrary, candidate Nixon was proposing a whole new overlay of special tax allowances as incentives for socially desirable projects, such as business investment in the Negro slums.

And on the most venerable and publicly noxious of the special advantages, the 27.5 percent depletion allowance for oil, enacted in 1926, Nixon during the campaign reiterated his consistent support over some twenty years. "I continue to believe that America's security requires the maintenance of the current oil depletion allowance," Nixon said at Cleveland on September 13 as the campaign began, vowing his support again and again on campaign stops through oil-conscious Texas. Nor did tax reform hold much allure for the Nixon men at the Pierre Hotel during the interregnum. Asked privately just before the inauguration whether the new administration might seek middle-class votes through tax reform proposals, an aide close to the President on both political and economic questions replied, "On any realistic list of our priorities, I would think tax reform would be pretty close to dead last."

Yet, just two weeks to the day after the inauguration, the President privately informed Congressmen responsible for tax legislation that he would sponsor some kind of tax reform in 1969, making that news public later in the week. By mid-April, tax reform was high on the formal list of legislative projects submitted to Congress. As the year wore on, it became the Nixon administration's single most important legislative proposal for 1969, so much so that Nixon could tell a news conference on September 26 in dead seriousness: ". . . my primary concern is to get tax reform . . . We need that tax reform above everything else."

Tax reform was but the first element of a domestic reform program, not even contemplated during the 1968 campaign, that gradually took shape as 1969 progressed and would reach fruition with the unveiling of Nixon's New American Revolution in the January 1971 State of the Union Message to Congress—a development no less surprising in its totality than the sudden emergence of Nixon as a tax reformer. Not only in the 1968 campaign but throughout his whole political career, he had shown little interest in either the substance or the politics of reform. That he should suddenly assume the strange new role of reformer soon after entering the White House is in no small part the accomplishment of that most remarkable figure of the early Nixon months in the White House: Daniel Patrick Moynihan.

Moynihan had no part whatever in the President's sudden conversion to tax reform but was at the heart of Nixon's new self-image as reformer. Second only to his desire to buttress the legitimacy of government by accepting the important domestic programs of the Kennedy-Johnson administration, Moynihan wanted to push Nixon on a reform course that, though progressive, was compatible with Republican principles in their broadest sense, e.g., giving the poor cash payments instead of social services distributed through a governmental apparatus. In those long sessions alone with the President in the Oval Office at day's end, Moynihan appealed to Nixon's love of history and particularly the history of great men by talking of Benjamin Disraeli's role as reformer. Queen Victoria's great Conservative Prime Minister, Moynihan told the President, had proposed social-welfare reform legislation that the Liberals would neither dare to propose nor hope to pass, and had thereby gained lasting political support for the Tories from the working class.* Could Nixon now be the latter-day Disraeli, actually passing social reforms that the Democrats would not even propose because of automatic rejection by Republicans in Congress? That was just the sort of idea guaranteed to intrigue Richard Nixon, who began talking about it to other aides. "You know very well," Moynihan quoted Nixon as saying, "that it is the Tory men with liberal policies who have enlarged democracy."

The analogy with Disraeli was more apt than Nixon may have realized. Disraeli's personal involvement in the social reforms his party sponsored was casual as he concentrated on foreign policy, precisely in the Nixon pattern. Indeed, there was a hothouse quality about the Nixon reform. The original soil of major elements in the Nixon reform program—tax reform, income maintenance for the poor, consumer protection, environmental control—had been the liberal wing of the Democratic Party. Nixon found himself on this soil purely by chance—the chance that Pat Moynihan happened to be around to plead for income maintenance, the chance that a great public outcry for tax reform coincided with the Nixon Presidency, the chance that consumer protection and environmental control came of age in 1969. Moreover, if there had not been such an unusual

---

*When he left the White House in January 1971, Moynihan gave Nixon a reading list including *Disraeli*, the best-selling biography by Robert Blake. Nixon later recommended it to others and sent an autographed copy to Representative Hale Boggs of Louisiana, House Majority Leader.

vacuum in domestic policy planning when Nixon took office, programs so inherently alien to Nixon could scarcely have taken root there.

This hothouse quality undermined the Nixon reform program through his first two years in the Presidency. Inadequately grounded in ideology, the reforms were subject to constant internal haggling and revision. Intrigued though he was by Moynihan's Disraeli analogy and try though he might, Nixon simply could not generate within himself or his staff the moral fervor with which he pushed the antiballistic missile, the Supreme Court nominations of Judges Haynsworth and Carswell or the sustaining of Presidential vetoes. The subconscious message was evident: Those were the vital matters, but reform? Well, that's something to help me in the history books, something for tomorrow.

There had been no political interest whatever in tax reform for five years when Joseph W. Barr, promoted from Under Secretary to Secretary of the Treasury for the last month of the Johnson administration, traveled to Capitol Hill on January 17, 1969, to deliver a valedictory before the Joint Economic Committee of Congress.

Throughout the Eisenhower administration, liberal Democrats had demanded tax reform by removing special tax advantages for rich individuals and businesses (some of which had been added by a Republican administration and a Republican Congress in the tax revision of 1954). But when the Democrats gained office in 1961, the long-anticipated reform was a bitter disappointment. Operating on the theory that Congress would swallow the bitter medicine if enough sugar-coating were added, President Kennedy combined the biggest single income tax reduction in history with a wide-ranging but not very tough reform (not including any change in the 27.5 per-cent oil depletion allowance); predictably, Congress took the tax cut and rejected much of the tax reform in the 1964 tax act. Since then, except for Senator Robert F. Kennedy's brief campaign for the Presidency in 1968 which ended in his assassination, no serious American politician had talked tax reform. A new package of tax reforms had been prepared by technicians at the Treasury late in the Johnson administration, but President Johnson kept them bottled up until after the 1968 election and then reluctantly released them not as a Presidential program but only as a Treasury proposal. Mr. Taxation in Congress—Representative Wilbur Mills of Arkansas,

Chairman of the House Ways and Means Committee—had always been an advocate of tax reform, and in 1968 had scheduled exploratory hearings for 1969 to consider the new Treasury proposals, though without much hope of any legislation resulting. But late in December 1968, after a meeting at the Pierre with the President-elect, Mills decided that support for tax reform, both in the new administration and among the general public, was so skimpy that he would postpone indefinitely even those exploratory hearings.

This nadir for tax reform could scarcely be affected by the *pro forma* Congressional testimony of a lame-duck Secretary of the Treasury on his last working day in office. But unbelievably it was. Special advantages in the Internal Revenue Code, Secretary Barr told the Joint Committee, would cost the government more than $50 billion in lost revenue in 1969. Then Barr recited the words that would change the course of Congress and the administration for the next year: "I will hazard a guess that there's going to be a taxpayers' revolt in this country if we don't do something about it." That revolt, said Barr, would come not from the poor but from middle-income ($7,000–$20,000-a-year) taxpayers outraged over "the high-income recipients who pay little or no Federal income tax."*

Joe Barr struck an amazingly responsive chord in an overtaxed electorate increasingly harassed and unhappy. His forecast of a taxpayers' revolt sent torrents of spontaneous mail demanding tax reform pouring into the White House, the Treasury (more there in February than in all 1968) and Congressional offices. Representative John Byrnes of Wisconsin, a highly conservative and highly conscientious Republican from Green Bay, Wis., and his party's senior member of the Ways and Means Committee, had been brooding about the need for tax reform. He now moved rapidly. Scheduled to speak before the Tax Section of the New York Bar Association in New York on January 30, Byrnes sounded a vigorous demand for tax reform and, at the same time, urged action on the new Republican officials at the Treasury. Not to be outdone, Mills scheduled hearings by the Ways and Means Committee for February 18.

"We now regard this as an idea whose time has come," Under

---

*Barr's testimony was widely interpreted as an attack on the incoming administration. Writing in the *Washington Post,* Frank C. Porter called it "an indirect dig at President-elect Nixon's campaign proposals for tax credits for business manpower efforts in the ghetto."

Secretary Charls Walker was saying privately at the Treasury, urging the White House to conform to the new mood and back tax reform. On the late afternoon of February 3, two weeks to the day after his inauguration, Richard Nixon, David Kennedy at his side, entertained Mills and Byrnes at the White House and told them he now favored passage of some tax reform bill in 1969, although his new team at the Treasury could not possibly submit their own detailed proposals for many weeks to come.

In fact, the strategy plotted at the Treasury by Walker, and delegated broad responsibilities for legislation by Secretary Kennedy, was to appease Congress and public opinion with a minimal bill for 1969, gaining time to prepare a comprehensive bill for 1970. But the rising public demand forced Treasury technicians into a round-the-clock schedule to prepare a broader bill for 1969. Even that was not enough after Congressmen returned home for the Easter recess in mid-April and confronted a taste of that taxpayers' revolt Joe Barr had forecast. The folks back home, making out their federal tax returns in time for the April 15 deadline, were outraged to find the 7.5 percent surcharge on the income tax passed by Congress in 1968 at President Johnson's request to finance the Vietnam war. If we have to pay more taxes, they asked their Congressmen, why can't we have tax reform? The House passed the extension of that surtax, as requested by Nixon, but Senate Democrats—following the leadership of Senator Edward M. Kennedy, the new Senate Majority Whip—held the surtax as hostage for tax reform. Nixon had no choice but to bow to the will of Congress and public opinion on tax reform.

That, indeed, was the story of Nixon's first reform program, legislation for which his press agents and speech writers would claim full credit. At first, totally uninterested in tax reform, then failing to delay major action until 1970 and finally cornered into agreeing on a bill much wider in scope than he preferred, the President was never the master of the situation. Not since the Landrum-Griffin Labor Reform Act in 1959 had major legislation been drafted in such great part by Congress without domination by the administration. Congress, in turn, was responding to public opinion, threatening to pass a truly landmark tax reform bill as public reaction rose, but then, when the spontaneous taxpayers' revolt inevitably began losing steam in midsummer, it began responding to lobbyist pressures and greatly scaling back the attacks on special tax advantages. Disappointing though the final product was, the tax reform bill ended up as the most complicated single piece of tax legislation ever passed by Congress. And yet, despite its great importance, the President's role throughout the year-long struggle was little more than that of a spectator—and a not very interested spectator at that.

Nixon's interest in the tax reform fight seemed fitful, perking up occasionally when something caught his fancy but generally not focused on the major legislative struggle of his early months in office. This led to ever-intensifying bickering between the White House staff and the Treasury, and an unresolved ambivalence between the desire for tax reform to attract the middle-class voters and an equally strong desire to fulfill commitments made during the 1968 campaign. Overall, there seemed to be a general slackness of purpose.

For example, even after Nixon decided to go ahead with a tax reform intended to clear away exemptions and special advantages, Counsellor Arthur Burns and his staff at the White House were still pressing for the program of special tax incentives as a substitute for direct federal spending that candidate Nixon had promised in 1968 —one hand undoing what the other was trying to do. Through the winter and early spring of 1969, Burns pestered the Treasury endlessly to come up with some proposals to send to Congress. But the Treasury tax experts protested to Burns that there was no precise way to write into law a tax advantage for a good social purpose as contrasted to an indifferent social purpose.* Burns' staff suspected it was getting a run-around from the Treasury, and it may have been correct. As late as April 14, the President's special message to Congress on forthcoming domestic legislative proposals promised "a program of tax credits, designed to provide new incentives for the enlistment of additional private resources in meeting our urgent social needs." After that, silence. Burns finally gave up trying to move the Treasury, and the President never again mentioned the only positive tax proposal he had put forth during the entire campaign.

*The classic case the Treasury threw up to Burns was that of the Washington Hilton, a deluxe hotel for high-priced convention trade built in what qualified as a low-income, high-unemployment area. Would the Hilton Corporation be eligible for tax credits under the Burns proposals?

The same lack of hard commitment by the President was obvious when the Treasury reform program, drafted under intense deadline pressure, came to John Ehrlichman at the White House in April. Although the Treasury plan—essentially the work of Edwin Cohen, who had left the University of Virginia law faculty to become Assistant Secretary of the Treasury for Taxation—did not satisfy Mills, Byrnes or the other tax reformers in Congress, it did have some teeth. It was based on a concept called "minimum tax," contained in the Democratic but not the Republican platform of 1968, which provided that everybody with an income, even those with income carefully derived from areas excluded from taxation, should pay *some* tax —a *minimum* tax. Once in the White House, however, the teeth began to be pulled under Ehrlichman's supervision.

Arthur Burns objected to the inclusion of income from capital gains in the new minimum-tax provision. Out it went. The ubiquitous John Mitchell told the President that income from municipal tax-exempt bonds, a lucrative and favored tax shelter for the very rich, should not be subject to the minimum-tax provision either. Mitchell, a bond lawyer who had made his fortune marketing just such municipal issues, told Nixon the provision could not pass the Senate—undoubtedly true—and was unconstitutional—palpable nonsense in the opinion of Treasury lawyers. Out it went. The Treasury's plan was being eviscerated in Ehrlichman's office while Secretary Kennedy was in Guatemala on a government mission, and the process of evisceration reached its peak on a day that Under Secretary Walker happened to be at the Greenbrier Hotel in West Virginia for a speech.

Realizing that the tax reform was too weak for Congress even in the form it left the Treasury, Walker sought and won a personal appointment with the President to save what was left in the bill. It worked. What Walker and Cohen wanted from Nixon was to retain at least some tougher tax treatment of capital-gains income, perhaps the biggest tax shelter of all. At the meeting, Walker, backed by Budget Director Mayo, gained the support of Mitchell (who kept his own hand close to all these internal negotiations) and finally got the President's approval. Ehrlichman, who had been proposing elimination of the capital-gains proposal, said not a word during the meeting.

But it was a Pyrrhic victory for the Treasury. With Nixon not focusing on these questions, and probably not a little bored by them, he was susceptible to the persuasions of the last advocate who faced him—particularly if that last advocate had the Texas charm and palaver of Charley Walker. A professional economist, a Treasury veteran of Eisenhower vintage and a big-time Washington lobbyist when John Ehrlichman was arguing zoning cases in Seattle's law courts, Dr. Walker did not hesitate to argue a point with the President and argue it hard. He was, in short, precisely the type of departmental officer Haldeman and Ehrlichman least liked. After winning that capital-gains case against Ehrlichman in April, Walker was subsequently stopped from getting to the President by Haldeman's Berlin Wall. Never again was a policy-maker from the Treasury able to confront the President alone as an appellant to argue a controversial case.

This deepening hostility between White House staff and Treasury, exacerbated by the President's vagueness, reached a hot boil on the most politically volatile aspect of the tax reform: the emotion-drenched and dollar-rich oil depletion allowance. Oddly, here was the only provision of the Internal Revenue Code on which Nixon had an inflexible pre-Presidential position. Whatever else was done to business or the oil industry, the President made clear that not a percentage point—not a fraction of a percentage point—of that 27.5 percent must be touched! When the Treasury's original proposal came before Nixon in April and he spotted a proposed taxation change for the oil industry, the first thing he asked was: "Now, this doesn't change depletion, does it? I'm committed on depletion." He was assured that although the proposal did take away some tax advantages for the industry, it left the 27.5 percent sacrosanct and inviolable. But that position became more and more difficult to sustain because of a decision in March by Mills that if his tax reform bill were to have any credibility with liberals, it must make some reduction in the depletion allowance. In other words, the Treasury's alternative was not enough for either Mills or the liberals.

To stave off a cut in the depletion allowance by the House, Cohen and his Treasury tax lawyers in late June came up with a new twist. Carefully worked out, it would keep the depletion allowance at 27.5 percent but require that every last cent of tax benefits from the allowance had to be plowed back into petroleum exploration. The Treasury men thought it a beautiful gimmick to take the President

off the hook, but the President never saw it. It went to John Ehrlichman, and there it stopped. He neither passed it on to Nixon nor
commented on it.* The Treasury lawyers were furious, but self-
effacing David Kennedy would not think of barging into the Oval
Office to stick the important proposal under Nixon's nose.

When the House version of the tax bill, passed on August 2, cut
the depletion allowance 7.5 percentage points to 20 percent, a difficult Presidential decision obviously had to be made. The Treasury
team of Kennedy, Walker and Cohen came running to Nixon's beach
home at San Clemente, Calif., where the President spent much of the
summer of 1969, to find out what position they should take in the
Senate.† The Treasury men carried with them a memorandum for
spelling out three possible options for the President: No. 1, fight the
House action; No. 2, accept it; No. 3, propose the petroleum exploration scheme that had never gotten to the President's desk a month
earlier. Of the three options, the Treasury thought No. 2 would be
rejected out of hand.

Present at the meeting with the President at his beach house
were Ehrlichman, Haldeman, Flanigan, Arthur Burns and Paul
McCracken. What happened or did not happen at that meeting
would become the source of disagreements, mutual misunderstandings and recriminations far into the future, all of it stemming from
the President's own fuzziness on this as on so many other domestic
questions. And, as happened in other controversial meetings, the
Nixon administration once again suffered from its chronic occupa-
tional disease: failure of internal communication.

One version, coming from inside the White House, is simple
enough. According to it, Ehrlichman's staff had earlier presented an
option paper to Nixon and he had *then* made his choice: Oppose any
cut in the oil depletion allowance. At the meeting, he relayed his
decision to the Treasury men.

Quite a different train of events, however, is remembered by
others who attended the meeting. "Well," asked Nixon, "is Congress
going to cut the oil depletion allowance?" Yes, he was told, but the

*It is entirely possible that Ehrlichman, then deeply engrossed in the drafting of
the welfare reform, never saw the Treasury proposal.
†This was the same San Clemente meeting that decided to support a reduction
in the corporate income tax. See pp. 197–98.

final figure coming out of the Senate would be higher than 20 percent. "Well," Nixon replied, "we might as well go with it. Let's just accept it and go on from there." The Treasury team did not bother to present its petroleum exploration alternative.

Returning to Washington, the Treasury men set to work preparing Kennedy's testimony for Senate Finance Committee hearings, with Walker writing the section on the oil depletion allowance. The prepared testimony, read to the committee on September 4, contained this sentence: "Although the Administration did not recommend a cut in domestic percentage depletion, *we accept the House approach* to increasing the share of the national tax burden borne by the petroleum industry."* Big Oil and its allies in the Republican Party were apoplectic, the oilmen crying betrayal and threatening to abandon Nixon in 1972, the politicians demanding that the White House reverse Kennedy or face the loss of campaign contributors galore, not to mention the state of Texas.

John Ehrlichman complied by giving them something very close to reversal. Telephoning Republican members of the Senate Finance Committee, Ehrlichman said Dave Kennedy must have been confused at San Clemente because Dick Nixon certainly would never, ever, support a cut in the depletion allowance.

But private assurances would not be enough. Among the Texas politicians who had written the White House in wonder over Kennedy's testimony was Barbara C. Culver, a county judge from the West Texas oil country. Ehrlichman authorized Harry Dent, White House political aide, to reply to Judge Culver with a repudiation of Kennedy. "The President continues to stand by his campaign commitments," wrote Dent, adding that Kennedy "is to be corrected very soon." The Dent letter was given to national wire services on September 25, the very day that James Allison, Deputy Chairman of the Republican National Committee, was interviewed by Margaret Mayer, Washington correspondent for the *Dallas Times Herald.* Allison, a Texan, also had been primed by the White House and he took aim at Under Secretary Walker, producing front-page headlines in Dallas. "Walker is the culprit, and I think they ought to fire him . . . ," said Allison. "I think he has operated on his own without considering what the President said during his campaign. Up to now

*Emphasis is added.

nobody's stopped him." With the White House press in an uproar, Press Secretary Ron Ziegler added to the confusion by saying the President opposed the cut in the oil depletion allowance but would not fight it hard and "will abide by the judgment of Congress."

The hostilities produced by that incident would not soon subside. The high officials at the Treasury were furious at Ehrlichman and the White House for undercutting them and, they felt, undercutting the President. "Some of them don't think Nixon's smart enough to be President himself," snapped one Treasury man. Walker happened to meet Dent for the first time, and it was not pleasant. For their part, Ehrlichman and his men blamed Walker, who had become the strong man at the Treasury, for all the trouble—blame that would prevent Walker from succeeding Kennedy as Secretary the next year. And the two most important Texas Republicans, Senator John Tower and Representative George Bush, unsatisfied with Ziegler's comments, awaited Nixon's press conference the next day, September 26, to clear up the confusion once and for all.

The President was asked, of course, about the oil depletion allowance. His reply, so typical of his political style at less than its best, is worth quoting in full.

Question: You told an audience in Houston last fall that you opposed reduction of the oilmen's depletion allowance. Do you still oppose it?
The President: As a matter of fact, I not only told the audience in Houston that, but that has been my position since I entered politics in California 22 years ago. It is still my position.

I believe that the depletion allowance is in the national interest because I believe it is essential to develop our resources when, as we look at the Mideast and other sections of the world, many of the oil supplies could be cut off in the event of a world conflict.

On the other hand, I am a political realist. I noted the action of the House of Representatives in reducing the depletion allowance. Also, my primary concern is to get tax reform—the tax reform which we submitted in April, which goes further than any tax reform in 25 years. We need that tax reform above everything else.

Some of the items that I recommended, the House did not follow my recommendations, and the same will be [true] in the Senate. When the bill comes to my desk, I intend to sign that bill, even though it does not follow all of my recommendations—provided that it does not require a revenue shortfall. That is more than I believe the Nation can stand.

In this remarkable answer the President reaffirmed his support of percentage depletion, not only as a 1968 campaign commitment, but as a conviction of long standing born of national security concerns; neither criticized nor defended but simply ignored Kennedy and Walker, then under assault by the White House staff; took credit for "the tax reform we submitted in April," though, for good or evil, the reform was almost entirely the product of Congress; elevated the reform to such a priority that it was worth a reduction in the oil depletion allowance, although, in fact, the reform had been watered down dreadfully by September 26; vaguely threatened a veto if the bill resulted in too large a net loss of revenue.

The final version of the bill approved by Congress in December set the depletion allowance at 22 percent, rather lower than the Treasury had expected. The reform, in general, was disappointing. Without an administration determined to achieve real changes, the early resolve of the Congress wilted before the insistence of the lobbyists and the subsidence of the grass-roots taxpayers' revolt. The immense tax reductions, nonsensical economically, attached to the bill by Congress, put it far out of balance from a revenue standpoint.* Still, on December 30, the President signed it, ending his first venture as a domestic reformer, with liberals unimpressed, Big Oil outraged and his fiscal problems for the rest of his term further complicated.

As a campaigner, Richard Nixon had voiced the horror over expanding welfare rolls that had been a set piece for Republican orators in the 1960's: ". . . for those who are able to help themselves —what we need are not more millions on welfare rolls—but more millions on payrolls in the United States of America," he said in his Miami Beach acceptance speech, thereby fixing a formulation that he was to shout at scores of balloon-filled rallies between August and November. That welfare had become an acute political issue, particularly important to the Republicans, was obvious by the time the midterm campaign of 1966 began. White manual workers, the backbone of Democratic voting strength, were outraged by the Negro exodus from the South—poor blacks who would immediately begin drawing welfare payments in Northern cities at the expense of middle-class taxpayers. That amounted to a forced redistribution of

*See pp. 196 ff.

wealth encouraged by rich Democratic liberals who themselves did not suffer much from the redistribution because of tax advantages provided them by the Internal Revenue Code. Just such antagonisms of class and race, rubbed raw by Republican oratory, was one reason why conservative Republicans, such as Governor Ronald Reagan of California, had made serious inroads into the vote of the white workingman in 1966. To Nixon's strategists, the welfare issue was a possible lever for the emergence of the Republicans as the majority party by the end of the 1970s.

But once off the campaign platform, what should Nixon do about welfare? The Miami Beach formulation was, of course, no practical guide. Even in the less frenetic moments of his radio speeches, candidate Nixon dealt in generalities. In his paid April 25 address over CBS radio, he called for an "improved and streamlined form" of welfare (not using the word "reform") with incentives "for families to stay together" and "for supplementing welfare checks with part-time earnings." These vague proposals did not seem to advance Nixon's overall view, set forth in the April 25 speech, of making "welfare payments a temporary expedient" and ending "the 'custodial' approach which began in the New Deal."*

As usual, Nixon in 1968 made much more clear what he did *not* want: the use of direct cash payments as income maintenance for the poor—either in the framework of a guaranteed annual income or the negative income tax being proposed by one of his outside conservative advisers, Professor Milton Friedman—to supplement or replace the welfare system. On May 15, 1968, Nixon said, ". . . at the present time, I do not see a reasonable prospect that I will recommend . . . a guaranteed annual income or a negative income tax. . . ." The prospect became no more reasonable later in Nixon's campaign—a fact that influenced his postelection task force on welfare, headed by economist Richard Nathan. The Nathan report was scarcely relevant to Nixon's campaign oratory about putting those on the welfare rolls onto the payrolls and, instead, would raise federal welfare costs by establishing national standards in minimum

---

*In fact, the New Deal was just as unhappy with the "custodial" approach. "What I am seeking is the abolition of relief altogether," wrote Franklin D. Roosevelt in a 1934 letter to Colonel E. M. House. "I cannot say so out loud yet, but I hope to be able to substitute work for relief." Roosevelt did not succeed and neither did Nixon.

payments to be met by the states. But Nathan, who was to become an Assistant Director of the Budget, made sure his task force kept away from the forbidden region of income maintenance.

That also was the view of Pat Moynihan, who, two years before entering the Nixon White House, had rejected both Friedman's negative income tax and the guaranteed annual income schemes of Democratic liberals but had endorsed a different form of income maintenance widely practiced by Western European governments—children's allowances, fixed cash sums to be paid to families for each child.* Feeling that such a scheme was too radical for any Republican administration to accept, Moynihan was prepared to concentrate on federal standards for welfare recommended by Nathan's task force against the predictable opposition from Burns.

What changed Moynihan's outlook and persuaded him to raise his sights was the first meeting of the Welfare Subcommittee of the new Urban Affairs Council (with Nixon not present) late in January a few days after the inauguration. Robert Finch, then still the self-confident Presidential confidant and leader of the progressive forces in the Nixon administration, presented a paper recommending revisions in the welfare law that he had inherited from the HEW bureaucracy. While avoiding the incendiary words "guaranteed annual income," that is precisely what it amounted to.

Wow, let's see what happens here! Moynihan said to himself. Strangely, nothing much did. Three Cabinet members present—Mitchell, Stans and Romney—missed the point entirely and failed to recognize Finch's paper as a direct contradiction of Nixon's campaign pledge against income-maintenance plans. Doubtless, Finch himself did not realize he was detonating a bombshell. Other than Moynihan, only one man present perceived the significance of the HEW paper: Dr. Martin Anderson, a brilliant young conservative intellectual who was Dr. Burns' deputy and was sitting in for him at that subcommittee meeting. As Finch read the paper Anderson's eyes almost popped out of his head.

As a veteran bureaucratic tactician, Moynihan decided the best ploy was to treat the income-maintenance proposals in Finch's paper as routine, everyday ideas that ought to shock nobody. He routinely

*Moynihan's proposal was contained in *The Crises in Welfare,* a background paper he prepared for a symposium on social welfare sponsored by Governor Nelson Rockefeller in 1967.

directed the Urban Affairs Council to make estimates of how much the proposals would cost. But Anderson would not stand for that and demanded a discussion of the merits of the plan. "Now, wait a minute," Anderson demanded. "Let's call a spade a spade."

"Anybody who wants to call a spade a spade," replied Moynihan in a gracious *non sequitur* of the kind he frequently employed to enliven the administration's councils, "should be made to use one." In a flash of intuition, Moynihan realized that the frame of reference on welfare had shifted dramatically leftward. When Anderson challenged the income-maintenance plan, Moynihan correctly perceived this as tacit evidence that Burns and Anderson now would be willing to accept Nathan's recommendation of minimum standards and that the real debate would be over income maintenance.

A few days later, appearing on our syndicated television show taped on January 29 for use on February 2, Moynihan went public on the income-maintenance question: "I feel the problem of the poor people is they don't have enough money and I would sort of put my faith in any effort that put more resources into the hands of those that don't now have them . . . Cold cash! It's a surprisingly good cure for a lot of social ills." Later in the program, however, when asked whether the American people would accept the concept of family-allowance payments, Moynihan replied, "I don't know. I think probably they wouldn't."

Nor did it seem probable that Nixon would accept it with Burns opposing Moynihan in what then seemed a mismatch in Burns' favor. On his side, Burns had the conventional Republican philosophy, shared by Richard Nixon with every fiber of his soul, that nobody ought to get paid for doing nothing. Besides, Moynihan's early draft of the welfare reform, containing a plan for income-maintenance payments to families, was put together rapidly with many technical deficiencies, all of which were quickly spotted by Burns and pointed out to the President. Finch was Moynihan's only ally in the Cabinet in the early going; all the rest were either unconcerned or actively supporting Burns. Finally, Burns thought the battle was very nearly won when, during an early meeting, the President said, "Look, one thing is certain. I'm not going to have a guaranteed annual income."

But Burns did not know his old friend Dick Nixon as well as he thought. He could not begin to imagine the quiet successes Moynihan would have with the President in those late afternoon chats in

the Oval Office and those beautifully written memoranda. As Moynihan put it to Nixon, the idea of substituting cold cash for bureaucratic services was a quintessentially conservative idea. Thanks to
Moynihan, Nixon for the first time began to think of himself as a
reform President, a Disraeli passing what the liberals dared not
propose. The welfare reform was described to him as the first truly
landmark social reform since Franklin D. Roosevelt's Social Security
was passed in 1935, and, as such, certain to be loudly applauded by
the most intractable Nixonphobes in the press and intelligentsia.
This appeal to Nixon's sense of history, his love of novelty and
his desire for approbation from those who had so long despised him,
far outweighed his conservative misgivings. Very early in the
game, Moynihan had defeated Burns in the battle for the President's
mind.

Still, one oppressive question weighed heavily on Nixon: How
could any social reform as radical as income maintenance be acceptable to that Nixon-Wallace constituency of 1968 which the President
and John Mitchell wanted to preserve for 1972? The answer came,
partly by accident, from George Shultz. The Secretary of Labor,
busy with other matters, had been only a tangential observer of the
Moynihan-Burns struggle. But later that winter during an Urban
Affairs Council discussion presided over by Nixon, Shultz commented, quite impromptu, that what Moynihan's plan needed was
something to take care of the working poor. That strongly appealed
to Nixon, who had been impressed by Shultz's quiet, intelligent
manner in such meetings. Shortly thereafter, Shultz was summoned
by Nixon to the Oval Office and asked to work out some proposals
that would put a greater premium on the need for everybody to work,
as Nixon had suggested back in that radio speech of a year earlier.
Shultz responded with precisely what the President wanted: work
requirements (all welfare recipients except the disabled and mothers
with preschool children would have to go to work if it was available)
and work incentives (the family allotments would go to the working
poor as well as the unemployed, thereby ending the existing situation
whereby a family head was better off accepting welfare than working).

Shultz's contribution to the welfare reform was to have far-
reaching implications. First of all, it was the making of George
Shultz. Henceforth he would be consulted by Nixon on all matters
of domestic importance and, in little more than a year, would gain

enough authority to approach the status of Deputy President. It was also, in perhaps lesser degree, the making of John Ehrlichman. Called upon to synthesize Moynihan's proposal, Shultz's addition and Burns' objections, Ehrlichman produced the final version—thereby pinning down his status as chief domestic-policy staffer in the White House, toward which he had been rapidly evolving all winter. It also firmly established the Nixon practice of using conservative rhetoric to hide an essentially radical program. Shultz's somewhat humdrum work requirements were exaggerated out of all proportion in relation to Moynihan's landmark income-maintenance scheme.* And, most immediately, it ended the last slim chance that Burns might defeat Moynihan's program. Once Shultz made his contribution, the issue was settled. Late in May, Nixon instructed Ehrlichman to tell Moynihan that he had decided, in principle, to accept his program.

But nobody told Arthur Burns! Through June and July, he worked to defeat the still-unpublicized plan. Doubtful now of his own ability to influence Nixon's thinking, Burns worked around Nixon, wooing other members of the Cabinet with remarkable success. George Romney, a liberal but also an ardent defender of the Puritan Ethic, inveighed endlessly against family payments. Burns also recruited Vice President Agnew, who told Nixon that the plan was ill-conceived in many ways—particularly, he said, in neglecting the welfare of children—and ought to be delayed until improvements could be made. Desperately anxious to roll out a domestic reform program of his very own, Nixon replied to Agnew that he would *never* have a program if it had to satisfy *everybody*. "I'm not sure this is just right," he added, "but we've got to make a start." Naturally, Burns did not neglect John Mitchell, the strong man of the Cabinet. Mitchell agreed with Burns' position and told him he would so inform the President. In formal Cabinet-level sessions, Mitchell said nothing about welfare (though he seldom said anything about any subject at such sessions); whether or not he mentioned welfare to Nixon in one of their daily private chats, it is clear he made no strong

---

*As reports of the new program began to leak out, the White House was anxious to stress Shultz's work requirements as the heart of the bill. Presidential aides were most unhappy when our column of July 25 predicted "a welfare reform that comes close to being an outright income maintenance program."

appeal. And by the summer of 1969, nothing less than a strong appeal from John Mitchell would have been enough to change Nixon's mind. Opposition from Romney, Agnew, Stans and the great majority of the Cabinet made no difference. "I have the pleasure of holding a poker hand nobody can beat," Moynihan told an aide.

The occasion to show that hand came at a Cabinet meeting that was one of the more curious episodes of the first year of the Nixon administration. Returning to Washington on August 3 from his wildly successful reception in Rumania, Nixon scheduled a Cabinet meeting for August 6 at Camp David, the Presidential retreat in the Catoctin Mountains of Maryland. In a euphoric mood after his Rumanian triumph, Nixon planned to have staffers from the White House and HEW brief the Cabinet, who would then debate the welfare reform. But Nixon really did not expect much of a debate. As soon as it became evident to members of the Cabinet that the President was committed, they would give their assent.*

And anybody with the slightest sensitivity could have seen that the President had his mind made up. He was absolutely delighted by the briefing by Robert E. Patricelli, a twenty-nine-year-old Deputy Assistant Secretary at HEW. Turning to an aide, Nixon asked of Patricelli, a Phi Beta Kappa, Fulbright scholar and Harvard Law graduate: "How do you get that smart?"

But most of the members of Nixon's Cabinet were not that sensitive. Burns was lobbying Cabinet members to oppose the program right up to the last minute and, once the briefing was concluded, again presented his objections. So did Agnew, Kennedy and Romney. In fact, Romney, incorrectly assuming that this was the last stage of the struggle for the President's mind, presented his arguments with that typical brand of Romney passion not once, not twice but three times. As the zealous Romney launched into his arguments

*Nixon attempted much the same ploy during the 1960 Republican National Convention in Chicago when, after being nominated for President, he called the party elders together to discuss the selection of a nominee for Vice President. Actually, Nixon had already made up his mind about choosing Ambassador Henry Cabot Lodge but wanted to have a charade of a debate which he would control in such a way that Lodge would seem to be the spontaneous choice of the party leaders. As it turned out, Lodge drew more opposition than support from the leaders, who were more than a little irritated when they finally realized Nixon had already decided on Lodge and was merely using them.

for that third time, a tight-lipped Haldeman turned to the man next to him and snarled, "If Romney says that once more, this will probably be his last Cabinet meeting."

The situation was becoming ludicrous: Cabinet members opposing a decision which they did not comprehend had already been made by the President; Nixon unwilling to curb them by admitting that the Cabinet meeting he had convened was not intended seriously to debate the question. It was Mel Laird who saved the day.

As soon as Romney finished his third tirade against the bill with Haldeman's temper rising, Laird broke in to object to the "Fair Share" name given the income-maintenance plan by White House aide William Safire. "Mr. President," said Laird, "I don't like the name of this thing at all. Fair Share. It sounds like Harry Truman's Fair Deal." It was that hoary bureaucratic ploy of deflecting unprofitable debate away from substance to labels, and it worked splendidly.* By this time, most of the Cabinet members had begun to realize that the President's decision had already been made and they had placed themselves in the impossible position of opposing it. So, eagerly, they pulled out their pencils and engaged in a protracted discussion of a new name for the income-maintenance program that they opposed. They decided on Family Security, but later it was changed to Family Assistance Payments (which quickly became known by its acronym, FAP).

Nixon was quite pleased by the four-hour meeting, taking some pleasure in the fact that he had acted against the wishes of a majority of his Cabinet. Immediately after the Camp David session, he reminded an aide of the famous but probably apocryphal Lincoln story that, when opposed by his entire Cabinet on issuance of the Emancipation Proclamation, Lincoln had declared, "The ayes are one, the nays are nine; the ayes have it."†

In a televised address to the nation on domestic programs three days later, Nixon unveiled his welfare reform with an income-maintenance plan of at least $1,600 per family, smoothed over by

*Nixon had used the same technique in April during the Urban Affairs Council debate on Model Cities. See p. 41.

†In that conversation with his aide, Nixon speculated that, had a vote of Cabinet members been taken it would have been 12 against him with only Finch, Shultz and Rumsfeld supporting the President's position. Nixon then thought a moment and changed his mind. No, he said, Laird would have voted for it too, making the vote 11 to 4.

conservative rhetoric ("There is no reason why one person should be taxed so that another can choose to live idly").

Just as programmed, the approval from left and right was remarkable. On the right, it was applauded by columnists James Jackson Kilpatrick and David Lawrence, the *Chicago Tribune,* and Representative James Utt of California (perhaps the member of Congress farthest to the right). On the left, it was applauded by columnist TRB of *The New Republic,* by the *Washington Post* and the *New York Times* and by Representative John Conyers of Michigan (perhaps the member of Congress farthest to the left). It was a high point for Nixon, Social Reformer.

But doubts set in quickly as to whether Nixon was sincere about pushing the bill through Congress or was merely seeking headlines. The charge was false, but there were grounds for making it. Through the rest of 1969, Nixon was so preoccupied with foreign policy that he seemed to have forgotten this hothouse project.* With welfare reform seemingly destined by a critical Wilbur Mills for burial in his Ways and Means Committee, some White House aides were already talking privately in the past tense—commenting that Nixon could go to the voters in the midterm 1970 campaign and tell the voters that Congress had failed to crack down on welfare chiselers by refusing to pass the President's legislation.†

The growing feeling among liberals that the President wanted to kill his own most liberal creation was encouraged on January 13, 1970, when Finch, in an address to the National Press Club, excoriated Mills for not acting on the bill. "This most revolutionary social proposal since the '30s . . . is being threatened with 'death by invisibility' at the hands of a Congress apparently too preoccupied with other matters even to offer alternative reform proposals of its own," said Finch. Chairman Mills was predictably enraged, commenting to friends that Bob Finch was either stupid or trying to kill the bill on Nixon's orders and that he felt the latter was true. In fact, it was not, although nobody unfamiliar with the mysterious inner workings of the Nixon administration could believe it. The truth was

---

*After his welfare message to Congress, Nixon did not mention the program on nationwide television and brought it up on only four other occasions in 1969, and each of those times only in passing.

†To some extent, he attempted just this in the 1970 campaign, albeit unsuccessfully. See Chapter XI.

that Finch had acted wholly on his own, without the knowledge of the President or his staff. Chief White House lobbyist William Timmons was horrified, not only for the sake of welfare reform but out of anxiety over the impact of Finch's speech on the administration's relations with Mills across the board. Less certainly, but quite probably, the genuine objective of Finch's harsh remarks was to prod Mills into action on the bill.

At about the same time, the conservative consensus on behalf of welfare reform was breaking up. Two days after Finch's Press Club speech, James Jackson Kilpatrick published a column that began: "President Nixon served up his welfare proposals last August, wrapped in a package of pretty rhetoric and tied with a bow of conservative blue. Sad to say, some of us who should have known better were fairly swept off our feet. I hereby repent." Kilpatrick's public repentance, widely syndicated and widely quoted, had a measurable effect in reducing conservative support for the program.

Then came the unexpected. Without warning late in February the Ways and Means Committee—under Mills' prodding—approved the welfare reform bill with scarcely a comma changed from the administration's proposal. The bill was passed with *too* much cooperation, warts and all, just as it left the White House, without the fine tuning usually expected from Mills as a subtle legislative craftsman. Irked by Finch's taunts, had Mills decided to let Nixon stew in his own juice by sending an imperfect bill to the Senate? Mills denied it. The White House believed it.

Senator John Williams of Delaware, the flinty conservative about to retire from public life, led adamant Republican opposition inside the Senate Finance Committee. As the administration made changes to conform to Williams' objections, however, the National Welfare Rights Organization—a radical organization of welfare recipients—energized liberals on the Finance Committee against it. Caught in this left-right cross fire, the welfare reform died of suffocation in the Finance Committee as the Ninety-first Congress ended.

But there were still hopes for passage in the Ninety-second Congress, and, in any event, welfare reform had been a high point of Richard Nixon's first two years. It displayed him as no mere Republican nay-sayer; it proved he could take a radical position. It was the source of his self-conception as a reformer. But its failure in a Democratic Congress demonstrated the limitations imposed on

Nixon as an American Disraeli able to accomplish what no liberal could.

If welfare reform was a high point in the emergence of Nixon as reformer, his anti-hunger proposals were close to a low point—reinforcing hostility to the outside world of liberals and revealing the inadequacy of cloaking progressive measures with conservative rhetoric.

As Nixon entered the White House, concern about hunger in America was rising as one of those evanescent political issues that flourish briefly and then subside. But with such voluble liberal Democrats as Senator George McGovern of South Dakota whipping up sentiment, politicians of both parties suspected, wrongly as it turned out, that hunger would be a major issue for the 1970 campaign. Moynihan's Urban Affairs Council staff set to work on the problem immediately and, in the spring, had some specific proposals for the President. On May 6 Nixon revealed to Congress his program for distribution of free food to the poor, and plans (following a Moynihan recommendation) to convene a White House conference on food and nutrition later in the year, pledging to "put an end to hunger in America for all time." On June 11 he appointed (again on Moynihan's suggestion) Dr. Jean Mayer of the Harvard Medical School, a world-famous nutritionist, as full-time Special Consultant to the President to run the conference.

There was nobody in the administration quite like Jean Mayer, a naturalized American citizen who fought with the French maquis during the Nazi occupation of France and served with the French Foreign Legion. Flamboyant, tough, liberal, and a registered political independent in Massachusetts, he did not follow the example of his Harvard colleagues, Moynihan and Kissinger, in fitting snugly into the White House as loyal Nixonians.* His primary concern was

---

*The difference was pointed up during the November 1969 antiwar demonstrations in Washington. Leaving the White House in the evening to attend a Georgetown dinner party, Mayer had to pass through the ranks of a silent procession, consisting mainly of young people, mourning the Vietnam war dead and protesting Nixon's war policy. Mayer felt guilty about being on the opposite side and having to pass what was, in effect, a picket line. When Kissinger arrived (late as usual) at the same dinner party, Mayer expressed his feelings and asked whether Kissinger, too, did not feel a little guilty. "Not a bit," snapped back Kissinger brightly. "Why should I?"

promoting his own ideas about combating hunger and malnutrition, not being a servant to the best interests of the administration.

As viewed by the White House staff, especially Moynihan, Mayer never joined the team but played the role of free agent. To Mayer, the White House staff, especially Moynihan, was excessively political. Peter Flanigan, anxious to make sure that no anti-Nixon oratory seeped out of the White House conference, insisted that Mayer get clearances from the FBI, CIA and IRS on all of the some four thousand delegates to the conference (including some seven hundred representatives of the poor, many of them with criminal records who were bound to fail an FBI clearance). Flanigan even insisted on a security clearance for the famed Archbishop Fulton Sheen of Buffalo because he was "a little pink." Through Flanigan, objections were relayed to Mayer over his attacks on the nutritional deficiencies of "fun foods." These objections came from food processors and included some powerful figures in the Republican Party (particularly Donald Kendall, chief of Pepsi-Cola). But more troublesome to Mayer was his fellow Harvardian and liberal, Moynihan. "Pat has turned out to be one hell of a pain in the neck," Mayer told a friend in the summer of 1969. What particularly irritated Mayer was that Moynihan was trying to exclude from the conference not only critics of Nixon but critics of Moynihan. Moynihan also blocked an invitation to Senator McGovern to address the conference on grounds that he would make a partisan attack on Nixon.*

But Mayer had weapons to use against the White House staff that Cabinet members, at least in 1969, either could not or would not employ. When political interference thrown up by members of the White House staff grew intolerable, Mayer *demanded* to see the President. If his demand was ignored, the White House staff realized, Mayer might well resign with an embarrassing public blast against the President. Invariably, when Mayer began pressuring to visit Nixon, the political interference that had been troubling Mayer magically vanished and this message was relayed from Haldeman: Now that we've taken care of your problem, do you *still* want to see the President? Just as invariably, Mayer would insist on keeping his appointment.

---

*Instead, Senator Walter Mondale of Minnesota was invited as the Democratic speaker. He responded by attacking Nixon with partisan zeal that McGovern would have been hard put to equal.

Those meetings with the President went well. Although Nixon pleaded budgetary limitations as the reason for not going quite so far as Mayer wanted in feeding the poor, he was characteristically polite and nonargumentative. Mayer perceived in both the President and Mrs. Nixon an empathy for those too poor to eat well, derived from their own backgrounds of relative poverty. Nevertheless, there were two basic problems between the President and the nutritionist from Harvard that made their final break inevitable.

The first problem was the inescapable incompatibility between Mayer's plans to feed the poor and Moynihan's plans to give them "cold cash." Considering budgetary limitations, Moynihan wanted every dollar available for Family Assistance Payments. So, when Moynihan and Nathan briefed the press on welfare reform at San Clemente, in August 1969, Nathan commented nonchalantly that the cash payments would take the place of the food-stamp program —newly expanded under Nixon's anti-hunger program. Mayer, left back in Washington while the entire White House had planted itself in San Clemente for the summer ("like a goddamn banana republic," Mayer groaned to an aide), was outraged—and impotent. For three days he was unable to contact either Ehrlichman or Burns in California. Finally, however, he got his message across: Make it clear that Family Assistance Payments do not preclude the food-stamp program or I'll quit. Nor was any doubt left that his resignation would be noisy. Consequently the White House staff authorized a statement by Ron Ziegler in San Clemente resurrecting food stamps. But Moynihan then quietly passed the word among his associates that once Mayer left following the White House conference in December, food stamps would be doomed. The President, fond of both Moynihan and Mayer and seemingly dedicated to both cash payments and food stamps, remained aloof—a common posture for him in intramural policy disputes.

The second problem was more basic and more general in application. While spending more money and devoting more attention to feeding the poor than any administration (including Lyndon Johnson's), Nixon did not want to talk about taking the hard-earned tax dollars of his middle-class constituency to feed the undeserving poor. In his application of the Disraeli theme, the President wanted to hide progressive reform with conservative rhetoric. To Jean Mayer, this was exactly wrong. Conservatives are interested mainly in money, said Mayer, and liberals are interested mainly in rhetoric. So, Nixon was getting the worst of two worlds by taking money away from the conservatives (who couldn't care less for rhetoric) and failing to provide the rhetoric craved by the liberals (who did not appreciate the money).

The question came to a head on December 1 on the eve of the White House Conference on Food, Nutrition and Health. Against Moynihan's wishes, Mayer had gained an audience in the Oval Office with the leaders of the conference to plead with the President to brighten up the limp address of welcome to the conference he had prepared for the next day. Mayer's argument was that a more sympathetic, more emotional approach—particularly rhetorical pledges to fight hunger—would dampen anti-Nixon sentiment that was roaring up among the conference's delegates. No more substantive measures were needed, said Mayer; only rhetoric. Cordial as ever, the President refused.

From the White House standpoint, the conference at the Washington Hilton Hotel was a fiasco. The President's cool speech got a comparably cool reception, his aides carefully noting that he was interrupted not once by applause. Once Nixon left the hotel, there was plenty of applause. "For God's sake, feed the hungry!" shouted the Reverend Ralph Abernathy, the civil rights leader, getting a standing ovation and setting the emotional tone of the conference. Leaders of the conference's eight task forces concentrated more on attacking Richard Nixon than on attacking hunger, calling his proposals "feeble and inadequate" and saying that he "has not reached the level of understanding we have reached."

"Ungrateful wretches," snapped Moynihan in the privacy of the White House, where there was a quiet resolve never to hold another such conference where arrangements got beyond their control and into the hands of a nonpolitical professor.*

The dreary postcript came in 1971. When he first accepted the post as special consultant, Mayer obtained a personal commitment from Nixon that a follow-up conference would be held a year later. But once Mayer returned to Harvard, nothing happened. The White

---

*Accordingly, the decennial White House Conference on Children scheduled for 1970 was put in the loyal hands of Stephen Hess, one-time speech writer for President Eisenhower, sometime aide to (and biographer of) Richard Nixon, and Moynihan's deputy on the Urban Affairs Council staff.

House simply did not want a recurrence of the 1969 conference. Two letters from Mayer went unanswered. Finally, Mayer made it clear to Dick Nathan, now in charge of the anti-hunger program, that he would publicly attack the administration if the follow-up conference was not held. It was subsequently scheduled, but in such a way as to make it almost invisible and to prevent a great outpouring of radicals. The place—relatively inaccessible Williamsburg, Va.; the date—February 5, 1971, the day of the Apollo XIV landing on the moon, an event that would dominate the news and preoccupy the press. Nixon did not attend. In fact, at the last minute, even Nathan found himself too busy to go. What little did appear in print about the Williamsburg follow-up was acidly hostile to Nixon.

Although he had done more to feed the hungry than any other President, Nixon did not—indeed, could not—capitalize on his achievement. The hunger issue had shown the limitations of the Tory playing radical reformer, Nixon-style.

Even before his inauguration, Richard Nixon had in his hands a memo from Roy Ash, president of Litton Industries, recommending that the application of sound business methods to the Executive Office of the President was overdue. "The many departments involved and the multi-faceted programs to achieve domestic goals preclude the same personal role in domestic affairs as he plays in foreign ones," wrote Ash, reinforcing Nixon's own convictions. "The President cannot and should not also be the 'domestic desk officer.' " What was needed, Ash continued, was a new mechanism inside the Office of the President to pull together and unify all domestic programs. The Bureau of the Budget, established during the administration of Warren Harding to coordinate fiscal affairs for the rapidly expanding federal government, could not perform this task because its "value system . . . has not been as much one of perceiving and articulating national goals and objectives as one of budget economizing—of making the proposed expenditures fit the funds available. By now, the connotations that go with the name 'Bureau of the Budget' substantially limit its broader effectiveness."

Thus an industrialist's memorandum written in the turgid prose of American business began the Nixon reform which would be most faithful to Republican principles, least political in intent and perhaps most permanent in its implications. Remembering the unsatisfactory and slow-moving reorganization commissions headed by Herbert Hoover during the Truman and Eisenhower administrations, Nixon and Ash agreed on a small blue-ribbon commission to propose quick reforms. A spacious office in the Executive Office Building next door to the White House was reserved for Ash, who would head a five-member Advisory Council on Executive Management. This was no hothouse flower but a typical Republican growth based on the party's deeply held feeling that it could apply sound business techniques to the chaos of government.

But, strangely, this type of reform interested Richard Nixon considerably less than the exotic concept of income maintenance or Pat Moynihan's heady talk of a new Disraeli. He did tell the council that he wanted reorganization to give him better control over the government, expressing dismay over his inability to make his wishes known to Cabinet members.* During the council's periodic reports, however, the President's eyes would glaze. "Is this going to be effective?" he would ask. "All of you have been in the business world. You should know how to do it." He wanted reassurance, but he did not want to get too involved in all the boring details.

Unlike the public proceedings of the Hoover commissions, the Ash council worked in utmost secrecy. Its staff members were forbidden to take home documents or even notes but had to deposit everything in "burn bags" for destruction, in the manner of the National Security Council staff dealing with top-secret material. Although their work would profoundly change the Bureau of the Budget, Budget Director Robert Mayo was kept in the dark. So were Cabinet members, threatened with further loss of influence as a result of the Ash reforms.

But the senior staff at the White House was well aware of the Ash council and the direction it was going in the summer of 1969: an expanded, reorganized Bureau of the Budget taking over management functions, plus an expanded, reorganized White House domestic staff for policy decisions. Don Rumsfeld made one audacious attempt to seize control of the domestic policy-making by transforming his Cabinet-level Council on Economic Opportunity, restricted

---

*One member of the Ash council, retired AT&T Chairman Francis Kappel, simply could not understand Nixon's problem. "When I'm not communicating with somebody in *my* organization," he said, "*I* just put on my hat and go see the man."

to poverty matters, into the instrument for domestic policy. But this role was destined for John Ehrlichman, who was mainly interested in making sure that the White House staff did not surrender too many powers—specifically, control over new legislation—to the reorganized Budget Bureau.

Other, less ambitious staffers at the White House had fewer personal concerns as they learned what the Ash council was up to. Wise Bryce Harlow wondered whether, in the name of efficiency, an immense institutionalized bureaucracy was being forged inside the White House that would forever after alter the nature of American government. With Ash council plans ultimately calling for some two hundred additional staffers in the Executive Office of the President, how could the Cabinet-level departments hope to retain any lasting influence? The plans even aroused some doubts among members of the Ash council. Francis Kappel, formerly of American Telephone and Telegraph, wondered why in the world so many new staff members were needed. Some thoughtful Ash council staffers pondered whether they were not duplicating the Soviet system, centralizing all functions of government within the Executive's immediate staff. Moreover, since Congressional supervision is geared to the Cabinet-level departments, their loss of power threatened to reduce the power of Congress to oversee the Executive and hence alter the Constitutional system of checks and balances. But whether any of this soul-searching got as far as the President is doubtful.

In October, the Ash council finished its recommendations for the Executive Office of the President and, through a staffer, asked for a date to present them to the President. Dwight Chapin, Haldeman's aide who managed the President's schedule, came back with a shocker. "It has been decided," he said, that the council would report not to Nixon but to Haldeman and Ehrlichman. Who had decided that? "It has been *decided,*" Chapin repeated. Clearly, Haldeman and Ehrlichman, fearful of what the council might do with the White House staff, wanted to maintain control of the report, passing muster on it and perhaps amending it before it got to Nixon. So Ash himself telephoned Haldeman and a compromise was arranged. The report would first go to Haldeman and Ehrlichman, but then, untouched, would automatically be relayed to the President.

Handed the report, Ehrlichman immediately snapped that he

didn't like it. "But, John," said Haldeman, "you haven't read it yet." When these two top aides realized the report would enlarge, not diminish, their power, they agreed to it without protest. The President's own approval quickly followed. In its original form, the plan proposed that the big new Budget Bureau be renamed the Office of Executive Management with an enlarged White House domestic staff to be organized under a Domestic Policy Council, consisting of all domestic Cabinet members (later to be renamed the Domestic Council).

As a first public step toward reorganization, Nixon on November 4 officially installed Ehrlichman as chief of the White House domestic staff, a function he had been performing for some time. With the Urban Affairs Council going out of business, Moynihan was given the Cabinet rank of Counsellor. Thereafter, he faded as a significant factor in making policy. But the Ash reforms were not perfected and made public until the following March.

Shortly before that, George Shultz, who would replace Mayo in charge of the reorganized Budget Bureau, was told about the plan. His only suggestion was that to remove the word "budget" from the new title—a word with historical connotations and implications of power—was a political mistake. The Office of Management and Budget (OMB) resulted. But when the new plan was formally presented to the Cabinet in a session at the Green Room of the White House on March 4, 1970, Romney and Volpe, typically outspoken, dissented with hostile questioning as soon as Ash finished his briefing. Would this not further dilute the power of Cabinet members to make policy?

The reply came not from Ash but from John B. Connally, the millionaire Houston lawyer, conservative Democrat, three-term former Governor of Texas, one-time protégé of Lyndon B. Johnson and Ash council member. Able to make black seem white, Connally, with eloquence and tact, calmed the fears of the Cabinet members. Nixon was duly impressed. Considering his difficulties with the Democratic Congress, he was further impressed and, later, took note for future reference when Connally traveled the corridors of Capitol Hill the next few days to lobby the Democratic powers there and persuade them that the new plan would not diminish their power to oversee the government. Surprisingly, Congress did not veto the reorganization, although the plan did, in fact, protect the executive branch behind the opaque walls of the White House as never before. Congress did not even debate the matter very much. With little debate, scant public attention and no great effort on his own part, Richard Nixon had effected a fundamental change in the very fabric of the federal government whose long-range meaning no one could even guess.

The President, who had not mentioned "reform" in his campaign, sent Congress a message on October 13, 1969, that said: "We intend to begin a decade of government reform such as this nation has not witnessed in half a century . . . That is the watchword of this Administration: *Reform.* "* In that message, Nixon listed welfare reform, draft reform, tax reform, revenue reform, Social Security reform, reform of the grant-in-aid system, electoral reform, District of Columbia government reform, OEO reform, reform of foreign aid and new initiatives to feed the hungry and control the growth of population. In his first State of the Union Message to Congress four months later, he would propose a major program for environmental reform.

Pat Moynihan had done his work well. Richard Nixon was embarked on a wide-ranging program of reform that could not have been envisioned nine months earlier. But there was no great public applause and more than a little public criticism. Columnists accused Nixon of zigzagging, going left on his reform administration after moving right on civil rights, the ABM and judgeship appointments. Liberals regarded the reform program as a lot of eyewash. But most of the trouble came from the right; *Human Events* magazine, the American Conservative Union, a group of House conservatives calling themselves the Republican Regulars, among others, were increasing their criticism of Nixon for having betrayed Republican principles—criticism undermining the Nixon-Mitchell premise that the fealty of the 1968 Nixon-Wallace voters must be maintained at all costs. Thus attacked from all sides, Nixon felt a written rationale of his overall program was clearly needed—giving it not only an ideological consistency but a Republican ideological consistency.

The task fell to William Safire, former newspaper reporter, ex-press agent, political lexicographer, resident White House

*Emphasis in the original.

quipster, and, officially, a speech writer for Richard Nixon.* It was first thought that Safire would write a speech for Nixon setting forth an ideological rationale for his program—the New Federalism—with delivery set for late 1969. But Nixon decided against it, feeling that the emphasis through his first year had been too much in crises management—that is, winding down the Vietnam war and holding down inflation—and not enough on positive accomplishment to justify a full-fledged ideological rationale. Instead, in December, Safire wrote a paper to be distributed quietly among the White House staff and a few newspaper correspondents called *New Federalist Paper #1* and signed by "Publius," the Roman moralist whose name was used by Hamilton, Madison and Jay in the *Federalist Papers*. Ehrlichman also had a hand in writing the paper, and, finally, Nixon reviewed it and made some changes.

The attempt to reconcile conventional Republicanism with Nixon's reform initiatives on the centralizing and decentralizing tendencies contained in his own program was not entirely successful. Safire described the process with the use of an oxymoron, "national localism," which went over, according to Safire himself, like "an absolute bomb." Nevertheless, Publius did manage a good working definition of the New Federalism:

> A sea-change in the approach to the limitation of centralized power—part of what is "new" in the New Federalism—is that *"States rights" have now become rights of first refusal.* Local authority will now regain the right to meet local needs itself, and gain an additional right to Federal financial help; but it will not regain the right it once held to neglect the needs of its citizens. States' rights are now more accurately described as States' duties; this is a fundamental change in federalism, removing its great fault without undermining its essential local-first character, and provides the New Federalists with two of their prime causes: the cause of regaining control, and the cause of fairness.†

"Regaining control" meant returning power to the people by use of decentralizing devices such as revenue sharing. "Fairness"

---

*Safire had first entered the Nixon orbit in 1959 at Moscow as publicity man for the model kitchen exhibit, where Khrushchev and Nixon had their famed debate. Needless to say, Nixon made Safire's job easy that day.
†Emphasis in the original.

meant the central government following the "national conscience" (as in the school desegregation issue).

White House staffers to whom the Publius paper was distributed were intentionally kept ignorant of Nixon's role in shaping it so they could be free to criticize it, and criticize it they did. Tom Charles Huston, a twenty-eight-year-old speech writer and former national president of the rightist Young Americans for Freedom, wrote a rebuttal titled *Federalism: Old and New—Or, the Pretensions of New Publius Exposed by Cato* (Cato, the Roman censor, had been used as a pseudonym by eighteenth-century English Whigs). The nub of Cato's argument—and indeed the unease of many doctrinaire conservatives over the drift of the Nixon program—was this: the formulation by Publius of a first-refusal right by states, after which the federal government would take action, "not only . . . is objectionable, it is revolutionary." To Cato, "power implies the right to say No and make it stick; it includes the right of a state to decide for itself whether a 'problem exists.' " Moreover, the Publius concept of a national conscience was derided. It denigrated "morality" to the status of "the temporary decision of a majority of those who happen to take the effort to think about it. . . ."*

Taking the Cato criticism into account, Safire wrote a revised version of the Publius paper which was delivered as a speech by George Shultz, still Secretary of Labor but by now a major spokesman for the administration, to the University of Chicago Graduate School of Business (where Shultz had been dean before coming to Washington) on March 19, 1970. Now the concepts toward which Publius had been groping were more clearly defined:

> In essence, the New Federalism calls upon us to act as one nation in setting the standards of fairness, and then to act as a congeries of communities in carrying out those standards. We are nationalizing equity as we localize control, while retaining a continued federal stewardship to insure that national standards are attained.

This was no stirring battle cry to send the multitudes into the street. It was far too precious to do that. But it *was* a rationale for

---

*The President's part in the preparation of the Publius paper was kept secret even after the Cato paper was written. In a discussion of the Publius-Cato debate, the February 23, 1970, edition of *Time* said, "The President encourages the intramural philosophizing but has no plans to embrace either interpretation."

the Nixon policies, although still something of a hothouse flower, compared with his appointments of Haynsworth and Carswell and his vetoing of money bills which sprang more naturally from instinct. Still, Richard Nixon—who had entered the White House with neither a program, nor a framework for one—now, one year later, had both.

IX

Time of Troubles

I feel deeply sorry for him. Every weapon he uses smashes in his hands.
—Sir Harold Nicolson on Winston Churchill, in
The War Years: Diaries and Letters 1939–1945

They could not positively prove it, of course, but some advisers around President Nixon in those days just before his bold gamble to send American troops into Cambodia were convinced he saw a similarity between his own adversity in withdrawing the nation from Vietnam and Winston Churchill's in ridding the world of Adolf Hitler. Others close to the President felt that he saw some similarity between the Cambodian intervention and Kennedy's throwing down the gauntlet to the Russians in demanding the removal of Soviet missiles from Cuba in 1962.

If so, the similarities were in the President's soul, not in the objective circumstances, because the circumstances of Cambodia could not conceivably offer Nixon anything like the universal and emotional backing that sustained Churchill during World War II or Kennedy in those brief days when American citizens gave him their total support to do whatever necessary to expel Soviet missiles from Cuba. To the contrary, in the public consciousness Cambodia was a distinctly marginal military undertaking that, whatever its actual significance as one factor in the Vietnam equation, widened the war to another country, and therefore must be bad.

Indeed, Nixon understood perfectly well that this would be the initial reaction by most Americans to the Cambodian invasion and, consequently, resolved to build it up to heroic proportions by rhetoric—his own rhetoric—to the consternation of his closest advisers. In short, he was attempting by the force of his own words to clothe the Cambodian intervention in apocalyptic terms that would persuade the American people that here was no mere military operation but an act of national courage, with high political significance directed not just at the enemy sanctuaries in Cambodia, not just at Hanoi, but at Moscow itself. Thus, as enunciated by the President when he announced his decision to "clean out" the sanctuaries, the enemy was defined in large terms as "the forces of totalitarianism and anarchy" and it was "our will and character" that were being tested. It was a calculated decision of endless implications that would affect the entire course of the Nixon administration.

The dominant Presidential mood was clearly perceived by Richard Nixon's closest advisers as he approached the point of decision on Cambodia, and it greatly disturbed them. Although the military aspects of the operation were difficult enough, the far deeper problem was the political reaction at home. For the President consciously to heighten and dramatize his rationale for intervention could only heighten and dramatize the political fury of the antiwar bloc, which had been almost brought to heel by the steady pace of U.S. troop withdrawals and the extraordinary decline in casualties (from almost two hundred a week during the last half of 1968 to just over one hundred a week in the last half of 1969). What worried Laird, Rogers, Kissinger and others of the tiny coterie close enough to the President to know about Cambodia in advance was that it might refuel the whole antiwar movement, anger the quiescent doves and compound Nixon's political problems at home.

Thus, in late April when the decision to enter Cambodia was forming, both Laird and Kissinger independently concluded that it might be better not to commit the President's personal prestige at all, but to let the world know about it in an announcement from Saigon by General Abrams. But it was now too late for that possibility to be seriously considered. In his own crisis-management formula, Nixon was now "keyed up and ready for battle."

When, on the afternoon of Thursday, April 30, a copy of the President's speech for that evening was sent to Melvin Laird for his perusal, he was horrified at the hyperbole. Asked by the White House for any comments he might have on the speech, Laird took the liberty of strongly recommending that Nixon remove from the text all mention of COSVN (Hanoi's Central Office for South Vietnam) as a key target of the operation. Laird tried to explain to Presidential aides that the COSVN shown on the map of Cambodia in the briefings given them by the Pentagon was no fortified bastion, no single entity, but a floating, amorphous command that slithered from one place to another in Cambodian jungles near the border of South Vietnam. Thus, the clear implication in the President's words that some very big Communist fish might be caught in the Cambodian operation—"the headquarters for the entire Communist military operation in South Vietnam" would be under direct attack, he said —worried not only Laird and Kissinger but the generals in Saigon, who knew that any such hope was illusory, and who further knew that their incursion might well be judged a failure.

So Laird forthrightly and in no uncertain words suggested that all reference to COSVN be struck from the President's text, and that the speech be toned down in general. The suggestion was ignored.

Even more to the point, Henry Kissinger gave a confidential briefing to reporters one hour before the President's speech specifically warning them not to expect any such grandiose results from the operation as the capture of COSVN, which he said might never be found and which wasn't the target of the operation anyway. That didn't change the President's text either.

Here, then, was the second time in six months that Nixon, discarding the advice of those he trusted most on foreign policy, had struck a hard rhetorical line to fit his own, not his advisers', concept of the political realities. In his November 3 speech six months earlier, that hard rhetorical line had hastened the resurrection of the doves, a political reaction more significant than the satisfaction it gave the hawks and Nixon-followers in the Silent Majority. On that occasion, Nixon's personal inclination had been bolstered by advice from his inner White House staff, particularly Haldeman. Now, six months later, the same thing was happening. Once again Haldeman, backed by Herbert Klein, the President's top public relations adviser, argued for a flag-waving speech designed to set an inspirational mood and encourage a patriotic response.

At five o'clock in the afternoon of April 30, Laird was informed by the White House that the speech would stand as Nixon wrote it, with no changes. That decision was made by Nixon despite the fact that Laird and Kissinger had agreed in talks together that day that the speech should be reshaped, its sensationalism removed. The President knew what he wanted, just as he had known what he wanted on November 3, and he plunged headlong into a text that, as one adviser said, made them "cringe."

The justification for the invasion of Cambodia was understood by everyone in the field in Vietnam, the Pentagon and the State Department. But from the very first, there was deep and bitter disagreement over whether and how to proceed. At the State Department, Secretary Rogers was tormented with anxiety over whether the invasion of a "neutral" country would add a dangerous new political and diplomatic dimension to the war. Laird was fearful about the domestic political costs of using American troops, and, for a while, he waged a low-keyed rear-guard action against such use. The American high command in Saigon, while enthusiastic about attacking the Communist sanctuaries along the border of South Vietnam, wanted assurance that the blow would really hurt the enemy, and that meant plenty of U.S. troops. For several years the generals had been pressing for an attack against Cambodia, just as they had against the Ho Chi Minh trail complex in central Laos. Always, political opposition in Washington blocked them.

Now, however, the situation had changed. For several years Prince Norodom Sihanouk, ruler of Cambodia, had permitted the North Vietnamese to use his country's eastern fringe, right up against South Vietnam, as sanctuaries for supplies and armaments as well as base camps for some fifty thousand Communist troops ready to assault the heavily populated, strategically vital southern part of South Vietnam. Most supplies for this war in the South had come from the Port of Sihanoukville on the Gulf of Siam. In early 1970, however, the Prince, becoming disenchanted with the growing Communist presence in his country, had closed down the vast warehouses in Pnompenh, where the Communists stored their supplies, and was quietly threatening other moves against Hanoi.

The changed mood of Sihanouk was an invitation to Washington and Saigon. If the sanctuaries posed an internal threat to Prince Sihanouk, they were a deathly hazard to President Nixon's Vietnamization program and the withdrawal of U.S. troops from South Vietnam. The theory of Vietnamization was built on Laird's assumption that the ARVN (Army of the Republic of Vietnam) would be able to protect itself and South Vietnam after the American withdrawal. To complete the withdrawal of U.S. combat troops while four North Vietnamese divisions remained poised on the border to attack the dwindling American force—or, after total withdrawal, the ARVN— was simply unacceptable to Nixon. If the sanctuaries could be broken up by a major assult it would take the enemy one year to restore them for a full-scale campaign against South Vietnam. During that year, the ARVN would (so Laird planned) be that much better trained and hence that much more prepared to go it alone.

Accordingly, Nixon sent Laird to Saigon in February to plot some action against the sanctuaries. Laird found American officials there agreed that the ARVN should be used as much as possible to maraud, harass and break up the Communist sanctuaries. He gave tentative approval, subject to reporting back to Nixon, with the understanding that under no conditions would U.S. ground troops be used. The Americans would limit their help to air and rescue missions.

Soon after Laird recommended this policy and before Nixon could approve it, however, a wholly unexpected event of vast importance for Vietnam occurred in Pnompenh. With Sihanouk on a world tour, a military group led by General Lon Nol seized power in a bloodless coup and greatly accelerated the anti-Communist line that had been slowly evolving under the Prince by ordering North Vietnamese and Vietcong troops to leave Cambodian soil immediately. Ignoring Lon Nol's demands, Hanoi began plotting his overthrow and dispatched its troops to key areas throughout Cambodia, setting off a small-scale war. Sihanouk, quickly shedding his recent anti-Communism, showed up in Peking to head a government-in-exile under Communist Chinese sponsorship. With Lon Nol far more hostile to the Communists than Sihanouk ever could have been, Nixon now authorized Laird to go forward with his plan for limited incursions.

But in doing so, Nixon ran into strong opposition from the State Department and the U.S. negotiating team in Paris. Large raids into Cambodia, they felt, would make the Paris peace talks even more futile. Moreover, the diplomats argued there might now be some chance to solve the Cambodian sanctuary problem by diplomatic means. Responding to the diplomats, Nixon suddenly ordered the ARVN raids across the border canceled, almost before they got started.

But if the diplomatic option failed, what would the United States do? Could Nixon risk the chance that the Communists, using their overwhelming military superiority against the underarmed and undertrained Cambodian army, might attempt an outright takeover of the country? Wouldn't that make a mockery of the whole effort in Vietnam all these years—to have neighboring Cambodia fall to the Communists overnight, as it were, while the Americans were "saving" South Vietnam?

In this mood of deepening crisis, Nixon ordered options drawn up for more serious moves in Cambodia, and Laird cabled General Abrams to submit contingency plans as soon as possible. There now started an internal debate of highest importance. On one side were Laird and Rogers; on the other side, the President and Kissinger, together with General Abrams and Ambassador Ellsworth Bunker in Saigon.

Abrams' obvious first choice for Cambodia was full use of American troops with no restricted rules of combat against the Fishhook area, a salient that jutted into the highlands of South Vietnam opposite some of the best American units, while the ARVN would strike the less important Parrot's Beak area to the south.

Laird's first choice was ARVN troops alone with no Americans at all to be used, not even the regular advisers to ARVN battalions who normally went into combat with them. The most that Laird was willing to accept was U.S. air support for the ARVN. The reasons for this stringent limitation on U.S. personnel were obvious—Laird's fear of domestic upheaval that would undermine the political gains Nixon had made since Vietnamization began.

There seemed to be no rush for decision in those early days of April, and the debate proceeded at a leisurely pace. From Saigon, the advice to Nixon became predictably louder: Use American troops and in sufficient numbers to make the incursions really hurt the enemy. Bunker and Abrams were pressing hard, with the full backing of the uniformed military at the Pentagon headed by Generals Wheeler and Westmoreland. In mid-April, intelligence reports that the North Vietnamese in the Fishhook area were starting to move west away from Vietnam and toward the heart of Cambodia, gave the hawks valuable new ammunition. The enemy game looked ominously clear: overthrow Lon Nol and establish a Communist government. Now Bunker and Abrams redoubled their efforts to win the

President's consent to an assault in force against the sanctuaries, *with* American participation.

Laird still held out for no American participation, but when the President asked him pointedly whether he could *guarantee* that the ARVN could successfully raid the sanctuaries alone, Laird had to answer that he did not know, that he could not be sure. Still, Nixon withheld a decision. Laird frantically sought military judgments that might convince him that the ARVN alone, with no U.S. ground help, could lay waste the sanctuaries. He could not get any.

Thus did Laird begin to see the inevitability of Nixon's decision. So did Kissinger, who knew from many past conversations with the President that in Nixon's philosophy a small objectionable act by a President does him as much political damage as a large objectionable act. In line with this philosophy, Nixon believed he would take almost as much heat from an ARVN invasion of the Cambodian sanctuaries, backed with U.S. air support, as from a U.S. assault. Moral: do it all at once and get it over with. Kissinger was tuned in to the inner decision-making process now at work inside the President far more than Laird was. To Laird, the difference in domestic political reactions to an ARVN assault (even with U.S. air support) as opposed to the outright participation of strong U.S. forces was fundamental and grave. Much closer to the American electorate than Kissinger had ever been, Laird wanted nothing so much as evidence to prove that the ARVN could go it alone in the Cambodian jungles. No such evidence was at hand. For his part, Kissinger, skeptical of Vietnamization from the start, never entertained the possibility that the ARVN could pull off a major operation without the help of U.S. ground troops.

The President summoned the National Security Council on April 22, but no decisions were made beyond the tentative one that there would at least be a large ARVN push against the Parrot's Beak. U.S. action against the Fishhook was discussed inconclusively. Now the pace picked up. Nixon had turned over the planning work to his special crisis panel, a group called Washington Special Action Group (WASAG), first constituted to handle the North Korean shooting down of a U.S. spy plane in the spring of 1969.* Operational plans

*WASAG was headed by Kissinger, and included the Chairman of the Joint Chiefs, General Earle G. Wheeler; the Deputy Secretary of Defense, David Packard; the Under Secretary of State for Political Affairs, U. Alexis Johnson; and the Assistant Secretary of State for Far Eastern Affairs, Marshall Green.

were demanded from the U.S. command in Saigon for an ARVN assault on Parrot's Beak.

Nixon was now tensing for what he strongly felt would be a major test of his will and the country's. Typically, priming himself for the impending crisis, he was spending more time alone, working late at night in his upstairs study in the Lincoln Room, wandering in and out of the Situation Room to chat with members of WASAG during their meetings. On April 24 he asked for operational plans for American troops to be used against the Fishhook, then flew to Camp David that afternoon—a giveaway that the long process of steeling himself for a major decision and the crisis that would follow it were coming to a climax. Kissinger joined him with the Fishhook plan on the next day, Saturday. They returned to Washington that afternoon and in the evening went down the Potomac River on the Presidential yacht, *Sequoia,* with Laird and Attorney General John Mitchell— Mitchell's presence being another sure sign that Nixon was on the verge of a very big and controversial decision. Later that night the President watched his second showing of the movie *Patton,* the new motion picture about General George Patton, whose bold decisions in World War II now reinforced Nixon's own resolve to risk the Cambodian intervention. Just as Mitchell in real life displayed those qualities of toughness and self-confidence that Nixon so much admired, and that so sustained him, so did Blood-and-Guts Patton epitomize the quality of deepest *amor patriae* that also appealed to Nixon, particularly in juxtaposition with the long-haired antiwar students who waved their Ho Chi Minh signs and North Vietnamese flags. The true American spirit was Patton, not the New Left.*

However, no final decision was made as the meetings of WASAG and the National Security Council increased in pace and tempo. Rogers was leaning very hard on the President to be cautious; Laird had grave reservations; and Kissinger was ambivalent, protecting Nixon's options to the end.

On Monday morning, April 27, Nixon huddled in the Oval Office with these three and Haldeman, but without his military advisers. The pros and cons were weighed all over again and domestic

---

*The impact of *Patton* on Nixon's Cambodia decision was felt by every close adviser who was aware of the President's repeated viewings of the film. A few weeks later, Secretary of State Rogers told a friend that the movie "comes up in every conversation" with the President.

political reaction was scrutinized. But now the reliability of the military advice the President was getting was questioned. Were the generals telling him what they wanted him to hear? Nixon decided to request Abrams' personal opinion on the Fishhook operation, cabling him outside regular military channels to ask for the "unvarnished truth." In response, Abrams strongly recommended a major American assault on Fishhook coincident with the ARVN attack on Parrot's Beak. That afternoon Rogers testified before the Senate Foreign Relations Committee on the administration's already announced plans for sending small arms and other military aid to the Lon Nol government in Pnompenh. Although pressed hard on what else Nixon planned, he could not, of course, tell what he knew. Nixon had decreed total secrecy, so much so that even some high-ranking officers in the Pentagon did not know what was coming.

Now, finally, Nixon was ready to decide. He retired to the Lincoln study Monday night with the familiar yellow foolscap, alone with his decisions and the shadows of history that filled the old mansion. Even then, his chief advisers did not know for sure what decision he would make. And when, very early the following morning, he called Kissinger to inform him that American troops *would* be used in the Fishhook region, Kissinger immediately produced his own yellow pad on which had been written all the caveats. Nixon glanced at Kissinger's list, then turned over to Kissinger his own list of caveats—how the operation might go foul, how the American people might overreact, what effect the U.S. interdiction might have on Congress. Each point that Kissinger had written out was on the President's list, drawn up the night before. It was his obligation, Kissinger told the President, to warn him about the full range of hazardous repercussions. Nixon replied yes, he understood, but sternly added that now that he had made his decision he did not want to see one backward glance or hear one recrimination if the operation soured.*

*On his omnipresent lined yellow pad, Nixon was discovered by Stewart Alsop, *Newsweek*'s Washington columnist, to have made a fairly complete list of both pluses and minuses on the Cambodian intervention. One of the President's pluses was that the intervention "may" encourage Hanoi to negotiate. Another was that it would speed Vietnamization. As for the minuses, Nixon wrote that the use of U.S. troops would provoke "deep divisions" in the United States, that it might cause the Communists to break off the Paris peace talks and that it might lead to a frontal Communist attack across the demilitarized zone separating North and South Vietnam.

Orders were dispatched to commanders in the field, and the President started work on the speech that would reveal his decision to the nation—the speech written without help or even the usual finishing touches by speech writers, the speech that made some of his closest advisers "cringe." No wonder. It bristled with a pugnacity unbecoming the head of the world's most powerful nation in addressing a poor and lowly state. "We will not be humiliated. We will not be defeated," the President cried. "If when the chips are down the U.S. acts like a pitiful helpless giant, the forces of totalitarianism and anarchy will threaten free nations and free institutions throughout the world. It is not our power but our will that is being tested tonight."

Nixon lashed out at Hanoi in terms usually reserved for a declaration of war, not an eight-week border raid. Hanoi he described as "a group which rejects every effort to win a just peace, ignores our warnings, tramples on solemn agreements, violates the neutrality of an unarmed people and uses our prisoners as hostages." All true, and had been true for years. There was only one explanation for the President's having invested this speech with such harsh, bellicose language. To make the decision acceptable at home, he wanted to create the appearance of a larger and more dramatic crisis than really existed, to place the Cambodian incursion in a Churchillian frame. He wanted to rally the same Silent Majority to whom he had appealed on November 3, and he tried to accomplish this not only by his appeal to chauvinism but by his attacks on domestic anarchists. "Here in America," he said, "great universities are being systematically destroyed"—also an obvious truth but one which could hardly be related, as yet, to the Cambodian decision. The clear purpose was to whip up anti-student support for the intervention. That was politically useful, but the tone was distractingly strident. By so polarizing American sentiment on the war into strong "pro" and "anti" viewpoints to an even greater degree than in his November 3 speech, the President was inadvertently crystallizing his opposition and thereby mortgaging himself to great political problems in the future.

Finally, the President's address that night came perilously close to an expression of self-pity—a self-revealing mood that had no place in the announcement of a military undertaking. His decision to send American boys into Cambodia, he said, might make him a "one-term President . . . but I have rejected all political considerations in making this decision . . . I would rather be a one-term President than be a two-term President at the cost of seeing America become a second-rate power and see this nation accept the first defeat in its proud 190-year history." Even if Nixon had been a sainted leader, few Americans would have cared whether the Cambodian intervention hurt his second-term election prospects. They were interested in the Cambodian decision's impact on *them* and the nation, not on the President.

These failings spoiled the impact of what could have been a tough, clean decision which in its military simplicity should have been clear to everyone. To make Vietnamization work, the ARVN needed time. If the Americans and the South Vietnamese could destroy enough stockpiled supplies in the sanctuaries to force the Communists to delay their replacement for one year, that would buy one year of grace from an enemy attack against South Vietnam. That was the whole purpose of the military aspect of the decision. A year later it would be seen to have worked.

As for the political aspect, Nixon really did want to show the Russians that America could take the initiative and was not to be taken for granted as a "pitiful helpless giant" unable to make swift and unexpected moves. Nixon had restrained himself, on the advice of Kissinger and Rogers, when the U.S. spy plane was shot down by the North Koreans.* He was watching the Russians build up Egyptian military power in the Middle East, unable to influence them in the slightest. He recognized that Hanoi was becoming persuaded that no American President could keep the war going much longer because of rising political fury at home. These were solid reasons for taking an approving look at the Cambodian operation. When they were added to the year of grace that a successful operation might well buy against an enemy attack on South Vietnam, the reason for action became better and more sufficient.

Domestic political reaction was hard to gauge in advance, but

---

*In his opening speech of the 1968 campaign at Concord, N.H., on February 3, Nixon referred to the hijacking of a U.S. Navy spy ship by the North Koreans as showing that under Lyndon Johnson "respect for the United States has fallen so low that a fourth-rate military power like North Korea will hijack a United States Naval vessel on the high seas . . ." He repeated this in nearly every speech prior to the nomination and included it in his acceptance speech at Miami Beach.

the President hoped that if casualties could be kept low, the politics of the intervention would be easily containable. In fact, spot polls by the White House three days after the intervention began showed Nixon's rating up three points. The military end of it was going so well that the President hoped to go to San Clemente for the weekend starting May 8. On Monday morning, May 4, that prospect looked excellent and his staff began to plan for it. In Cambodia the operation was justifying the 70–30 odds that military experts had put on it in favor of success. Nixon was understandably satisfied. Despite some violent public criticism of his rhetoric and college disturbances and demonstrations, his difficult decision was beginning to pay dividends. All that was before Kent State.*

The education of Richard M. Nixon as an accomplished student of world affairs who by the summer of 1970 was pursuing a clearly identifiable foreign policy, based on talking sense with the Russians, had been marked by slow, steady progress. There was now a sophistication, both in discussing the big problems and in applying reason to their solution, that had not always been Nixon's distinguishing mark. In 1959, toward the end of his Vice Presidency, Nixon had shown a surprising lack of subtlety and sophistication that not only reinforced the Soviet conviction that he was not really safe to do business with but infuriated none other than Dwight D. Eisenhower.

It happened at Camp David on September 27, the last day of Soviet Premier Nikita Khrushchev's visit to the United States. Eisenhower and Khrushchev had been at Camp David for two days, talking about Soviet-American problems and a possible summit meeting in 1960. On Khrushchev's last day before flying home to Moscow, Eisenhower gave him a luncheon to which he asked several Cabinet members and other leading officials of the government, including the Vice President.

As his guests sat down for Sunday lunch at the long table in the main camp, Nixon began shooting hard, offensive questions at Khrushchev, as though he wanted to resume their famous Kitchen Debate the previous July 24 in Moscow, in which Khrushchev and Nixon had exchanged sharp words and pointed fingers. Oblivious to his rudeness, Nixon kept up his questioning long enough to make the

*The political aftermath of Cambodia is discussed in Chapter XI.

back of Eisenhower's neck redden with embarrassment for himself and anger at Nixon. "Ike wanted to pick Dick up by the nape of the neck and drop him out in the woods," one of Eisenhower's luncheon guests said later. But Eisenhower was powerless to intervene. It might look to Khrushchev as though he were disciplining his Vice President, and such a breach in the common front was out of the question. Nixon finally stopped his badgering, but with no indication he understood that his conduct was offensive to Eisenhower or, more to the point, to Eisenhower's guest, Khrushchev.

Nixon had always been regarded as the American *bête noire* by the Russians, going back to his days as a successful (and scrupulously fair) Congressional Communist-hunter. He was infamous in Moscow as the toughest, hardest-line anti-Communist in the higher reaches of the American government. His advice to Eisenhower in 1954 to authorize an air strike by Navy carrier planes in the Gulf of Tonkin against the Vietnamese Communists in the battle of Dienbienphu was widely known. Considering his conduct in Khrushchev's presence in the Kitchen Debate and later at Camp David, the prospect of good relations between Nixon and the Russians did not look promising.

The new President, of course, had been fully aware of this handicap from the outset. He moved in several ways, both by public statements and private messages, to correct the Soviet impression that he would be difficult to deal with. He was resolved to prove to his own countrymen that, with his reputation as a hard-line anti-Communist, he would actually have greater negotiating freedom with the Russians than, say, a liberal Democrat. He was equally resolved to prove to the Russians that his pledge to replace confrontation with negotiation was the most serious pledge he had made in the field of foreign policy. The first test of that pledge, the Strategic Arms Limitation Talks (SALT), was in one sense the most uncomplicated test, because it was a head-to-head negotiation with the Russians alone, unlike the Mideast negotiations which involved highly unpredictable third and fourth parties. But in another sense, SALT was anything but uncomplicated, involving as it did the highest mysteries of nuclear science and technology, abstract formulations dealing with strategic balances, assured destructive capabilities, deterrence and other concepts susceptible to differing interpretations in Washington and Moscow.

An agreement of some kind with the Russians that would come out of SALT was Nixon's deepest hope, and one of his first acts as President was to order the most comprehensive study of strategic arms problems that had ever been made by the U.S. government. By contrast, although Lyndon Johnson became infatuated with the idea of talks with the Russians about harnessing both offensive and defensive weapons, particularly after his meeting with Soviet Prime Minister Aleksei Kosygin at Glassboro, N.J., in July 1967, preparations did not begin to equal those ordered by Nixon in January 1969. Johnson never did get his meeting with the Russians because of the Soviet invasion of Czechoslovakia in August 1968, just before the talks were to begin.

Nixon's insistence on thorough study and planning for the SALT talks showed his serious intentions. It took time, delaying the start of the talks until autumn of 1969. At that point the President was confident that at the very least a freeze on strategic weapons was all but certain, and had privately informed some of his top diplomats to that effect early in 1969. In talks with Soviet Ambassador Anatoly Dobrynin, Nixon was the exact opposite of the goading tough guy of a decade earlier. He was earnest and somber, leaving no doubt that he regarded success in the talks as indispensable insurance for the survival of the human race. There was no demagoguery here, no false pride and no placing of blame. The President was forthright about the infinite dangers of the arms race, and he made clear his sincerity to the Russians.

But for one reason or another—the historic defense psychology of the Russians and their paranoid demands for overlapping layers of security; disagreements on basic nuclear-weapons' data collected by the Americans and the Russians and its technical complexity; unwillingness of either side to make a first major concession; suspicion and fear of one side for the other—almost a year after the talks started, not only was there no comprehensive agreement, but no limited agreement, no ceiling, no real progress at all beyond the most complete exposure of each side's possible positions ever laid on the table. For Nixon, this impasse was becoming oppressive by the summer of 1970. He had gone far out on the limb in his first press conference after the Cambodian intervention, predicting flatly with no qualification that "there will be an agreement" in SALT. But beneath that unfulfilled prediction was a growing sense of uneasiness that negotiating with the Russians was proving to be fully as difficult in Nixon's Era of Negotiations as it had been in the past for Nixon's predecessors. And as that uneasiness was just beginning to gain a depressing grip on the President, the Russians in 1970 suddenly and unpredictably confronted him with two flaring crises: one in Cuba, one in the Middle East.

The first crisis was the discovery of alarming evidence in late summer that a Soviet base for nuclear submarines was under construction at Cienfuegos, in Fidel Castro's Cuba. Kissinger alerted the press to this disturbing development in one of his frequent background sessions with Washington reporters.* He spelled out the President's concern over this apparent Soviet violation of the agreement reached between Kennedy and Khrushchev in 1962 to end the Cuban missile crisis, with headlines resulting.

Nixon was not bothered about any sudden shift in the military or nuclear balance as a result of the Cienfuegos base; he knew he had plenty of options to discourage the Soviets. The root of his worry was deeper: Did this blatant effort to install a nuclear submarine base so close to the U.S. coast signal a basic change in Soviet intentions toward Nixon and the United States across the board, endangering SALT and all other negotiations? Was it a sign of a new Soviet offensive, based on Nixon's ever-growing political problems in Vietnam, the new rapprochement between West Germany and the Soviet Union and the fact that Moscow now had at least a nuclear parity with the United States?

The President did not know the answer. He dealt with the issue by sending a no-nonsense hands-off demand to Moscow and got a reply that seemed satisfactory. But the larger issue—the possibility that the Russians were now playing a calculated pressure game against him—was a source of the President's rising alarm, based partly on the Cuba sub base, partly on the deadlocked SALT talks (where no progress was visible), and partly on the rapid deterioration of the once hopeful prospects in the Middle East.

Of these trouble spots, it was the Middle East that was now, in

---

*Nixon was using Kissinger regularly for press briefings on foreign and military developments of more than usual import, leaving the State Department in a inferior role.

the summer of 1970, confronting the President with his gravest crisis, ruthlessly testing his pledge to end the era of confrontation. The trouble had started in late 1969, when Secretary of State Rogers and his Assistant Secretary in charge of the Middle East, Joseph Sisco, agreed under Soviet insistence to revise their plan for an Israeli-Egyptian settlement.* After Rogers accepted the Soviet version, it was then sent to Moscow, with high anticipation of Soviet approval. But weeks passed in silence. Then, without warning, the Kremlin rejected it out of hand. The decision shocked both Rogers and Nixon.

Here, then, was a most brutal test for the President: first, in the broad context of his overall program, having to negotiate with Moscow on everything; and second, in the narrower but more critical sense that his concept of a Big Power agreement as being essential to settle the Middle East was beginning to look foolish. As soon as the Russians—and, of course, President Nasser of Egypt—rejected the October formulation, Israel's powerful political allies in the United States intensified their campaign to undercut Nixon's concept that a Big Power agreement was the first step. The Russians had now proved their untrustworthiness, said Israel's American friends. The President should ignore the Big Power approach and, instead, let the two parties—Israel and Egypt—work out a settlement between themselves. Nixon met that challenge courageously and directed Rogers, rebuffed on his first attempt, to advance quickly to his second-stage move: a cease-fire along the Suez Canal. Anything less than a continuation of the administration's highly activist policy, Nixon felt, would further diminish U.S. influence and further deepen Soviet influence in the Arab world.

With Israel now, in early 1970, able to bomb with impunity deep in the Egyptian heartland and stage lightning raids on Egyptian military posts, Nixon decided to hold up new American military equipment for Israel, including another fifty Phantom fighters, despite rejection of his Sinai settlement plan. He pledged to maintain the balance of military power, but Israel now obviously enjoyed total air superiority, and held a technological base that gave her towering dominance over neighboring Arab states, including Egypt. Thus, Nixon—again—courageously held off the American-Jewish clamor for more weapons for Israel and ordered Rogers to keep top pressure on the diplomatic front.

*See Chapter IV.

By June the cease-fire proposal was ready. On July 23 it was accepted by Egypt. Israel said yes on July 31, and it went into effect on August 7, stilling the guns and the jets along the Suez Canal. But this glorious success, unimaginable a year earlier, was all too short-lived. Almost at once, the Egyptians started violating the stand-still agreement—a collateral agreement to the cease-fire that forbade any military build-up within a line fifty kilometers on either side of the Canal. The American U-2 spy plane was ordered into action by Nixon from an air base on Cyprus, but instead of getting it aloft for photographs the moment the cease-fire started, it was not airborne until two days later. The essential base-period, from which military movements could be accurately measured, did not exist. With Israel screaming betrayal, the Egyptians completed a massive movement of new SAMs (surface-to-air missiles) into the forbidden zone and did it with clear complicity, if not the active help, of the Russians.

Thus, once again, a case could be made that as a negotiator Nixon—the hardened anti-Communist of the previous twenty years —was being taken to the cleaners by the Russians. The Russians had done him in on his settlement formulation the previous December. Now they were doing him in again on his hard-won cease-fire. But in both cases, there were extenuating circumstances. After all, Egypt *had* been under heavy air attacks from Israel using bases on Israeli-occupied *Egyptian* territory. After all, the Russians did *not* have total control over their Egyptian clients. Nor had the Russians signed anything themselves in agreeing to the cease-fire stand-still. They had given what the United States took to be their word to cooperate, but with their typical brand of injured innocence the Russians looked at the ceiling when the United States sought redress, as if to say, Who, me?

This Soviet performance produced the sharpest welling up of anger Richard Nixon had felt since taking office. Far more than what happened the previous December, it raised ugly questions of Soviet intentions, forced Nixon into a reexamination of his basic negotiation strategy and for a brief time led him to speculate about revenge, on grounds that the Russians were playing fast and loose.

The mood did not last long. Nixon increased shipments of military aid to the Israelis, ostensibly to reestablish the power balance along the Canal (although his advisers doubted that the missile movement had disturbed it to any great extent), and—most impor-tant—continued on his predetermined path of a negotiated settle-

ment. Nothing could have given surer testimony to the President's
determination to follow his promised path of negotiation than the
self-control he displayed in this second appearance of Soviet flim-
flam, during the drawn-out Middle East negotiations, at just the time
his hopes for a breakthrough on SALT were also being dimmed. He
chose to ignore Soviet conduct and press on toward his negotiated
settlement. Then, all at once, the Middle East exploded in another
sector, far from the Suez Canal, in a crisis that called for all the
President's wisdom, and that conclusively proved how right he had
been all along in insisting that the Big Two could leave the area to
its own devices only at the greatest risk to themselves.

In Jordan the Middle East crisis was not Israel versus Jordan,
but the army of Jordan's King Hussein versus the Palestinian com-
mando organizations, principally Al Fatah. For almost three years
the army and the commandos had been at swords' point. The army
wanted a quiet front between Jordan and Israel, fearful of the terrible
retaliation that Israel consistently visited on Jordan for attacks
across the Jordan River into the Israeli-occupied West Bank. But the
commandos, claiming to speak for more than two million Palestinian
refugees, kicked out of Israel in 1948 and 1949 and from the West
Bank in the 1967 war, wanted only revenge for the outrageously
wretched lives they had been living.

By mid-September of 1970, soon after the spectacular epidemic
of skyjacking by Palestinian commandos, President Nixon became
suddenly aware that the off-and-on struggle between army and commandos was about to break into full-scale civil war. If King Hussein's army should lose that war, or appear to be losing it, Israel
would step in to help the King. Using one of the world's most
efficient and experienced air forces, backed up by highly mobile army
units, the Israelis would smash Syrian tank units that threatened to
join the commandos. They might also attack the Palestinian commandos. Although the Israeli high command opposed it at the time,
an Israeli preemptive air strike against those Soviet missiles that had
been moved up to the Suez Canal by Egypt, far to the west of Jordan,
could not be ruled out if the Israelis were drawn into an attack
against the Syrian tanks. Should that happen, the Russians would be
under irresistible pressures to assist their Egyptian friends. Without
any great stretch of the imagination, even a fool could perceive the

volatile source of World War III in the Jordanian civil war that broke out in earnest on September 17. And President Nixon was no fool.

As feared, some 250 Syrian tanks crossed the Jordanian border on September 19 and 20. The President's problem was acute. It was necessary to array so powerful a flotilla of naval power in the Eastern Mediterranean, and to alert U.S. airborne troops in Europe of such magnitude—and to do all this with worldwide publicity—that the Russians would know beyond doubt that direct U.S. intervention was a probability if Hussein started to go under. In pursuing this course, Nixon confronted private, ominous warnings that the British, French and lesser European powers not only would not support such intervention but might publicly oppose it.*

As in every grave international emergency, the real work of the Presidency was done quietly behind the closed doors of the White House at odd hours of the night and day. Having set the public scene with his well-advertised fleet movements in the Mediterranean, the President then set the private scene with himself, Kissinger and Sisco as the three principal actors. Working both in the President's Oval Office and in Kissinger's own office on the first floor of the West Wing of the White House (where Kissinger had recently been moved from the White House basement), these three arrived at the following policy: first, all options would be kept open, including possible direct U.S. intervention; second, the Soviet Union, which was in the midst of a major propaganda attack on the United States for allegedly interfering in the Jordan affair, must be warned most solemnly that the United States rejected that propaganda and that the situation was far too dangerous for propaganda; third, the Soviet Union must be told frankly that if the Syrian tanks did not withdraw, President Nixon could not predict what actions the United States might take.

The President directed Sisco to make points two and three to Yuly Vorontsov, Minister Counselor of the Soviet Embassy, who was summoned to the State Department on September 20. As for U.S.

---

*In 1958, Eisenhower *did* intervene with U.S. military power in the Middle East to prevent a potentially hostile government from taking over in Lebanon. He dispatched U.S. marines by naval vessels from Norfolk, Va., to Beirut. There was no reaction from Moscow or anywhere else. In those days, Soviet power in the Eastern Mediterranean was no more than a gleam in the Kremlin's eye.

intervention, Nixon, Kissinger and Sisco, with Secretary of State Rogers, Secretary of Defense Laird and Admiral Thomas H. Moorer, the new Chairman of the Joint Chiefs, occasionally sitting in on highly informal meetings, agreed that direct U.S. intervention might be necessary on one of two levels: first, and least dangerous, to "rescue" hijacked American tourists then being kept hostage on a remote desert airfield in Jordan; second, and more perilous, in response to an outright appeal for military help from King Hussein. Both of these options were open during the entire crisis.

At one meeting between the President, Kissinger and Sisco that lasted for almost three straight hours in Kissinger's office, Nixon took telephone calls from Israel and foreign capitals in Europe to discuss how various countries were handling the question of skyjack hostages and to explain the developing U.S. position on the Jordanian civil war crisis. It was decided that the far more preferable intervention would be to rescue American hostages—a good pretext for putting sizable forces around the airport at Amman and on the ground where the hostages were being held captive. That show of force, it was decided, should be warning enough to Syria. But even that limited intervention was regarded by Nixon as certain to be politically costly in the long run to the U.S. reputation in the Arab world. Intervention in response to a plea from King Hussein, on the other hand, would not only damage the United States in the Arab world but expose the King himself to vicious criticism—"tool of the imperialist Americans"—by the other Arab countries.

On Monday, September 21, Nixon held top-secret talks with Israeli Ambassador Yitzhak Rabin. The gist of these talks—there was no written word or pledge of any kind—was an understanding that if the Syrian tanks continued their advance, got to Amman and joined the Palestinian commandos in trying to overturn King Hussein, the Israelis would attack. Implicit in that understanding was that the United States would protect Israel's rear—at the Suez Canal —with the reinforced Sixth Fleet.

The "hot line" teleprinter between Washington and Moscow was never used during the Jordanian crisis. Nixon's quiet warning was transmitted verbally by Sisco to Vorontsov, the Soviet Minister Counselor. The President's strategy had one objective: to convince the Russians of the need to persuade the Syrians to turn their tanks around and get them out of Jordan, or unpleasant events would occur.

Here, not Cambodia, was the crisis that presented Nixon with the terrible drama of Kennedy's confrontation with the Russians at Cuba in 1962, with overtones of Armageddon. As one of Nixon's advisers said later, "Peace hung by the thinnest of threads." But unlike Kennedy's Cuba crisis, the imminent danger of war that would put Washington and Moscow in nuclear confrontation was far less publicly exposed than it had been in 1962. Nixon's stage was grander, his diplomatic and military problems more diffuse and complex, but the most exciting parts were played in total secrecy, beyond the capacity of the country to see and judge.

What saved the decision on intervention—either by Israel or, as it might have become necessary, by the Americans—was Hussein's spectacularly successful air attack, backed up by armor, against the Syrian tanks. Just how hard the Russians pressed the Syrians would long be debated, but it was plain that pressure was applied. By September 22, the Syrian tanks had started their withdrawal. With that first hard evidence that his mixture of quiet diplomacy and noisy mobilization of military power was working, Nixon quickly turned off the public drama. The crisis was over before its extreme urgency was known to all but a handful of the President's most intimate advisers.

Here was an example of Nixon not allowing rhetoric to interfere with a skillful display of quiet diplomacy. Nor was there any semblance of patting himself on the back after the crisis ended or the planting of newspaper stories about the country's good fortune in having a President who could keep his cool under intense pressure. The Jordanian crisis brought out what was best in the way Nixon could handle himself and the situation he faced—in sharp contrast to the less critical situation surrounding the intervention in Cambodia. The principal reason for that contrast was the proximity of direct Soviet involvement in the one and the absence of any likely Soviet interference in the other. In short, Richard Nixon was at his best when he was involved directly with the Soviets and when the stakes were highest.

The urgency of the Jordanian crisis caused an abrupt change for the better in Nixon's consultation with Congress, sadly deficient during the days just before the Cambodian intervention. The President briefed the leaders of both parties in the White House on

September 22, then invited the Senate's most prestigious Democratic oligarchs to discuss with him and Kissinger the unfolding drama in the mansion that evening. Georgia's Richard Russell, Mississippi's John Stennis and North Carolina's Sam Ervin talked for hours about the danger of World War III if Nixon's plan for Jordan boomeranged, but there was remarkable unanimity of support for the Nixon-Kissinger scenario. On the following day, State Department officials went before the Senate Foreign Relations Committee for a similar exercise. Even that arch-Nixon-critic, Chairman William Fulbright, gave the President high marks.

How different that was from the supersecrecy that had enveloped the days before the Cambodian intervention. On that occasion, Bryce Harlow, chief of Congressional liaison, discovered only hours before the President's speech announcing the intervention that an amendment barring U.S. combat troops from Cambodia was about to be attached to the Defense procurement bill on the floor of the House. The Armed Services Committee, hawkish though it was, had agreed to slip it into the bill in total ignorance of the fact that Nixon was about to send U.S. troops into Cambodia.

When this was learned by Harlow, Haldeman called a crisis meeting in the White House to discuss ways of expunging the amendment without giving away the President's invasion plan. If the usual consultation with Congressional leaders had been held on Cambodia, the existence of the amendment would have immediately become known. And that was precisely the course that Harlow, skilled in the ways of the Congress, had strongly advised: secret consultation with the leaders so that they would not be taken unawares and learn about the intervention in the President's speech to the nation. Harlow had been overruled.

With this background, the Haldeman meeting convened in a mood of tension. As it progressed the emotional strain showed through. Finally, Harlow turned abruptly to Haldeman and whispered, "I told you, Bob, we couldn't get away with doing it this way."

Five months later in the Jordanian crisis, that mistake was not repeated.

Despite his skillful handling of Jordan, the year 1970 was a time of foreign troubles for Richard Nixon. SALT was still stalled, with pessimism rising. The Russians were frustrating, or at least not advancing, the President's determination to negotiate an Arab-Israeli settlement.

The imminence of disaster in the Middle East persuaded Nixon to make a quick eight-day trip through the Mediterranean area in late September, a trip announced in the heat of the Jordanian crisis with one object: to show the U.S. flag. Concentrating on military objects, the President sailed with the Sixth Fleet, inspected NATO's base at Naples and balanced off the ideological contradictions bordering the Mediterranean with quick visits to Fascist Spain and Communist Yugoslavia. He capped the trip with a sentimental stop in Ireland, where his wife visited distant relatives (and none could be found for Nixon). Then home on October 5, having pressed hard his point that the Americans had vital interests in the Mediterranean and the Middle East that they would, if necessary, go to war to protect.

It was during this trip that President Gamal Abdul Nasser of Egypt, charismatic leader of the Arab world and Israel's blood enemy, died of a heart attack. President Tito of Yugoslavia chose to receive Nixon in Belgrade rather than attend Nasser's funeral—a choice that dramatized the rising concern among Mediterranean countries, particularly Communist Yugoslavia, over Russia's growing power there.

Despite the success of the Nixon flag-showing, the mere fact that he felt the journey necessary showed how much more critical the Middle East had become in the autumn of 1970 than it had been two years earlier. No, 1970 had not paid the dividends Nixon had every hope to collect from his policy of positive diplomacy abroad. But if 1970 was unkind abroad, at home it had been far worse: one setback after another, dominated by the domestic trauma induced by the Cambodian intervention and its fearful aftermath.

X
May 1970

The Universities have been to this nation, as the wooden horse was to the Trojans. . . . I despair of any lasting peace among ourselves, till the Universities here shall bend and direct their studies to the setting of it, that is to the teaching of the absolute obedience to the laws. . . . The core of the rebellion, as you have seen by this, and read of other rebellions, are the Universities; which nevertheless are not to be cast away, but to be better disciplined.

—Thomas Hobbes, in *Behemoth: The History of the Causes of the Civil Wars, and of the Counsels and Artifices by which They were Carried on from the Year 1640 to the Year 1660*

A society which comes to fear its children is effete. A sniveling, hand-wringing power structure deserves the violent rebellion it encourages. If my generation doesn't stop cringing, yours will inherit a lawless society where emotion and muscle displace reason.

—Vice President Spiro T. Agnew, in his commencement address, Ohio State University, June 7, 1969

At that moment on the evening of April 30, 1970, when Richard Nixon announced to the world that American troops were crossing the border into Cambodia, he could justly say that the terrible fears of 1968 for the tranquillity of the republic had not been realized. There had been no mass rioting in black ghettos since the spring of 1968. Although the late winter and spring of 1969 had been a violent and turbulent one on college campuses, the following autumn had been relatively quiet and, now, with just one month of the 1970 spring term remaining, there were few signs of unrest. Seemingly, the blacks and the young had heeded Nixon's admonition in his Inaugural Address "to lower our voices . . . stop shouting at each other. . . ." The appearance of quiet in the ghetto and on the campus was one cause for the sense of well-being that permeated the White House in the early spring of 1970.

Beneath the surface were causes for concern. The mutual alienation between the blacks and the young on the one hand and the President on the other was even deeper now than it had been when Nixon took office. Although the wave of mass ghetto rioting had subsided, organized violence by black urban guerrillas and uncontrolled street crime was on the *increase* in the inner city. Although campus violence had subsided during the 1969–70 school year, the American university was in serious danger of being politicized by the left with attendant erosion of academic freedom and standards of education. What was most potentially dangerous, however, was the failure of the President to develop a coherent philosophy and strategy in dealing with a possible large-scale revival of violent revolt by the blacks and the students.

How would Richard Nixon react to massive rioting on campus or in the ghetto? Massive retaliation and repression? Appeasement? Vacillation? A combination of all these? What the country could be thankful for was that the black inner city remained quiet into the spring of 1971 with no sign of a return to massive rioting—possibly because the blacks had realized they had lost far more than the white majority in the bloody disturbances of 1964–68, possibly because they feared all-out repression from Nixon and Mitchell, possibly because they had spent their self-destructive energies and could not summon new strength to go into the streets. The potentialities for national dislocation and tragedy were always greater in the black inner city than on the white college campus, and Nixon could be grateful he did not have to cope with uprising in the ghetto.

The campus was to prove disaster enough. When the Cambodian operation triggered student disturbances throughout the land unprecedented in the nation's history, Nixon had no prepared ideological or tactical position to fall back on. He swayed between repression and appeasement, his ambivalence helping to produce the first deep public ruptures of his administration. When it was over, his

Presidency would never be quite the same again. And all this was presaged by the President's handling of the student question in his first year in office.

Nixon's predilection was to sharply criticize the radical students and their permissive sponsors on the faculty who were turning the American university into a political cockpit built to Latin American specifications. When Columbia University was brought to its knees in the spring of 1968, candidate Nixon called it "a national disgrace," adding that the sanctioning of the rioting by "these professors who fawn on student violence" is "far more reprehensible than the disgraceful action of the students they encouraged." It was Nixon's strongly held conviction, and it was good politics.

But once Nixon was in the White House, he was advised by Daniel Patrick Moynihan to refrain from such criticism, which would have been his normal response. As an old-fashioned liberal intellectual devoted to academic freedom, Moynihan was even more deeply appalled than Nixon by student radicals and permissive professors. But he felt the President would help neither himself nor the campus crisis were he to intrude into the affairs of the campus. The test following Moynihan's advice came on April 28, 1969, when President Calvin Plimpton of Amherst College wrote Nixon that campus unrest would continue "until you and the other political leaders of our country attack more effectively, massively, persistently the major social and foreign problems of our country." As part of widespread student disturbances running continuously from late winter into the spring of 1969, Amherst had been shut down for two days by student strikers, and Plimpton's provocative letter to Nixon was one of the oldest political tricks in the book: pass the buck to the President of the United States.* Nixon followed Moynihan's advice neither to respond in kind with an equally provocative attack nor to respond with honeyed words of self-guilt—but just not to respond at all.

The reply to the Amherst letter (though it was not designated as such) was given by Nixon in his address at tiny General Beadle

---

*One Amherst undergraduate who was not favorably inclined toward either Plimpton or the student majority pressuring Plimpton was senior David Eisenhower, grandson of General Eisenhower and son-in-law of President Nixon. Metaphorically speaking, young Eisenhower told newsmen, Plimpton had written the letter to Nixon with a "gun at his head" held by the student strikers.

State College in Madison, S.D., a speech in whose preparation Moynihan played a major role.* It was the most closely reasoned, even-tempered, philosophically consistent statement on the campus problem that Nixon had yet made and was to make during his first two and one-half years in office. He calmly rejected Plimpton's suggestion that the turmoil on the campus was the government's responsibility and defended the opportunities for dissent afforded by the democratic system. Then, in language infinitely more restrained than the Amherst letter and without, even by implication, threatening federal intervention in campus affairs, Nixon turned to the Plimptons of America and said: Physician, heal thyself.

> . . . no group, as a group, should be more zealous defenders of the integrity of academic standards and the rule of reason in academic life than the faculties of our great colleges and universities. But if the teacher simply follows the loudest voices, parrots the latest slogan, yields to unreasonable demands, he will have won not the respect but the contempt of his students; and he will deserve that contempt. Students have some rights. They have a right to guidance, to leadership and direction; they also have a right to expect their teachers to listen and to be reasonable, but also to stand for something—and most especially, to stand for the rule of reason against the rule of force.

Nixon wisely adhered to the Moynihan hands-off policy through 1969 and into the spring of 1970, following a policy neither of repression (he opposed federal sanctions against student demonstrators) nor of conceding the justice of the Amherst letter's indictment of the government for the uproar on the campus. This was not difficult for him. The President was largely interested in other matters; there was little room in his narrow attention span for campus problems. But when he did talk about the campus, he displayed four separate strains of thought, some consistent with the General Beadle

---

*Nixon was at General Beadle State College to dedicate a library named in honor of Senator Karl E. Mundt of South Dakota, a very conservative Republican and Communist-hunting colleague of Nixon's on the House Un-American Activities Committee two decades earlier. The President's advisers did not want him to speak at a more prestigious college for fear of antiwar demonstrations directed at him by students. On the next day, June 4, Nixon delivered the commencement address at an equally safe haven, the U.S. Air Force Academy at Colorado Springs, Colo.— those two speeches marking his first appearances before students as President. Nor did he venture onto the college campus with significantly greater frequency in 1970 and into 1971.

State College speech and some not; these, four strains not easily reconcilable, were destined to result in confusion and irresoluteness when the President confronted the great post-Cambodian crisis of 1970:

1. *Condoning of violence on the campus cannot be tolerated.* In a February 22, 1969, letter to the Reverend Theodore M. Hesburgh, president of the University of Notre Dame, Nixon said the rule of reason, not force, must govern a university, adding, "Whoever rejects that principle forfeits his right to be a member of the academic community. The university administrator who fails to uphold that principle jeopardizes one of the central pillars of his own institution and weakens the very foundation of American education.*

2. *Liberal higher education in America is in grave danger and must be saved.* In a March 22, 1969, written statement on campus disorders, Nixon said that a matter of great personal concern to him "is the preservation of the integrity, the independence, and the creativity of our institutions of higher learning. Freedom—intellectual freedom—is in danger in America."

3. *When you get right down to it, the campus and the students are no concern of mine:* ". . . there is really very little that we in Washington can do with regard to running the university and college campuses of this country," Nixon told his press conference of September 26, 1969. "We have enough problems running the nation, the national problems."

4. *Come on now, kids, I want to be your friend!* "We are concerned when we see on the campus of this country the frustration boiling up into violence, and we want to find answers with you," he told members of the Association of Student Governments meeting with him in the East Room of the White House on September 20, 1969.

Underlying the President's own ambiguity was a broad variety of views available within his administration—ranging from Finch to Agnew, from Dr. James Allen to Bryce Harlow. Allen, holding the

---

*This tough-talking strain was followed more vigorously by Attorney General Mitchell and particularly by Vice President Agnew, who began his memorable series of polemical addresses with an attack on "effete. . . . hand-wringing, sniveling" permissiveness toward student rebels in his Ohio State University commencement speech of June 7, 1969. Agnew's performance as a polemicist is detailed in Chapter XI.

dual office of U.S. Commissioner of Education and Assistant Secretary of HEW for Education, took a soft line extremely sympathetic to student rebels and their faculty allies. Harlow, besides reflecting Congressional impatience with the campus rebels, had little personal empathy for the shaggy-haired campus dissenters.

On Sunday, June 15, 1969, Allen attended the worship service at the White House, chatted afterward with the President and then was asked by Harlow if they could talk for a bit. The conference took place in Harlow's office between Allen, Harlow and Bud Krogh, an assistant to Ehrlichman handling education problems. Allen was testifying the next morning before the House Education and Labor Committee on a bill sponsored by Representative Edith Green, the powerful and independent-minded Democrat from Oregon, that would require college administrators to file with the U.S. Office of Education plans for dealing with campus disorders. Here was a litmus test to reveal soft- and hard-liners on the campus question. As perhaps the leading soft-liner in the administration, Dr. Allen was going to testify in opposition to the Green bill on the grounds that it constituted intrusion of the federal government into the academic community. That was what was bothering Harlow that Sunday morning. Apart from his personal affinity for the Green bill, there was the matter of Republicans and moderate-to-conservative Democrats on the committee—whose support Nixon badly needed on other matters—supporting the Green bill. Harlow did not like the idea of the administration's top spokesman being on the other side of the fence. So, he asked Allen, why not change your testimony to say: Mrs. Green, I don't agree with your position in principle but maybe we can work out *something*—you know, a compromise. Allen flatly refused. This was a matter of deep principle with him, he told Harlow and Krogh. "Jim, we are *very* disappointed," an unsmiling Harlow replied in his soft Oklahoma drawl. Allen testified against the bill, and on July 1 the committee defeated it by a vote of 18 to 17. His testimony may well have made the difference.*

---

*In the July 7 issue of the *New York Times*, Warren Weaver reported on the attempt of two White House aides (not identified by name) to pressure Allen into changing his testimony. Weaver's account read as though it had come from Allen, and an embarrassed Allen offered his resignation to Secretary Finch at HEW. Finch declined it.

What makes the incident so strange is its ambiguous quality. A decision not to oppose the Green bill had been made by two of the President's most senior advisers, Bryce Harlow and John Ehrlichman. Why, then, was Allen not *ordered* to avoid opposing testimony? No such orders came from Harlow or Ehrlichman's man, Krogh. Chatting with Allen after the worship service that Sunday, the President did not mention campus problems. Nor did he ever refer to the Green bill in talking to Allen. How Richard Nixon felt about the whole campus crisis was mist-shrouded and insubstantial, as would become quite clear nearly a year later.

The welcome quiet of spring 1970 on the American college campus, vastly more serene than the year before, abruptly ended on the evening of April 30, 1970, with the beginning of the Cambodian operation. The next morning, May 1, students across the country were marching, picketing, striking, blocking entry to classrooms. Some 2,300 students at Princeton immediately agreed to plans for a student strike. At the University of Maryland in the suburbs of Washington, students ransacked the Reserve Officers' Training Corps office in a violent struggle with police that resulted in damage estimated at $10,000 and fifty injuries. Calls for Nixon's impeachment as President came from the National Student Association, student body presidents from ten colleges and sixty-eight members of the Cornell faculty.

Richard Nixon was in a combative mood. Confident that he had done the right thing in Indochina, the President, in a postcrisis mood of euphoria, unleashed all his natural hostility toward the campus dissenters that he had successfully curbed for more than a year. That morning of May 1, as the campus riots began, a Presidential limousine carried him across the Potomac to the Pentagon for a briefing on the Cambodian developments. The war news was good, and Nixon's spirits soared. The briefing over, he talked informally with two high civilian officials who had briefed him:

> You see these bums, you know, blowing up the campuses. Listen, the boys that are on the college campuses today are the luckiest people in the world, going to the greatest universities, and here they are burning up the books, storming around about this issue. You name it. Get rid of the war there will be another one. Then out there [in Vietnam] we have kids who are just doing their duty. They stand tall

and they are proud. . . . They are going to do fine and we have to stand back of them.

Appeasement of the student rebels was clearly the farthest thought from Nixon's mind. Although a nationwide student strike was getting under way with participation by more than 100 colleges, Nixon felt the campus reaction would subside as the initial shock of Cambodia faded and, in any event, was far less important than the general public's approval of the operation. So, he was not in a receptive frame of mind on Monday, May 4, when he received a letter drafted by President James M. Hester of New York University and signed by the presidents of thirty-six other colleges and universities. Pleading with Nixon "to consider the incalculable dangers of an unprecedented alienation of America's youth and to take immediate action to demonstrate unequivocally your determination to end the war quickly," they "urgently requested" a meeting with the President. When Press Secretary Ron Ziegler advised the press that the request likely would be rejected, Dr. Allen went to the White House to urge Moynihan and Ehrlichman to recommend such a meeting. They disagreed, arguing that the university administrators had been presumptuous and arrogant in their demands.

"This is not the way you treat a President," said Moynihan.

"This is not the way you keep a campus quiet," Allen shot back.

Moynihan and Ehrlichman prevailed. Nixon turned down the request. But as he was doing so, an event that would radically change the course of the post-Cambodian reaction and irrevocably affect the course of his administration was taking place in rural Ohio in the college town of Kent.

Kent State University, with 19,000 coeducational undergraduates, was a typically politicized state college where the faculty and administration had increasingly permitted excesses of student protest. Kent State's reaction to Cambodia was predictable, immoderate and massive, culminating in a Saturday night riot on May 2 in which the Reserve Officers' Training Corps building was burned down. Govenor James Rhodes of Ohio declared martial law at Kent State that night, dispatching units of the 145th Infantry, Ohio National Guard, to the campus. The demonstrations continued. On Monday, May 4, National Guardsmen sought to clear an area of rock-throwing student demonstrators, then opened fire without warning. When the guns had stilled, four students were dead and eleven wounded.

In its hard-line mood that had prevailed since April 30, the administration reacted to Kent State with an air of I-told-you-so. Agnew called the tragedy "predictable and avoidable," adding that it pointed up "grave dangers which accompany the new politics of violence and confrontation." At the White House, Ziegler said the killings "should remind us all once again that when dissent turns to violence it invites tragedy." The President himself expressed hope "that this tragic and unfortunate incident will strengthen the determination of all the nation's campuses" to strongly oppose "the resort to violence" as a method of dissent.

Not in the foreseeable future would the spokesmen of this administration be so self-confident about what was happening on the campus. Nixon did not even faintly envision the emotional torrent that the Kent State incident would set off across the country—on the campus, off the campus, in the administration.

The quantum jump in campus disorder was the first result. Fires did $100,000 damage on Long Island University's Brooklyn campus. Govenor Ronald Reagan closed the University of California with its 280,000 students as radicals attempted to seize control of the academic process. Three students were stabbed in a demonstration at the University of New Mexico. Nearly 40,000 students and faculty marched from the University of Minnesota to the state capitol. A half-million-dollar fire was set at Colorado State University. Students at the University of South Carolina took over the first floor of the adminstration buildings and ransacked the treasurer's office.

The list was endless. Overexcited student extremists, followed by temporarily radicalized moderates, thought the moment of revolution was at hand, and the self-assurance quickly fell away from the Nixon administration as the President viewed the carnage. Throughout official Washington, there was soul-searching and in no man was it deeper than in Wally Hickel.

When Governor Walter Hickel of Alaska was designated Secretary of the Interior in late 1968, he seemed among the least likely members of the Cabinet fated to side with student demonstrators. A self-made millionaire in the old rugged individualist mold, he showed his utter insensitivity to the deep public concern over man's ruination of his environment as soon as he was appointed. In a Washington press conference of December 18, 1968, the Secretary-designate fired a barrage of anticonservationist statements and affirmed that he saw no virtue in "conservation for conservation's sake."* This was the starting point for the education of Wally Hickel. To win confirmation by the Senate (two days later than the rest of the Cabinet), he had to swallow each and every one of his statements of December 18 in the presence of environmentalist Democratic senators on the Senate Interior Committee.

But, surprisingly, Hickel's conversion to the environmentalists' camp was a genuine one. His was a major contribution in forming the strong legislative program for protecting the environment that President Nixon submitted to Congress in his 1970 State of the Union Message. Suddenly he became the nation's most militant conservationist, blocking a proposed jetport that might damage the ecology of the Florida Everglades, taking action on his own to suspend federal leases to Union Oil Co. for drilling wells off Santa Barbara, Calif., prosecuting Chevron Oil Co. for culpability in oil spills in the Gulf of Mexico. In the good gray Cabinet of Richard Nixon, the Secretary of the Interior was a colorful, engaging individual.

He was not the favorite among Nixon's inner circle. Mitchell and Ehrlichman grumbled that Wally Hickel was a "poor administrator," unable to coordinate the far-flung undertakings of the Department of the Interior. But other Cabinet members who were equally poor administrators were in far less trouble. Hickel's high, piercing voice, Rotarian enthusiasm, profanity and table-pounding enthusiasm grated on the nerves of the President and his men. In an administration where the ego was supposed to be subdued or at least under tight control, Hickel's ran wild. Nixon's fascination with the film *Patton* had been based on admiration of the general as the kind of leader he would like to be; Hickel was equally fascinated, but saw George Patton as the kind of leader he himself was. "My God!" shouted Hickel, as he watched the film. "That's *me.*"

Nixon himself may have had some premonition at the time of Hickel's swearing in that his Secretary of the Interior was going to give him a little trouble. Recalling that earlier Secretary of the Interior under Franklin Roosevelt, "Old Curmudgeon" Harold Ickes,

*In that memorable press conference, Hickel also said conservationists wanted to "lock up lands for no reason. . . ." Other Hickelisms that day: "If we set standards too high, we might even hinder industrial developments. . . . In some areas, you might even have to use a subsidy to solve it." "A tree looking at a tree really doesn't do anything, but a person looking at a tree means something."

Nixon said humorously that one objective Ickes had set for himself was to "keep the President humble," adding, "Secretary Ickes was the one who once said that the President is not a descendant of a sun-goddess. And I am sure that Secretary Hickel will assume that great responsibility to see that this President also remains humble." Then, in a remark that later events would inscribe with even more irony, Nixon took note of the fact that Hickel had been the last of his Cabinet to win confirmation. "So," the President said, "if I may present him now with the Biblical scripture, 'The last shall be first,' as far as this Administration is concerned."

What disturbed the Nixon inner circle most about Hickel was his incessant combativeness in administration circles. A 1937 Golden Gloves boxing champion back home in Kansas, Hickel defied the unwritten Nixon edict that Cabinet members should be seen and not heard, often sounding off on subjects far removed from the province of the Interior Department. He was becoming Richard Nixon's *bête noire,* in no small part because of the happenstance placing of seats around the Cabinet table. When the President, after reading a paper at a Cabinet session, would lift his eyes, they would be staring directly across the table at the round, smooth, slightly chubby, animated, smiling face of Wally Hickel.

That Hickel was going to be a pest became obvious as early as April 1969, when he broke into a Cabinet meeting to deliver a polemic against the tight-money policy then carried on by the Federal Reserve Board. Hickel brought his hand down hard on the Cabinet table one time, thundering: "This fiscal policy is wrong!"* The rising interest rates in combination with high taxes, he continued, would bring about ruinous inflation. Hickel had violated the rules. Such matters were supposed to be discussed by those in authority in the Quadriad, not in general Cabinet sessions. David Kennedy, Secretary of the Treasury, seated next to Hickel, gave him a frosty banker's stare. Nobody else said a word. The silence was deafening —and embarrassing.† Nixon, with his usual good manners, saved the day. "Wally's got a point," he said. "We'll listen to it; we don't have to agree." But Nixon was not really interested in monetary policy in

---

*No economist, Hickel was referring to monetary policy, not fiscal policy.

†After the meeting, Clifford Hardin, Secretary of Agriculture, approached Hickel and told him most of the Cabinet in reality agreed with him. That only made Hickel more angry.

April 1969. The incident was meaningless from the standpoint of economic policy; not until August of that year was an effective campaign against tight money waged within the administration, and Hickel—far from the economic decision-making process—had nothing to do with it.* But the incident marked him off as a troublemaker.

Nor did the White House appreciate the way Hickel so vigorously lobbied for his projects. In August 1969, at San Clemente, Hickel made an impressive presentation in Cabinet for an expensive, long-term parks program. "This is what I want," the President said, delighted at a program whose benefits would immediately reach the taxpayer-voter. But the money managers seated around the Cabinet table—Kennedy, Mayo, McCracken and Burns—were not so happy. "Young man," Arthur Burns lectured Hickel later, "don't be so cocky. You haven't got all this money yet." He surely did not. As the effectiveness of Hickel's dynamic presentation faded, a Nixon interested in many matters more important than parks, yielded to the imperatives of fiscal austerity. Hickel never did get the money.

In the housecleaning contemplated for the Cabinet after the 1970 midterm election, Hickel was scheduled to be the first to go. Nor was the unhappiness totally one-sided. Hickel felt his lack of influence in the administration and most acutely his lack of access to the President. He had seen the President privately only twice since the inauguration. Moreover, his new-found militancy for protecting the environment had put him in close touch with the ecology movement on campus and in closer communication with students than most members of the administration. Increasingly he felt that Nixon, Agnew, Mitchell, et al., were unnecessarily alienating the students. In the weeks before Cambodia–Kent State, Hickel tried to arrange a private meeting with Nixon to discuss this problem. Failing that, he tried to give his message to Ehrlichman, who could then pass it on to Nixon. But Hickel could not even reach Ehrlichman. For him, the Berlin Wall was impenetrable.

Hickel's deepening frustration came to a peak that horrible first week in May 1970. The Cambodian operation, the Kent State incident, and the Nixon-Agnew reaction to it, impelled Hickel on May 6, two days after Kent State, to dictate an impassioned letter to the President that began:

*See pp. 193–94.

I believe this Administration finds itself, today, embracing a philosophy which appears to lack appropriate concern for the attitude of a great mass of America—our young people.

Addressed either politically or philosophically, I believe we are in error if we set out consciously to alienate those who could be our friends.

Today, our young people, or at least a vast segment of them, believe they have no opportunity to communicate with Government, regardless of Administration, other than through violent confrontation. . . .

Reminding the President that the British Crown had failed to listen to the young voices of Patrick Henry and Thomas Jefferson two hundred years ago, he contended that "history . . . clearly shows that youth in its protest must be heard." Hickel delivered this admonition, based on such premises, to the President: "Let us give America an optimistic outlook and optimistic leadership. Let us show them [youth] we can solve our problems in an enlightened and positive manner." He also called on Nixon to muzzle Agnew: ". . . a continued attack on the young—not on their attitudes so much as their motives, can serve little purpose other than to further cement these attitudes to a solidity impossible to penetrate with reason." Before closing ("Faithfully yours, Wally"), he suggested that the President "consider meeting, on an *individual* and conversational basis, with members of your Cabinet"—in other words open up the Haldeman-Ehrlichman Berlin Wall.*

Even if the confidentiality of this remarkable letter had been scrupulously protected, it was so critical of the administration's conduct of public affairs that, properly, it should have been accompanied by a letter of resignation. But, in fact, its confidentiality was not protected. Within hours after it was written and before Nixon had received it, an aide to Hickel slipped the letter to the press—apparently without Hickel's authorization—and its full text appeared in the morning newspapers of May 7.† Not even then did Hickel, unaware of such proprieties, submit his resignation.

The anger and frustration of Richard Nixon and his closest

*Emphasis is added.
†At his press conference of May 11, Nixon made a little joke about Hickel's letter reaching him by faster means than ordinary mail: "I hope he [Hickel] gives some advice to the Postmaster General. That was the fastest mail delivery I have had since I have been in the White House."

advisers can be imagined. Just at the moment when the American college was racked by arson, violence and revolution, when the country seemed in the process of disintegration, the President was stabbed in the back by a member of his own Cabinet! There was no need for long debates. Hickel *had* to go. He had eliminated himself by embarrassing the President in his most vulnerable moment.

But there were political reasons why Hickel could not be sacked forthwith. He remained the most formidable political figure in Alaska. With Republicans facing close elections for the governorship, the Senate and the state's lone Congressional seat in Alaska in November 1970, it would not be prudent to alienate Wally Hickel. Indeed, if fired right now, he might go right back to Alaska to run for his old job as governor as an anti-Nixon Republican. If he were kept on the job through the 1970 election, he could not run for the governorship or a Senate seat before 1974.

Far outweighing Alaskan politics in these calculations was Hickel's sudden new importance nationally. With his letter of May 6, he had become an instant folk hero on the college campus. The calculation necessary at the White House was this: Would Wally Hickel be more dangerous in the 1970 campaign as a tame Secretary of the Interior making innocuous campaign stops for Republican candidates or as a fired-up insurgent who had just been sacked and now was traveling the lecture circuit with anti-Nixon polemics? The obvious answer was made all the more obvious by the stark sense of terror, close to panic, pervading the White House after Kent State. The early post-Cambodia hard line was turning to appeasement, and that meant Hickel could not be fired now at the risk of further inflaming the campus.

The solution was what lawyer Ehrlichman wryly referred to among friends as an "interlocutory decree." Hickel would be sacked, but he would not leave until *after* the election. To make this effective in the eyes of the public and particularly Hickel's new campus constituency, it should not seem now to the public that Nixon was in any way displeased with Hickel. There then began an amazing charade of Nixon heaping praise on Hickel while conservatives, not realizing what was going on, gnashed their teeth in rage.

At his press conference of May 8, Nixon had not a single word of criticism for the man he had decided to fire under interlocutory decree. "I think the Secretary of the Interior is a man who has very strong views," said Nixon. "He is outspoken. He is courageous. . . . As far as his views are concerned, I will, of course, be interested in his advice."

At the same time, key Presidential aides were treating Hickel with maximum care in conversations with the press. The comments by Ehrlichman at an off-the-record session with newspaper correspondents at Costin's Restaurant in downtown Washington, the evening of May 13, are particularly remarkable and worth quoting at some length, considering Ehrlichman's part in the decision to sack Hickel. Although the dinner conversation was off the record, Ehrlichman was implanting in the correspondents the false impression that Nixon-Hickel relations were most cordial—in hopes they would write precisely that. Ehrlichman said:

> The stories I've read are just incredible. They are totally without foundation. Neither one of them [Hickel or Nixon] now feels there is a problem. If we let the newspapers run our Cabinet, we'd be running pillar to post. He's [Hickel] at peace on this. He's not exercised.
>
> He was in and out of Richard Nixon's office [during meetings to discuss the President's environmental program] maybe 40 times. He's seen him maybe 20 times since. Most probably what he meant was that he hadn't had a chance to meet with Nixon alone on matters of broader interest than just departmental matters. But that's not the way we run the White House. There's always a staff member present when Cabinet people come in unless it's just a personal visit. The President is an awfully busy man. He doesn't have the time just to put his feet up on his desk and say: "How are you, Wally? What's on your mind these days?"

Having launched this campaign to convince the outside world that all was well between Dick Nixon and Wally Hickel, there remained the corollary problem of dealing with Hickel himself. On May 7, the day Hickel's letter was published, John Whitaker, the White House aide handling Interior Department problems, visited Hickel in an attempt to cool him off. It was less than successful. Hickel got the impression—incorrect actually—that the White House was unaffected by the shock waves that Kent State had set off. Even after Nixon's kind statements about Hickel at his press conference on May 8 and Hickel's courteous response that young people "should be reassured by the President's determination to work together with all those millions of Americans who share his loyalty to the nation, if not always the same views," the trouble had not been smoothed over. Hickel still had not seen the President himself or even heard from him personally.

So Hickel was still in a prickly mood on Sunday evening, May 10, when CBS newsman Mike Wallace and a film crew went to Hickel's red-brick rambler in Kenwood, Md., an upper-middle-class suburb of Washington, to interview him for the network television show *60 Minutes* two days later. Recounting his difficulties in reaching either Nixon or Ehrlichman prior to Kent State to tell them of his concern with the alienation of youth, Hickel told Wallace that the White House staff is now "angry over timing" of the letter.*

On Tuesday, May 12, Ehrlichman, unaware of what had been told Mike Wallace, scheduled a chat with Hickel. What happened at that meeting, crucial to an understanding of what would happen months later, is in dispute.

The White House version is that Ehrlichman, then and there, fired Hickel but asked him not to say anything about it until after the November 3 election out of loyalty to the party and to the President. Hickel agreed and kept his word.

Hickel's friends give this colloquy to support a quite different version:

Ehrlichman: "We've got to set up a meeting between you and the President."

Hickel: "Do I have any problem with the President?"

Ehrlichman: "No, but he's upset, and we've got to set up a meeting.

Hickel: "Was there any problem with the President before I sent the letter?"

Ehrlichman: "No, none at all."

By any measurement, the latter version has greater credibility. It would be hard to imagine a man of Wally Hickel's ego and explosiveness accepting such a humiliating arrangement, or even if he had, living with it for four long months. Nor does Hickel's aggressive pace during those four months, still trying—and still mostly failing—to affect administration policy, lend credibility to the White House

---

*Hickel's son, Jack, nineteen, a University of San Francisco student, also interviewed by Mike Wallace, said he opposed the Cambodian operation and added of his father: "I think he was probably against it too." He was, but made no public criticism of the military operation proper.

version of a man living on borrowed time, under the weight of an interlocutory decree. The most charitable reconciliation of the two versions is that Ehrlichman *thought* he was sacking Hickel with a delayed impact and that Hickel did not understand it that way—just barely plausible in an administration that had enormous difficulties in firing anybody and where breakdowns in internal communications led to incessant misunderstandings.

What is not in dispute is that Nixon personally did *not* fire Hickel that spring. When Mike Wallace's interview ran on *60 Minutes* the evening of May 12, Nixon and Ehrlichman were irritated all over again and their determination that Hickel must go was reinforced. Nevertheless, a few days later, Hickel was summoned to the Oval Office for his third private visit with the President since the inauguration. Although Nixon had already decided his fate, the meeting was totally cordial.

"Mr. President," asked Hickel bluntly, "do you want me to leave?"

Richard Nixon threw up his arms. "That's one option I've never considered," he told Hickel.

It worked. Press sensation about the Hickel letter died down. Hickel lapsed back into the relative anonymity of a Nixon Cabinet officer. But at the White House, that "interlocutory decree" was not forgotten.

The treatment of Hickel in early May 1970 was, therefore, a White House ploy, born out of deep apprehension over the revolution on the campus, and consequently casts a shadow over the credibility of what was done directly to combat that revolution.

By the time Richard Nixon received Secretary Hickel's letter, the euphoria and self-confidence of May 1 had vanished in the aftermath of Kent State and its trail of flames and violence across the country. The observations from the White House immediately after the Kent State tragedy that violence begets violence did not long survive the nationwide holocaust. For the first time since he took office, a sense of panic enveloped Richard Nixon and the men around him, revealing self-doubt, lack of philosophical moorings and a pragmatism gone wild in dealing with one of the most difficult and intractable social issues of the nation: the student revolution. The Nixon hard line of May Day would be bent by panic into a policy that increasingly resembled appeasement, then would, as the flames of the campus died, shift back toward a hard line in preparation for the 1970 midterm election campaign. It was a performance that was to infuriate the campus, dismay conservatives and leave high officials inside the administration unhappy and perplexed.

Through all this period, the President seldom consulted the three Ivy League professors on his own White House staff: Pat Moynihan (Harvard), Henry Kissinger (Harvard) and Martin Anderson (Columbia). By conventional standards, Moynihan and Kissinger were liberals, Anderson a conservative. But all three agreed on the essence of the campus problem, believing that the fate of liberal education in America was at stake and that the roots of the problem were many and tangled: the affluence of modern youth, the decline of the intellectual tradition on the campus, the breakdown in all forms of authority, the spinelessness of college administrators who were more fund-raisers than schoolmen. All this was tending to politicize the university, with Vietnam a catalyst, not a cause. But as the university crisis reached a climax in the spring of 1970, Nixon turned not to his professors but to more intimate aides with a less informed and less profound view of the campus situation, and in particular to John Ehrlichman. His son a student at Stanford, Ehrlichman saw the problem simplistically as one of lack of communication. Failing to perceive the cosmic proportions of the campus crisis, Ehrlichman felt the problems could be solved merely by reassuring the students of the President's good will. In that off-the-record session with newspaper correspondents of May 13, Ehrlichman said:

> Our relationship with the kids stems from the feeling that no one is listening to them. They assume that there is a sort of active dislike of students in the Administration. We assume from the start that we disagree on Cambodia. We can live with that; they can live with that. But they want to be reassured that they are not being put down as a class. . . . It's like a kid who has been repudiated by his father. . . .

From this deceptively simple view of the problem came the moves toward appeasement born of the post-Kent State panic. On May 5, the day after the killings, six Kent State students came to Washington to see their Congressman, Representative J. William Stanton, an Ohio Republican, who met with the students and then telephoned the White House, arranging a meeting that day for them with Ehrlichman. Deeply impressed, Ehrlichman arranged for them to see the President the next day. At that meeting the students told Nixon that the upheaval on campus was caused by the Vietnam war and the lack of communication between student youth and the federal government. The three professors on Nixon's staff could have told him that Vietnam was at best a catalyst and certainly not a cause in the campus crisis, that communication was no problem and that the government knew all too well what the students were saying and vice versa. Indeed, Nixon often had said this himself in private, most recently in his harsh remarks of May 1 to the civilian officials at the Pentagon. But amazingly, in the new post-Kent State soft line, the President tended to agree with the students, informing them that his four basic goals might "minimize" student dissent—ending the Vietnam war, avoiding similar wars in the future, slowing the arms race and ending military conscription.

Although on the day of the Kent State killings Nixon had brushed aside the plea by thirty-six college presidents to see him, he now asked Ehrlichman to arrange a meeting with a smaller group. On May 7 he conferred with eight college heads, who proceeded to deliver the conventional academic view, not much different from what the Kent State undergraduates had given him a day earlier, that the crisis was the fault of the Vietnam war and the Nixon administration. The joint statement read to the President by Nathan Pusey of Harvard criticized antistudent remarks by members of the administration (presumably including the President's own May 1 reference to "bums" but aimed primarily at the steady antistudent barrage from Agnew) as a cause in fostering the revolution on campus.* Nixon listened courteously and attentively and gave everybody present the unmistakable impression that there would be no more student-baiting from Richard Nixon, Spiro Agnew or anybody else in his administration.

Among the eight college presidents conferring with Nixon, the

*The eight college heads included two former colleagues of Nixon's in the Eisenhower administration: Malcolm C. Moos of the University of Minnesota, who had been an Eisenhower speech writer, and W. Allen Wallis of the University of Rochester, who had been executive director of the Cabinet Committee on Price Stability, headed by Vice President Nixon. Others, besides Pusey, were William C. Friday of the University of North Carolina, Alexander Heard of Vanderbilt and Edward H. Levi of the University of Chicago.

President was particularly impressed by a soft-spoken Southerner: Dr. G. Alexander Heard, Chancellor of Vanderbilt University. Kissinger had a high regard for Heard and, in the only part he played in the spring crisis, suggested that the President name him as temporary liaison with the colleges. Considering Kissinger's hard-line views on the campus question, it was a curious recommendation. Heard was well respected but, like most college administrators, instinctively sided with student dissent and echoed current complaints of the student body. Two days later, on May 9, Dr. Heard was named not as the President's spokesman on the campus, but as the ambassador of the campus to the President. "The President demonstrated to me his willingness to listen," Heard told the press. "I will do my best to help him hear." Here again was the conception beloved of the students themselves: that the problem was mainly one of communication.

At his nationally televised press conference on the evening of Friday, May 8, Richard Nixon seemed unusually tense and ill at ease, and excessively eager to show an open face to the rampaging students, thousands of whom, nonviolent but volatile, were now in Washington and surrounding the White House itself. The neo-Churchillian heroics of April 30 were a memory from another age, as Nixon pledged an early return of the American troops from Cambodia.* As for the student demonstrations, never had he been so conciliatory. The same President who on September 26, 1969, had said that "under no circumstances will I be affected" by student antiwar demonstrations now had changed radically, saying of the student demonstrators:

> They are trying to say that they want peace. They are trying to say that they want to stop the killing. They are trying to say that they want to end the draft. They are trying to say that we ought to get out of Vietnam. I agree with everything that they are trying to accomplish.

While denying that he would muzzle Agnew (who that very night delivered an attack against "choleric young intellectuals"), as implied by the eight college presidents, the President said meaningfully, "I would hope that all the members of this Administration would have in mind . . . a rule that I have always had . . . : When the action is hot, keep the rhetoric cool."

*See p. 245.

The press conference ended at 10:30 P.M. As often was the case in a time of crisis after he had completed a public performance that so drained him emotionally, Richard Nixon was in a state of hyper-excitement, unable to think of sleep. A confirmed addict of the telephone at such moments, he talked with friends—placing and accepting calls, mainly from the West Coast, until 2:30 Saturday morning, then finally went to bed. But his mind was on the 100,000 student demonstrators converging on Washington, staying awake all night at the great marble memorials along the Mall in preparation for the next day's protest rally. He had curtly ignored the antiwar demonstrations of the previous fall, making certain that the press knew he was inside the White House watching a college football game over television while hundreds of thousands marched outside on October 15. His attitude now, in his new mood of reconciliation, was far different; he was anxious to make contact with the students and try his hand at "communication." So, after sleeping fitfully for an hour, Nixon arose, placed another telephone call, and then, in-forming only his valet, Manolo Sanchez, and the Secret Service, set forth by limousine from the White House at 4:55 A.M., arriving at the Lincoln Memorial five minutes later. There, Nixon found some eight students whose numbers soon grew to fifty.

The hour-long exchange that followed was to Nixon, he told Garnett Horner of the *Washington Evening Star* immediately after-ward, one of the most interesting experiences of his life. "I know you think we are a bunch of sons-of-bitches," said the President to the students. Attempting to achieve empathy with them, he remembered his own days as a law student at Duke University when his own perceptions of world politics were not always correct. At that time, he told them, he felt Neville Chamberlain was "the greatest man living" and Winston Churchill was "a madman," only coming to realize his error later. ("I doubt if it got over," he confessed to reporter Horner two hours later.) The President urged the students to keep their demonstration peaceful, adding, "Remember, I feel just as deeply as you do about this." Clearly, he wanted no face-to-face debate on Cambodia. Instead he launched into a long, descriptive travelogue discussing interesting places he advised the students to visit while they were still young—Japan, Mexico, China (if possible), Indochina (!), India, Iran, the Soviet Union, Hungary, Czechoslo-vakia. Touching on the problems of black separatism, the urban crisis and environmental pollution, the President finally moved around the little crowd to talk with the students.

Here, however, his congenital difficulty in making easy conversation betrayed him. When he met a group of students from Syracuse University, then closed down by the antiwar strike, he could only blurt out a question about whether Syracuse would return to the powerful football teams of the recent past. Meeting some students from his native state of California, whose whole system of higher education was then paralyzed, he asked whether they enjoyed surfing. These irrelevancies are what the students carried away in their memories from their rare meeting with the President of the United States.

From the Lincoln Memorial, the President visited a deserted Capitol (to show it to Manolo Sanchez, who had never seen it), and thence to the Mayflower Hotel in midtown Washington, where, unnoticed, he breakfasted in the Rib Room on corned beef hash with a poached egg. By 7:30, he was back at the White House, seeking out the first reporter he saw, Horner, to tell him of the morning's events.

It was a unique outing for Richard Nixon, of a kind not seen before in his Presidency and, as of mid-1971, not seen again. The most sequestered President since Herbert Hoover—hidden behind the iron grillwork of the White House—he had suddenly sallied forth to meet with potentially hostile demonstrators. It was the only reprise of his abortive "Bring Us Together" slogan of election night, 1968.* But more than that, it was the symbolic high point of his post-Kent State effort to appease the student revolution and, as such, revealed the limitations of that tactic.

The fact that he had been so eager to brief the press in detail on his conversation at the Lincoln Memorial showed that Nixon thought his effort at "communicating" with the students had been a highly successful one. But those students who had been at the Memorial, when interviewed later by reporters, were negative, and dwelled on his irrelevancies about football and surfing. Reading those comments, Presidential aides were bitter, feeling the students were distorting a deeply meaningful experience so as not to lose status with their peers. In truth, however, the President's remarks as he described them himself—the Chamberlain-Churchill analogy, the little travelogue, the admonition against black separatism on the

*See pp. 33–35.

campus—scarcely seemed likely to appeal to a college undergraduate of 1970 who was politicized enough to travel to Washington for a demonstration. The incident, indeed, reflected the limitations of the Ehrlichman-Nixon concept that all that was really necessary was communication. The differences between the student left and Richard Nixon could not be resolved by an early-morning saunter on the Mall.

Nixon's soft line scarcely inhibited the convulsions on the American college campus, and there was yet more tragedy to come. In the early hours of May 15, a demonstration on the campus of all-Negro Jackson State College in Jackson, Miss., ended in tragedy with state highway patrolmen opening fire on student demonstrators. Two died, eleven were wounded.*

Five days later, on May 20, the President met with the presidents of fifteen predominantly Negro colleges for more than two hours at the White House to discuss the Jackson State tragedy and general problems affecting black higher education.† The statement read by President Herman Branson of Central State University, Wilberforce, Ohio, was intentionally harsh. "The increasing alienation of black youth" was blamed in no small part on "the policies and practices of your Administration" and especially the rhetoric of Spiro Agnew and John Mitchell.

By virtue of both his inclination against face-to-face confrontation and his new conciliatory policy toward the campus, the President did not refute the statement. But a strange incident occurred after Branson finished reading the joint statement, showing that Nixon's patience with such constant haranguing from the campus community and his confidence in the new soft line were both wearing thin. John A. Peoples, Jr., president of Jackson State, pulled from his briefcase a series of photographs showing the killings at his college. Nixon leafed through the photos, then suddenly sat bolt upright and said, "Look, what are we going to do to get more respect for the police from our young people?" The law-and-order theme of autumn

---

*However, the Jackson State killings did not have nearly the convulsive effect of those at Kent State. The explanation given by many black leaders was racism. With some justification, they argued that the deaths of white students were more meaningful to liberal Americans than the deaths of black students.

†The meeting had been requested by the black educators just prior to the Jackson State killings.

1968 had suddenly transcended the soft line of spring 1970—a hint of what might be coming in the 1970 campaign. The Negro educators bristled, and tense silence enveloped the room. A bit rattled, the President then turned to Deputy Attorney General Kleindienst and asked him to brief the college presidents on how the new Law Enforcement Assistance Administration in the Justice Department was going to work. The black educators glowered as they listened to what they regarded as a *non sequitur* of stunning proportions. Nixon said little else in the course of the meeting.

But he had not yet abandoned his soft line. Just as Heard's appointment had emerged from the May 7 meeting with the white college presidents, Nixon was most impressed with President James E. Cheek of Howard University at the May 20 meeting, and two days later he named him a consultant to Heard—to be not Nixon's representative to the black colleges but the ambassador of the black colleges to Nixon. With the Heard and Cheek appointments, the Nixon soft line, born of tragedy and violence and the fear they instilled, set up a trap soon to be sprung on the President himself. That was quite evident to Pat Moynihan and Marty Anderson. But they were not consulted by the President.

On May 21, six days after the Jackson State killings, Dr. James Allen prepared for two gripe sessions (called "informal exchanges") with government workers under his supervision in the Office of Education which were to encapsulate the deep resentment that Cambodia–Kent State had caused within the federal government, and the Nixon administration's lack of purposefulness in dealing with it.

Nowhere was there more turbulent anti-Nixon feeling in May 1970 than at the sprawling Department of Health, Education and Welfare, the most liberal of federal departments in both its Presidential appointees and its civil servants.* The rising tide of anger of the civil servants in one of HEW's biggest divisions, the Office of Educa-

---

*Immediately after Cambodia, HEW civil servants began pressing for a meeting with Secretary Finch. It was finally scheduled for May 19 in the HEW Auditorium, but one hour before the meeting, Finch was rushed off to the hospital with a nerve ailment in his arm. Under Secretary Veneman, explaining to the employees that Finch was hospitalized and that he would read a prepared statement by Finch, was hissed and booed. Veneman was hissed again in reading the Finch statement's defense of the Cambodian operation.

tion, had led Dr. Allen to agree to the two "informal exchanges." He, too, was troubled. On April 27, three days before the move into Cambodia, Allen took a public stand for school desegregation that made clear his unhappiness with the President's desegregation statement of March 24 (from whose preparation Allen had been excluded).* Arriving at his office on May 1, the day after the President's Cambodian speech, Allen found his staff in an uproar. Anthony J. (Toby) Moffett, Jr., head of the newly formed Office of Students and Youth in the Office of Education, came in to chat.

"What are we going to do, Toby?" asked Allen.

"Don't ask me," Moffett replied, "I resigned in the middle of the speech last night.†

Allen was not prepared to take such precipitate action and, instead, began three weeks of torment and indecision. When Hickel's letter made the headlines on May 7, Allen's aides urged him to send a similar message to the President. But still Allen held his peace. His choices, he knew, were threefold: say nothing; support Nixon on Cambodia; oppose him. Finally, he decided on the third option, feeling his loyalty to the educational community ran deeper than his loyalty to the Nixon administration and that, as its representative in the Nixon administration, he must reflect the educational community's agony over Cambodia.

Knowing on May 22 that he would be asked about Cambodia, he had typed out a statement breaking with the President on Cambodia—the first sub-Cabinet officer to make such a break *publicly*.‡ At the first "informal exchange," when the question came up, Allen read in part from his typed statement:

> My professional competence does not include answers in this area. But I find it very difficult to understand the rationale to move into Cambodia, or indeed, to continue the war in Vietnam. . . . Our concern

---

*See pp. 172–73.

†In truth, Moffett did not resign until May 7 and then based it not primarily on the Cambodian operation itself but on "irresponsible" statements by Nixon, his reference to student demonstrators as "bums" and his comments immediately following the Kent State killings.

‡Another Assistant Secretary at HEW, James Farmer, had been criticizing the Cambodian intervention since May 1 whenever anybody asked him. But no newsman asked him, and no newsman was around when anybody else asked him. As a result, there were no repercussions, and Farmer stayed in office, resigning on December 7, 1970.

must be in dealing with the disastrous effects on the education of young people in this country.*

Even less thoroughly versed in the niceties of government protocol than Hickel, Dr. Allen did not immediately resign. Months later, he would acknowledge that his resignation was certainly called for. But in those tense days he did not take for granted that he would be leaving. Indeed, his fellow top-level officials at HEW privately congratulated him for his forthrightness.

When Allen returned to his office from the HEW Auditorium, he found a message waiting for him from the White House that he should proceed there immediately to see Ehrlichman. Allen assumed, naturally, he was going to be fired. But when he arrived at the White House, he found that Ehrlichman wanted to talk about the details of the President's proposal of $1.5 billion to help school desegregation in the South.† The meeting ended without Ehrlichman saying a word about Cambodia. Before leaving, Allen felt obliged to tell Ehrlichman that he had broken with the President on Cambodia and that the *Washington Evening Star* was now on the streets with the story. Not even lifting an eyebrow, poker-faced John Ehrlichman said he had not yet seen the story and made no other comment.

Now began a waiting game of nerves. Nixon well knew that Allen simply could not continue in a sub-Cabinet-level post after so personal a rebuke to himself implied in Allen's public break on Cambodia. But in that crisis month of May of 1970, the panicky sense of lost confidence that followed Kent State still persisted, and the President did not want to risk throwing fuel on the campus conflagration by *firing* Allen; he wanted Allen to *resign,* and do it quickly (and hopefully as quietly) as possible. Indeed, Ehrlichman

---

*The full statement by Allen, which he read in its entirety to the second meeting: "I find it difficult to understand the rationale for the necessity of the move into Cambodia as a means of supporting and hastening the withdrawal from Vietnam, a withdrawal that I feel must be accomplished as quickly as possible. What concerns me most now is what our responsibility is in dealing with the disastrous effects that this action has had on education throughout the nation and the confidence of millions of concerned citizens in their government."

†Ehrlichman wanted Allen's approval of the $1.5 billion subsidy, even though he had not been consulted in the planning for it because Senator Jacob Javits of New York, a leading Republican liberal, would not press it in the Senate unless Allen did. However, Allen insisted on a softening of the proposal's anti-busing implications, changes which Ehrlichman agreed to at that May 21 meeting.

asked Secretary Finch at HEW to pressure his education chief to resign immediately. But Finch, playing out the string and about to leave his desk of torment at HEW for the tranquillity of Cabinet-level Counsellor's post in the White House, was not about to push out the distinguished educator he had lured to Washington from his sinecure in Albany.*

A few days after his meeting with the civil servants, Allen visited Walter Reed Army Hospital to see Finch, convalescing from the nerve ailment in his arm and utterly exhausted after his unhappy fourteen months at HEW.

"Some of the boys in the White House would like me to resign," commented Allen as they chatted in the warm sunshine on the Walter Reed balcony.

"I know," replied Finch. "I've been telling them to keep their shirts on. I tell them this: I'll talk to Jim Allen, but I'm not for his resignation." The main reason for haste, Finch explained, was the runoff election for governor of Alabama coming up in a few days. George Wallace was running to get back in the Statehouse and was campaigning in large part against the Nixon administration. Nixon's political aides, for their part, would have dearly loved to see Wallace eliminated then and there with no chance to cause Nixon trouble in the 1972 Presidential election. Nixon political operatives were telling Finch of their fears that Wallace would use Allen's apostasy on Cambodia as proof positive that all the leftists were hiding out in the Nixon administration.†

The waiting game continued for a full twenty days—Allen refusing to resign, Nixon not yet daring to fire him. Finally, at around 5 P.M. on June 10, Allen was summoned to Robert Finch's huge office at HEW. Finch motioned Allen to the couch in the corner. There they sat in silence for endless seconds—Finch's head bowed. It was Allen who broke the silence.

"We've come to the end of the line, I guess," he said.

That shattered Finch's reverie. "I have been instructed to request your resignation," he said.

"Is this Cambodia?" asked Allen.

"Yes," Finch replied. "I guess so."

*See p. 60.
†Wallace won and, of course, Dr. Allen's views on Cambodia were not a campaign issue.

Allen then started to talk about what he had hoped to do at the Office of Education, attempting to break the tension with pleasantries, but Finch interrupted him, saying, "I'm too upset to talk now. Will you come here at nine o'clock in the morning for coffee, and we'll announce it then?"

Allen agreed, expressing pleasure that this would give him time to draft a proper resignation. He then left the Secretary's office, five minutes after he had entered it.

As Allen walked back to his own office, somebody intercepted him with an HEW press release revealing that Allen's resignation (then unwritten) had been proffered and accepted.* Arriving at his own office, Allen tried to get Finch on the telephone but could not. Nor did he hear from the Secretary the next day. Of course, there was no coffee session in his office at nine o'clock. Two weeks later Finch, now a Presidential Counsellor and looking like a man relieved of a terrible burden, apologized to Allen and told him the White House had simply announced the resignation without informing him.

Quite apart from the display of bad manners shown by the White House in the sacking of Allen, the incident revealed how deep the President's self-doubt really was that spring. There were undisputable grounds for firing Allen once he publicly denounced the Indochina policy. But Nixon, after waiting twenty days to be taken off the hook by a resignation, did not even announce then that Allen was being sacked because of Cambodia. Indeed, many months later, high officials in the White House and HEW still would not admit that Cambodia had *anything* to do with Allen's firing. They used that old cliché about his being a "poor administrator" (also the favored weapon against Hickel), and argued that Allen had put too much emphasis on a new "right-to-read" program for poor children while neglecting basic educational programs (while, in fact, the excessive emphasis on "right to read" stemmed from the excessive interest in it by the President and ex-schoolteacher Pat Nixon).

But the fact that Dr. Allen was finally fired on June 10, though the real reason—Cambodia—was shrouded and would remain so, was a clear bugle blast that Nixon was beginning to recover from the Kent State trauma and regaining his confidence. Now the soft policy

*The similarity to the firing of Leon Panetta is striking. See pp. 157–59.

would harden, causing still greater confusion in what Richard Nixon really thought about the campus crisis.

Even after the soft-line policy had crested and begun to recede in early June, there was yet one more reinforcement that Nixon would add to his self-constructed trap on campus policy: the Scranton Commission.

The idea of a Presidential commission to investigate campus violence and explore ways of peacefully satisfying campus unrest came in early May from Bernard Segal of Philadelphia, a distinguished Republican lawyer and national president of the American Bar Association. Ehrlichman quickly took to the idea as part of the soft line then at its peak. Pat Moynihan, for one, knew the commission was trouble from the beginning; in effect, Nixon was putting his imprimatur on a commission that could only cause him trouble, with one political segment or another, no matter what it reported. The campus question was essentially a political problem with overtones of broad public policy and ideological conviction. As such, it should not be delegated to a commission of either experts or public-spirited citizens but ought to be decided by the President himself. Finally, the Scranton Commission was a direct violation of Moynihan's rule of more than a year earlier that the President ought to do his best to keep his hands off the campus. But neither Moynihan nor Marty Anderson, who would have said the same thing, was consulted.

The President's intense interest in the commission when it was being set up in May was evident by his selecting as its chairman the man he had originally wanted to be Secretary of State: William Warren Scranton, the former Governor of Pennsylvania.* Scranton's sympathy for student dissenters was well known, but that was not thought to be an impediment with the soft line prevailing at the time. With Scranton and Ehrlichman working together, a President's Commission on Campus Unrest was formed whose verdict would be preordained: Overlook the acute politicization of the campus and blame the government for the woes of the campus.

By the time Nixon unveiled the Scranton Commission on June 13, the return toward the hard line had begun to set in and misgivings

*See p. 22.

about the commission among White House aides were manifest. The commission's only student member came in for special attention from Agnew, who had never accepted the soft line. Joseph Rhodes, Jr., a twenty-two-year-old junior fellow at Harvard who had been student body president at the California Institute of Technology, was practiced in the intemperate rhetoric of the day's student activists. Governor Ronald Reagan supplied Agnew with quotes from Rhodes' public statements saying that Nixon and Agnew "are killing people" and that Reagan was "bent on killing people for his own political gain." Agnew called for Rhodes to get off the commission —a call that by now was viewed with considerable sympathy inside the White House and perhaps by the President himself. But it was much too late to get rid of young Mr. Rhodes.*

It was, indeed, much too late to avoid the springing—step by step—of the complicated trap Nixon had set for himself. The first step came on June 8, when eight young White House aides, dispatched by the President a week earlier to find out what was being thought and said on the college campus, returned to Washington with their reports. They need never have left, considering their obvious conclusions: the students blamed Nixon, Agnew and the Vietnam war for their present malaise. Thus did the President's own aides publicize the battle cry of the campus dissenter.

Next, the memoranda started to pour in to the President from the "ambassadors" of the campus whom Nixon had named—Heard of Vanderbilt and Cheek of Howard. "We do not believe that our national government really understands that a *national* crisis confronts us," Heard said in a June 19 memorandum to the President, adding that Nixon's Cambodian operation had caused a severe leftward shift of students.† On July 6, Heard wrote that Nixon was not communicating with the students and that his attempt to do so in his famous stroll to the Lincoln Memorial had backfired. Talking about Syracuse football and California surfing, said Heard, "offended students who felt immersed in a national tragedy, like telling a joke

---

*Besides Scranton and Rhodes, members of the commission included President Cheek of Howard; James F. Ahern, Chief of Police, New Haven, Conn.; Erwin D. Canham, Editor-in-Chief, *Christian Science Monitor;* Lieutenant General Benjamin O. Davis, Director of Civil Aviation Security, Transportation Department; Martha A. Derthick, Associate Professor, Boston College; Bayless Manning, Dean of the Law School, Stanford University; and Revious Ortique, Jr., attorney, New Orleans.

†The emphasis is Heard's.

at a funeral." On July 22, Cheek put the blame for all that ailed the nation's black colleges squarely on the shoulders of the federal government.

In short, the educators named by Nixon to tell him what ailed the campus were, predictably, telling him the fault was his. When word of this leaked out, Nixon sought to set the record straight by releasing all the memoranda on July 24, thereby compounding the self-injury. Along with the memoranda to the President from Heard and Cheek, the White House released a list of Heard-Cheek recommendations headed by one which did nothing more than place semi-official sanction on the politicization of the university: ". . . the President [should] increase his exposure to campus representatives, including students, faculty and administrative officers, so that he can better take into account their views and the intensity of those views in formulating domestic and foreign policy."

At the same time that the Heard-Cheek material was being released, the Scranton Commission was taking testimony at Kent State, Jackson State and Washington that intersected on this one point: the campus malaise was almost entirely the product of the Vietnam war and, therefore, Richard Nixon's fault. Nobody was a bit surprised when the commission's major report on September 26 blamed the President for not exerting moral leadership. But the damage had been done in the tone of that summer's hearings that clearly favored the student dissenters.

On Capitol Hill, conservative Republicans were sickened. Nixon clearly had made no headway among the majority of the campus community, who despised him. But, these conservatives felt, he had alienated that minority on the campus—say, no more than 20 percent—that was looking for leadership against the politicization of the university and for the restoration of traditional values. And in the White House itself, there was a sudden realization by July that Nixon's May efforts had triggered a constant stream of pro-student, anti-establishment propaganda, devoured by the communications media and clearly inimical to his own interests. White House aides who had been praising the student protesters now began to leak stories undercutting the Scranton Commission and its permissive bias.

Even before the Heard-Cheek memoranda were officially released, the President began his counterattack. The colleges were now in summer recess. The panic of early May was forgotten; the anti-student bias in the rest of society was remembered. So, at his

press conference in Washington on the afternoon of July 20, Nixon
said:

> I noted that the Scranton Commission hearings had been interpre-
> ted by some as indicating that the evidence was mounting to a conclu-
> sion that one way to bring peace on campus was to end the war in
> Vietnam.
> Well, that of course would not be news. I am not sure if it would
> bring peace to the campus. . . . I want peace on the campus but my
> major obligation is to adopt policies that I consider will bring peace
> to the world.

Nixon was beginning to fight his way out of the trap, set by his
own White House aides and Chancellor Heard and the Scranton
Commission, that there was some unbreakable link between the
Vietnam war and campus uproar. Ten days later, on July 30, in a
press conference from the Century Plaza Hotel in Los Angeles, the
President finally gave the lie to that argument:

> . . . we have to recognize that for university presidents and professors
> and other leaders to put the blame for the problems of the university
> on the Government primarily . . . is very short sighted.

The President went on to say his administration was ending the
war, ending conscription, dealing with problems of the environment
and reforming the governmental structure.

> But once all those things are done, still the emptiness, the shallow-
> ness, the superficiality that many college students find in college cur-
> riculums will still be there. Still when that is done, the problem we have
> of dissent on campus . . . dissent becoming sometimes violent, some-
> times illegal, sometimes shouting obscenities when visiting speakers
> come to campus, this is not a problem for government—we cannot
> solve it. It is a problem which college administrators and college facul-
> ties must face up to.
> We share our part of the blame. I assume that responsibility. We'll
> try to do better. But they have to do better also.

So, for the first time since the National Guardsmen had opened
fire at Kent State, Richard Nixon suggested that the problems of the
campus were not purely external and, indeed, were rooted in the
psyche of the national middle-class youth and their antipathy toward
the pallid education they were being given. The soft line was buried,

and the change toward a new hard line began. From both the President and Vice President, it would grow harder and harder as the 1970 campaign neared.

Long before that 1970 campaign began, an article of faith at the White House was that no lasting damage had been done the Nixon administration by that terrible May of 1970. In fact, so the argument went, the only long-range harm had been that the Senate's endless debate, extending well into the summer, on the Cooper-Church amendment to bar future use of American troops in Cambodia had created the logjam that forced a lame-duck session of Congress. Otherwise, the Nixon men felt, the Cambodian operation had turned out well politically—popular enough with the people to be a political asset. Maybe there had been some backing and filling about the campus scene in May, but who could blame us? And, anyway, didn't the colleges return to full schedules in September without any trouble?

But this argument overlooked the injuries that can be sustained by a President and his administration, leaving invisible scars that persist after superficial healing. The indirection with which the President handled the indiscretions of Walter Hickel and Dr. James Allen on Cambodia, through the fear of losing political ground by firing them outright, sat badly with many high officials. Throughout May, Nixon often seemed as though he had no fixed opinion on the college crisis: he would shift one way when the campus was in flames and another when the students had left for summer recess. The political ineptitude in setting up investigations and study that were *guaranteed* to result in anti-administration propaganda shocked Republican partisans. But worst of all was the panic with which Richard Nixon and his closest advisers handled themselves in his first grave domestic crisis. Was it his Bay of Pigs to be remedied in some future recurrence of the May troubles, as Kennedy redeemed the Bay of Pigs with stunning success during the Cuban missile crisis? Or was it a characteristic pattern of action, to be repeated at some future time if similar or graver domestic turmoil should confront him?

XI

Agnew, Nixon and the 1970 Campaign

He [Agnew] thinks the prospects for the Republican Party are tantalizing. America, he believes, is now witnessing the emergence of a new Republican majority. As he sees it, "that new majority can dominate the political life of the final third of this century, as the Democratic Party dominated the middle third."

—Haynes Johnson, in
the *Washington Post,* March 29, 1970

Will Americans be led by a President elected by a majority of the American people or will we be intimidated and blackmailed into following the path dictated by a disruptive and militant minority—the pampered prodigies of the radical liberals in the United States Senate?

—Vice President Spiro T. Agnew, at
San Diego, California, September 10, 1970

It was bright and sunny with just a breezy hint of autumn on the morning of September 10, 1970, at the U.S. Coast Guard terminal of Washington National Airport. The national midterm election campaign of the Republican Party was about to get under way. Vice President Spiro T. Agnew would fly that morning to Springfield, Ill., starting a speaking tour for Republican candidates that would stretch, nonstop and unrelenting, across the continent.

As Secret Service agents went through the laborious process of examining all luggage to be brought on the Vice Presidential plane, using new X-ray equipment to search for bombs, there was an air of excitement usually associated with the beginnings of Presidential campaigns. This would be no mere Vice Presidential jaunt but the major national effort to get President Nixon's appeal for a friendlier Congress to the American people. As such, its broad outlines were shaped from the Oval Office of the White House. Agnew's own somewhat drab staff had been shunted aside and replaced with four of Nixon's most impressive staffers for full-time duty with Agnew: Counsellor Bryce Harlow as chief of staff, speech writers William Safire and Patrick Buchanan, and Dr. Martin Anderson as chief researcher.* By now, Ted Agnew had become the most spectacular, most controversial, most exasperating political figure in the country. Accordingly, seats on the chartered Eastern Airlines jet were filled with Washington's top political correspondents—guaranteeing maximum coverage for Agnew's words.

Staff, press and Secret Service waited in the warm sunshine outside the Coast Guard terminal for the Vice President, who was more than a half-hour late—delayed by a last-minute strategy conference with the President at the White House. Finally a black limousine drove onto the runway, and Agnew emerged—tall, immaculately groomed (looking, as ever, as though he had just stepped out of a Bond clothing ad), smiling a tight unchanging smile. Walking briskly to a battery of microphones set up outside the plane, he told television interviewers that he would "carry the Nixon message to the people" in an effort to "alter the makeup of the Congress sufficiently to give the President more support." He described Nixon as "enthusiastic about the campaign" but unable to "participate significantly . . . because of his involvement with the very sensitive and important matters of state." So, said Agnew, "I will carry that burden . . . for this campaign."

Asked about the issues, Agnew was, as usual, succinct: ". . . one of the principal issues is whether policies of the United States are

---

*For the fall campaign Agnew also had taken on Carl DeBloom, executive editor of the *Columbus* (Ohio) *Dispatch* as his press secretary and Victor Gold, a Washington public relations man expert in the techniques of handling the press on a political campaign, as DeBloom's assistant.

going to be made by its elected officials or in the streets. I think that's the primary issue."

Agnew was then informed that Lawrence F. O'Brien, Chairman of the Democratic National Committee, had proposed that he should be taken off the government payroll while campaigning between now and Election Day.

"Well," said Agnew, "I don't think I have to back up to the pay window." Then with a flourish he boarded the plane for Springfield and a campaign whose implications would be discussed and considered for years into the future.

For on that day of September 10, 1970, the fates of Spiro T. Agnew and the Republican Party had coincided. His campaign strategy was the party's. His success or failure would be the party's. This identity of fortune, which would have momentous consequences for Richard Nixon and his administration, had been a long time coming.

For a Vice President, Spiro Theodore Agnew was improbable, if not wholly unique. Defying all those celebrated dicta of American politics, starting with John Adams' description of the Vice Presidency as "the most insignificant office that ever the invention of man contrived," Agnew had lifted himself in a brief two years from the almost total obscurity that surrounded him at the Republican convention in Miami Beach (where, according to one enterprising pollster, most people thought "Spiro Agnew" was some kind of shellfish) to third place on the list of Most Admired American, ranking after Nixon and evangelist Billy Graham. Some Republican politicians would perhaps have placed him even higher, ahead of Richard Nixon himself.

Agnew liked telling stories about some of his hapless predecessors, most particularly Thomas R. Marshall, Woodrow Wilson's undistinguished Vice President. To Marshall, a Vice President—any Vice President—was "like a man in a cataleptic state. He cannot speak." Not so Spiro Agnew. What had sent him miraculously soaring toward the political heights in the spring and summer of 1970 was, in fact, not anything he did but everything he said. He became the most hotly discussed politician in the country with his hard divisive talk, his frontal attack, his disdain for "pusillanimous pussyfooting" and his uncanny ability to make liberals scream in pain and anger. By the summer of 1970, Agnew had become a one-man road show pouring uncounted gold into Republican treasure chests from Harrisburg to New Orleans, from Des Moines to Honolulu— leaving behind him some party faithful convinced they had just seen the Republican true believer they had been waiting for all their lives, but also leaving others deeply concerned that "that fellow Agnew" was wrecking his party and tearing his country apart.

In one year, Agnew had become an issue in himself, a phenomenon in some ways bigger than his President and bigger than his party. And yet, no prophet attempting to peer into the Agnew future in 1962 could have suggested that this stolid son of Greek immigrants might someday symbolize within his own person the deepest hates and the most passionate longings in a dangerously polarized society. For the Agnew rise after 1962 was even more improbable than Nixon's after that same year, a year that saw one go down to defeat in California, and the other, riding the political waves of a bitter Democratic primary battle, get elected county executive of Baltimore County. In that heavily Democratic area, no other Republican wanted to run. Agnew won the nomination by default, the election by a fluke. It would not be the first time that fortune favored his career.

Ted Agnew lost his first campaign for public office, a race for circuit court judge in Baltimore County in 1960; Baltimore County (the suburbs surrounding Baltimore but not the city itself) was Democratic territory. Thus, four years after he was elected county executive in 1962, Republican Agnew was marked for certain extinction as the Democrats bound up their wounds and prepared to take him on in 1966. In light of this, Agnew had been quietly lobbying party leaders for months for a crack at the nomination for governor. He had nothing to lose. He drove to Washington to ask whether either Representative Rogers Morton or Representative Charles Mathias, the state's two Republican Congressmen, wanted to run for governor. Mathias said absolutely not. Morton equivocated briefly, then also said no. Both agreed to back Agnew, and both knew Agnew wouldn't have a chance. But then, in another stroke of good fortune, the presumed Democratic nominee, Carlton Sickles, lost in the primary to perennial candidate George Mahoney, whose racist appeal was certain to alienate large numbers of Democratic voters, sending them into the Republican column on Election Day.

It was then that Morton and Mathias began to realize that Agnew, far from a certain loser, might be the next governor of Maryland. Earlier in the campaign, the two Congressmen were talking about Agnew, and Morton commented that Agnew was not always an easy man to get along with. Mathias agreed, and said that if Agnew was elected governor, he would be hard to handle. "Don't worry about that," said Morton. "That's one thing that can't happen!"

There was only one issue in the campaign: Mahoney's promise to preserve racial discrimination in housing and state employment. Running hard on a platform on nondiscrimination, Agnew defeated Mahoney and walked into the governor's mansion at Annapolis, the hero of the racial moderates and liberals. At once he began courting Governor Nelson Rockefeller of New York, then covertly plotting his 1968 bid for the Republican Presidential nomination. Agnew moved to polish his moderate-liberal credentials, pushing through the Legislature the state's first fair-housing legislation (and the first in any state south of the Mason-Dixon Line) and placing more Negroes in state jobs than ever before in history. Agnew owed his election to black voters. He paid them back handsomely.

But even then, signs appeared of aloofness, wariness about becoming too involved with Negroes, an emotional withdrawal. Rabbi Israel Goldman, Vice Chairman of the Maryland Commission on Human Relations, discerned in the governor a disinclination to get personally involved with social-welfare problems, particularly in the racial field. "My impression is that he is a person who likes to work from the top and isn't very eager to get down among the masses," Dr. Goldman told an interviewer. "Some of the things for which he is criticized stem from this fact: that he doesn't relate to people, he doesn't get down to the people's level."

But as the Republican governor of a Democratic state, elected on a moderate program with backing from blacks and Jews, Agnew had political credentials useful to a Republican Presidential candidate in 1968, and Rockefeller's men were looking for just such a Republican governor to head the Draft Rockefeller movement covertly supported by Rockefeller himself. Rockefeller's first choice to run the Draft Rockefeller Committee was former Governor William W. Scranton of Pennsylvania, but Scranton turned it down. Then he turned to Agnew, once again in the advantageous position of moving into a vacuum no one else wanted to fill. The committee was announced on March 15 and Agnew filled the chairmanship with zest —for all of six days! Between Agnew and Rockefeller there was the distance of the latter's great wealth and high position, and Agnew seemed to bask in the reflected glory of Nelson Aldrich Rockefeller. It was understandable, then, that this fascination with Rockefeller turned to cold withdrawal when Rockefeller announced on March 21, 1968, that after all he would not be a candidate for the Presidency —a tactical decision for delay (later, Rockefeller became an active candidate). The most lasting impact of the delay was to propel Spiro Agnew into history. Rockefeller did not even have the wit to telephone Agnew before going on television, to inform him that he was pulling out of the race. By chance, at the very hour of Rockefeller's live telecast, Agnew's regular biweekly press conference was scheduled to be held in the State Capitol at Annapolis. Assuming along with every one else that Rockefeller would announce his candidacy, Agnew and the assembled capitol press corps watched the program from the governor's office. When Rockefeller took himself out of the race, the humiliation to Agnew was made all the more bitter and unforgivable by the fact that it was witnessed by the Maryland capitol press corps.*

Agnew and Nixon had only one serious talk before the Rockefeller fiasco, a January 1968 meeting in New York City during a meeting of the National Federation of Republican Women. They spent more than an hour talking together at a party given for Nixon by State Senator Louise Gore of Maryland, a strong Agnew supporter, and hit it off well. But at that time Agnew's heart belonged to Rockefeller, and Nixon knew it. It was the Rockefeller snub that brought together these two politicians, so alike in personal characteristics—shy and remote, both were fighters who knew how to go for the jugular, and both from the wrong side of the tracks had clawed their way up the political ladder, intensely suspicious of the Eastern

*Rockefeller had been given a list of nine prominent Republicans, all backing his prospective candidacy, with strict instructions to get each on the telephone before going on the air. A few minutes before his telecast, just as Rockefeller was about to begin his telephone calls, an aide came rushing in to suggest a last-second change in his script. The script, said the aide, was more important than any telephone calls. Rockefeller ran out of time. Many hours after the broadcast, he finally put that telephone call in to Agnew, but the breach was beyond repair.

establishment. Within ten days after Rockefeller's tactical withdrawal from the Presidential race, Agnew went to New York and spent two hours talking politics with Nixon at his Fifth Avenue apartment. After that, the contacts, both by phone and in personal chats, steadily increased. It became obvious to a very few astute politicians that Nixon may have had more in the back of his mind than merely Maryland delegates to the Miami Beach convention.*

Shortly after his Fifth Avenue meeting with Nixon, there occurred a seminal event in Agnew's strange political career that was to change its course forevermore—generated by his own deep-seated animus toward extremists, the recommendations of political advisers to chart a more conservative course and the incalculable aftereffects of the Rockefeller fiasco. Appalled by the rioting in Baltimore following the assassination of Martin Luther King, Agnew summoned eighty black leaders to the executive mansion in Annapolis on April 11 and administered a dressing down that caused most to leave in anger—instantly transforming his position in racial politics. These responsible leaders, he said, should have spoken out clearly and loudly against less responsible black leaders—the "circuit-riding, Hanoi-visiting, caterwauling, riot-inciting, burn-America-down type of leader." In the weeks between April 11 and the Miami Beach convention, Agnew lost no opportunity to elaborate on this theme. At the annual National Governors Conference in Cincinnati in July just before Miami Beach, he summoned national political reporters to his hotel suite and delivered a slashing attack on the Poor People's Campaign, led by Ralph Abernathy, then camping on federal land in Washington. In passing, he suggested that Richard Nixon was best suited to deal with such menaces.

At Miami Beach, Richard Nixon quietly tossed forward Agnew's name at each of the three postnomination meetings held in his suite at the Hilton Plaza. Each time there was silence. Agnew? No one in the inner circle—Mitchell, Haldeman, Finch—was against Agnew. But no one knew enough about him to be for him. Thus,

*The Maryland delegation split, 18 for Nixon to 8 for Rockefeller, on the first and only ballot at Miami Beach after a long holding action during which the Rockefeller delegates, headed by Senator Charles Mathias, persuaded Agnew to go to the convention as a favorite son. He did so, but before the balloting infuriated Maryland Rockefeller delegates by coming out for Nixon.

Nixon's choice fell with considerable surprise on the ears of even his closest political associates. When Nixon announced it the next day to the press, the reaction was not surprise but shock.*

But what was surprising to Nixon's inner circle and shocking to the press was infuriating, insulting and unforgivable to liberal Republicans—a sure signal that Nixon was going full speed for a law-and-order campaign.

Talking with reporters just before he left Miami Beach, a euphoric Richard Nixon revealed that he saw in Ted Agnew "a mystique" that would entrance the American people. His forecast was premature. Nixon's enthusiasm at Miami Beach soon faded as Agnew's eagerness to slash away at the Democrats backfired through maladroit rhetoric. He called Hubert Humphrey "squishy soft on Communism," made ethnic slurs, said that "if you've seen one city slum, you've seen them all." A long-time Nixon speech writer, Stephen Hess, was quickly shunted to the Agnew campaign plane to try to keep the candidate's foot out of his mouth. By election time, the most that the Nixon circle hoped for was that Agnew would not lose any votes. On Inauguration Day, 1969, Ted Agnew's stock was at a low point.

On January 21, 1969, the day after his inauguration, Richard Nixon, admirer of Woodrow Wilson, took Wilson's desk from its resting place of many years in the Vice President's ceremonial office in the Capitol and put it in the President's Oval Office in the White House. Aside from losing the Wilson desk, Vice President Agnew had very few experiences, good or bad, in the early days of the administration. On the same day that he lost the Wilson desk, he went to the East Room of the White House to help the President thank Republican campaign workers for their part in the campaign, and gave a brief talk that summed up his own conceptions of the role he was about to fill. The "principal" part of that role was this: "Whatever the President wants is what I want. I envisage that as the principal role of the Vice Presidency—to implement the policies of the Chief Executive." Then, having referred to Nixon as "a towering

*David Broder of the *Washington Post* was less shocked than most of his colleagues. On May 17 he wrote that Nixon "has been paying keen interest to Agnew as a Vice Presidential nominee."

source of strength to me," he thanked the campaign workers and left the White House, as he put it, to "make my way to the tender mercies of the Senate."

Agnew quickly tried but never could pull off his Constitutional function as President of the Senate. He had never sat in a legislative body, knew nothing about the culture, habits or sensitivities of the hundred senators and found himself with less to do than at any time in his life. That discovery is one every Vice President sooner or later makes for himself, but the reaction to it varies. Some, like Franklin Roosevelt's first Vice President, John Nance Garner, and Harry Truman's Alben Barkley, had spent most of their adult lives on Capitol Hill, so the adjustment to a life of relative ease was not so difficult for them. But for Agnew, there were no friends on Capitol Hill and not even many acquaintances.

He attempted at first to promote the President's programs in the Senate but his ignorance of senatorial form and custom brought an abrupt end to these efforts. Worried about losing Republican support in the Senate for the surtax extension in July 1969, the White House suggested that Agnew do a little judicious lobbying with Republican senators. Just before the roll was to be called on the vote, Agnew quietly stepped off the rostrum and walked over to importune several Republicans known to be leaning away from the surtax extension bill —a violation of senatorial propriety and the role of the Vice President. One of these was Senator Len Jordan of Idaho, who took immediate, sharp offense. Not only did Jordan brusquely tell Agnew to go off about his business but took it up at the weekly meeting of Republican senators. Jordan, a conservative who seldom made trouble about anything, delivered a little lecture about separation of powers, then enunciated what became known as the Jordan Rule: whenever the Vice President lobbied a senator about anything on the floor, he should vote the opposite way, whether or not it violated his principles and convictions. There was no dissent. After that meeting, Senator Gordon Allott of Colorado, Chairman of the Senate Republican Policy Committee, politely informed Agnew that no Vice President had ever been allowed the liberty of lobbying senators on the floor.

The Jordan incident brought an effective end to Agnew's career on Capitol Hill. The first Vice President since Henry Wallace twenty-four years earlier elected without previous Congressional experience, he now determined that he could do Nixon little good in the Senate. After July 1969, Agnew functioned only perfunctorily as presiding officer over the Senate and seldom worked out of his Capitol office, preferring his handsome suite in the Executive Office Building next door to the White House.

Minor chores handed him by the President made him no happier than presiding over the Senate. For example, on February 14 Nixon placed Agnew in overall charge of all matters between the federal government and state and local governments. That assignment, a typical one for Vice Presidents, meant nothing at all in the way of power but a great deal in the way of picayune detail. Every President has wanted to use his Vice President as much as possible as a buffer between himself and boring governmental chores. On February 14 Nixon talked about Agnew's "important responsibilities" in intergovernmental relations. In fact, Agnew, like every Vice President who had preceded him, knew that no matter how a President dressed up the duties he handed his Vice President, only rarely did they matter.

Agnew also came to loathe the ceremonial functions of his office, which struck him as irrelevant and merely time-consuming. He agreed to give a formal luncheon on June 11, 1969, for the Patriarch of the Armenian Apostolic Church, His Holiness Khoren I. Engraved invitations went to more than thirty guests, including Senator Everett M. Dirksen of Illinois, Republican leader of the Senate, seven other senators and several prominent members of the House. Agnew arrived late, just in time to get there before the meal was to be served. He stood behind his seat while Khoren I and his other guests took their chairs, proposed a toast to His Holiness, then without another word said goodbye and walked out of the room, never to return. Not only did his sudden disappearance puzzle the guest of honor but it infuriated the senators, who had taken time out of their own day to attend the luncheon for one reason only—the fact that the Vice President had invited them.

Those early days as Vice President were regarded by Agnew as miserable and unproductive. He was not one to sit on the sidelines for long. It was in that same month of June 1969 that he decided to start speaking out on fundamental issues that had been irritating him at least since his break with the Negro leadership of Maryland in April 1968. He had been smarting over the liberal reaction to that event, as well as the liberals' conviction, buttressed by unending press criticism, that he was nothing more than a political primitive who didn't understand the subtleties of the Negro revolution, the disillusionment of the nation's youth and the dangerous political divisions that were steadily widening. He struck first at the growing campus violence, choosing as his forum not some safe platform before, say, a national veterans' organization, but the huge, turbulent campus of Ohio State University, where, at graduation ceremonies on June 7, he made his memorable assault on the "sniveling, hand-wringing power structure" that "deserves the violent rebellion it encourages." The story made page one of the *Washington Post*. Spiro Agnew had returned to the headlines in a speech replete with the syntax and choice of words—alliteration, highly colored adjectives, extensive learned quotations and other tools of the polemicist—that were to make him the most quoted Vice President in this century.* Cynthia Rosenwald, a thirty-two-year-old Baltimore housewife who had been Agnew's speech writer as governor of Maryland, continued to do the writing and research for Agnew's speeches as Vice President. But the basic prose of the Ohio State speech and his other early polemical efforts as Vice President was his own.† As he would tell another audience almost two years later, looking back to that summer of 1969, he was now about to embark on a career unique for any Vice President: "I forsook the comfortable code of many of my predecessors, abandoned the unwritten rules—and said something."‡

Ohio State was only the prelude for what came in New Orleans, on October 19, setting off a flash alarm throughout the press and political community of an emotional intensity not felt in almost twenty years, not since Senator Joseph R. McCarthy's Wheeling, W. Va., speech escalated the hunt for Communists in the government. Speaking at a $100-a-plate dinner billed as a Citizens' Testimonial Dinner (but in fact a straight Louisiana Republican Party fund-raiser

---

*In a single speech he made as governor of Maryland, Agnew quoted Voltaire, H. G. Wells, George Wallace ("academic freedom can get you killed"), Walter Lippmann, William Ernest Hocking, Swedish journalist Victor Vinde, Nicholas Murray Butler, Charles de Gaulle and Descartes. He is also an inveterate chaser of long esoteric words, which he likes to pepper into speeches. He used to read regularly a section called "Increase Your Word Power" in the *Reader's Digest*.

†Miss Rosenwald (Mrs. Peter Benno) left Agnew to spend full time with her children in March 1970, long before his celebrated midterm election campaign.

‡This was contained in Agnew's speech to the Middlesex Club of Boston on March 18, 1971.

with conservative Democrats in attendance), Agnew fired his blast at "a spirit of national masochism . . . encouraged by an effete corps of impudent snobs who characterize themselves as intellectuals." The speech, which he wrote himself one Saturday morning in his office in the Executive Office Building, was his sharpest attack on anti-Vietnam war protesters—coming between the two big antiwar demonstrations in Washington in October and November 1969. It was an immediate sensation, driving a wedge down the center between, on the one hand, the antiwar forces—intellectuals, the students, liberals and a growing body of moderates—and on the other, the Silent Majority, to whom Nixon himself was about to appeal in his November 3 war speech.* In New Orleans, throughout the rest of the South, and wherever there were war hawks and recruits for what Kevin Phillips called "the coming conservative cycle of American politics," Agnew became an overnight hero.

Eleven days later, Agnew invited the newly elected Republican leader of the Senate, the liberal Hugh Scott, and his liberal junior Pennsylvania colleague, Senator Richard Schweiker, to fly with him to Harrisburg for another fund-raiser. Both were concerned about traveling with the ever more controversial Agnew, but it was difficult to say no. In his Harrisburg speech, Agnew strongly defended his New Orleans speech, and for the first time directly linked the "mature and sensitive people of this country [who enjoy the] freedom of protest" with "avowed anarchists and Communists who detest everything about this country and want to destroy it" by exploiting the freedom of protest. For a liberal Eastern state, this was strong medicine, much stronger than Agnew's speech at New Orleans before a basically conservative audience. But the central-Pennsylvania Republicans, many of them rural-based, and the conservative party money men who turned out to hear Agnew loved every word of it. Only the two senators with him were disturbed by the Vice President's trenchant tone. On the way back to Washington in Agnew's plane that night, Scott and Agnew never once discussed the speech.

There had been, up to this point, little coordination between Agnew and the White House on the hardening political line being taken by the Vice President and the increasingly angry repercussions. Agnew, in fact, saw Nixon infrequently. But that did not mean he

*See pp. 85–86.

was doing anything that the President disapproved of. On the contrary, Agnew's chief of staff, Stanley Blair, attended the regular 8 o'clock staff meeting presided over by Haldeman every morning during 1969. Those meetings kept Agnew informed on the mood of the moment, including Nixon's private attitudes toward the subjects Agnew concentrated on: the media, antiwar demonstrations, campus riots, the developing political strategy.

The White House, repeatedly pressed to disavow or criticize the Vice President, repeatedly refused to do so. Agnew's speeches were his own to give, said Ron Ziegler, and no wraps would be placed on him by the President. Between the New Orleans and Harrisburg speeches the President himself, asked at an October 30 White House ceremonial function to comment on the New Orleans speech, praised Agnew, saying he had "done a great job."

But on the next day, October 31, Senator Albert Gore, fighting for his life in Tennessee, delivered the type of remark about Agnew that was becoming common among Democrats. The Vice President, said Gore, was becoming "our greatest disaster next to Vietnam"— thereby beginning a long-range political feud, carried on by hurled invective, that would not culminate until a year later. Whatever was said by Gore and the Democrats, the mail coming into the Vice President's office was running 60 to 1 in favor of Agnew during the first week of November, and the best or worst was yet to come.

On November 13 Agnew dropped his most explosive bombshell against an enemy far more formidable than any students, new leftists or black extremists: the powerful television networks, exerting more influence over the style and pace of American life than all other cultural or media outlets put together.

The occasion at Des Moines, Ia., was a meeting of the Midwest Republican Conference, which was dull until the Vice President took the podium to blast the network commentators who had "expressed, in one way or another, their hostility" to the President's November 3 Vietnam speech in their brief commentaries immediately following it. He also attacked venerable Democrat Averell Harriman—former Governor of New York, former Secretary of Commerce, former Assistant Secretary of State, many times former Ambassador—who had been asked by the American Broadcasting Company to fill the commentator's role following Nixon's speech. Harriman, said Agnew, used the occasion "to justify his failures" as President Johnson's chief negotiator at the Paris peace talks in 1968. Then Agnew got to the heart of the matter:

> The purpose of my remarks tonight is to focus your attention on this little group of men who not only enjoy a right of instant rebuttal to every Presidential address but, more importantly, wield a free hand in selecting, presenting and interpreting the great issues of our Nation. . . . We do know that, to a man, these commentators and producers live and work in the geographical and intellectual confines of Washington, D.C., or New York City—the latter of which James Reston terms the "most unrepresentative community in the entire United States." Both communities bask in their own provincialism, their own parochialism. . . .
>
> In tomorrow's edition of the *Des Moines Register* you will be able to read a news story detailing what I said tonight; an editorial comment will be reserved for the editorial page, where it belongs. Should not the same wall of separation exist between news and comment on the nation's networks? We would never trust such power over public opinion in the hands of an elected government—it is time we questioned it in the hands of a small and un-elected elite. The great networks have dominated America's airwaves for decades; the people are entitled to a full accounting of their stewardship.

Agnew attacked the network anchor men (but named only NBC's David Brinkley) for having "made their minds up in advance" about the President's hard-line speech that evening. He claimed that network reporters by "a raised eyebrow, an inflection of the voice, a caustic remark dropped in the middle of a broadcast can raise doubts in a million minds about the veracity of a public official or the wisdom of a government policy." Altogether, it was Agnew's sharpest effort to drive a wedge between the American public and the major source of their news. To the "effete corps of impudent snobs" had now been added the giant television networks and their highly paid commentators.*

---

*Some of the harshest criticism of the Des Moines speech came from the *Washington Post*, which charged him with delivering a typical Agnew "tirade . . . that would have carried twice the force had it been accurate and even-handed, but that is not the Vice President's way: never use a scalpel when a meat ax can do the job." Seven days after Des Moines, Agnew journeyed to Montgomery, Ala., to attack the Washington Post Co. (owners of the *Post, Newsweek* and radio and television properties in Washington, D.C.; Jacksonville and Miami, Fla.; and Cincinnati, Ohio), calling this an example of "the growing monopolization of the voices of public opinion."

Important though the Des Moines speech was, it was far eclipsed in significance by the little-known fact that it had the President's specific sponsorship. In the Ohio State, New Orleans and Harrisburg speeches, Nixon and his inner circle had been appreciative onlookers. The words had been written by Agnew and his own staff. But now, the White House took an active interest. The idea for the Des Moines speech (the Media Speech as it quickly became known at the White House) came from Pat Buchanan, who had discussed it with President Nixon. Buchanan, a young conservative who had been an editorial writer for the *St. Louis Globe Democrat* before joining Nixon in 1965, was in charge of monitoring the media at the White House to see what they were saying about the President. Thus, what Agnew asserted in the Media Speech exactly duplicated Nixon's own convictions—even to the language. A leading newspaper editor was astounded by Agnew's Media Speech; he had heard exactly the same words from Nixon during a private meeting several weeks earlier. Indeed, White House aides had heard such talk endlessly from the President. Agnew edited and reedited the speech given him by Buchanan, but he was not striking out as a free agent this time. Henceforth, Pat Buchanan would play a major role in the composition of all the Vice President's major speeches.

In addition, the White House envisioned Agnew's newly escalated polemics in part as a means of decreasing the visibility of John Mitchell as the Democrats' leading target. Mitchell had been warned by his friends in the legal profession that his stature as the nation's lawyer-in-chief was being whittled down by his role of gut-fighting, pro-Southern, anti-Negro politician. Now Agnew would take over the heavy hitting—and with it the heavy receiving.

Thus the President was carving a role for Agnew as the avenging angel of the Silent Majority to deal out awful retribution to establishment power centered in the East which was, to Nixon and Agnew, aloof and remote, absorbed in its own self-interest and prepared to foist its will on provincial America. Agnew, said the President in his December 8, 1969, press conference, had "rendered a public service" with his criticism of television reporting (but, added the President, in one of his characteristic little balancing acts, television had been treating Nixon fairly).

After the Media Speech, the nationwide demand for Spiro Agnew at fund-raising dinners could not be satisfied. The Vice President was sought after by conservative, liberal and in-between state party leaders to fill their $100-a-plate banquet tables. Suddenly, without anybody quite realizing how, Agnew had become a truly formidable figure traveling the Republican banquet circuit in the winter of 1969–70.

But even then, Agnew was sowing seeds of discord in the Republican Party that would produce a bitter harvest in the autumn. From the very start of Agnew's searing polemics at New Orleans, there were those with deep misgivings—including the Republican National Chairman, Rogers Morton. Agnew's tough line against antiwar demonstrators had served a useful purpose, said Morton, but now it was time to "take a quieter approach." For the next year, state Republican leaders who agreed with Morton were torn between the desire to capitalize on Agnew's phenomenal fund-raising skills and the fear that he was driving voters away from the party. On February 20, 1970, the liberal-led Minnesota Republican Party conducted its best fund-raising dinner ever at the St. Paul Auditorium with Agnew as the speaker. But Agnew ignored their requests that he mute his rhetoric in deference to their attempts to woo the youth vote away from Hubert Humphrey, running again for the Senate (at St. Paul, Agnew accused leading Democrats of "a weird desire to suck up the political support of organized dissidents").

By mid-1970, more and more moderate-to-liberal Republicans were questioning the value of close association with the Vice President. When Agnew went to Cleveland on June 20 for a fund-raiser, the only Republican member of Congress from Ohio at the head table was Senator William Saxbe. No admirer of Agnew, Saxbe had been invited personally by the Vice President to fly aboard his plane from Washington to Cleveland. He could scarcely say no. But Republican Congressmen from the Cleveland area did say no, boycotting the affair. So did Representative Robert Taft, Jr., of Cincinnati, facing a difficult race for the Senate. Portents of the future were already in clear perspective.

In the first half of 1969, while Agnew was making his unsuccessful effort to find happiness amid the Senate and his ceremonial functions, Richard Nixon was coming to some immensely significant political conclusions of his own: if the 1970 campaign was handled skillfully he could snatch the Senate away from its top-heavy Democratic control and make small gains in the House—a remarkable feat that would reverse history, give Nixon unstoppable velocity toward reelection in 1972 and energize the Republican Party. History was against it: for the party in power at the White House the record of the twentieth century for midterm elections showed the average loss of House seats at 41 for the White House party (excluding 1902 and 1934, when the White House party *gained* seats) with an average loss in the Senate of 7 seats. Nixon's main interest for 1970 was the Senate. As he began to study his candidate raw material and measure his possibilities of success, Nixon came to be positively enamored with the idea of bringing home a Republican Senate in 1970. To do that, a net gain of 7 seats was essential, giving the Republicans 50 seats. The 50–50 tie would then be broken by Agnew as President of the Senate, thereby enabling the Republicans to organize the Senate, dominate and run its committees and take control of the legislative machinery—the first time the Republicans would be controlling either chamber since the Republican Eighty-third Congress was elected with General Eisenhower in 1952.

Central to this thesis was candidate selection. Never before had a President involved himself so intimately in the selection of Senate candidates and worked so hard to recruit good ones—as it happened, mainly members of the House. In larger or smaller part because of exhortations from the President, these outstanding Republican Congressmen agreed to desert their safe seats in the House to run a hazardous race for the Senate: George Bush of Texas; William Brock of Tennessee; Lowell P. Weicker, Jr., of Connecticut; J. Glenn Beall, Jr., of Maryland; Thomas Kleppe of North Dakota; William V. Roth, Jr., of Delaware; Clark MacGregor of Minnesota; Robert Taft, Jr., of Ohio; Laurence J. Burton of Utah; John Wold of Wyoming.

It was an excellent record of candidate recruitment, but there were conspicuous failures. Nixon's first choices for the Senate in Maryland and North Dakota, Representatives Rogers Morton and Mark Andrews, would not run. Nor would Representative Peter Frelinghuysen in New Jersey or Governor Paul Laxalt in Nevada. The failure to get Laxalt in particular showed the inadequacies of the Nixon political operation. Laxalt, Nevada's most popular Republican, wanted to leave public life and certainly did not want to challenge Democratic Senator Howard Cannon, but he might have been persuaded if the persuading had been properly handled. It was not, one reason being that John Mitchell rejected appeals early in 1969 from White House political aide John Sears to throw major administration resources into developing 1970 candidate material. Laxalt wanted absolute assurances that if he ran for the Senate he would have adequate financing. Failing to get that assurance and not wanting to run anyway, he finally turned the President down.

The unprecedented intervention by the White House into candidate selection extended to one seat that there was no chance to win. Murray Chotiner, who had slipped onto the White House staff as a political aide in 1970 after a year's quiet service in his bureaucratic Siberia, was having breakfast with Washington's leading political reporters on June 10, and began running through the list of prime Senate races. When he came to Massachusetts, he commented that a fellow there named McCarthy not only was planning to run against Senator Edward M. Kennedy but had an excellent chance to beat him. Not one of the political reporters present had ever heard of McCarthy, whose first name Chotiner could not remember. In fact, John J. McCarthy turned out to be a rich right-winger whom White House aide Charles Colson (one-time assistant to former Senator Leverett Saltonstall of Massachusetts) persuaded to run in the Republican primary against liberal Republican Josiah Spaulding, a former Republican state chairman, who had long since announced his own candidacy, had support from all state party leaders and was extremely well financed.* The Colson-Chotiner thesis was that Senate nominee McCarthy would slash away at Kennedy and not for a minute exempt the Chappaquiddick affair, whereas blueblood Spaulding would run a me-too liberal campaign and be too gentlemanly to mention the senator's personal problems. Since neither McCarthy nor Spaulding had a chance in the world to win, why not pick the man who would rough up Teddy Kennedy and diminish his chances to be Nixon's opponent in 1972? What this thesis omitted was the overall effect of right-winger McCarthy on the rest of the

---

*Actually, McCarthy was Colson's second choice. His first was cartoonist Al Capp (creator of *Li'l Abner*), a former liberal who had moved sharply to the right but was not a Republican and had no party experience. Shocked at rumors that the White House was courting Capp, Governor Francis Sargent of Massachusetts telephoned Colson in Washington to check it out. The governor was even more deeply shocked when he learned from Colson it was all too true. But Capp would not run.

Republican ticket, including Governor Francis Sargent, in liberal Massachusetts. Even after Spaulding easily won the nomination from McCarthy, the party leaders in Massachusetts did not forgive the White House or Richard Nixon (who probably knew nothing about the Colson-Chotiner ploy).*

In Florida, White House aides played a far more dangerous game with candidate selection while Nixon was preoccupied with foreign crises. The President had personally asked the veteran Representative William Cramer to run for the Senate race being vacated by a conservative Democrat, Spessard Holland. With Florida close to becoming a Republican state, there was an excellent chance for Cramer. Then, suddenly, G. Harrold Carswell, on the heels of his defeat by the Senate for a seat on the Supreme Court, was persuaded by Cramer's Republican archenemies, Senator Edward Gurney and Governor Claude Kirk—strongly supported by White House political aide Harry Dent—to run for the Senate.† Cramer smashed Carswell in the primary by almost 2 to 1, but the cleavage in the party guaranteed the defeat of Cramer in the general election for a seat that Nixon had been counting on.

Perhaps the fiasco in Florida, the bumbling in Massachusetts, the lost opportunity in Nevada and other such errors might have been avoided had there been an overall field general for the midterm campaign with the power to go all-out for Laxalt's candidacy in Nevada, to order Colson to keep hands off Massachusetts, to restrain Dent in Florida and give countless other orders. But there was none. John Mitchell sensed this. He would confide to friends after the election that the Republicans lost the midterm Congressional election for two reasons: first, Nixon as chief campaigner talked and acted as though he were running for sheriff, not as the great leader of an underdog party; second, and more important, there simply was no coordinated campaign for the Republicans in 1970—no campaign at all, but just a bunch of individual races.

Mitchell, the 1968 campaign manager, was the one Republican

---

*Long after the 1970 election, Kennedy said privately that Colson had a valid point, that McCarthy would have caused him far more trouble than Spaulding (who, predictably, never mentioned Chappaquiddick). But like Colson and Chotiner, Kennedy had little interest in the future of the Massachusetts Republican Party.

†See pp. 164–172.

inside or outside the administration whom most state party leaders and most of the party's candidates desperately wished were in active control of the Congressional campaign. Mitchell, however, with the sole exception of the single most important race in the whole country—New York's Senate campaign—neither sought nor was asked to take any role at all in the 1970 campaign. Some of his friends thought he saw the depth of the problems involved and chose to opt out. Whether or not that was true, by 1970 Mitchell had become more deeply involved in Justice Department affairs and seemed to have no desire to run a jerry-built midterm campaign. Anyway, the White House *never* names a campaign manager for midterm campaigns; after all, the President is not running for office himself. But what made 1970 different was the unprecedented intervention in state races by the White House on a scale that demanded a Mitchell-type czar to keep the loose ends straight.

Instead, power was widely divided. At the Republican National Committee, Chairman Rogers Morton and Deputy Chairman James Allison were in an adversary position against the White House political aides: Chotiner, Dent and Colson. When the President himself was concerned, Haldeman entered the picture in a commanding fashion. Harlow and Finch had major but undefined roles. Agnew was to have his say. And Richard Nixon, lacking the steadying influence of Mitchell, would suddenly barrel into the campaign of 1970 in a way that would deeply affect both it and his Presidency.

While the White House and Republican National Committee were seeking out the best candidates for the Senate, an ideological underpinning for all these state campaigns was slowly evolving.

At bottom, of course, was John Mitchell's grand strategy of combining the Nixon and Wallace votes of 1968 into a Republican majority—a strategy that by its very nature entailed a right-of-center posture. This Mitchell strategy, in turn, was further refined by the most-talked-about political book of 1969: *The Emerging Republican Majority* by Kevin Phillips, a young, conservative lawyer from the Bronx who had worked under Mitchell during the 1968 campaign and gone with him to the Justice Department briefly as a political aide in 1969. Phillips' book advanced the thesis that—with the conspicuous exception of the Northeast heartland of liberalism, the Pacific Northwest, Minnesota, and black and Latin voters anywhere

—Americans had had their fill of liberalism and were looking for a
new conservative political doctrine built on the needs of the suburbs,
the South, what he called the Sunbelt (running from Southern California through the New Southwest to Florida), and the white, especially the ethnic Catholic, labor force. This could become a national
Republican majority under Nixon, while the dying Democratic
Party of Franklin Roosevelt's coalition of the 1930s gave way to a
new and distinctly minority Democratic Party, combining the black
and Latin minorities with the "privileged elite of the Northeast"
(which he saw as "blind to the needs and interests of the large
national majority").*

Although the President publicly disavowed any interest in Phillips' book, the truth was that its precepts were devoured and relished
by the White House. Nixon himself—even if, as he said, he had not
read *The Emerging Republican Majority*—had no substantive disagreement. Increasingly it became obvious that the President and his
men wanted to aim at the Kevin Phillips audience. Thus, the 1970
campaign theme worked out by the White House almost exactly
fitted the Phillips thesis, playing hard to just that audience—the
ethnic Catholic workingman, the suburban homeowner—so concerned about the drug addiction of their children, the rising cost of
social-welfare programs to benefit blacks, and the general air of
permissiveness. In the air at the White House, then, was a rising
dream that the 1970 midterm election not only would reverse historical patterns but would also begin a great political realignment that,
in 1972, would engulf the old and dying Democratic Party and place
Nixon at the head of a new Republican majority.

In the eyes of the White House, prospects for this were enhanced by one aspect of the troubles of May 1970. On May 8, during
the wave of violent student demonstrations, antiwar students

---

*Nixon and some of his aides were upset by Phillips' book, not because they
disagreed with it but because it was overly candid in revealing a harsh political
strategy—particularly in regard to a Republican abandonment of the Northeast. On
September 26, 1969, when asked about *The Emerging Republican Majority*, Nixon
gave this carefully prepared answer: ". . . I have not read the book . . . I believe
the Republican Party should be a national party. I don't believe in writing off any
section of the country . . . To the extent that the book advocates theories that are
inconsistent with that principle, of course, I would disagree with it." Mitchell also
denied ever reading the book.

paraded through the Wall Street financial district in New York City where Mayor John V. Lindsay, antiwar and pro-student, had ordered the flag at City Hall to fly at half-staff in honor of the students killed at Kent State. It was then that hard-hatted construction workers stormed the student demonstrators in Wall Street, and while smiling policemen looked on, beat them up, shouting, "All the way, U.S.A."—then off to City Hall to raise that flag to full-staff. On May 11 two thousand construction workers marched throughWall Street in support of Nixon and the war. That started a nationwide flurry of hard hats (trade union men and habitual Democratic voters) parading and demonstrating for Nixon. The political revolution predicted by Kevin Phillips seemed at hand. The high-water mark came on May 26, when Nixon received twenty-two union leaders, including Peter J. Brennan, president of the Building and Construction Trades Council of New York, and Thomas Gleason, general president of the International Longshoremen's Association and a member of the AFL-CIO Executive Council, who gave him a construction worker's hard hat with the legend "Commander-in-Chief" printed in bold letters on the front.

In the summer of 1970 the developing strategy at the White House was further hardened by a new book, this one by two Democratic liberals, Richard M. Scammon (election analyst and Census Bureau Director in the Kennedy days) and Ben J. Wattenberg (speech writer for Lyndon Johnson and Hubert Humphrey). Their book, *The Real Majority,* became must reading at the White House because it found an electorate that was mostly unyoung, unblack and unpoor deeply influenced by something new in politics—The Social Issue, consisting of attitudes about violence, protest, race, students, dissent, crime, promiscuity, pornography and drugs. "It was change that some few Americans perceived as beneficial, but measurably large numbers did not," said *The Real Majority*. "Most voters felt they gained little from crime, or integration, or wild kids, or new values, or dissent." If so, the Republicans clearly had a better chance with them than the Democrats.

But this ideological hardening and the goal of building a majority Republican Party were not totally compatible. The emphasis on ideology and the President's private tirades against liberal Republicans inevitably promoted a spirit at the White House that ideological considerations would have to outweigh party considerations. Without anybody's saying it in so many words, White House thinking was evolving toward the position that if a Republican majority in the Senate was unobtainable, the President could achieve at least an *ideological majority*.

That this might directly contradict hopes for a stronger Republican Party did not seem to have been considered by anybody. For instance, in the State of Washington, Nixon decided very early that he would do nothing to oppose the bid for reelection of Senator Henry M. Jackson.* Though a liberal on most domestic questions, Scoop Jackson had fought vigorously for the Nixon position on the Vietnam war, for the antiballistic missile and most other defense questions, and for the supersonic transport. The cries of anguish from the Washington Republican Party that this open coddling of a Democrat would deeply undermine party morale had no impact on the White House. But the State of Washington was only a small measure, compared with Virginia and New York, of how far Nixon would go toward stressing an ideological majority.

Governor Linwood Holton of Virginia, a moderate Republican and one of Nixon's earliest key supporters for President in 1967, pleaded with the President in White House chats to back State Senator Ray Garland, a young college professor, for the seat occupied by Senator Harry Flood Byrd, Jr. Byrd had switched from Democratic to Independent, ostensibly out of pique at the leftward movement of the Democratic Party, but actually to protect his place on the ballot. Had he stayed in the Democratic Party, he might well have lost the primary election to a moderate. With Byrd running as an Independent, Nixon himself decided, sub rosa, not to back Garland in hopes that if Byrd was elected as an Independent he might either switch all the way and become a registered Republican, or at least vote with the Republicans to organize the Senate in January 1971.

In truth, no matter what misleading hints he may have tossed out to Nixon, Byrd was not about to insult the Democratic grandees who had for so many years been his father's best friends and whom he himself had known since his youth. Nevertheless, Nixon did everything he could to help Byrd and hurt Garland, without actually endorsing Byrd. Garland was denied funds from the Senate Republi-

---

*Jackson was Nixon's first choice to be his Secretary of Defense. See p. 24.

can Campaign Committee and Byrd was invited to San Clemente in the early summer of 1970, ostensibly to be consulted on Senate legislation but actually to have his picture taken with the President and published on front pages the next day all over Virginia.

If any doubt remained, this ensured Byrd's victory, to the chagrin and detriment of Governor Holton's budding Republican Party, Holton had been snubbed by the high command of his party despite his record; his progressive Senate candidate had been deliberately shunned for an archconservative Democrat-turned-Independent. More than any other state, Virginia showed how far Nixon was prepared to go beyond conventional party considerations to bring in a Senate that would meet his ideological specifications—more than any other state, that is, with the important exception of New York.

Prior to his appointment to the U.S. Senate by Governor Nelson Rockefeller on September 10, 1968, Representative Charles E. Goodell had been a hard-working conservative Republican from upstate New York who was considered to have an excellent future in the House. A lieutenant of Melvin Laird (who maneuvered to get him on the House Republican leadership team in 1965), Goodell had an unassailable record for party regularity and a penchant for hawkish bellicosity on Vietnam and other national defense matters. Although in his nine years in the House he had been inching toward more progressive positions, his appointment to fill the vacancy left by the assassination of Senator Robert F. Kennedy was assailed by the *New York Times* and other liberal sources.

In the face of such criticism, Goodell moved leftward with breath-taking speed and abruptness in order to build a base of support for November 1970, when he would be contested for his Senate seat. By 1969, he had become a hair shirt for Nixon and his policies. On September 25, 1969, he proposed a December 31, 1970, cutoff date for withdrawal of all U.S. troops from Vietnam. He was one of only two senators (Senator George McGovern of South Dakota, a leading Democratic dove was the other) to address the November anitwar rally sponsored by far-left organizations. He was one of the first Republicans to attack Agnew publicly in 1969. In short, Goodell had become an anti-administration battering ram. No liberal Republican was attacked more virulently in private by Nixon than Goodell. Moreover, in New York, there was an alternative to Republican Goodell: Conservative Party candidate James L. Buckley, brother of

William F. Buckley, Jr., conservative ideologue columnist and editor (of the *National Review*). Jim Buckley had run surprisingly well against liberal Republican Jacob Javits in 1968. Now with Goodell and Representative Richard Ottinger, the Democratic nominee taking the same liberal line, Buckley might conceivably weld together enough votes from the Conservative Party, from ethnic, hard-hat Democrats and from the growing body of anti-Goodell Republicans to beat both Goodell and Ottinger in the nation's most liberal state. Moreover, as a registered Republican from Connecticut, Buckley would vote with the Republicans to organize the Senate in January 1971.

There was one other element in the possible strategy of marking Goodell for defeat: the reaction of Governor Rockefeller, who, in the early part of the 1970 campaign, was running uphill for his fourth term in office. Rockefeller had an ironclad deal with Nixon that the President would make no overt move in New York State without first clearing it with the governor. Rockefeller had grave doubts about linking his own campaign to Goodell's because of the swelling anti-Goodell sentiment among registered Republicans. Hence, Rockefeller wanted to avoid getting tied too closely to Goodell. That fit Nixon's strategy for keeping his options open until he could ascertain whether Buckley's chances really were strong enough to entertain a White House purge of a sitting Republican senator—a step that would deeply trouble the liberal-to-moderate elements in his party.

So, having traveled different but very similar roads for the past eighteen months, Vice President Agnew and the White House campaign strategy were converging on the same point in the late summer of 1970. What Agnew had been saying and what strategy was becoming were so nearly identical that his role was inevitable—an inevitability enhanced by the fact that Agnew had kept to the hard line during the May crisis while the rest of the administration, Nixon included, had abruptly but temporarily left it.* Now everybody was back on the hard line.

At a campaign-planning session in the Executive Office Building on August 10, Agnew was briefed by the Republican high command, including Haldeman, who rarely appeared in such sessions.

*See p. 288.

Also there were Senator John Tower of Texas (Chairman of the Senate Republican Campaign Committee), Chotiner, Harlow and James Allison (Republican Deputy National Chairman).* Agnew laid down several edicts, including his determination to campaign for Representative William Cowger in Louisville, Ky., to repay Cowger's campaign for him in 1962 when he ran for County Executive. But the important business that day was the *style* of the upcoming Agnew campaign, and Haldeman spelled out the President's plan to make Democratic spending a major theme, blaming the Democrats for the still-worsening inflation.

Later in August the President assigned the four top-drawer aides—Harlow, Buchanan, Safire and Anderson—to travel with Agnew, and this team mapped out a political journey that would take the Vice President to thirty states.† They also perfected the tactics that would accompany the broad strategy which had been apparent for so long. Seeking a pejorative phrase to use against Democratic liberals that would demean them in the eyes of crucially important blue-collar workers and suburban householders who had been voting Democratic over the years, Buchanan hit upon the term "Radical-Liberal," or, as Agnew himself shortened it, "Radiclib." Harlow, senior member of the Agnew advisory team, defined what constituted a Radiclib. A Radiclib wanted to get out of Vietnam even if it meant turning it over to the Communists; wanted to reduce Pentagon spending below the peril point; was weak and permissive on the law-and-order issue; and voted extra billions of inflationary appropriations to domestic-spending bills.

*Prior to this meeting, Nixon relayed a request to Don Rumsfeld to consider running the entire 1970 campaign. Rumsfeld flatly declined the offer on grounds this was incompatible with running the antipoverty program. That Nixon would consider Rumsfeld, who had never run a national campaign or been very close to one, to take on such an assignment indicated the haphazard quality of the 1970 planning.

†The target seats laid out were held by these Democratic incumbents, most of them liberals: Vance Hartke of Indiana, Harrison Williams of New Jersey, Stuart Symington of Missouri, Joseph Tydings of Maryland, Philip Hart of Michigan, Joseph Montoya of New Mexico, William Proxmire of Wisconsin, Quentin Burdick of North Dakota, and Howard Cannon of Nevada. Non-incumbent liberals on the list were: Adlai E. Stevenson III of Illinois, Hubert H. Humphrey of Minnesota, Joseph Duffey of Connecticut, Representative John V. Tunney of California, Philip Hoff of Vermont, Representative Richard Ottinger of New York, and Howard Metzenbaum of Ohio.

That the President would not himself be taking to the hustings was a foregone conclusion by then. The plans for him were to attend "nonpolitical" regional briefings for newspaper editors in several cities around the country that autumn—always, by happy coincidence, in a state with an important Senate race so that the Republican candidate could be photographed with Nixon. But he had no intention of actively campaigning about the country.

That was underlined in early September when the President accepted a luncheon invitation from Representative William Colmer of Mississippi, the crusty old chairman of the House Rules Committee. All the powers in the House, Democratic and Republican, were gathered at lunch in the Speaker's dining room to eat delicious fresh shrimp flown up from the Mississippi Gulf Coast just for Mr. Colmer. After lunch, Nixon rose to thank his host and then added a remarkable statement: he wanted to take this opportunity, he said, to tell those present that he definitely *was not going to take a major role in the forthcoming campaign*. He wanted the leaders of both parties to know that, he said. In the opinion of those who heard the President, he meant every word of it.

On Wednesday morning, September 9, the President spent two hours briefing the four-man Agnew team on the eve of the Vice President's trip. He talked more about the details of the campaign tour, the politics that Richard Nixon dearly loved, than of a grand strategy. Never had a President shown such expertise, such intimate knowledge of an advance man's work. Indeed, he was the super-advance man, explaining why Agnew must go to Casper and not Cheyenne in Wyoming the next day, revealing tricks of the trade. He noted that after his peripatetic campaigning in 1954, 1958 and 1966, he felt nostalgic about not going out on this midterm campaign and was envious of the enriching experience awaiting the Agnew team—an omen of what was to come.

On the next morning, September 10, while his party waited at the airport, Agnew received final instructions from the President at the White House. Nixon sharply emphasized his thesis that the Democratic liberals must be chased so far into left field by Agnew's rhetoric that the great middle-roading Democratic public would desert them and vote Republican. Blame them for the cost of bread to the housewife, for failing to vote Nixon's law-and-order crime bills into law, for a permissiveness that was ruining America's children, for pornography and drugs, for being ready to sell out to Communism abroad.*

This Presidential instruction to Agnew was the result of both Nixon's own convictions and advice from Murray Chotiner and other White House aides. Haldeman himself agreed and pushed it hard, and though he knew little about national politics, his voice, added to the others, was vital. Mitchell, on the sidelines, knew instinctively that the law-and-order, Radiclib strategy would not and could not sustain the campaign. Mitchell felt Agnew had worked that issue so hard before the real campaign began that it would grow stale by November. But Mitchell was silent, not asked for his views and not volunteering.

However, as the Agnew campaign was readied for takeoff, the strategy laid out to reverse the tides of history in off-year elections was being undermined by two factors, both fully realized by the Agnew team.

The first was that the Democrats had also read Scammon and Wattenberg's *The Real Majority* and had, though belatedly, awakened to The Social Issue. Democratic Senate candidates suddenly had come out for law and order. In Illinois, Adlai E. Stevenson III took to wearing an American flag in his coat lapel in the style of superpatriot candidates. In Minnesota, Hubert Humphrey reversed his stand and came out against gun controls.† In California, Representative John V. Tunney made speeches about law and order.

The second factor was The Economic Issue, described in *The Real Majority* as being fully as dangerous to Republicans as the Social Issue was to Democrats. And just at the worst possible time for Nixon his economic Game Plan was collapsing, resulting in job layoffs that Nixon in *Six Crises* a decade before had strongly implied would never be permitted to damage Republican political prospects in *his* Presidency. As the Agnew campaign neared final preparation, the dark cloud of unemployment was becoming the most ominous

---

*This factual error crept not only into Agnew's speeches but also into the President's when he began his campaigning in mid-October. In fact, the Democratic Congress had passed several Nixon anti-crime bills, including the authorization of more federal judges and the District of Columbia crime bill, a sweeping and highly controversial law.

†Wattenberg was a speech writer for Humphrey in the 1970 Senate campaign.

and obvious fixture in the political sky. From a January unemployment rate of rock-bottom 3.9 percent, unemployment had steadily climbed. By August it was 5.1 percent, the highest level since October 1964. For construction workers, the jobless rate had reached 12.2 percent—and these were the very hard-hat workers who played so large a part in the Kevin Phillips equation. Soon the General Motors strike would send unemployment soaring still higher.

The strategy of the Agnew team was to ignore unemployment and, instead, put the Democrats on the defensive on The Social Issue, thus forcing the Stevensons, Humphreys and Tunneys to spend so much time validating their own law-and-order credentials and answering Agnew's charges that they would have no time to campaign on The Economic Issue. At his September 10 meeting with Agnew, the President stressed just this point.

Departing from Washington on September 10 for Springfield, Agnew traveled cross-country to Casper, Wyo., and then the next day to San Diego, quickly establishing the level of dialogue. The "great question," he said in San Diego, was this: "Will America be led by a President elected by a majority of the American people or will we be intimidated and blackmailed into following the path dictated by a disruptive radical and militant minority—the pampered prodigies of the radical liberals in the United States Senate?"* He contrasted the "progressive President carrying out his mandate for reform" and the "reactionary Congress in the grip of bitter men." He appealed to "the workingmen of this country" to join the Republican ranks and become "the cornerstone of the New Majority." As planned, Agnew dominated the evening news telecasts and the newspapers' front pages.

By the end of September, the Nixon agents traveling with Ag-

---

*This Agnew theme was not limited to political campaigning. He really believed what he said about "pampered prodigies," and when his fourteen-year-old daughter, Kim, wanted to wear a black arm band to school to protest the Vietnam war, he had forbidden it, as he told columnist Stewart Alsop, because Kim could not explain to his satisfaction why she was against the war. According to Alsop, writing in the November 3, 1969, issue of *Newsweek*, Agnew said, "Kim, I have given you the arguments for not just getting out [of Vietnam] and you just haven't given me a logical argument against it. So there will be no black arm band and no participation in a demonstration."

new knew that, as one of them later put it, "we had the Liberal Establishment in total rout." So successful had Agnew's scorching blasts been in gaining and holding the big media play and putting the Democrats on the defensive that the bread-and-butter issue was still submerged in the political debate. But Republicans were far from universally happy, particularly after Agnew replaced Democrat Albert Gore of Tennessee with Republican Charles Goodell of New York as his No. 1 target.

During his first week of campaigning early in September, Agnew suggested that not all Radiclibs were Democrats. The general assumption was that he was talking about Charley Goodell, as indeed he was, but he was awaiting a green light from the White House before charging ahead. For weeks Agnew had been undercutting Goodell in conversations with the President; for weeks he had been straining at the leash to go after Goodell. Just before leaving on his flag-showing tour of the Mediterranean on September 26, the President agreed that Buckley looked far more like a winner than Goodell in the New York Senate race. The trick, he told Agnew, was to let the voters of New York get a strong impression that the Nixon administration wanted Buckley elected and Goodell defeated, but to do it with subtlety. Nixon gave Agnew carte blanche to fire his harpoon at Goodell when he thought the occasion right. He was barely out of the country when Agnew, during a television interview in Minot, N.D., on September 30, suddenly, without warning or prepared speech, lashed out at Goodell as a "radical liberal" who was deliberately undercutting the President's foreign policy and was lending encouragement to "dissident elements" trying to tear down the system. Goodell, said Agnew, "has left his party"—but he quickly added that he was *not* supporting Buckley. "I'm merely saying that I am not supporting Senator Goodell." But Agnew's nonsupport of the Conservative candidate was more apparent than real. On October 5 the Vice President's attendance was well publicized at a New York City luncheon to raise money for Buckley—in effect, an endorsement.

Presidential Counsellor Robert Finch, in charge of the campaign speakers' bureau which assigned Cabinet members and other administration officials for political speeches, took sharp exception to Agnew's interference in New York, claiming the White House was maintaining a hands-off policy toward Goodell. Agnew fired back immediately. He had not been sent into political battle carrying the

Nixon banner just for a "frolic," he said. "I'm out here doing a job for the Administration. And while everything I say has not received the express clearance of the President, I have a sense of purpose and definition in what I'm attempting to accomplish." Agnew knew what Finch apparently did not: Nixon very much wanted Goodell brought down and Buckley elected.

That became clearer on October 12, when the President visited Connecticut, the scene of a furious Senate race, for one of his "non-political" regional meetings with editors. For his return trip from Hartford to Washington, Nixon took off from Westchester County Airport in New York, just across the Connecticut state line. He had alerted the camp of James L. Buckley, but no one else, so that when he arrived at the airport, Buckley-for-Senator partisans were there to be photographed with the President. It was a small but significant boost.

Apart from Finch and a few other dissenters, the Nixon political high command was well pleased by the anti-Goodell campaign. Agnew's attack was shrewdly timed and phrased. He had now made it respectable for New York Republicans to vote for Buckley, but at the same time had transformed Goodell into a martyr, so that Agnew-hating liberal Democrats might vote for him instead of Ottinger, thereby throwing victory to Buckley in a three-way race. Even John Mitchell, who concerned himself only with this race, was smiling.

What was not fully perceived by Nixon, Mitchell and their lieutenants was how, inside the moderate-to-liberal wing of the party, Agnew's attack on Goodell had created consternation, fear and anger. Was this the first step in a partywide purge, to force all Republicans into the Nixon-Agnew mold? Chairman Morton immediately reiterated his strong support for Goodell (and was promptly dismissed as a mere "party functionary" by the high-riding Agnew). So did moderate and liberal Republican senators, who wondered whether they might not be next, if not in 1970, then in 1972.* But in this as in Washington State, Massachusetts and Virginia, Nixon showed little interest in the health of the party.

Beyond the turmoil it caused within the Republican Party, Agnew's onslaught against Goodell produced one seemingly small incident that was to prove the beginning of Spiro Agnew's decline

---

*Senator Hugh Scott described Goodell as a "disaster" because of his political apostasy, then quickly added, "But he's *our* disaster."

in the campaign of 1970. In the draft of one speech he was writing for Agnew, Safire referred to Goodell as "a political Christine Jorgensen"—a coarse analogy between Goodell's quick conversion from conservatism to liberalism and the sexual transformation of a young male nurse as a result of an operation in Denmark into the female Christine Jorgensen. Reading Safire's draft aboard the chartered jetliner, Agnew laughed his small, contained laugh and said he liked it. Bryce Harlow, however, thought it was in bad taste. Everybody agreed, and the remark was deleted.

But it was lodged in Agnew's consciousness. In a free and easy conversation in New Orleans, with editors of the *New Orleans Times Picayune* and *States Item,* Agnew blurted out that Goodell was "the Christine Jorgensen of the Republican Party." He later told aides he assumed the meeting was off the record, but, in fact, it had been made clear it was *on* the record. The remark received front-page treatment, and Agnew, in character, subsequently defended it with vigor.*

Unimportant by itself, the Christine Jorgensen incident was the final verbal straw resulting in widespread revulsion. Such obvious lack of taste and discretion unlocked fears and apprehension that had been building up inside the Republican Party. Agnew was no longer so welcome. In California, where the Republican ticket was running into unexpected trouble, state party officials ruled out a second visit by the Vice President on grounds that it would hurt their candidates.† And with the guttering of the Agnew campaign, The Economic Issue began to glow for the Democrats.

Sometime early in October as the Agnew attack grew tiresome, the Democrats finally got off the defensive on The Social Issue and

---

*When Miss Jorgensen protested Agnew's use of her name, the Vice President did not let the matter rest, but turned his guns on her, describing her as a "publicity seeker." Long after the campaign of 1970, Agnew still could see nothing wrong with having used the analogy. All his aides, however, could.

†Even before the Agnew campaign began to go downhill, however, party officials had made the Vice President *persona non grata* in several states. He was specifically told by Pennsylvania party leaders not to come to Philadelphia (although he did make fund-raising speeches in Pittsburgh and Harrisburg). He did not go to New England (except for one fund-raiser in Hartford, Conn.), stayed out of New York (except for that private fund-raising luncheon for Buckley) and was politely told to stay out of Ohio, heartland of Old Guard Republicanism.

assumed the offensive on The Economic Issue. The attack came in a rush, and the statistics pushed it along faster, with several hundred thousand General Motors workers on strike in Michigan, Ohio, Illinois and Indiana, with the press and the evening newscasts filled with news of the budding recession.* All those dreams of bringing the hard hats into the Republican Party on the basis of The Social Issue were being destroyed by the hard realities of The Economic Issue.† Thus, Democratic National Chairman Lawrence F. O'Brien struck precisely the right note when he charged that the newly unemployed "have no feeling that anyone in power sees their plight —or gives a damn." In fact, that concern was also being felt, sharply and uncomfortably, by more and more Republicans.

Bryce Harlow, for one, was worrying. It was now time to strike a different note, thought Harlow; the law-and-order theme *must* be varied somewhat or the result could be overkill. Harlow sensed, too, that the economy was getting far more attention in voters' homes and workers' plants than law and order, and wondered whether the campaign should not begin to switch to that subject and pitch the campaign on a generally higher level for the final three weeks.

This concern struck Harlow with such force on October 5 during Agnew's swing through Florida that from a Florida airport he put in a long-distance telephone call to Haldeman in the White House. Harlow suggested that Haldeman arrange a top-level political meeting so that the serious questions of strategy could be thrashed out. The meeting was held the next day in the Roosevelt Room at the White House, with Haldeman presiding and Harlow, Dent, Chotiner, Rumsfeld and several others taking part. Harlow spelled out his concern that thirty-five days of Agnew's campaign had given the country—and the opposition—such powerful political medicine that it might be well to slack off and move to something

---

*Political aides at the White House felt that the news selection for these programs presented a pessimistically biased picture of the economy and therefore helped the Democrats.

†The concurrent dream of wooing President George Meany of the AFL-CIO away from the Democratic Party had faded even before the recession began in earnest. Meany had been wined, dined and consulted by Nixon for months. But once Agnew began his campaigning, the old labor baron snapped back as a reflexive Democrat, charging the Vice President with hitting "phony issues" and engaging in "inflammatory rhetoric."

else, most likely the economy and Nixon's success in winding down the Vietnam war. After explaining his case, he then went around the room, asking each person for comment. Nobody there agreed with him. Rumsfeld said nothing at all. Chotiner, totally wedded to the law-and-order theme, wanted only to smite the Democrats harder and so recommended. Haldeman reported the consensus to the President, who fully agreed. Moreover, Harlow found little sympathy for his growing concern within the Congressional high command—Senator John Tower and Representative Bob Wilson, chairmen of the Senate and House campaign committees, Representative Gerald Ford, the House Republican leader, and National Chairman Rogers Morton (who was barely on the fringe of this sort of high White House political strategy). When Harlow had completed all his checking and double-checking, he told Haldeman, "I am not getting the message to change."

Harlow was not alone, however. Robert Finch had long been troubled by Agnew's lurid attacks on the Democrats. On the road much of late September and early October with special responsibilities for California, Finch telephoned Nixon several times after the President returned from his trip to the Mediterranean on October 5. Finch was troubled by his press conference in Omaha, when nearly all the questions were about unemployment, low farm prices, high farm costs, and the developing recession. Now Finch pleaded for a change of signals. But Nixon was adamant. Pressed by Chotiner and Haldeman, the President told Finch that only the Democrats would profit if the Republicans suddenly started to explain why the unemployment rate was going up so fast. That, he said, was "a Democratic issue."

Accordingly, despite the warning of Harlow and Finch, Nixon clung to the campaign theme adopted in those early discussions in August—a decision of great importance, since he was about to take to the road himself to an extent no President ever had in a midterm campaign.

Having returned from abroad on October 5, Richard Nixon went to his Florida villa at Key Biscayne over the weekend of October 10 and 11. His top political advisers—Chotiner, Dent, Morton, Finch, Rumsfeld and even John Mitchell—were busy elsewhere. But H. R. Haldeman was there, and the President decided on a breath-taking gamble: to campaign not just in three or four states, nor just in ten or twelve, but in twenty-three different states between October 17 and Election Eve, November 2. Only those two and Mitchell, who kept in touch by telephone, knew the full extent of that campaign commitment Nixon made to himself over the October 10–12 weekend down in Florida. Nobody else was consulted. Chotiner and Dent undoubtedly would have concurred. But Harlow would not have. Neither would Morton, whom Haldeman had kept at arm's length from all campaign planning. Finch had already made clear his own reservations, and Rumsfeld was talking to his White House friends in words that would have burned Agnew's ears. If *he* were running for office in 1970, ex-Congressman Rumsfeld said, he would not want Agnew coming onto *his* home ground. Agnew, thought Rumsfeld, was raising lots of money and losing lots of moderate Republican and Democratic votes with the excesses of his rhetoric. For Nixon to campaign on the same theme would simply compound the damage, he contended.

But Nixon had made up his mind. This was the politics he loved: out on the campaign trail with a carefully memorized speech ripping the Democrats. Nixon tended to think of politics in terms of campaign appearances, not grand strategy. Nor, as he longed to replace Agnew on the trail, did he consider the personal risks to his Presidency of such unprecedented barnstorming. Here was the ultimate risk, the higher significance of operating without the restraint of a campaign manager. There was no one to turn Nixon around.

Richard Nixon left Washington on the cold, windy morning of October 17 for his first swing of the campaign: to Vermont, New Jersey, Pennsylvania and Wisconsin. The President's campaign theme became dramatically clear even before *Air Force One,* gleaming in the frigid cold of a Vermont snowstorm, taxied up to the large hangar at Burlington International Airport, where a couple of thousand citizens had turned out. In that crowd were several hundred anti-Nixon students, who had come to the mountaintop airfield to heckle the President. Only a handful were actually allowed into the hangar, the rest roped off outside near the President's pathway into the hangar. Police officials explained why. The White House wanted a few hecklers admitted to the hall but just enough to make themselves heard without being able to drown out the President or cause serious trouble. In short, Nixon wanted a foil for his hard law-and-order, anti-permissive theme. That was clear before the President landed.

What happened immediately after he landed, and the huge craft came to a stop near the hangar, revealed something else about the coming campaign: whenever a chance arose, the White House would overplay, not minimize, hostile actions by anti-Nixon demonstrators. The reason was obvious: to stimulate hatred of the demonstrators and sympathy for the beleaguered President, which would engulf The Economic Issue.

When the door of *Air Force One* opened and the President stepped out, waving at the generally friendly crowd, a small flat piece of concrete about half the size of a dollar bill spun out of the crowd of obscenity-chanting demonstrators, who were roped off near a corner of the hangar at least fifty yards from *Air Force One,* flew close to the ear of a reporter standing on the apron and watching Nixon at the top of the portable ramp, then hit the ground and splintered into a dozen pieces less than halfway to the foot of the ramp. This was the famous rock-throwing incident at Burlington that White House aides took such pains to explain later to members of the press who had not seen it because the flat projectile landed fully twenty-five yards from *Air Force One.*

When Nixon spoke later that day at Ocean Grove, N.J., he inserted the rock-throwing incident into the law-and-order speech that he had been polishing all day, and that he would continue to polish and embroider until the campaign ended:

> This is a great and good country. I have flown over it. I have visited its towns and cities. I respect those who may have different points of view, as you do.
>
> But I also want to say this—there is a small group in this country, a small group that shouts obscenities, as they did at the last meeting, that throws rocks, as they did at a meeting earlier today in Vermont; a group of people that always tear America down; a group of people that hate this country, actually, in terms of what it presently stands for; who see nothing right with America. And those people night after night appear on our television screens and people here in the United States get the impression that that, if it is not the present of the America, may be the future.
>
> Let me tell you what the facts are: that is a minority today; it is

not going to be a majority in the future because the majority are the people I see standing in front of me here in this audience.

And I want to tell you now as I leave what you can do. Don't engage in violence. You don't have to use the epithets. The way to answer them I can tell you—and it's time for the Great Silent Majority to speak out—the way to answer them is with the most powerful voice known in the history of man. That is the voice of the vote, at the ballot box.

Quite apart from the sudden escalation of a small flat sliver of loose concrete into "rocks," here were all the elements of the Nixon campaign theme bunched into a single quick passage of rhetoric, far from the postelection call of "Bring Us Together." Those three weeks of the Nixon campaign revealed the President's limitations as a strategist. Long afterward, one of his wisest advisers was to say privately that Nixon had made a "major miscalculation" in duplicating Agnew's exacerbation of The Social Issue. The President, he said, should have spent the final three weeks on a different political errand "telling the country to look at the great future if we only will work together." As Mitchell succinctly told friends later, Nixon was "running for sheriff."

The full extent of the President's still-expanding campaign gradually seeped out in private conversations between his aides and local politicians on that first four-state day of campaigning. The logic of expanding to twenty-three states what only a few weeks earlier had been a far more limited campaign—and, at that lunch with Representative William Colmer in early September, the promise of no campaign at all—was intriguing. Nixon compared the ordeal of choosing which states to campaign in to the ordeal that John Wanamaker, the Philadelphia merchant and Republican politician, faced in deciding how much advertising to buy for his store. According to Nixon, Wanamaker figured that half his advertising was productive, half was wasted, but he never could decide which half was which. Consequently, he kept paying for a maximum advertising budget. Similarly, the President couldn't decide which states to campaign in, which to ignore, so he campaigned in every single state where he thought his Republican senatorial candidates might have a chance. He prop-stopped in Ohio, North Dakota and Missouri on October 19, in Tennessee, North Carolina and Indiana the following day, in Maryland on October 24. Then, on October 27 and 28 in an unprecedented Presidential effort in a single state for a Senate candidate, he made four stops in Florida for Representative Cramer, already writ-ten off as a lost cause by every realist.* On October 28 Nixon made two stops in Texas for the Senate candidate he favored above all others, Representative George Bush, and then went on to Illinois on October 29, where Senator Ralph T. Smith had even less chance of beating Stevenson than Cramer had in Florida. From Illinois, Nixon flew to Minnesota for his friend Representative Clark MacGregor—like Cramer and Smith a certain loser—then stopped in Nebraska, and finally in San Jose, Calif., where, at 7:30 in the evening of October 29, understandably weary, he delivered his basic campaign speech.

There were some regional variants in that basic campaign speech; at Longview in segregationist East Texas, Nixon added a passage extolling the neighborhood school and condemning busing of students to achieve racial balance. But for the most part, one speech was very much like another, and all were pure Nixon. No speech writer had written these. The repetition of phrases, the talking down to the voters with unadorned prose and simplistic ideas, the constant search for applause lines—all these were pure Nixon—lines written down by him in longhand on yellow legal notepads and then memorized.

The basic speech of 1970, as finally honed and perfected, began by defending his Vietnam policy ("What we have done is after five years of men going into Vietnam, we have been bringing them home"), then pledged to continue fighting crime and inflation. The Social Issue attack on protesters, begun at Burlington, Vt., had been

*The Florida trip produced an example of the deep-seated enmity between the White House and the Republican National Committee. Senator Edward Gurney specifically asked that Deputy National Chairman James Allison, who had managed Gurney's campaign for the Senate in 1968, travel with the President on his Florida tour. Haldeman's man, Dwight Chapin, telephoned Allison to say there would be no room for him on *Air Force One.* When Gurney learned of this snub to Allison, he called it to the President's personal attention and the decision was reversed. Chapin told Allison that a place had now been found for him. When Allison arrived at Andrews Air Force Base to board *Air Force One,* Herb Klein informed him that if any reporters should ask how many Senate seats the Republicans would gain in the election, he should say two. Allison thought at the time that the gain would likely be more than two seats, and he informed Klein that he would tell them, the press, what he really thought if asked. Klein insisted that as part of the President's offical party Allison adhere to the White House line.

polished to perfection ("I can tell you that the violent few that you see on your TV screens are not a majority of the American youth today and they will not be leaders of America tomorrow"). It was basically a hard-nosed, conservative speech. When he mentioned his innovative welfare-reform program, denounced by the U.S. Chamber of Commerce as well left of center, Nixon used the most conservative rhetoric to describe its purpose: "If a man is able to work, if a man is trained for a job, and then if he refused to work, that man should not be paid to loaf by a hard-working taxpayer in the United States of America."

The basic speech lasted about forty-five minutes—very long, considering its lack of dramatic tension, and it would tend to get longer when he was tired. He was tired the night of October 29 at the San Jose Municipal Auditorium, the President's sixth speech in four states that day. Finishing the speech, he walked to the parking lot and the first serious disorder of the campaign: a much larger than usual throng of hostile, antiwar, anti-Nixon youths who shouted the usual obscenities but with more than the usual passion.

Nixon made a rapid calculation. He jumped up on the hood of his custom-made, bulletproof Lincoln and stood there for an instant, his face creased in a smile, the fingers of his right hand in the V-for-victory salute that had been appropriated by antiwar protesters. The crowd took Nixon's use of it as provocative. Then, just as quickly, he slid off the hood and climbed into the back seat of his limousine, a stone just missing his head as he hurried into the car. As the motorcade began to weave its way out of the parking lot, the crowd, now infuriated, closed in, throwing eggs, rocks, whatever came to hand, cracking windows in the press bus and denting the Presidential limousine. Opinions differed, as they always do in a sudden dramatic episode, as to exactly what happened, but there was no disagreement on one thing: Nixon was the target of by far the most hostile act of his Presidency. Nixon's political advisers, both on the road and back in Washington, were jubilant.* All through the

*There was, however, a minority view in the White House that felt a part of Nixon's strength was that he could travel anywhere in the country, whereas Lyndon Johnson, harassed and tormented by violent protesters everywhere, had been a prisoner in the White House his last months in office. These aides felt the San Jose incident blurred the distinction between Nixon and Johnson and made it seem that not all that much had changed in the nation during the two Nixon years.

three weeks of Nixon's campaign, they and the President had been milking piddling little incidents as examples of the horrors of left-wing dissenters. Early on the day of the San Jose incident, the high-pitched voices of some hundred teenagers and subteenagers got nowhere when they tried to heckle the President at a huge airport rally in Rockford, Ill. That had been the usual level of heckling on this swing, but San Jose was something else. The election was only five days away, enough time to give the San Jose incident maximum exposure, to build it up as the centerpiece of the entire Nixon-Agnew campaign, to exploit this near tragedy—or was it a lucky break?—in such a way that it would encapsulate the law-and-order issue in a form far more dramatic than anyone in the Republican high command could have hoped. In that effort, nothing would be spared, but its result would fall far short of the hope. By overreacting, Nixon would expose his hand too baldly, look too eager and become the victim of overkill.

On October 27 the Bureau of Labor Statistics added five major urban areas (including Los Angeles) to its list of "substantial unemployment areas," defined as likely to have at least 6 percent unemployment for two successive months. That raised to 38 out of 150 major labor areas the number in the "substantial-unemployment" category, the largest number since 1964 and 33 more than had been on the list just one year earlier, in October 1969. Naturally, the Democrats tried to make the most of the recession that was clearly setting in.

So it was that the San Jose incident seemed a heaven-sent opportunity for the Republicans. With Nixon calling the turn, they seized it and ran with it. The Republican National Committee had long since reserved network television time for the President to address the nation the next night, October 30—to be the first and only national TV performance by him in the 1970 campaign. According to the plan, the President's speech that night at the gaudy Anaheim (Calif.) Convention Center on the edge of Disneyland was to be video-taped for nationwide coast-to-coast telecast an hour later. A happy coincidence! thought Nixon. He assigned William Safire, who had been transferred from the now largely ignored Agnew campaign, to write a tough law-and-order speech based on San Jose. Safire did so, and Nixon then rewrote it, toning it down considerably. But then, in a snap decision whose importance would only become known a few days later, he decided that his first speech to the nation in this campaign should not dwell so heavily on terrorism and law and order. It should be the basic campaign speech, with a paragraph or two about San Jose thrown in.

Safire's speech would then be saved for the next morning's airport rally at Phoenix, Ariz., which would not be nationally televised. As planned, Nixon gave it there and it received only limited attention in the press. It was, indisputably, a hard-boiled speech:

> The terrorists, the far left, would like nothing better than to make the President of the United States a prisoner in the White House. Well, let me just set them straight. As long as I am President, no band of violent thugs is going to keep me from going out and speaking with the American people whenever they want to hear me, and wherever I want to go. This is a free country, and I fully intend to share that freedom with my fellow Americans. This President is not going to be cooped up in the White House.

His next two speeches were in Albuquerque, N.M., and Las Vegas, Nev., and in both Nixon soft-pedaled the San Jose incident. In both, too, he allotted special time to defending San Jose, whose city fathers had been bombarding him with messages that their town was getting a bad name because of all the publicity from the rock-throwing incident. But at Salt Lake City, Utah, in the last stump speech of his campaign, he returned to the San Jose theme, attacking the "ugly demonstrators . . . shouting their four-letter obscenities . . . terrorizing the people who were going in, throwing bricks, rocks, and chains at the cars that went by, damaging the Presidential limousine, breaking windows in the press buses and in the police cars . . . I say that those who carry a 'Peace' sign in one hand and who throw a bomb or a brick with the other hand are the superhypocrites of our time."

That set the stage for the surrealistic climax on Election Eve, November 2. Nixon earlier had discussed with Haldeman and other close aides the possibility of an Election Eve telecast—usually in terms of a fireside-chat format, with the President talking calmly and conversationally to his fellow citizens. But Nixon decided that no such program was called for—that is, until San Jose. Sensing a dynamic element in the San Jose unpleasantness that could trigger a Republican sweep, he suddenly decided to televise nationally that tough Phoenix speech on which he and Safire had collaborated. The only date left was Election Eve, and time was duly purchased by the Republican National Committee on the three networks.

Typically, neither Morton nor anybody else at the National Committee was consulted. It was, indeed, Richard Nixon's decision, and it showed a startling lack of appreciation of politics in the video era. An Election Eve appeal, by definition, must be soft-sell, restrained, "cool," in the phrase so beloved of the medium. The Phoenix speech was hard-sell, frenetic, "hot." It was a startling blunder, and it was to be further compounded.

The Phoenix speech had been video-taped by several television stations, one of which, unknown to the White House, achieved a perfect copy in color. But the tape that Safire purchased was black-and-white, with a very poor sound track. Sent to Hollywood to edit the speech for television presentation, Safire at once noted its poor quality. In a telephone conversation with a Haldeman lieutenant, Jeb Magruder, in San Clemente on the afternoon of November 2, Safire fully informed him that the Phoenix tape was not of the best quality, but could be made usable. After checking (presumably with Haldeman), Magruder called back with this word: We're going with it.

At 7:30 P.M. Eastern Standard Time, on the National Broadcasting Co. television network, this shoddy tape, with ear-scraping sound, showing the President in an arm-waving stump speech attacking "terrorists" and violent thugs, was immediately followed by a restrained, quiet appeal for Democratic votes by a Lincolnesque Senator Edmund Muskie of Maine, sitting behind a desk in the living room of an attractive house in Cape Elizabeth, Me. His speech was superb, the color telecast technically flawless.* With Muskie following Nixon's fifteen minutes and calling on the voters to repudiate what he called the Republicans' "politics of fear," even partisan Republicans conceded that the contrast could not have been more disastrous for Nixon. John Mitchell felt that the Election Eve telecast

---

*Muskie's speech was written by Richard N. Goodwin, speech writer for many Democratic Presidential candidates. Funds to pay for the telecasts were raised by a committee headed by Averell Harriman. The triumph opened up a big lead for Muskie against his rivals for the Democratic Presidential nomination.

undermined whatever impact had been achieved by the three weeks of campaigning by the President. Moreover, the entire process—fifteen minutes of frenetic, scratchy-sounding Nixon, fifteen minutes of calm, smooth Muskie—was repeated twice more that evening for the nation, on ABC at 8:30 and on CBS at 9. For Republican partisans, flabbergasted and distraught, the evening had a macabre air about it.*

But so did the whole campaign. Built on nothing more substantial than high-flying dreams and Spiro Agnew's rhetoric, it was damaged by the economic problems that always seemed to undo Republicans, and with three weeks to go, by the President's sudden participation on an unprecedented scale. Now all Richard Nixon could do was desperately hope for returns that would be better than any reasonable person could expect on Election Eve.

The election results were mixed, perhaps shaded slightly in favor of the Democrats. The Republicans had lost 9 seats in the House—a better record than usual for the White House party, but not all that good considering the very low base from which they started; Democrats controlled, 254 to 181. The Republicans took a licking in governorships, losing a net of 11, so that Democratic governors now outnumbered Republicans again, 29 to 21. In the Senate, Republicans did reverse the historical trend by picking up a net gain of 2 seats. Some bitter enemies of Nixon—Democrat Gore in Tennessee and Republican Goodell in New York (the two men most grimly marked for defeat by Agnew)—were eliminated. Senate seats switched from Democratic to Republican in Connecticut, Maryland and Ohio, but Republican seats were lost in Illinois and California. From the Nixon-Agnew standpoint, the victory of James Buckley in New York was particularly gratifying. But there were disappointments, led by the failure of George Bush to win the Senate seat in Texas and including similar failures in Florida, North

*When asked about the incident during a nationally televised interview with network correspondents on January 4, 1971, the President sought to shunt responsibility to unnamed subordinates: ". . . I think that was a mistake. As a matter of fact we apparently felt at that time that the [Phoenix] speech said some things that needed to be said, but having it rebroadcast the night before election is not something that I would have perhaps planned had I been, shall we say, running the campaign. Incidentally, when I am the candidate, I run the campaign."

Dakota, and Indiana. The result was a Senate with 55 Democrats and 45 Republicans, which was far from control, "ideological" or otherwise, by Nixon.* Most distressing to long-range Republican hopes of becoming the majority party based on the Nixon-Mitchell strategy was the Democratic resurgence in the South, where the party regained governorships in Arkansas and Florida, holding the fiercely contested governorship in South Carolina and retaining Senate seats once given up for lost in Texas and Florida (while losing both races for governor and the Senate in increasingly Republican Tennessee).

By any conventional standard, there was not much for either party to get excited about. The results generally would have been shrugged off had not the President's wildly exuberant hopes been so widely proclaimed, had not Spiro T. Agnew monopolized the front pages and evening newscasts with his acid attacks from mid-September to mid-October, had not Richard Nixon from mid-October to Election Day carried on a campaign of unprecedented, white-hot intensity. But all those things *had* happened and the Republican performance would necessarily be judged in the light of these events. And that guaranteed that the election would be followed at the White House initially by stridently exaggerated claims of success, then by intense and remorseful self-examination, and finally by significant change for the second half of the Nixon administration.

*Actually, the breakdown was 54 Democrats, 44 Republicans, 1 Conservative-Republican (Buckley of New York), 1 Independent (Byrd of Virginia). On the vote to organize the Ninety-third Congress, Buckley voted with the Republicans and Byrd with the Democrats to make it 55 to 45.

XII

Starting Over Again

. . . as a President, I am the leader of my party. That is one of my jobs. And in a campaign, I try to lead my party. But this is a non-campaign year and now I am going to wear my hat as President of the United States and that is where I will be on this program and on other programs for the balance of '71.

—Richard M. Nixon, in a televised interview
with four network correspondents, January 4, 1971

On Thursday, November 5, two days after the 1970 midterm elections, ten senior Washington correspondents—most of them syndicated columnists, their views ranging from ultraconservative to slightly right-of-center, all with a record of having treated Richard Nixon with sympathy during his Presidency, some of them outright Nixon partisans—were summoned to the White House to see the President.* Arriving there, they were ushered into the Map Room on the ground floor. They were soon joined by the President, accompanied by Counsellor Robert Finch, Communications Director Herbert Klein and Press Secretary Ronald Ziegler. Nixon noted that this

---

*They included Clark Mollenhoff, who had resigned from the White House staff effective July 1, 1970, to return to the *Des Moines Register and Tribune* as Washington bureau chief. Others present were Columnist Stewart Alsop of *Newsweek*, Columnist Willard Edwards of the *Chicago Tribune* and syndicated columnists James Jackson Kilpatrick, Nick Thimmesch, Richard Wilson, William S. White, and Roscoe and Geoffrey Drummond.

paneled room derived its name from Franklin D. Roosevelt, who taped maps to its walls so that he could closely follow the battles of World War II, thereby following a suggestion made to him by Winston Churchill. Lyndon Johnson had converted it into a lounge and ready-room for Secret Service agents, on duty around the clock to be ready to serve as Presidential bodyguards on a quick unscheduled trip. But, Nixon told the correspondents, he takes no quick unscheduled trips and had restored the room to its former elegance.

Then Nixon got down to the business at hand. Not since July 30 in Los Angeles had he submitted himself to questioning by the Washington press corps—a hiatus not seen since Herbert Hoover's day. Now he would entertain questions from this select, presumably friendly group, though his answers would not be for direct quotation. He spoke for thirty minutes, mostly about the election results two days earlier, then answered questions, almost all concerned with the election returns, for another thirty-five minutes.

The President gave the impression of a man well pleased. As he told the story, the prospects in Senate races were particularly bleak when he began campaigning, implying that is was *his* activity that turned the results around. In particular, he thought he had materially contributed to Republican victories against Democratic incumbents in Maryland and Tennessee. Disregarding the continued fat Democratic majorities in each house, he called the results gratifying. As for the net loss of 11 governors' offices to the Democrats, that was a matter of state issues. Anyway, he went on, the governors no longer have the impact on Presidential campaigns they once had. He was delighted in particular, he made clear, with James Buckley's triumph in New York. Nor did he concede Republican failure in the South, pointing to the Senate victory in Tennessee and the gain of one House seat in Virginia. The Republican catastrophe in Florida he wrote off as the result of factionalism. As for 1972: unbounded optimism.

That session of November 5 was the high point but not the end of a frenetic propaganda campaign by the White House to transform the gloomy results of November 3 into a shining victory. It began in the small hours of Wednesday, November 4, when Vice President Agnew, interviewed on national television, called the election a great victory for President Nixon by giving him an "ideological majority" in the Senate. That interpretation had been suggested to him by Bryce Harlow, but Agnew, unlike realist Harlow, was genuinely happy about the results of the election. Watching the returns on television with several Cabinet members from his apartment in the Sheraton Park Hotel, he had been ecstatic over the defeat of his enemies, particularly Goodell in New York and Gore in Tennessee. On the next morning at San Clemente, Nixon picked up the line. "I would call this a victory," he said, claiming a "working majority" in the Senate. "I believe that our hand has been strengthened," the President concluded. It did not work. The press consistently analyzed the election as a defeat for the Republican Party, for Richard Nixon and for Spiro T. Agnew.* Angered, the President ordered a propaganda barrage to counteract the press accounts. On Thursday, November 5, Ziegler said the President was "delighted" with the "tremendous success" in the election. On November 6 Klein credited the President's heavy campaigning with turning the national complexion of election from defeat to victory for the Republicans, and contended the overall strategy had paid off. On November 9 the friendly columnists who attended Nixon's exclusive press conference published their accounts; a similar description of the President's views appeared in *Time,* and Ziegler told the rest of the press once again just how satisfied everybody at the White House was with the balloting. On November 10 hundreds of editors and Washington correspondents received a letter from Finch, claiming a "clear success" for Nixon, whose policies had been "clearly endorsed" by the nation.

The result of the mass campaign: negative. A typical reaction came from Ted Lewis, conservative columnist of the conservative *New York Daily News,* who wrote:

> What comes through in all this contrived effort to interpret the election as a substantial plus for Nixon is the almost hysterical character of the oversell effort. It is as if even a shadow over the dimensions of the claimed victory is unacceptable. Nixon must be protected from all that claims that he only half succeeded. He must be pictured as an authentic Mr. Big or he could be in trouble two years from now. . . .

*For example, our column appearing two days after the election reported "widespread ridicule by Republican politicians of absurd White House interpretations" and added that those politicians "now doubt Mr. Nixon's ability to handle the economy as a political question."

Could it be that Nixon cannot accept defeat or a questionable victory? Does, for example, his unglamorous defeat for Governor of California in 1962 still force his ego to insist on measuring election results in terms of total victory or defeat?

Indeed, the frantic propaganda campaign flowing from Washington, San Clemente and Key Biscayne in early November 1970 was peculiarly the product of Richard Nixon and seemed intimately related to a personal need for expiation. Those White House aides who had worked on the campaign genuinely felt the election had been a modest success (Bryce Harlow compared it with the midterm Eisenhower elections of 1954 and 1958 and found its outcome far more pleasing), but were appalled by the hyperbolic claims of triumph from the President and from Finch, Klein and Ziegler at the President's direction. As for many high officials in the White House and elsewhere in the administration who did not actively participate in the 1970 campaign, they agreed with the press analyses far more than they cared to admit. Such officials believed the President had suffered severe damage from the election, not so much because the outcome had fallen short of hopes as because Nixon had come across as a hard, divisive politician, an image framed by the Election Eve disaster and the contrast with Muskie. To these officials, the strident postelection claims of a victory that did not exist only enhanced that image.

Outside the iron grillwork of the White House, the reactions of Republicans were far less restrained, far more shrill. For the first time since Nixon's inauguration, workers and leaders of his own party were denouncing him, still privately and not for publication but with increasing despair and anger. Something had gone wrong in the way the Nixon administration was running the government, they were saying, though they did not know quite what. What they did know, however, was that the campaign had been a disaster, and the attempts from the White House to make it seem a triumph only worsened matters.

Clearly, in November 1970, the Presidency of Richard Nixon had hit bottom. Thus, as his second year in the White House neared its end, two questions were being asked in political circles: Did the President believe his own propaganda? Did he reject those in his own administration who saw in the ashes of the 1970 campaign the portents of disaster for 1972? In a short time it became clear that the answer to both was definitely no. So complex was Nixon that he could feel menaced by the critical analyses of the 1970 campaign to the point that he had to launch a hysterical effort to negate them; and yet at the same time he could be so aware of their validity that on the day after the election he was able to begin an introspective effort to find out what had gone wrong and try to correct it.

Thus, at the very moment of the ludicrous propaganda campaign, the White House was simultaneously immersing itself in self-criticism and self-analysis. Pat Moynihan, though a Democrat and not formally involved with considerations of political strategy, told his friends in the White House that the trouble with the Nixon administration and Republicans generally was that they talked not about the things that made people happy but the things that made them unhappy—war, crime, welfare-cheating, discord. Don Rumsfeld was saying much the same thing in memoranda urging a more positive tone for the second two years of the administration. A few days after the election, Nixon and the administration's senior officials met at the President's winter home at Key Biscayne for a frank session of introspection. The result was a five-hour clinical, unemotional discussion of what had gone wrong in the past and what could be done in the future. A few days later another, smaller session involving Nixon, Mitchell and a few aides produced the unanimous recommendation that Nixon must henceforth *be the President*—no mere politician or campaigner but the Chief Magistrate of the Republic.

Never far from the heart of these discussions was the personality of the central figure: the shrouded, brainy, brooding, contradictory man who sat in the Oval Office.

For nearly two decades, friends and aides of Richard Nixon had pondered how he could be made more attractive to the American people, how his intelligence and capacities could be brought home to them, instead of being obscured and even hidden by a personality that, always difficult in its personal relationships, was absolutely impossible in mass relationships.

Yet, even in these most private discussions restricted to his own staff, unwritten limits were imposed on how far anyone could go in reaching behind the barrier of the President's private life. In one such meeting, William Timmons raised a question regarding the President's peripatetic girdling of the continent from sunny Key Biscayne to sunny San Clemente. As chief of Congressional liaison, Timmons reported, he heard much harsh criticism from Republican Congressmen that the newspaper stories about Nixon's villas, his vacations and his living the good life did not go over well with the home folks. Bristling, Bob Haldeman glared at Timmons, who had inadvertently touched on a sore point. The President's trips, he said, were not a matter of going on vacation. Nixon felt that conducting the affairs of state periodically in California and Florida was necessary to give the impression of decentralizing the government. Moreover, Washington was where the enemies were gathered, particularly his enemies of the press. But beyond that, Timmons' question looked to Haldeman like an effort to penetrate the deeply guarded private life of the President, and he was not about to permit it.*

Within two weeks after the election, the President and his men were in general agreement about what had to be done, not only to make him viable for 1972 but to prevent the second two years of his term from being sheer disaster. Foreign policy, it was decided, was no problem. With American troops moving out of Vietnam on schedule and opposition to the war proving to be no great issue in the 1970 campaign, it was assumed at the White House that this was an asset for Nixon. The President himself, noting the small, ineffective groups of antiwar hecklers he had met in his autumn campaigning, assumed that the peace movement was more dead than alive and that without it, there would be little or no opposition to his Indochinese policies in the halls of Congress. False though these ideas would prove to be a few months later, they seemed valid enough in November 1970. Other problems were more pressing at the White House and they came in roughly this order:

1. *The President.* It was not put in so many words, but the President and his advisers agreed that the image of Nixon, the hermit

*Soon thereafter, Nixon received medical justification for his love of San Clemente and Key Biscayne. On December 30 the President underwent a full-scale medical examination at the U.S. Naval Hospital in Bethesda, Md., outside Washington. Brigadier General Walter R. Tkach, the White House physician, reported to the press that Nixon was in excellent condition but needed more exercise and more rest in the sun and, therefore, should spend more time at his two vacation homes. The President said, "I feel that until the Senate takes time off to take some sunshine, I can't take any either."

leader, walled off from the people, antagonistic to the nation's youth, unpleasant and unapproachable, possessed by foreign affairs while he neglected the pressing domestic needs of the nation, must be changed. That would entail transformations in substance as well as style.

2. *The Economy.* The recession, which had cost the Republicans such losses in the 1970 campaign, had to be stopped quickly without setting off a greater inflation than now existed. That entailed greater changes in the Game Plan for the economy than the President had yet been willing to consider.

3. *The Program.* A more forward-looking, more progressive program had to be offered to Congress and the nation. The President had to be shown to favor something besides the antiballistic missile and G. Harrold Carswell.

4. *The Cabinet.* It had gaping holes that had to be filled for reasons of both image and policy. At Interior, Hickel had to go under the interlocutory decree of the previous May.* But other changes seemed in order, starting with Kennedy at the Treasury, Romney at Housing and Urban Development, and possibly others.

5. *Congress.* Relations with Capitol Hill were deplorable, though exactly what to do about it was a more difficult problem. The consensus in the White House: new lobbyists for the President plus a softer line toward Congress.

6. *The Vice President.* By virtue of his overexposure in the 1970 campaign, he should be seen and heard a great deal less, and, if possible, toned down.

Put together, this amounted to a recasting of the administration in mid-course, an extremely sensitive task for any administration. But for the Nixon administration, it was to prove particularly difficult. The changes outlined in the early weeks of November were to get caught up in the very same conflict between intent and execution that had become the administration's hallmark over the previous two years; an inbred confusion that made an agony out of accomplishing stated tasks, large and small.

Whatever else Richard Nixon decided about remodeling his administration for the second two years, his first task (left over from May) should have been the sacking of Walter Hickel as Secretary of

*See p. 282.

the Interior. There had been no change of heart at the White House about letting him stay on, although, of course, the reasons for his dismissal would have been more obvious to the public had he gone immediately after his letter of May 6. Still, the removal of a Cabinet officer should have presented no great difficulties. But beginning with Ray Bliss and extending to Leon Panetta, Robert Mayo and James Allen, this administration had been congenitally unable to fire anybody cleanly and with good style. Hickel was to prove no exception. At a time when Nixon wanted to project a more positive image, the tag end of the Hickel affair would again evoke memories of a closed administration, harshly rejecting all dissent.

It had been an unhappy autumn for Hickel. The crisis of May had brought no easier access to the President. The Agnew campaign had seemed to him to expressly violate the warnings he had put forth in his May 6 letter to the President. While he wanted to play the college campuses and convert his new constituency among the students to Republicanism, he was kept under wraps with speaking assignments among business groups. But worst of all for Hickel was the constant stream of news leaks from the White House, all of them quite accurate, that he would be fired once the election was over. As early as August, he went to Ehrlichman to protest the rumors, and he thought then that he had received a sympathetic ear and promises that they would stop.

They did not stop. Campaigning in Pittsburgh in October, Hickel read a newspaper story predicting that if the Republicans gained control of the Senate he was certain to be fired. This time he called Finch, who happened to be in Colorado Springs, Colo., and informed him that such newspaper accounts were hurting the cause. "People come up to me and tell me, 'Wally, if they're going to fire you, I'm not going to vote Republican,'" Hickel informed Finch, who reassured him that the planted stories would stop.

But once the election was over, White House aides put Hickel's name at the top of the list in conversations about changes for the next two years. So, a day or so after the election, an irate Hickel went to see John Mitchell. But Nixon himself, it soon became clear, was still procrastinating, unable to order the *coup de grâce* to be administered to Hickel.

"I can take anything," Hickel told Mitchell, "but the White House says that 'Hickel's going to get fired,' or an aide says that 'he's leaving after the election' or Ziegler says 'we're thinking about this.' Now, look: either you cut that horseshit out or fire me. I can take it, but it's disrupting my department."

"Wally," Mitchell replied to him, "I've never heard them mention the fact they were going to fire you."

"Then, John, cut that horseshit out," Hickel shot back. "You're doing a disservice not to me but to the government."

The rumors continued. Late in November, it was determined at the White House that the unpleasant task must be performed, and the man to perform it was, of course, John Mitchell. Nixon preferred not to have to face Hickel, who predictably would not make the task easy. At the White House, grim, unsmiling John Mitchell was thought to be the man who could stare down Hickel and not be intimidated by his bulldog pugnacity.

"Wally," Mitchell began, as he sat down in Hickel's office, "we've been talking this over, and it would be better if you just quietly resigned."

With that, almost anybody else in the Cabinet (save perhaps Romney) would have sent his resignation to the President within a half-hour. But not Hickel. Undisturbed by the niceties of protocol, he was not going to make things easy for the White House. "John," he replied, "I'm just not going to go through that." He then explained that his only differences with the President himself were over economic theory, that he still wanted to work inside the administration, and that his departure would do the President more harm than good. It was the beginning of a dialogue that lasted exactly fifty-five minutes. Clearly, John Mitchell was not administering the quick, clean *coup de grâce* that the White House had hoped for.

Mitchell protested that "there's so much turmoil" over Hickel that it would be better for all concerned if he left quietly. Hickel insisted that this could "really backfire," that under no condition would he resign *quietly*.

"The only man who could ask me to quit would be the President," said Hickel. "John, anytime the President wants my hat, he can have my hat."

The meeting ended with Mitchell leaving with these words: "Wally, sit tight until you hear from me."

To Hickel, those words meant that he had convinced Mitchell that his dismissal would be a mistake, that he ought to be retained, and that the Attorney General would use his massive influence toward that end. In fact, they meant no such thing. Mitchell merely felt that Hickel wanted direct word from Nixon. He was urging Hickel to keep quiet until that word came, rather than blast off publicly about their meeting. But Mitchell had failed to fire Hickel. The unpleasant confrontation would still fall to the President.

A few days later, on Tuesday evening, November 24, in an interview over CBS television, Hickel revealed that Mitchell had called on him to discuss his future—a hint that his resignation had been requested. To the very end, Hickel was infuriating the White House by bringing out these unpleasant matters in public. Over national television, Hickel made clear that only the President could fire him. "I'm going out with an arrow in my heart and not a bullet in my back," he said.

On the next day, the arrow was shot. But the stage for it was set with curious indirection. At 4 P.M. on November 25, Thanksgiving Eve, George Shultz telephoned Hickel and asked him to the White House for a twice-postponed meeting over the Interior Department budget request. When he arrived, Hickel found John Whitaker, the White House liaison man with the Interior Department, Caspar Weinberger, Shultz's deputy at the Office of Management and Budget, and two other budget officials—but not Shultz. Irritated, Hickel said he would not even discuss the budget until the man who could make the decisions, Shultz, was present. The five men waited. No Shultz. Finally, a telephone call to Whitaker that the President himself now wanted to see Hickel. Before he left, Hickel murmured some message for Shultz about the budget meeting that presumably would be held once Hickel returned from his meeting with the President. Hickel remained unaware that his last moments in the Nixon administration were at hand. As he left the room, Whitaker commented, "The Secretary won't be back."

Hickel was ushered into the Oval Office for his fourth meeting with the President since the inauguration. With Ehrlichman at his side, Nixon now was forced to engage in the face-to-face confrontation he deplored. To the man who had so irritated him these past six months, he began with a courteous statement about how well Hickel had performed his tasks at Interior after a difficult beginning. The conversation continued in sidewise fashion until Hickel asked the President to come to the point. He did, talking about a lack of mutual confidence. Finally, he asked for Hickel's resignation forthwith. The rest of the half-hour session was taken up largely by Hickel, who spelied out his personal philosophy to an uncomfortable Nixon (at one point asking Ehrlichman for confirmation that he had recommended as early as late winter 1969 that the administration follow a progressive course).

At six o'clock on Thanksgiving Eve, Ziegler announced that the President had asked for and immediately received Hickel's resignation—a public dismissal of a Cabinet officer rare in the American system.* "The President feels," said Ziegler, "that the required elements for a good and continued relationship which must exist between the President and his Cabinet members did not exist in this case."

But that did not end the Hickel affair. For months, Whitaker had been complaining that the Interior Department under Hickel was being run by an unholy combination of dreary civil servants and Wally Hickel's cronies from Alaska. Harry Flemming, patronage chief at the White House, had been unhappy since the beginning about Hickel's appointment of non-Republican civil servants to key posts. Now Haldeman, who had replaced Peter Flanigan as Flemming's superior at the White House, was ready to move. A purge list was prepared a few days before Hickel's dismissal.† Once Hickel was gone, Haldeman dispatched White House personnel aide Frederic V. Malek to the Interior Department to act quickly. Old-timers could not remember anything to approach the massacre. Setting himself up in the office of Deputy Under Secretary of the Interior, Malek summoned the six high-level Interior officials on his purge list and said to each in identical language: "We want your resignation, and we want you out of the building by five o'clock."

The sluggish hesitation with which Hickel was sacked and the

---

*The last such public firing occurred in 1952, when President Truman sacked former Senator J. Howard McGrath as Attorney General. Far more common, however, were firings which were presented to the public as resignations—for example, in 1967 when President Johnson eased out Robert S. McNamara as Secretary of Defense.

†Acting Secretary Fred J. Russell, under White House orders, also moved quickly to reverse two of Hickel's conservationist decisions: orders banning all commercial billboards on federal lands and banning imports of products from eight species of whales that Hickel had designated as endangered.

lightning brutality that struck down his aides indicate perhaps the contrast between the personal styles of Richard Nixon and H.R. Haldeman. Taken as a whole, the mass dismissals at Interior scarcely fit the postelection aims of the White House for a more positive image. The White House, of course, had not heard its last from Wally Hickel, who now became a folk hero to the Republican left (he was quickly named man of the year by the Ripon Society, a liberal Republican youth group). His dismissal was mourned by the press and by the same conservationist senators who had fought his confirmation in January 1969.* And, as in the case of James Allen, the President never did explain the real reason Hickel was sacked: disloyalty to administration policy. Again, administration officials tried to explain it in terms of getting rid of an inefficient administrator.

Sloppy though the dismissal was of Hickel and his team at Interior, the President experienced even greater difficulty in what should have been routine shifts to begin the second half of his administration. Somehow, as he neared nearly two years in the White House, Richard Nixon still was not able to shape the administration to his own specifications.

Near the top of the Nixon purge list after the 1970 election, just below Hickel, was George W. Romney, Secretary of Housing and Urban Development. No two men could be so dissimilar as Nixon and Romney, the bombastic, evangelistic auto salesman who had challenged Nixon briefly for the Presidential nomination and then made a quixotic bid against Agnew for the Vice Presidential nomination at Miami Beach.† Romney did nothing without fervor, and now, at HUD, he had turned his fervor toward seeking more federal money for the hard-pressed cities, toward more and cheaper housing, toward racial integration of the lily-white suburbs. Although Romney did have partisans in the White House who admired his drive and ability to be critical of administration spending priorities without ever being critical of the President himself, the majority feeling there

---

*Senator Gaylord Nelson of Wisconsin, a Democratic conservationist who had led the fight against Hickel's confirmation and voted against him, said of his dismissal: "It turns out he had a great instinct for what was right and the guts to act on his convictions."

†See p. 52.

—shared by the President—was one of irritation. Particularly irritating was Romney's campaign to integrate the white suburbs—attacking the sensibilities integral to Nixon's dream of a majority Republican Party. As for Romney, the aloofness of The Germans at the White House and of the President himself was equally puzzling. "I don't know what the President believes in," a disconsolate Romney, unable to switch spending away from defense to the cities, told a friend in the summer of 1970. "Maybe he doesn't believe in anything."

What tipped the balance in the President's mind toward getting rid of Romney was the availability of a superb replacement: Donald Rumsfeld. Over the past eighteen months, the President had been increasingly impressed by Rumsfeld's keen mind, industriousness, self-confidence and unbreakable loyalty to the President.* He liked Rumsfeld by his side and had him there often during his three-week campaign of 1970. Nixon agreed that Rumsfeld had served long enough running the antipoverty program. He seemed an ideal man to clean up HUD. Like Dr. James Allen and Wally Hickel, Romney was regarded at the White House as a poor administrator. Rumsfeld had done sterling work in making some sense out of the administrative chaos he inherited from the Democrats at OEO and was eager to cut loose at HUD.

John Mitchell, serving once again as Richard Nixon's unsmiling angel of death, paid a visit to Romney shortly after the election. By all accounts, it seems that Mitchell did not specifically ask Romney to quit, but rather danced around the edge by suggesting that he might want to—or so, at least, Romney told friends. What was clear from the meeting was that Romney might prove to be just as sticky as Hickel in refusing to resign quietly. Since Romney had been

---

*Rumsfeld's loyalty particularly impressed the White House during the 1970 campaign. Representative Allard K. Lowenstein, an aggressive antiwar Democrat from New York, was one of Rumsfeld's closest personal friends. He had received help from Rumsfeld, then a Congressman, in a successful race for Congress from a marginal Long Island district in 1968. But Rumsfeld regarded himself as no longer a free agent in 1970 now that he had left Congress for the White House. When Lowenstein's Republican opponent asked for Rumsfeld's public endorsement, he complied on grounds that he could do no less as a member of Nixon's Cabinet. The cost of the endorsement was Rumsfeld's long friendship with Lowenstein, who lost the election.

considerably more discreet than Hickel in avoiding any public criticism of the President and had suppressed his misg. vings about Nixon's Indochina policy, there would be less solid grounds for firing him. Even before the Hickel firing, there were doubts at the White House whether the benefits of getting rid of Romney would be worth the fuss.

The hard-boiled image given the President in the firing of Hickel and his aides at a time when he wanted to seem more soft-boiled saved Romney's Cabinet post. Rumsfeld was relieved at OEO and, keeping his Cabinet rank, was named a Presidential Counsellor— that post designed with such lofty dimensions for Arthur Burns but now a way station, with neither duties nor responsibilities, for administration officials temporarily or permanently between jobs.* If and when Romney left HUD, Rumsfeld presumably would move in, but that might not be before the election of 1972.

Just as he was unable to get Romney out of HUD, the President was unable to get the man he wanted for Ambassador to the United Nations (which had carried Cabinet rank since 1953). As a gesture toward a bipartisan foreign policy, Nixon had always wanted a liberal Democrat for this post. At the Pierre Hotel in late 1968 he made a pass at Senator Eugene McCarthy, and then had more serious negotiations with Sargent Shriver, the Kennedy brother-in-law who was then ambassador to France. It was a near thing, but Shriver made too many demands, and with time running out, Nixon went to a competent but colorless Foreign Service officer, Charles W. Yost, who had retired at age sixty-six with the rank of career ambassador. Now, two years later, the President again began thinking about a liberal Democrat at Turtle Bay, and his penchant for novelty made an unimaginable twist: Why not Pat Moynihan at the UN!

When sought out by the President, Moynihan was agreeable. He had always insisted that he would serve Nixon for only two years, and, indeed, his effectiveness had sharply waned in 1970 with Ehr-

*After the 1970 election, with Counsellors Harlow and Moynihan returning to private life, there would be two White House staffers of Counsellor rank: Rumsfeld and Finch. Both gradually became more and more invisible until Haldeman made plans in the spring of 1971 to move them out of the White House into new (and larger) offices next door in the Executive Office Building. Finch was willing, but Rumsfeld balked at a move that would take him so far from the President. Both stayed at the White House.

lichman and Shultz tightly controlling the domestic policy-making apparatus. Moreover, he was deprived of staff and responsibilities as a Presidential Counsellor. As for Harvard, if he did not return by January 1971, he would lose his precious tenure.* But after the excitement of the past two years, Moynihan was less than excited about returning to academic life, where his old colleagues were displaying the intolerance of the liberal intellectuals toward Richard Nixon and all his works. So Moynihan accepted the UN post, and the President kept it quiet, savoring the little surprise he would spring on the world.†

Unfortunately for the shock effect, however, Moynihan had to inform Harvard he probably would not be coming back, and the word spread through the Boston grapevine. On November 20 the *Boston Evening Globe* published a copyrighted story by Charles L. Whipple disclosing Moynihan's selection for the UN. Nixon had told scarcely anyone—and certainly not Ambassador Yost, who thought he was to serve through an entire four years. Angered by their chief's humiliation, Yost's staffers began pressing for a reversal of the President's decision. So did the entire Foreign Service establishment and its friends in the press, outraged that the President should name anyone with so little experience in foreign affairs as Pat Moynihan. The shrill attack was led by the *New York Times,* which in an editorial of November 25 said Moynihan had "none of [Yost's] qualifications and practically no experience in diplomacy," adding: "He is likely to be bored stiff at the glacial pace of the UN diplomacy, but however that may be, he is simply not qualified for the job."

Stunned by the intensity of this attack, embarrassed that he had been the source of the Boston leak, and influenced by the fact that his wife and children (who had stayed in Cambridge during his two years in Washington) did not want to move to New York either, Moynihan apologetically informed Nixon that he had changed his mind and would be returning to Harvard after all. But Yost was

---

*Henry Kissinger stayed on at the White House and lost his tenured position at Harvard.

†Moynihan's personal planning had advanced so far that he had won agreement from Stephen Hess to serve as his chief deputy at the UN. Hess, who had been Moynihan's top lieutenant on the staff of the Urban Affairs Council in 1969, was running the White House Conference on Youth in 1971.

finished. On December 15 the President announced he would be replaced not by a liberal Democrat but by a Republican, Representative George Bush of Texas, who had been defeated in his race for the Senate. Bush knew even less about foreign policy than Moynihan, but was immeasurably less controversial. The Foreign Service establishment, unable to launch a second attack, acquiesced.

One postelection appointment that gave Nixon no trouble was Hickel's successor at Interior. Since the May crisis, the President had made up his mind. It would be Rogers C. B. Morton, the man Nixon had wanted in the first place and who now was only too happy to relinquish his ambiguous position at the Republican National Committee.* But picking Morton's replacement as National Chairman—a Presidential labor of minuscule proportions—meant a repetition of Nixon's frequent difficulty in decision-making and his continued vagueness about what to do with the National Committee.

When it first became obvious during the summer that Morton would replace Hickel at Interior, there was some talk at the White House of Robert Finch becoming National Chairman. When such speculation got into print, however, Southern Republican leaders protested bitterly over the elevation to the top party post of the man they had described to their precinct workers and money men as the Svengali leading Nixon toward racial integration. Long before the election, Finch removed himself from consideration for the post. Actually, Nixon's first choice was Bryce Harlow, about to resign as Presidential Counsellor. The President asked Harlow on two occasions after the election to replace Morton, but Harlow said no both times. He had not planned to stay at the White House more than two years anyway, and was anxious to get back to running Procter and Gamble's Washington office. Besides, Harlow's difficulties with Haldeman and Ehrlichman were increasing, and he might have wondered whether as National Chairman he would have any more contact with the Oval Office than Morton did. And, just as two years earlier, Rumsfeld's name also came up.† But this time he made clear to the President that he did not want and would not accept the job. The isolation of Rogers Morton at the National Committee was a major influence in the decisions of Finch, Harlow and Rumsfeld to avoid the job.

*See pp. 24–25.
†See p. 72.

But there was one eager volunteer. Early in December, just before he was about to leave the government, Harlow received a visitor at his White House office: Senator Robert J. Dole, a forty-seven-year-old freshman senator from Kansas. A conservative who said little and attracted no special attention during eight years in the House, Dole's political personality changed abruptly upon election to the Senate in 1968 when he noticed that the most articulate and publicized Republican senators tended to be liberals who often opposed the President's programs. Spotting a vacuum that existed for Nixon's de facto spokesman in the Senate, he moved immediately to fill it, defending the President on his most controversial proposals: the antiballistic missile, the Haynsworth and Carswell nominations, the supersonic transport, Vietnam, the Cambodian operation— much to the irritation of some Senate Republican elders, including Minority Leader Hugh Scott, who felt freshmen senators should be seen and not heard. But Dole's help was deeply appreciated at the White House. Now, in December 1970, Dole told Harlow that he would like to continue to defend the President's policies from a broader platform, as Chairman of the Republican National Committee. Harlow liked the idea, and so did Nixon.

But not Hugh Scott, who feared Dole would become the party's official watchdog on the Senate floor, censuring Scott himself whenever he strayed from the administration line. Nor did the state chairmen and members of the National Committee, who felt Morton had not spent enough time at party headquarters, and who did not like the prospect of another member of Congress devoting only part-time to the National Chairmanship.

With Dole apparently vetoed, there now began an endless, aimless period of proliferating candidacies. Scott put forward his own political lieutenant from Pennsylvania, Robert Kunzig, now Director of the General Services Administration. The party's money men put forth one of their own, a prodigious fund-raiser from Delaware named Thomas Evans (who was backed by John Mitchell). Nixon further confused matters by asking Morton to sound out Representative Thomas Kleppe of North Dakota, just defeated in a race for the Senate, for the job. Kleppe, who had no desire whatever to be chairman, was amazed and noncommittal. What followed was two full months of nothing happening as the deadline (January 14–16) neared of the Republican National Committee meeting in Washington. Nixon seemed only intermittently interested.

Thanks to the lack of a strong contender and a nonaggression pact between Dole and Scott, negotiated by Morton and Mitchell, Bob Dole was back in the picture. As for complaints by state party leaders that they wanted a full-time party chairman, John Mitchell had a solution: Dole would be chairman and make speeches around the country, but Tom Evans of Delaware (operating as Mitchell's man) would be co-chairman with the power to hire and fire staffers. No Republican National Chairman had ever had such limitations imposed on him, and the usually docile members of the National Committee rebelled. When they met in Washington on January 14, Nixon had to appeal to them himself (via amplified telephone call to a meeting at the National Committee) to quell their opposition to the Dole-Evans arrangement.

In the listless search for a successor to Morton, Nixon had shown by his own momentary preferences that he had no clear idea whether he wanted a front-man making stump speeches (Morton) or a nonpolemical technician (Bliss) at the National Committee. Harlow would have been both, Kleppe would have been neither, Dole was orator but not technician, Evans was technician but not orator. In fact, Nixon was only sporadically and vaguely interested in the whole process. As Haldeman had said the previous May, the regular party apparatus did not count for much with the President.* He was waiting for the day, near the end of 1971, when Mitchell would quit as Attorney General to become full-time manager of his 1972 campaign. The man actually running the National Committee until then, Tom Evans, was Mitchell's stand-in.

The battle fumes of the Hickel affair were still redolent in the Washington air, the rumors of Romney's departure were still strong, the Moynihan-UN fiasco had just been played out, and the disjointed search for a new Republican National Chairman was just beginning on Thursday evening, December 10, 1970, when the press gathered at the White House to question Richard Nixon over nationwide television. It was the twelfth press conference of his Presidency (fewer in that span of time than any President had held since Hoover), and at none of the previous eleven conferences had the correspondents been nearly so belligerent. That stemmed in part

*See p. 74.

from irritation over the passage of four months without a regular news conference. Not once during the midterm campaign had the President been available for interrogation. But more than that, the hostility permeating the East Room that December evening stemmed from the killer instinct of the Washington press corps. The correspondents sensed that Richard Nixon was down, and they were after him in full cry.

And indeed, quite contrary to the Pollyannish claims dispensed publicly, it was in fact well known and understood inside the White House that Nixon and Agnew were down and needed rapid rehabilitation. In the case of the Vice President, that would require a lowered profile after that horribly damaging campaign. But in the Nixon White House, this was not done by anything so simple as the President calling in the Vice President and telling him to keep his mouth shut for a spell. In the Nixon White House, Presidential aides who were on close terms with Agnew got the word from the President and passed it on to the Vice President that perhaps he should try being more positive, try selling administration programs rather than ripping away at Democrats, student radicals and black extremists.

In the case of the President, the problem was far more difficult. Within the framework of a loose center-right ideology, Nixon must now give off a softer image, show more charity toward his enemies, put more stress on positive programs than on attacking the Democrats, give the impression of having a more vital interest in domestic problems and, if at all possible, display a little human warmth.

The press conference of December 10, his first major appearance over national television since the election, was intended to start erasing the memory of his abrasive campaign appearances. On balance, it was a success. In contrast to the obvious animosity of the reporters, the President seemed restrained and noncombative. In response to provocative questions implying that he had failed to heal the divisions in the country, Nixon noted that "there's always going to be a generation gap and . . . differences between the races," then added calmly and softly:

> The problem is trying to mute those differences, to mitigate them to the greatest extent possible, and to develop a dialogue. I think we have made some progress in that respect, not as much as I would like.
> I am concerned about our relations with youth. I do believe that

as we make progress in bringing the war in Vietnam to a close . . .—
I was glad to note, for example, that the casualties this week were down
to 27, which was a fourth of what they were a year ago and an eighth
of what they were two years ago. One [casualty] is too many, but that's
an improvement.

This was not the Nixon of the 1970 campaign excoriating protesters. The new soft line surfaced repeatedly throughout the news
conference. For the first time, he admitted he had erred earlier that
past summer when he blurted out that accused mass slayer Charles
Manson was guilty, although Manson's murder trial was then in
progress in Los Angeles and he had not yet been convicted. "I think
that's a legitimate criticism," Nixon now conceded. "I think sometimes we lawyers, even like doctors who try to prescribe for themselves, may make mistakes."* In contrast to his haranguing the
Democratic Congress throughout the 1970 campaign, he now said
he "can only hope that in the year 1971, Democrats and Republicans
will work with the President . . ." He said that "under no circumstances" would he again back a third-party conservative candidate
against a Republican nominee as he had backed Buckley over Goodell in New York, adding that "I personally expect to support all"
Republican candidates for the Senate in 1972, even though "some of
them are, as you know, members of what is called the liberal wing
of the party. But they are Republicans. We welcome them. We want
them! We need both."

Yet, not all the rough edges had been removed. There remained
the quintessential Nixon, who simply could not be totally submerged

---

*Nixon's classic gaffe on the Manson case occurred in impromptu remarks, filmed
for television, at the Federal Office Building at Denver, Colo., August 3, 1970. Here,
his deeply imbedded distaste for the press betrayed him. Charging that newspapers
and television were glorifying Manson in their coverage of his trial in Los Angeles,
Nixon blurted out, "Here is a man who was guilty, directly or indirectly, of eight
murders without reason." Immediately afterward, Press Secretary Ron Ziegler tried
to mitigate Nixon's blunder by saying, "If you take the President's remarks in the
context of what he was saying, there is no attempt to impute liability to any accused
[sic]. The gist of his statement was just the contrary." When the Presidential party
returned to Washington, a further statement was issued by Nixon: "I've been
informed that my comment in Denver . . . may continue to be misunderstood despite
the unequivocal statement made at the time by my press secretary." Not until that
December 10 press conference, four months later, did the President admit his
offense, inexcusable for a lawyer.

either by the force of his own personal will and self-restraint or by the image-making efforts of his aides. Asked about Romney's efforts to integrate the white suburbs, the President reverted to the Nixon-Mitchell grand political strategy. "I believe that forced integration of the suburbs is not in the national interest," he said curtly, without adding the conciliatory proviso that perhaps *un*forced integration in the suburbs might be a positive good. Having avoided all comment on the Scranton Commission report since its issuance on September 26, Nixon still avoided touching that prickly subject. He had just "last night or early this morning" sent his reply to Governor Scranton and so could not comment on it until Scranton received it. That old animus against the press, never very far from the surface, appeared again in response to a question from Robert Semple of the *New York Times* noting that many people—including "some columnists"—wondered whether he was giving the country a "clear sense of direction." Nixon concluded a conciliatory answer by saying caustically, "I particularly hope I can give it [a clear sense of direction] to the columnists. I want them to have a sense of direction, too."

There was, in short, only so much that could be done to soften Richard Nixon and make him more positive. A long, turbulent career had permanently imprinted on his political style a collection of hates, prejudices and habits that were immutable. The Nixon image was simply not that changeable. In the long run, his hopes for political rehabilitation before the 1972 election depended less upon his personality than on the success of his programs—in particular, of his economic program.

On November 5, 1970, two days after the election, signals began pouring out of the President's Council of Economic Advisers that a change in the economic Game Plan was in order. "Economic policy like other [policies] have to be responsive to the national will," said Paul McCracken, chairman of the council. Two days later, another member of the council, Herbert Stein, flatly predicted a return to full employment by mid-1972. What the council members were proposing was clear enough: a switch to an expansionary economic policy to fight the recession and give up the struggle against inflation. That would be an attack on one of the two serpent heads of Nixonomics —the one that had caused by far the most damage in the just-completed election. An all-out attack on the recession, consequently, was being pleaded for by Republican politicians who had suffered badly in 1970 and feared even worse for 1972.

At the Treasury, Secretary Kennedy and Under Secretary Walker were appalled. They argued privately that victory over inflation was in sight if only the government did not panic by throwing more fuel on the fire. After all, the Treasury men reasoned, the recession that had been induced in a so far unsuccessful effort to slow down inflation had been costly to the President and the party in the election. Why make the switch now *after* the election? There would be time enough to step up the economy, if need be, before the 1972 election. So the Treasury readied itself for a major debate inside the administration over economic policy.

That only showed how out of touch with the White House David Kennedy had become. In fact, McCracken and Stein were reflecting Richard Nixon's own views—views that had hardened long before the election but that he had concealed. Those views had begun with a revealing impromptu Nixon remark, delivered offhand at an informal untelevised press conference in the Oval Office back on July 20. Asked about the prospects for a balanced budget, the President conceded publicly for the first time that the budget would be unbalanced, then added:

> We expect the economy to be moving upward for the last half of this year and to continue to move upward during fiscal 1972. . . .
>
> Our goal is a period when the economy will be working at full employment, which is a goal we think we can achieve during fiscal year 1972 [ending July 1, 1972], and is, of course, to operate with a balanced budget.

Never before had Nixon so publicly embraced the Democratic policy of priming the pump in bad times. But more important, and *without* prior consultation, he had casually set a goal of full employment by mid-1972. Since the economy would not "be moving upward" in the second half of 1970, as Nixon forecast, that goal would be unattainable; but to come even *close* would involve a much more expansionary policy and a dumping of the precious Game Plan. Finally, Nixon's remarks of July 20 revealed, though in imprecise terms, the influence of George Shultz, who had taken over as director of the newly reorganized Office of Management and Budget on July 1.

In a White House shy on professionalism, Nixon was enamored of Shultz's cool professional competence. Clearly, Shultz was eclips-

ing John Ehrlichman as the most formidable shaper of domestic
policy on the President's staff, just as Ehrlichman had feared.*
Shultz was immediately given charge of the 7:30 staff conference
each morning formerly presided over by Ehrlichman, handling it
with more businesslike dispatch and less flamboyance, saying less
and listening more than Ehrlichman.† A clue to the revised standings
in relative power at the White House came in late summer during
a visit to Nixon at the White House by Senator Robert Dole of
Kansas. Dole expressed chagrin at his inability to contact John
Ehrlichman and told Nixon he would like to meet him someday.
"Ehrlichman?" retorted the President. "Don't worry about him."
Then, picking up his telephone, he said, "I'll put you in touch with
somebody who *really* counts: George Shultz."

As one who really counted, Shultz was able to implant his
economic views on Nixon as nobody else had in the first two years
of the Nixon administration. By November 1970, Shultz had convinced Nixon of the worth of these economic views:

Full-Employment Budget: This concept was behind the President's talk at his July 20 press conference and was thereafter refined
and clarified in Nixon's mind. An old proposal by liberal economists
for the past generation, it envisioned a budget being balanced with
expenditures fully as high as revenue would be *if* there was full
employment (that is, unemployment at around 4 percent). Thus,
with unemployment well over 6 percent, the President could claim
a budget balanced on the full-employment theory, even though, in
fact, there would be a substantial actual budget deficit—sheer heresy
for a conservative Republican.

Money Supply Expansion: As an exponent of Professor Milton
Friedman's theories, Shultz wanted the money supply expanded not
only at a steady rate but at a faster rate than the Federal Reserve
Board, under Arthur Burns' leadership, seemed to have in mind.

Incomes Policy: In a slight break with Nixon's iron opposition
to any incomes policy of significance, Shultz was advocating an
attempt to hold down prices and wages, an attempt limited to the

---

*See pp. 239–40.

†Ehrlichman stopped attending the 7:30 meeting when Shultz first took it over
but, fearful of being shut out of day-by-day events, soon returned to it. Thereafter,
Ehrlichman sat at the opposite end of the table from Shultz and played a major part
in discussions.

withdrawal of artificial government supports that tended to raise them—such as import quotas and labor union privileges—but *no* interference in the free market economy. That meant continued opposition to Burns' proposal for a return to wage-price guideposts.

Long before Election Day, Nixon was committed to an expansionary policy that would run a considerable deficit, but never mentioned it because of his conviction that conceding anything at all was wrong with the economy would play into the Democrats' hands. The Treasury's postelection opposition crumpled quickly.

But the Nixon-Shultz money-supply-expansion and incomes policy quickly collided with Arthur Burns, the man who had recommended George Shultz as Secretary of Labor but never thought of him as an economist skilled enough to draft the grand design of the nation's economic policy. On the morning of November 20 in a meeting at the White House, Nixon—reflecting Shultz's viewpoint—urged Burns to expand the money supply at a faster rate. In response, Burns reiterated his old position that some incomes policy, some government restraint on wages and prices, was necessary. As a specific example, he urged Presidential suspension of the Davis-Bacon Act, which gave construction workers on federal projects high prevailing union-wage rates. That suspension would do two things: wave a big stick at the building trades unions to hold down their unconscionably inflationary wage settlements and greatly reduce the cost of construction performed under government contract.

Thus, partly to appease Burns and ensure a steady money supply, it was decided that Nixon's scheduled December 4 speech to the annual banquet of the National Association of Manufacturers in New York would not only promise an expansionary economic policy but do a little Shultz-style jawboning against oil price increases (a protected industry) and construction-labor wage increases—thus balancing condemnation between labor and management.

One very early draft of the NAM speech actually contained a proposal to subject oil companies to antitrust prosecution by repealing an immunity law unless they rolled back a 25-cent-a-barrel crude-oil increase; it was eliminated before it even got to the White House speech writers.* The suspension of Davis-Bacon suggested by

---

*This law was the Connally Hot Oil Act, authored in 1935 by Senator Tom Connally of Texas, no relation to the man who would be Nixon's Secretary of the Treasury.

Burns was still intact in a late draft but was thrown out by the President on the recommendation of former Labor Secretary Shultz, who argued that antagonizing the hard-hat unions would be bad politics. Thus, the speech contained only toothless jawboning against Big Oil and the construction unions.

Anxious to have Burns' cooperation in expanding the money supply, Nixon sent an aide and the final draft of the NAM speech to the marble palace of the Federal Reserve Board a few blocks from the White House so that the chairman could have a look at it. Arthur Burns was far from pleased and downright unhappy about the failure of the speech even to mention the Davis-Bacon Act. "George Shultz gets over to the Budget Bureau," Burns grumbled to a friend, "and he suddenly becomes an expert on politics." In a lecture at Los Angeles, three days after the President's NAM speech, Burns made clear that he still felt a full-fledged incomes policy—including "a high-level price and wage review board"—was necessary to justify a possible inflationary expansion of the money policy.*

In the early months of 1971 Nixon edged ever so cautiously closer to a working incomes policy. He forced a partial rollback of a Bethlehem Steel price increase by threatening to end the import quota on foreign steel—a withdrawal of artificial government aid that fell within the boundaries of the Shultz doctrine. Nixon finally did suspend Davis-Bacon after first weighing a flat freeze on construction-industry wages and prices proposed by James Hodgson, Shultz's hand-picked successor as Secretary of Labor, but opposed by Shultz. Thus ended Nixon's adamant refusal through his first two years as President to intervene in wage-price decisions. But he was still far short of a full-scale policy to hold down wages and prices on a systematic basis. Bitter memories of his OPA days, reinforced by George Shultz's doctrinaire opposition, were still strong.

If the NAM speech on December 4 was hesitant about an incomes policy, it left no doubt about the switch to an expansionary policy, asserting that Burns had made a "commitment" to keep the money supply expanding "adequately," and for the first time advocating his policy of deficit spending under the label of the full-employment budget:

*Many observers, including some key Democratic Senators, misinterpreted what was happening as a carefully orchestrated scenario between the White House and the Federal Reserve with Burns sending up trial balloons for future Presidential action.

. . . we plan our budget on the basis that it would be balanced if we were at full employment and the economy were producing full tax revenues, not when the economy is below that point, and, consequently, our budget policy will be responsible in holding down inflation, but it will also be responsive in encouraging expansion.

The tuxedo-clad captains of industry, listening to the President speak at the Waldorf-Astoria Hotel's ballroom, may have been confused by details of the full-employment budget concept, but they had no trouble grasping the meaning. While defending the battered old Game Plan and declaring that "the worst of inflation is over," the President was really abandoning the Game Plan and saying that inflation was by far the lesser evil when compared with recession. The question posed nearly two years earlier of whether Richard Nixon would rather fight inflation than be elected to a second term was now being answered.* After a nationally televised interview with four network-television correspondents on January 4, 1971, Nixon turned to one of them (Howard K. Smith of ABC) and commented, "I am now a Keynesian in economics." He meant that he was embracing the advice of Lord John Maynard Keynes that high government spending and large budget deficits are desirable in times of economic recession—advice spurned and downgraded by Nixon and other orthodox Republicans for nearly two generations. Smith aptly commented that the President's belated embrace of Keynesian economics was "a little like a Christian crusader saying, 'All things considered, I think Mohammed was right.' "

Just how clearly the fight against inflation was being placed in a secondary position became clear when the budget for the year ending July 1, 1972, was submitted to Congress on January 29, 1971. The deficit was calculated at $11.6 billion (under the full-employment budget concept, it would have produced a surplus of $100 million, the President said). But this was based on revenue generated by an economy boiling along at the level of a $1,065-billion Gross National Product—a ludicrously high figure in the opinion of most economists.

The derivation of the $1,065-billion figure goes back to Nixon's pledge the previous July of full employment by mid-1972.

*See p. 178.

McCracken and Stein knew that was impossible to achieve from the first but felt the next budget must reflect an economic condition at least close to that. Thus, the Council of Economic Advisers proposed that the next budget contain two figures for the Gross National Product—one an *estimate* of $1,055 billion (about $10 billion higher than the consensus among private economists) and the other a *goal* of $1,065 billion. But Shultz and Nixon balked. How could the federal government set an economic goal and then admit it was going to fall $10 billion short of that mark? The $1,065 billion alone was retained in the budget, the goal becoming the estimate! In truth, most economists expected a deficit of over $20 billion, or over $40 billion in red-ink spending for two years, with the budget running wildly out of control after that. That was the true extent of Nixon's abandonment of the Game Plan.

Equally important in its implications for the future was a change of vast importance in his economic team that Nixon decided to make just after the election. David Kennedy's disappointing tenure at the Treasury had to come to an end, and Nixon knew that the self-effacing Kennedy, a Mormon who was no Hickel or Romney, would be happy enough to leave a post that had become increasingly unpleasant. To replace him, Nixon wanted somebody who could sell dynamically his new, expansive economic program (along with his new legislative proposals) to the press, the Congress, the business community and the nation. Dr. Charls Walker, who in two years had performed most of Kennedy's duties in dealing with Congress and the press, fit that description perfectly and was eager for the advancement. But the tax-reform fight had left irremediable scars on the relationship between Walker and White House aides John Ehrlichman and Peter Flanigan, who convinced Nixon that Walker would be a mistake. They wanted a prominent bank president from Wall Street or the West Coast. But after two years of Kennedy, the President was wary of bankers. Besides, frustrated by the failure of his novel plan to install Moynihan at the United Nations, Nixon wanted another surprise that would shock Washington, and, perhaps, energize his drowsy administration for the two years ahead.

Nixon had been impressed by John B. Connally on the Ash Council on Government Reorganization.* Like John Mitchell, Con-

*See p. 240.

nally had the imperious air of authority, self-possession and master-fulness that Nixon lacked and, therefore, so admired in others. Soon after the 1970 election the President began talking to his close aides about Connally and asking their opinions. But nobody even faintly guessed that the President was thinking about the Treasury, and he kept his thought to himself (certainly not mentioning it to Connally's mentor in Texas Democratic politics, Lyndon B. Johnson). In three meetings over a ten-day period, Nixon appealed to Connally to join his administration. A reluctant lover in this affair, which surprised him as much as it would everyone else, Connally at first refused and then finally said yes. At last, Nixon had that stunning surprise that he hoped would reinvigorate the Cabinet. It was announced on December 14, shocking Wall Street, Capitol Hill, Texas and the world.

From Nixon's standpoint, the move seemed eminently sensible. He finally had his Democrat in the Cabinet, albeit a very conserva-tive Democrat who for the past decade had led the Tory wing of the Texas Democratic Party. Texas Republicans gasped at Nixon's audacity—some would call it betrayal—in bestowing this honor on their great enemy, but Connally's presence in the Nixon administra-tion could only help the President's chances to carry Texas in 1972, which might be vital to his reelection. He brought strength to a Cabinet that was weak, and would be weaker when Mitchell resigned to become campaign manager for 1972. And here was a glib, Stetson-wearing supersalesman who could make Nixon's new economic game plan make sense to the nation. The only drawback was the lack of paper qualifications by John Connally, lawyer-businessman-politi-cian, to be Secretary of the Treasury. But that seemed irrelevant; there never had been a Secretary *better* qualified than David Kennedy.

Why Connally should take the job was a little more puzzling. He had spent only seven years in public life (one as Secretary of the Navy under John F. Kennedy and six as governor of Texas), and, friends thought, he missed the excitement of wielding power and influencing affairs. Perhaps, as Connally himself said, Nixon did appeal to his love of country. Perhaps, as Connally told his friends, Nixon did remind him that just making money, as Connally was doing, could not satisfy a man's inner yearning. But, far more impor-tant, John Connally was a man of Presidential proportions, and with the Democratic Party moving rapidly leftward, he had no chance whatever of achieving his goal there. In the Republican Party, with Spiro T. Agnew badly wounded by his 1970 campaign, was there a long-shot possibility that he could be Richard Nixon's running mate in 1972?

In the interim, Connally became the only noneconomist, the only businessman and the only politician on a Quadriad consisting of economists Shultz, Burns and McCracken. Unlike them, he had an open mind on almost all economic questions (Arthur Burns said to friends that he thought Connally was "educable"). How he would act in a crisis was anybody's guess. But with his access directly to the President assured, the certainty was that he would act, and act without recourse to doctrine. That would, indeed, be something new in President Nixon's management of the economy.

When Richard Nixon returned from his autumn campaigning, he had the profound misfortune of facing the very same Ninety-first Congress he had been condemning from one end of the country to another. The Senate, immobilized all spring and summer by the meandering debate on the Indochina situation, had so frittered away its time that it could not complete its work before the election and thus forced the first lame-duck session of Congress since the Korean War twenty years before. Having denounced the Democratic leadership for its irresponsibility, among many sins, the President now had to deal with those same leaders to salvage something out of his legislative program.

This dramatized a situation that had existed all through 1970. Whereas the Congressional liaison staff, headed by William Timmons, was trying to achieve a working relationship with the Democratic leaders of Congress, other Presidential aides were trying to issue an indictment of blind partisanship against those leaders, a record that the Republicans could run against not only in 1970 but in 1972 as well—a view shared by the President. Timmons was trying to build up the record of the Ninety-first Congress; Nixon was trying to tear it down.

But now, Nixon's first postelection mood was to show a less truculent face to the nation. In that spirit was his conciliatory comment at his December 10 press conference that Democrats in 1971 "will work with the President" for essential programs. But lame-duck sessions containing so many members of Congress who would not return for the next session in January are always mischievous—

a quality magnified when Congress and the White House are controlled by different parties. It would be an absolutely safe bet that the lame-duck session of 1970 would try Nixon's patience.

The session lived up to the worst expectations. Senator Russell B. Long of Louisiana, mercurial chairman of the Senate Finance Committee, went on a rampage that succeeded in tying into one messy package three major pieces of Nixon legislation already passed by the House—the welfare reform (including Family Assistance Payments), a trade bill containing quotas on textiles (proposed by Nixon) and shoes (opposed by Nixon), and a Social Security payment increase. The lame-duck session adjourned without enacting any of the three. Despite a strenuous lobbying effort by the White House, legislation to continue the supersonic transport was defeated in the Senate; the plane barely got a brief stay of execution, with its final fate to be determined by the Ninety-second Congress. Four separate appropriations and authorizations bills containing economic and military aid for Vietnam, Laos and Cambodia were held up in session-end blocking maneuvers by antiwar senators. Nixon, somewhat sullen and irritated by having to bother with Congress, as he always was, curtly turned down a State Department request that he personally lobby key Senate and House members to untangle the aid bills. Nevertheless, they did finally pass, more or less intact—representing one of the few successes of the lame-duck session. But most of the time the Senate, under Mansfield's permissive leadership, was a snakepit of endless talk with four separate filibusters under way on a single December afternoon.

For most of that lame-duck session, Nixon held his peace, venting his anger only privately, complaining to aides that he was unable to get off for a badly needed rest at San Clemente or Key Biscayne, furious at Long's madcap maneuvers and Mansfield's lackluster leadership but not appealing to either of them. Thus, when the long, garrulous, unproductive Ninety-first Congress finally adjourned *sine die* on January 2, 1971, all his bottled-up antagonism boiled to the surface in an angry statement he issued on January 5. Timmons' Congressional liaison staff was, unbelievably, not even consulted about the final form of this attack on Congress and learned, to its horror, of Nixon's intemperate remarks along with the rest of the country.

In the final month and weeks of 1970, especially in the Senate of the United States, the Nation was presented with the spectacle of a legislative body that had seemingly lost the capacity to decide and the will to act. When the path was finally cleared, vital days had been lost, and major failures insured.

In probably no month in recent memory did the reputation of the whole Congress suffer more in the eyes of the American people than in the month of December 1970. In these times when the need to build confidence in government is so transparent, that was good neither for the Congress nor the country. Let us hope that it never takes place again.

Even a partial listing of the vital legislation rejected, or left unenacted, by the departing 91st Congress provides a yardstick of just how far this Congress fell short of the mark of becoming the Great Congress —that it might have been.

That was an authentic outpouring of authentic Nixonian wrath, in the same genre as the post-Carswell outburst. But it served a far less useful political purpose than did the denunciation of the Senate in April 1970. There was no question that the January 5 statement would provide excellent Republican campaign ammunition for the next election, but the next election was not until 1972. For now, the tactic at the White House was supposed to be the soft line, a smile and an honest attempt to get along with Congress better in 1971, with a huge new outpouring of legislation ready to be introduced. So, the January 5 statement, far from being planned, was an automatic release of pent-up emotion showing the President's deep-seated animosity against Russell Long's procrastinations and Mike Mansfield's pleas of impotency. He had encountered these procrastinations and these pleas in face-to-face conversation with the senators, smiling a tight little smile and listening without a trace of rancor in his voice. The emotion built up inside and poured out in a rush on January 5.

What also made that statement a clear disclosure of Presidential pique rather than conscious strategy was that the President had just named a new chief of Congressional liaison, who was embarked on a determined policy of kindness toward Congress.

The reason for the change could be traced to the Attorney General. For months, John Mitchell had been advising that the fault lay with Bill Timmons and his hard-working staff, and the President believed him. Mitchell's argument was that Timmons, who had spent his entire career on Capitol Hill as a staff aide, simply did not have the stature to deal with House members and senators. He was, indeed, a ready-made scapegoat. Once the election was over,

Mitchell had his candidate for a replacement: Representative Clark MacGregor, who had sacrificed his safe House seat in a hopeless run against Hubert Humphrey for the Senate in Minnesota. Gregarious, aggressive, bright, and a veteran of ten years in the House, MacGregor had favorably attracted Mitchell's attention in 1968 as an early Nixon supporter in a state dominated by Rockefeller sentiment. Now Mitchell convinced Nixon that MacGregor was just the man for Congressional liaison.

When this word began to seep out, it naturally alarmed Timmons (who, in what had become standard practice in the Nixon White House, had not been consulted). Timmons went to Haldeman, who confessed having talked to MacGregor but said his would be a policy-making post with no responsibility over Congressional liaison. Thus, it was with some surprise that Timmons learned on December 1 that he had acquired a new boss; MacGregor was named White House Counsel *with* direct supervision over all Congressional liaison. In a procedure that after two years had become a familiar pattern, Nixon neither advised Timmons of any displeasure with his work, nor gave him personal prior word of his forthcoming demotion. Indeed, in a White House reception shortly after his demotion, the President went out of his way publicly to praise Timmons for the splendid way in which he had handled Congressional affairs.

MacGregor had advantages in his new post that Timmons lacked, including easy access to the President and the powerful patronage of John Mitchell. But MacGregor fully agreed with Timmons that a major problem with Congressional relations was the President's tendency to lash out at Congress, coupled with the obvious contempt that Haldeman and Ehrlichman made so clear they felt for Congress. With a big new legislative program being readied, improving Congressional relations would be all the more important. As a starter, MacGregor arranged a series of White House briefing sessions for Congressmen, preached a policy of greater tolerance for Congress among Presidential aides and distributed buttons reading I CARE ABOUT CONGRESS to his staff.*

Breakfasting with a group of correspondents at the National Press Club on January 14, MacGregor spoke frankly about his prob-

*However, Timmons and the other lobbyists inherited by MacGregor refused to wear the buttons. MacGregor did not press the matter.

lems. He told how he was trying to get senior White House officials —unnamed, but obviously Haldeman and Ehrlichman—to spend more time getting to know Congressmen and their views. Heaping praise on Timmons and the rest of the liaison staff, MacGregor placed the blame for the problems in Congress squarely on the Haldeman-Ehrlichman group: "It's natural if you haven't served in the House or Senate that you see some [members of Congress] who are not the best examples of competence and intelligence, to feel that everybody's that way." He added that the President's January 5 denunciation of Congress was prepared without his knowledge. Asked by a correspondent what that statement had accomplished, MacGregor said bluntly, "Nothing."*

When they read a detailed account of MacGregor's remarks in the next morning's *New York Times,* Haldeman and Ehrlichman were outraged—not only by the criticisms of themselves, unheard-of in the Nixon White House, but by MacGregor's indiscretion in daring to suggest that *any* act of the President had no purpose. The word spread through the White House staff that Clark MacGregor, barely on board, was out of favor and might soon encounter the Berlin Wall blocking his access to the President.

Beyond that, MacGregor would face the same problems Bryce Harlow and Bill Timmons had encountered. Once the Democratic Congress dug in its heels and refused to swallow the large portions of legislation that Nixon was preparing, the I CARE ABOUT CONGRESS slogan would become not only obsolete but obscene as the President, by reflex action, opened fire again and Ehrlichman and Haldeman returned to their Congress-baiting ways. The probability for this happening was high, because the heavy new diet of legislation Nixon had prepared was certain to prove indigestible.

At that Key Biscayne meeting shortly after the election, the

*At that breakfast, MacGregor also criticized the omission of Senator Muskie from the White House ceremonies December 31 when Nixon signed the anti-water-pollution bill, although Muskie had pioneered, authored and managed the bill through to passage. Such heavy-handed politics, said MacGregor, would be "a thing of the past." The omission of Muskie was traceable to a rare case of bad judgment by Timmons, who did not want to see a front-runner for the Democratic Presidential nomination given publicity at a White House forum. In fact, this omission gave Muskie more publicity than he would have received had he been invited.

President and his aides spent a great deal of time talking about a positive, politically popular legislative program for the next year. It was determined, moreover, that the token revenue-sharing program of $500 million in federal money distributed to the states would be greatly expanded.* Besides revenue sharing, a broad domestic program that had been developed over the past year by John Ehrlichman's Policy Council staff would be presented by Congress as part of a more progressive, more positive Nixon image. By Christmas, it was determined that the revenue sharing would be substantial: a total of $5 billion in new money.

At precisely the moment Nixon was denouncing the Congress as "a legislative body that had seemingly lost the capacity to decide and the will to act," he was drafting a legislative program of massive proportions. Its basic outlines were unveiled on the evening of January 22 in the President's State of the Union Message. Nixon proposed "six great goals" of domestic legislation to Congress:

1. The welfare reform left over from the old Congress.

2. "Full prosperity in peacetime" with passage of Nixon's full-employment budget.

3. An expanded program to clean up the environment.

4. A national health insurance program.

5. A big revenue-sharing program "to reverse the flow of power and resources from the states and communities to Washington and start power and resources flowing back from Washington to the states and communities and, more important, to the people all over America."

6. A massive reform of the federal government, coming from the Ash Council, that would leave State, Treasury, Defense and Justice as the only Cabinet-level departments intact and consolidate all others into four new departments: Human Resources, Community Development, Natural Resources and Economic Development.

All this was described by Nixon in cosmic terms, appropriating the "power-to-the-people" slogan of the revolutionary New Left:

. . . what this Congress can be remembered for is opening the way to a New American Revolution—a peaceful revolution in which power

---

*Revenue sharing was first proposed by Representative Melvin Laird of Wisconsin in the late 1950s. It was first seriously advocated inside an administration by Walter Heller, Chairman of the Council of Economic Advisers, in 1964 but was rejected by President Johnson after opposition from organized labor.

was turned back to the people—in which government at all levels was refreshed and renewed, and made truly responsive. This can be a revolution as profound, as far-reaching, as exciting as that first revolution 200 years ago—and it can mean that just five years from now America will enter its third century as a young nation new in spirit, with all the vigor and the freshness with which it began its first century.

At the same time, the President described the program as the antidote to a deepening public disillusionment with the governmental process. "Let's face it," he said. "Most Americans today are simply fed up with government at all levels." By strengthening state and local government and reorganizing the federal government, he said, "we can make government more creative in more places."

Some skeptics on the White House staff, while recognizing the program as an excellent one, thought the high-flown prose style of the State of the Union Message (provided by speech writer Raymond Price) and the New American Revolution label (supplied by speech writer William Safire) ludicrously inappropriate. Moreover, as positive and friendly toward Congress as Nixon sounded (in the final words of the message he called on the legislators to "make this the greatest Congress in the history of this great and good country"), what would happen when his program foundered? There would be trouble for *all* parts of the Revolution, particularly revenue sharing, which would dilute Congressional power by automatic transfer of money to the states and, therefore, predictably infuriate all the committee chairmen—especially Wilbur Mills, whose Ways and Means Committee would handle the bill. These same chairmen also would oppose the governmental reorganization as a threat to their power.

Nevertheless, the public reaction was strongly positive. "Mr. Nixon's State of the Union Address was distinctive, innovative, and committed to both some proper concerns and some excellent ideas," said the lead editorial in the *Washington Past,* scarcely an apologist for the Nixon administration. From more usually pro-Nixon quarters there were cheers. Columnist Joseph Alsop called it "bolder and more innovating than anything heard from a President" since the early days of Franklin D. Roosevelt.

And then something very strange and politically improbable happened. The image of the progressive, positive, nonpartisan President that Nixon had been trying to purvey since Election Day suddenly began to take hold. The criticism and incessant backbiting perceptibly decreased. The nervous looks at the White House disappeared, replaced by something close to euphoria. Ehrlichman confidently predicted that this high, new mood would continue right through to Election Day, 1972. John Mitchell, scarcely addicted to euphoria, was talking the same way to his friends. But Ehrlichman and Mitchell, two extremely able men, were new to national politics. They were making two miscalculations. First, they had vastly overestimated the public impact of the New American Revolution, a program far too intellectual to sustain public acclaim. That would be particularly true with the soon-to-be discovered fact that no part of it would pass Congress without months, perhaps years, of tedium. In short, the New American Revolution would be forgotten in an astonishingly short space of time. Second, and more important, they had misjudged the continuing—indeed, what would shortly be the growing—political volatility of the Vietnam war. The times of trouble for Nixon were to resume all too soon.

XIII
Meeting
Adversity: 1971

*Every Presidency runs its own fever chart—a jagged
line of highs that look unassailable and lows that can
seem bottomless while they last. Richard Nixon has
lately fallen into a low cycle—perhaps the lowest of
his two years in office.*
                                    —*Newsweek*, April 5, 1971

*Vietnam is the wound in American life that will not
heal, however soothed it may seem for long stretches
under the balm of continuing U.S. withdrawals.*
                                    —*Time*, April 12, 1971

When Melvin R. Laird, Secretary of Defense, returned to Washington on January 15, 1971, from one of his periodic inspection trips to Indochina, he carried in his briefcase a proposal from Saigon—unanimously backed by the South Vietnamese government and Army, the U.S. high command and U.S. Ambassador Ellsworth Bunker—for a direct military assault on the Ho Chi Minh Trail in the Panhandle of Laos. This was the complex of roadways and trails running south from North Vietnam through the Panhandle into Cambodia, the lifeline of Hanoi's legions fighting in Cambodia, southern Laos and, most important, South Vietnam.

Of all the dreams of glory that had filled ambitious military minds since serious U.S. intervention in the war in 1965, cutting the Ho Chi Minh Trail was the most bewitching. Plans had been drawn up countless times under countless generals, but always, because of the cost in manpower and the risks in international politics, the White House had said no. Robert S. McNamara, as Secretary of Defense, resisted increasing military demands for an attack against the Trail by promising to deploy an electronic wall—running from the South China Sea along the southern edge of the Demilitarized Zone (DMZ) separating North and South Vietnam to the border of Laos, thence south down the South Vietnamese-Laotian border. It was never feasible and ended as a pathetic patch of electronic sensors in the DMZ area.

Now, on January 15, Laird had in his briefcase the most serious plan ever formally presented to a President for a massive in-and-out invasion of Laos and a cutting of the Trail. One new factor militated for such an action in the late winter of 1971: the withdrawal of American troops and the necessity of protecting from enemy attack the constantly depleted numbers of those remaining. The justification was similar to the one that persuaded the President to risk the earlier invasion in April 1970 of the Cambodian sanctuaries.*

At first Laird, in Saigon, was skeptical about the Laos plan, but one feature of it made it instantly more attractive than the Cambodian operation: there would be no U.S. troops. First, to use them in Laos was illegal under the terms of the 1970 Defense Appropriations Act. Second, they would not be needed, because Communist forces arrayed along the Ho Chi Minh Trail were far smaller than those in the Cambodian jungles. Third, and finally, it was time to see how South Vietnam's much-improved army, the ARVN, would perform without American troops alongside. Although U.S. air support would be provided in vast quantities, the real work would be Saigon's. With American withdrawals moving ahead at a 12,500-a-month pace, it was important to learn just how good ARVN really was.

Laird knew the political cost at home might be very high, but he had been won over to the plan in Saigon. It was the President who was skeptical. Thus, the tables were reversed from the previous April, when most of Nixon's advisers were skeptical about Cambodia. Now even Secretary of State William P. Rogers, so negative about the Cambodian invasion, gave his blessing to Laos; without American troops participating, Rogers saw a diminished political risk both at home and abroad. Henry Kissinger, as usual, presented

*See pp. 245 ff.

Nixon with a series of options that neither pushed Nixon into this new and risky undertaking nor pulled him out. Those options, however, pointed toward accepting Saigon's proposal.

But locked within the President were far greater reservations now than he had held about invading Cambodia. As Nixon perceived the operation against the Ho Chi Minh Trail, it might indeed buy more time for safe withdrawal of American troops by reducing the supplies essential for the enemy to launch an attack against South Vietnam. It was all very well to see how ARVN would react alone in the field, as Laird proposed. But Nixon remembered what happened at home after Cambodia: the Kent State tragedy and the subsequent emotional upheaval that so profoundly affected his Presidency.* Could it happen again? Nixon's White House inner circle also was far more wary now than it had been in May 1970. Now H. R. Haldeman was following the President's lead and worrying about another campus outbreak.

Laird convinced Nixon with his argument that even temporarily stemming the flow of war supplies from moving down the Ho Chi Minh Trail was essential to prevent a build-up, and thus deny the enemy a base for a major campaign against South Vietnam during the 1971 and the 1972 dry seasons. Complementing the Cambodian intervention, it would give ARVN one more year of small-combat seasoning and protect the American rear in the final stage of troop withdrawal. Furthermore, Laird informed Nixon that the operation simply could not be a disaster; American transport helicopters were available in huge numbers to ferry ARVN troops in and out of the narrow stretch of mountainous Laotian terrain, never more than twenty miles from the border of South Vietnam. So Nixon said yes. In acquiescing, he privately told Laird and the Joint Chiefs that this would be the very last major operation in South Vietnam in which the United States would take a large role.

In a February 2 meeting with Laird, Rogers, Kissinger and Admiral Thomas H. Moorer, Chairman of the Joint Chiefs of Staff, Nixon expressed his hope that the decision to move against the Ho Chi Minh Trail would not stimulate new antiwar excesses or upset the relative domestic tranquillity. Whether it did or not would, he knew, turn on whether his administration could convince the American people that this was not enlarging the war, was not carrying the

*See pp. 275–77.

war to still another country, was not a prolongation of the war, but would indeed have the effect described by Laird on February 9 to the Senate Armed Services Committee: "We have not widened the war. To the contrary, we have shortened it."

So the troubled late winter and early spring of 1971 started with still another military adventure in Vietnam, an adventure of uncertain duration and high political risk. Richard Nixon's misgivings were justified. Laos would trigger what nothing else in the long war had done: powerful domestic pressure for setting a deadline for final withdrawal of U.S. troops that would come not from radicalized campuses but from the great political center in the U.S. Congress, both Democratic and Republican.

The operation went sour from the start. In an effort to conceal exact targets along the Ho Chi Minh Trail to be hit, the U.S. command in Saigon on January 29 ordered an unprecedented news embargo, approved routinely by the President, on all aspects of the operation. But news outlets in Tokyo and elsewhere soon had the heart of what looked like a very big story, and it was fed to the American public from these secondary sources. This infuriated politicians and press, arousing new suspicions. The fact that the North Vietnamese correctly estimated precise targets of the ARVN invaders showed conclusively that the enemy needed no American news reports to learn exactly what was coming. The enemy's chain of intelligence, with links into the heart of the Saigon military establishment, was excellent.

Nixon had learned one lesson from Cambodia. Then, he had rejected recommendations from top advisers, including Laird, that he stay out of the limelight, let the Cambodia invasion be announced in Saigon and play down the operation as a routine.* Now, as the Laos operation began, he said nothing. Presidential silence was complete for fully ten days. Then, on February 17, Nixon held a nontelevised press conference, another concession to the low profile he had temporarily assumed, and without truculence or flag-waving, tried to put the operation into perspective: ". . . the operation has gone according to plan," said Nixon, and quoted General Abrams as saying that, against stiff Communist resistance, the ARVN "are fighting . . . in a superior way" and "are proceeding in a way that

*See pp. 246–47.

he [Abrams] believes is in accordance with the plan and holding their own against enemy attack."

The Laos operation ended on March 24, six weeks earlier than scheduled. A full evaluation of the operation would not be made for many months and, in fact, was a muddied picture. Some ARVN units had fought well, some not so well. Both the North Vietnamese and South Vietnamese had suffered very heavy casualties; whether Communist losses were so heavy that they would inhibit offensive action into the 1972 dry season remained to be seen. American losses seemed scarcely of a scale to provoke widespread domestic upheaval: 174 killed in action; 1,027 wounded; 42 missing in action; 107 helicopters lost (and hundreds more brought down by enemy gunfire, retrieved and made to fly again).

What turned Laos into a political disaster at home were the pictures on the television screens, night and morning, particularly at the tail end of the operation when some panicked ARVN troops, trying to escape the withering fire of the North Vietnamese, clung to the skids of American helicopters evacuating both the wounded and ARVN units cut off by the encircling enemy. To Nixon and his staff at the White House, a major part of the trouble was what they regarded as outrageous bias on the part of the news correspondents in Indochina (most of whom were, in fact, opposed to U.S. involvement). The President's habitual irritation with the media was now rubbed raw, revealing itself mostly in private remarks to his staff but occasionally in public. With Nixonian self-pity, the President told a televised press conference of March 4: "Now, I realize that night after night for the past three weeks on television, there is a drumbeat of suggestion, not from all but from some commentators. And I can understand why they disagree, from the same ones who said that Cambodia wouldn't work, that this isn't going to work."

To compensate for what it regarded as biased and unfair press coverage (and, in fact, television did seem to give a distorted picture), the White House opened a propaganda barrage far greater then the postelection effort the previous November to paint a Republican victory.* Despite a serious Pentagon effort not to permit any exaggerated claims, they came in profusion. The propaganda included the mailing to editors across the country of a February 8 column by Joseph Alsop praising the President for having undertaken the Laos

*See pp. 347 ff.

operation and charging that Senator J. William Fulbright of Arkansas, Chairman of the Senate Foreign Relations Committee, was "eager to be proved right by an American defeat." As a public relations tactic, the decision to mail Alsop's column backfired.

The major propaganda coming from the White House was the unprecedented Presidential exposure in a series of television appearances and newspaper interviews reminiscent of, though not so shrill as, Lyndon Johnson's exposure to the press at the height of the Dominican Republic crisis in April 1965.* But whereas Johnson then had most of the people with him and was trying to build a *total* consensus behind his intervention in the Dominican Republic, Nixon was trying desperately to save the little support he had. He was trying to reverse the political reaction that in his political consciousness he had felt was probably inevitable if he gave the go-ahead in Laos.

The Gallup Poll dropped the President's approval rating to its lowest point, 51 percent, in a sample taken at the height of the Laos operation between February 19 and 21. That was a five-point drop from his 56 percent approval rating the previous month, and eight points below Dr. Gallup's findings after the Cambodian incursion of 1970. Shortly after that Gallup finding, it was decided by Nixon's public relations experts to give the American people the largest concentrated dose of this President on television and in interviews with journalists. The purpose was to stimulate an immediate upward movement in the polls and thus prevent further deterioration of the President's position on Capitol Hill and in the nation.

In quick succession, in the six weeks ending March 22, Nixon made these appearances: an interview on February 9 with conservative Peregrine Worsthorne of the *London Sunday Telegraph;* a non-

*On April 28, 1965, President Johnson ordered marines into the Dominican Republic to put down a revolt that American diplomats in Santo Domingo feared might be taken over by Communists. To defend this action, Johnson embarked on a high-pitched, high-profile propaganda campaign that backfired badly. In *Lyndon B. Johnson and the World,* Philip L. Geyelin wrote that Johnson's "irrelevant rationalizations and often inaccurate reconstruction of events . . . conspired to turn an essentially unmanageable and, in some ways, unavoidable crisis in a fundamentally unstable and crisis-prone Caribbean nation into a crisis of confidence in the President himself."

televised press conference on February 17; a special televised press conference on March 4 limited to foreign policy questions; an interview on March 8 by columnist C. L. Sulzberger of the *New York Times;* an interview on March 11 by Barbara Walters of NBC's *Today* show for broadcast on March 15; an interview on March 11 by nine women reporters for publication on March 13; a one-hour live televised interview on March 22 by ABC's Howard K. Smith— a rate of exposure to major media outlets of more than one a week.* The President's basic theme was defense of the Laos operation, which ended unofficially two days after Nixon had his televised conversation with Howard K. Smith. To Sulzberger, he made the astonishing statement that he "seriously doubted if we will ever have another war," adding for emphasis: "This is probably the very last one." To Smith, who prodded him on his decline in the polls and his diminished credibility, he pleaded for understanding and sympathy on the war:

> Now we are reaching the key point—the key point when we see that we are ending America's involvement in a way that has been the longest, the most bitter, the most difficult war in our nation's history. And once we go over that hump, *once the American people are convinced that the plans that have taken so long to implement have come into effect,* then I think the credibility gap will rapidly disappear. It is the events that cause the credibility gap, not the fact that a President deliberately lies or misleads the people. That's my opinion.†

All to no avail. The mid-March Gallup poll, published on March 31, showed Nixon down another point, to precisely 50 percent approval—still another new low. No matter how much propaganda poured out of the White House, Nixon could not prevent a nightmarish mass psychological reaction in the country.

Many Americans simply did not believe him, did not believe that U.S. troops were not being used.‡ Many refused to believe

---

*Several *Times* correspondents in Washington had for some time been requesting an interview with Nixon. But the President chose the European-based Sulzberger, one of the few *Times* writers sympathetic to his Vietnam policy.

†Emphasis is added.

‡In an Opinion Research poll taken on February 7 and 8, almost 50 percent of more than 1,000 citizens sampled believed that U.S. troops were taking part in the Laos operation.

anything their government was telling them about Vietnam—a psychology of doubt that was perpetuated in part by a suspicious press. Despite statements to the American people that were more open and candid than any Johnson had ever made, Nixon had been unable to dispel this doubt. He had pulled American troops out of Cambodia just as he had said he would. He was continuing troop withdrawals just as he said he would. But when he and his top lieutenants claimed that the Laos operation would *shorten*, not widen, the war, he was met by disbelief. That was just one measure of the frustration over the long war.

The operation in Laos, limited though it was, was the unexpected catalyst that brought into the open this politically preeminent fact: public opinion had sustained very nearly all it would or could in Vietnam. The fact that President Nixon had almost halved American troops in Vietnam made little difference. Nor did the dramatic decline in battlefield deaths, down from an average weekly 278 throughout 1968 to 51 during the last six months of 1970. What Americans were now concerned about was not the fact of a *perceptible* ending of the war but the need for a total and *immediate* ending of the war; not the declining battlefield casualties, but the frightening, well-documented reports of growing drug addiction and near mutiny of U.S. troops; not the heroic exploits in the field that President Nixon, as Lyndon Johnson before him, took pains to dramatize with Medal of Honor sessions at the White House, but the alarming reports of American atrocities which heightened their conviction that this war had already lasted too long for a purpose too few could understand.

Until the Laos operation, all this had been hidden from view. Now this public disaffection became so apparent to politicians that the vital center in Congress, both Republican and Democratic, which had been so important to the support of the war for both Johnson and Nixon, was being swept by antiwar passion.

It was obvious first in the Democratic majority. Until the spring of 1971 the Democratic left (referred to in Nixon's White House as the "crazies") had not the glimmer of a chance to push through the Democratic caucus, much less the House itself, any resolution setting a deadline for pulling the last American out of the war. Now, in mid-March, the President's Congressional liaison staff was becoming

frightened that a break in the center toward a strong antiwar position
was in the making. But neither the President himself nor his Congressional lobbyists could do very much about stopping such a movement in the House majority party.

The ranks of the House Democratic establishment were becoming filled with enemies of the war. Representative Thomas P.
O'Neill, a Massachusetts regular who had come out against the war,
was elected House Democratic Whip—the first dove in the party's
hierarchy in the House. Representative Phil Landrum of Georgia, a
respected leader of Southern Democratic conservatives, was turning
against the war. Two Chicago Democratic regulars—Representatives Daniel Rostenkowski (Mayor Richard J. Daley's lieutenant in
Washington) and Roman Pucinski—came out against the war. Their
joining the opposition was no mere political ploy to embarrass a
Republican President. Their constituents were pushing them into it.
The switch by Rostenkowski and Pucinski was instructive. Daley,
running for his fifth term as mayor on April 6, had given a major
campaign speech calling on Nixon to move fiscal priorities away
from the war.

On March 31, by the razor-edge vote of 101 to 100, the House
Democratic caucus rejected a resolution setting December 31, 1971,
as the deadline for final withdrawal of all American troops and,
instead, adopted a substitute that followed the example of Senate
Democrats, setting the deadline by the end of 1972.

The President's own House Republicans, in the center and on
the right, were not far behind. A letter that a year earlier would have
been unthinkable was sent to the President in early April signed by
eight conservative Republicans asking him to speed troop withdrawals, set a deadline beyond which no draftees would be sent to Vietnam and "consider" setting a troop-withdrawal deadline. Its signers
included such staunchly pro-Nixon conservatives as James Broyhill
of North Carolina, John Hammerschmidt of Arkansas and Garner
Shriver of Kansas.* But Nixon kept aloof. Instead of calling these

*As measured by the Americans for Constitutional Action (ACA), Broyhill had
a conservative voting record of 90 percent; Hammerschmidt, 80 percent; and
Shriver, 79 percent. Other signers, and their ACA records, were: Donald Brotzman
of Colorado, 73 percent; Howard Robison of New York, 70 percent; Tim Lee Carter
of Kentucky, 67 percent; William Steiger of Wisconsin, 65 percent; William S.
Broomfield of Michigan, 65 percent.

conservatives to the White House for a cozy chat, he passed the letter off with a routine acknowledgment signed by William Timmons. That was one sign of how far the antiwar movement had progressed: the President no longer made a personal effort to deal with it, as he had in his first year.

Nor was Nixon willing to make concessions to his critics that might limit his freedom of action. In Congress and in the administration, Republicans hoped that the President would make a dramatic gesture—at best, setting a troop-withdrawal deadline of his own but, more realistically, increasing greatly the rate of troop withdrawal or pledging no more ground combat action of any kind for Americans.

But when his big foreign policy speech was delivered on April 7 over national television, it did no such thing. With the Laos operation still fresh in the country's mind and under rising pressure from centrist Congressman of both parties, the President carefully avoided characterizing the Laos invasion as either success or failure. Only time could tell, he said. But one thing was clear: Vietnamization "has succeeded." He then announced a slight increase in the troop withdrawals, from 12,500 to 15,000 a month.

> As you can see from the progress we have made to date and by this announcement tonight, the American involvement in Vietnam is coming to an end. The day the South Vietnamese can take over their own defense is in sight. Our goal is a total American withdrawal from Vietnam. We can and will reach that goal through our program of Vietnamization if necessary.

He called on Hanoi, as he had countless times in the past, not to force the Americans to pursue Vietnamization but to negotiate an end to the war at the Paris peace talks. Then, coming to grips with the rising demand for a preannounced troop-withdrawal deadline, he said:

> Let me turn now to a proposal which at first glance has a great deal of popular appeal. If our goal is a total withdrawal of all our forces, why don't I announce a date now for ending our involvement? Well, the difficulty in making such an announcement to the American people is that I would also be making that announcement to the enemy. And it would serve the enemy's purpose and not our own.
> If the United States should announce that we will quit regardless of what the enemy does, we would have thrown away our principal

bargaining counter to win the release of American prisoners of war, we would remove the enemy's strongest incentive to end the war sooner by negotiation and we will have given enemy commanders the exact information they need to marshal their attacks against our remaining forces at their most vulnerable time.

That speech was unquestionably the least belligerent statement on Vietnam yet made by Richard Nixon. There were no threats of escalation, no threats of renewed bombing, no threats of maintaining a perpetual residual force in Vietnam. Had it been delivered on November 3, 1969, it would have been hailed as most conciliatory. But on April 7, 1971, as just another appeal for patience and trust, it was a bitter disappointment on Capitol Hill.* The growing ranks of Congressional backers of a deadline felt even more restive, more discontented, more intent on forcing a date for complete withdrawal. They even studied the prospect, still remote, of imposing a forcible limitation of expenditures to stop the war. Nixon would undoubtedly disregard any such strictures. Nevertheless, with all the remarkable progress he *had* made in winding down the war, the ineluctable force of American politics on the war issue was working against him, frustrating his Presidency and threatening his future.

The unhappy truth was that Johnson's war had, indeed, become Nixon's war in the simplistic convention of American politics. The long, arduous struggle by Nixon to tame the war and end U.S. participation, to transfer the principal combat role from the Americans to the South Vietnamese under the sensible policy of Vietnamization and at the same time drastically reduce American involvement in Asia, had gone far, but not far enough or fast enough to prevent Johnson's war from becoming Nixon's war. Considering all he *had* accomplished in Vietnam, this was perhaps the cruelest irony of Nixon's Presidency. He had forced the generals to submit, had drastically reduced the flow of manpower into the Asian jungles, had shown courage in risking the political tumult of Cambodia and

*Nixon's leaders in the Senate, Senators Hugh Scott of Pennsylvania and Robert Griffin of Michigan, issued highly encouraging statements after being briefed by the President. They reported Nixon indeed had a deadline in mind, that it would be before the 1972 election and that his long-term view of Vietnam was not to keep residual forces there indefinitely. But they were contradicted by the White House. Ron Ziegler denied that Nixon had a "specific date" for final troop withdrawal.

Laos, but protesters still marched and opposition continued to build against "Nixon's war."

Now time was running out on him in Vietnam. Just how far it had run was clear from a macabre event growing out of the war that was unparalleled in American politics. The President, at his best—courageous and determined—on the war itself would be at his worst on this corollary issue: the Calley case.

Charged with murdering 102 unarmed South Vietnamese civilians on March 16, 1968, at the hamlet of Mylai 4 in South Vietnam, First Lieutenant William L. Calley, Jr., twenty-eight years old, was convicted on March 29, 1971, of the premeditated murder of twenty-two civilians.

With the choice of penalties limited to either life imprisonment or death, the military jury of six officers sentenced Calley on March 31 to serve the rest of his days in jail. He could keep his uniform and pay-and-allowances until the case had been reviewed under the legal procedures laid down in the law, ending with a final review by Secretary of the Army Stanley Resor. As Commander in Chief, Nixon had the right to step in at the end of the line—or, technically, anywhere along the line. But since the sentence was not death, there was no *obligation* for the President to involve himself at all.

The trial had started on November 12, 1970—as much a trial for procedures of military justice and for the moral fortitude of the armed forces as it was for the unfortunate lieutenant. The offense, epitomizing the brutality of the Vietnam war, evoked contrary reactions that intersected at the same point. To doves, Calley's crime was a mirror image of American immorality in Indochina: the lieutenant had become a scapegoat for the sins of Presidents, Secretaries of Defense and four-star generals. To hawks, Calley was raised to heroic stature as the American warrior, tethered and restrained by politicians refusing to permit the military to seek victory. The result was a public reaction of unprecedented spontaneity and volume, an uproar of anger, consternation and bitterness that had brought the American people, for very different reasons, to a common conclusion: the war had become a corrupting cancer.

On March 31 the White House announced that five thousand telegrams had been received in the two days between the verdict and the sentencing, "about 100 to 1 in favor of clemency." Another fifteen hundred citizens had telephoned, almost unanimously in favor of clemency and outraged at the outcome of the trial.

Senator Abraham Ribicoff of Connecticut, an antiwar liberal Democrat, appealed to the President for clemency. Calley, he said, should not "be made to bear sole responsibility for all wrongdoing." Senator Frank Moss of Utah, ranking third in the Senate Democratic hierarchy, said he would introduce a resolution asking Nixon to reduce the sentence. The South, a bastion of support for the war, was inflamed. Senator Herman E. Talmadge of Georgia, speaking "as a former combat soldier myself" and a supporter of the war, said he was "saddened to think that one could fight for his flag and then be court-martialed and convicted for apparently carrying out his orders." Governor George Wallace, addressing a joint session of the Alabama Legislature, said he was asking the director of the State's Selective Service System to investigate whether the draft could lawfully be suspended in Alabama; later, Wallace visited Calley in his quarters at Fort Benning, Ga. The Quitman, Ga., Draft Board wired the White House it would not induct any more young men; local draft boards in Athens, Ga., and Elizabethtown, Tenn., resigned en masse.

But the mood at the Pentagon was far different. Secretary of the Army Resor and Under Secretary Thaddeus R. Beal, General William Westmoreland (Army Chief of Staff), General Abrams (the field commander) and their aides had crossed the Calley bridge eighteen months before when, overruling the barely contained anger of the Army officer corps and backed by Secretary Laird, they had decided that Calley's crime must be investigated. Then, having established a reasonable case that he did in fact commit murder, they steeled themselves for the general court-martial. For those men the ensuing months had been the most painful of their lives. When the verdict was handed down by the Vietnam combat veterans who constituted the jury, they braced themselves for what they knew would be a violent reaction. Their first post-trial decision was to release Calley from the Fort Benning stockade and permit him the relative freedom of his own quarters, thereby obviating his transfer to federal prison at Fort Leavenworth, Kan. An order to release him had been prepared and the Western White House at San Clemente, where the President was enjoying the sun, was duly notified.

In the tumult spreading across an unhappy land, Nixon at San

Clemente kept a public silence. As was so often the case when he was away from Washington, the President took to the telephone on March 31, the day the life sentence for Calley was announced. It was early evening in Washington, late afternoon in San Clemente. How many calls he placed across the continent is unknown; in all probability, there were many. For certain, there were at least two telephone calls from the President to powerful members of Congress, one Republican and one Democrat, both strong supporters of the Vietnam war.

One went to Representative Gerald Ford of Michigan, House Republican Leader. Noting that the White House had been swamped with protests, Nixon said he wondered what the picture was in Congress, then asked Ford to take discreet soundings in the House to learn political reaction to the fact that he was considering a wide range of options in granting clemency to Calley. Ford did so and, naturally, found enthusiastic Congressional support for such intervention. Although Ford never heard the President say that one of these options was an outright pardon, several Congressmen who were then sounded out the next day by Ford, as the President had asked, thought they understood that a pardon was in fact one of the options.

The other call from Nixon went to the popular, influential Representative Olin Teague of Texas, Chairman of the House Veterans Committee and just elected Chairman of the House Democratic Caucus. Nixon asked Teague what he thought of the Calley affair. Teague replied that Calley was a pathetic case and never should have been an officer in the first place. But, said Teague, he had always been against the court-martial. Now, he said, he favored a far more lenient sentence than life at hard labor. "Well, then," Nixon replied, "why don't you get out and talk that up with some of the other members." Following the President's advice, Teague the next day told a meeting of House Democratic deputy whips that "high officials" were moving toward clemency for Calley. Again, almost surely incorrectly, there was an impression that a complete pardon was possible (though Teague did not seek to give that impression).

Thus, before he had said a word publicly, the President was both checking political reaction and trying to drum up support for his intended intervention.

On the next morning, April 1, the Army's decision to release Calley from the Fort Benning stockade was dispatched to San Clemente. That same morning, the President preempted the Army with a public announcement: he had instructed Admiral Moorer, Chairman of the Joint Chiefs, to order the Army to release Calley from the stockade and return him to quarters pending the outcome of the final appeal—precisely what the Army had already decided to do. At San Clemente, Presidential aides put out a story that Nixon had awakened from his sleep and suddenly decided he must do something about the Calley case to show respect for the U.S. uniform. Actually, he had placed those two calls to Capitol Hill hours before he went to bed.

In fact, the President—working closely with chief domestic aide Ehrlichman, not the national security aides who usually advised him in military dealings—had decided upon a massive intervention in the Calley case. On Saturday, April 3, he assaulted the objectivity of the lengthy military appeals procedures by announcing that he would personally review the case "before any final sentence is carried out."

If Calley was well on the way to becoming a hero, Nixon's intervention seemed to put the power and majesty of the U.S. government on his side, with its implication that he had indeed been victimized. The intervention impugned the punctilious objectivity that the Army had imposed on the trial and the legal mechanics that had governed the trial. The Army's three reviewing authorities still to hear the evidence and judge the court's verdict were put in an impossible position.

The private explanation at the White House was that the President was so deeply concerned about containing the national outrage that he felt bound to say something that would cool the passion and keep it from getting out of hand. This is roughly what Nixon said on April 30 at his televised press conference, the first chance reporters had to question him about his intervention:

> . . . I felt that it was proper for me to indicate that I would review the case because there was great concern expressed throughout the country as to whether or not this was a case involving, as it did, so many complex factors in which Capt. [sic] Calley was going to get a fair trial.*

That, surely, was part of the truth. But there was also the fact that the President had been on the telephone fully two days *before*

---

*Nixon persisted in referring to him as "Captain" Calley, both at this press conference and on a previous occasion. In the April 30 press conference, he called him "Captain" on three separate occasions, although his questioners properly referred to Lieutenant Calley.

Ehrlichman informed the world that he had decided to review the case, whipping up public sentiment that would only heighten passions he said he wanted to cool. Thus, he was not just responding but leading, and leading in a way that exposed certain things about him.

It revealed, for one thing, a nonchalance about legal forms remarkable in a lawyer (as previously seen in his injudicious comments on the Charles Manson case).* Questioned at a press conference back on December 8, 1969, Nixon prejudged the Mylai Incident at a time when criminal charges were pending against Calley and others by saying, "What appears was certainly a massacre and under no circumstances was it justified." In that same press conference, Nixon showed a vigorous intent to prosecute the case, asserting that "we shall see to it that what these men did, if they did it, does not smear the decent men who have gone to Vietnam in a very . . . important cause." Contending that the incident "should be brought before the public," the President then seemed concerned mainly that a military court-martial might not be adequate to reveal these facts. Thus, when he had a chance to stop the court-martial at its source, he was leaning in precisely the opposite direction. The change in his position suggests a darker side of Richard Nixon that many voters could never quite define but that, throughout his extraordinary political career, had repeatedly tainted his record. In that troubled spring of 1971 the tragic Calley case was a major political opening for the President, particularly because it involved the South, so basic to the Nixon-Mitchell grand strategy. If he intervened, he would place himself at the head of that outraged army of citizens infuriated with the trial.

The President's aides and Nixon himself felt that his intervention had cooled the public's passion, for the outcry over Calley died down nearly as rapidly as it had begun. But there was another possible explanation—that the Calley outrage had already run its course when Nixon intruded upon military justice, and that his intervention was not only politics but bad politics. Indeed, there was a perceptible anti-Nixon reaction, best summed up by an extraordinary letter written directly to the President by the young Army officer who had been chief prosecutor in the trial. On April 3, Captain Aubrey M. Daniel, III, a twenty-nine-year-old Virginian about to finish his Army tour of duty, wrote his Commander in Chief: "The

*See p. 366 n.

greatest tragedy of all will be if political expediency dictates the compromise of such a fundamental moral principle as the inherent unlawfulness of the murder of innocent persons." The President, said Daniel, should have provided the moral leadership of the nation and led it to support "the law of this land on a moral issue which is so clear and about which there can be no compromise."

Richard Nixon had been at his worst in the Calley case. A man able to make decisions on the grand scale in world affairs with courage and prudence, he was flawed by an instinct that often and unerringly sought *tactical* advantage in the short-range situation without proper attention to long-range *strategic* considerations. He was moved to follow, or even influence, the mob on Calley without contemplation of what further damage he might be inflicting on a system of laws under direct assault by his worst enemies on the left.

Indeed, the Calley case, though distinctly a product of the Vietnam war, seemed divorced from the conflict in Nixon's mind. Henry Kissinger and Melvin Laird were not actively consulted on it. This was for the President a further concession to his and John Mitchell's strategy of combining the Nixon-Wallace vote into a new Republican majority for 1972. Here was George Wallace, newly installed again as governor of Alabama, breaking months of quiet to rampage all over the South lionizing Lieutenant Calley! In his instinctive effort to counter this, Nixon allowed himself to do damage not only to the process of military justice but to the entire legal system, and to seem to countenance in the eyes of the world what he had once called a massacre. The moral costs of following the Nixon-Mitchell strategy had been high—the slowdown on civil rights, the Haynsworth and Carswell fiasco, and now the Calley intervention—with no assurance of what electoral success it might bring in 1972.*

*Nixon's high hopes in the South for 1972 were dealt a possibly serious blow on April 20, 1971, when the Supreme Court ruled 9–0—the two Nixon appointees, Chief Justice Burger and Justice Blackmun, concurring—in favor of compulsory busing for racial integration. This renewed the old battle between HEW (which wanted to rewrite agreements with Southern school districts to conform to the new high-court edict) and Justice (which once again cautioned a go-slow policy). At Justice, Mitchell still was the most formidable figure in the Cabinet. But at HEW, Secretary Eliot Richardson, a steel-nerved aristocrat, was an infinitely more formidable figure than Bob Finch. Richardson's activist policy in carrying out the Supreme Court decision won Mitchell's approval for a strong busing plan for Austin, Tex., and signs pointed to similar strong plans in other Southern cities. If that happened, the Nixon-Mitchell strategy of placating the South could be undermined.

. . .

Following the lame-duck session of 1970, Ehrlichman and his staff reexamined the supersonic transport to decide whether it was worth trying to save in the new session coming up in 1971. There were considerations of foreign policy, international balance of payments, ecology, aviation progress, unemployment, the aviation industry, and the federal budget. Nixon, still feeling the SST was essential to what he called the country's "sense of nation," decided to go ahead.* Characteristically, little attention was given to the prospects of winning in Congress (preliminary head counts pointed to a possible loss in both the House and Senate). Equally characteristically, no attention whatever was given to the political danger that a losing SST fight posed for the President: a defeat harmful to his political prestige just when he was seeking to shrug off the effects of the 1970 election.

In fact, the votes on the SST came at precisely the worst time, in late March, when the Laos operation and the sudden loss of the center on Vietnam was dropping Nixon into the very depths of his Presidency. All the energetic White House efforts to mobilize industry and organize labor behind the SST much more effectively than in 1970 were to no avail. Congress killed the project. Clearly, Republicans in both the House and Senate were defecting from the President in massive numbers (five defections among the usually well-disciplined nine-man Republican leadership team in the House) to show both their disapproval of the President and their verdict that he was in deep trouble, and therefore easy to oppose. The issues of economy and ecology raised by the foes of SST were secondary to a grass-roots revolt against the President. When a Democratic supporter of the SST chided its principal Cabinet sponsor, Secretary of Transportation Volpe, about the large number of Republican defections, Volpe's retort was: "They weren't voting against SST. They were voting against John Ehrlichman and his German Mafia in the White House."

It was, as Howard K. Smith suggested at the start of his March 22 interview with the President, Nixon's "winter of discontent"—soon to extend into spring. His descent in the polls continued, Dr. Gallup's mid-April sample showing another new low: 49 percent.

The war and the Calley case associated with it were not alone responsible. The economic malaise persisted. Despite all the heavy

*See p. 53.

deficit spending, unemployment remained over 6 percent into the summer and the business recovery was sluggish. Inflation persisted, the 1957–59 dollar having dropped in value to 70.8 cents, compared with 80.6 cents when Nixon took office. Still, the President stuck stubbornly to the Game Plan, presided over by George Shultz. As the problem of Nixonomics persisted, Republicans and businessmen pleaded with the White House to do something, to do *anything*. To no avail. White House aides excoriated Wilbur Mills and Arthur Burns for even suggesting a tax cut and incomes policy. But working quietly behind the scenes for the politically essential change was John Connally.

In mid-August, with the Hoover-haunted specter of unemployment under a Republican President growing more distinct, Richard Nixon finally succumbed to Connally, Burns, and practically everybody except George Shultz. In Nixonian style, he called a crucial meeting of the Quadriad at Camp David the weekend of August 14–15 to consider stunning economic decisions that Nixon had already made. On Sunday evening, August 15, the President took to national television to repudiate the Game Plan (without admitting it). In springing his spectacular surprise in typical Nixon style, he grandiloquently referred to his new economic plan as "the most comprehensive new economic policy to be undertaken in this Nation in four decades." That may have been an exaggeration, but it was no exaggeration to say that the President had repudiated his old policy on every score: 90-day wage-price freeze to be followed by an incomes policy, stimulative tax cuts (including the revival of the old investment credit), a 10 percent tariff superimposed on imports, new spending cuts, postponement of welfare reform and revenue sharing.

How well all this would work in the future (particularly the wage-price freeze) remained to be seen. But for now, there was euphoria. Wall Street went wild, Republican politicians sighed in relief and the nation seemed to take on new confidence. It was the first solid domestic triumph of 1971 for Nixon. The bright progressive image of the New American Revolution had long since faded as his reform proposals bogged down in Congress and, by spring of 1971, the President had become a bit abrasive in public appearances.

So, too, Spiro Agnew. By mid-March, he had grown restive pushing Presidential programs, and his aides felt he might be losing hard-core conservative backing without compensating gains in the center or left. With Nixon and Mitchell declining to say positively that Agnew would stay on the ticket in 1972, the Vice President might need some zealots on the right to make sure that purging him would extract too high a cost for the President. Besides, Agnew was a true believer in his own polemical attacks on the media, on youth and on protesters. He *liked* delivering them.

Hence, without consulting the President or his chief aides (discussing it only with Presidential speech writer Pat Buchanan), Agnew returned to the attack, casting aside the low-profile advice he had received from the White House. On March 18, before the Middlesex Club in Boston, he resumed his war with the media in a full-scale attack on CBS in particular, and the national media generally.

He was off and running again, restraint cast aside, his low profile gleefully discarded. But his polls continued to sink, dropping below 50 percent even among Republican voters. Inside the White House, many felt Agnew must go in 1972 for Nixon to be reelected, a judgment reinforced by the Vice President's comically inept round-the-world trip that summer, climaxed by a gratuitous attack on American black leaders delivered from the heart of Africa.

Moreover, Agnew had collided head-on with Nixon's most spectacular foreign policy initiative: a move to break a generation of total estrangement between the U.S. and the People's Republic of China.

Little noticed at the time of Nixon's nontelevised press conference of February 17 was his strong assurance to Red China: it had nothing to fear from the invasion of the Laos Panhandle; the assault on the Ho Chi Minh Trail was "no threat" to Peking and "should not be interpreted by Communist China as being a threat against them." Although the U.S. press was running speculative scare stories about possible Chinese intervention, the President was confident there would be such intervention only in the event of a ground or airborne assault against North Vietnam itself. Thus, despite his refusal to publicly knock down braggadocio threats from Saigon that the ARVN might invade North Vietnam, Nixon had issued absolute orders that there would be no crossing the DMZ unless North Vietnam first mounted a major attack of its own into South Vietnam across the 17th parallel. The closely guarded reason for that Presidential order would become dramatically clear a mere six weeks later in what would be by far the flashiest event of the President's relentless effort to fulfill his pledge to negotiate, not confront.

When Premier Chou En-lai of Red China arrived in Hanoi on March 5 at the height of the fighting in Laos, the North Vietnamese wanted a public commitment from him. They wanted assurance that if the Americans attacked North Vietnam on the ground, as the North Vietnamese politburo desperately feared, the People's Republic would intervene, as it had when General Douglas MacArthur approached the Yalu River in North Korea more than twenty years earlier. But Chou, a shrewd politician and one of Communist China's few leaders who knew what the outside world was all about, refused to play that game. Chou and the Americans were already deep in a little game of their own, one of the most secret and suspenseful going anywhere in the world. Starting with his quick decision to make the visit to Rumania in the early summer of 1969, Nixon had lost no opportunity to make his signals to Peking clear: an end of the twenty years of separation between Washington and Peking was very much wanted by the Americans.*

Having outlasted the ravages of the Cultural Revolution and felt the rising passion between Peking and Moscow, Chou also wanted to end the long period of isolation between China and the United States. He had no intention of letting Hanoi interfere with those plans. If he had said what the North Vietnamese wanted him to say, the threat of war between the United States and Red China would have postponed, perhaps ended, any chance of making mutual contact during the Nixon years. So Chou blandly heard out the North Vietnamese, then remarked that he was certain that strong and resolute North Vietnam could handle the running-dog American imperialists without help from China. He then packed up and went home to Peking.

In the White House, President Nixon noted the reluctance of Premier Chou to threaten the Americans. He and Kissinger had been orchestrating a *pas de deux* for months with the Chinese Communists, using a variety of secret, third-party contacts. Public awareness that something was up was heightened when Nixon on February 25, in his State of the World Message to Congress, referred to the People's Republic of China—the first time since Chiang Kai-shek was driven from the mainland in 1949 that a high U.S. official had not called it Red China or Communist China in an official state-

*See p. 100.

ment.* The President also remarked to aides, and the word was passed around Washington, that he hoped China would open its doors to American tourists and he hoped he might someday go himself. In this mood, Nixon and Kissinger now computed that the Chinese move would come sometime in early summer (though they had no hard evidence).

Thus, on April 6 when the American ping-pong team, playing in a world tournament at Nagoya, Japan, was invited to come and play in Peking, Nixon was surprised only at the timing. But he was not nearly so surprised as everybody else, including the State Department, which tended to underestimate what was happening. The department's China experts predicted privately after the first few days of the ping-pong visit that the President would do nothing about relaxing trade barriers until the summer, if then. In fact, Nixon responded immediately with a trade gesture, as the Chinese had responded—although somewhat slower—to his decision to ease passport restrictions on March 15. The President and Kissinger were playing those cards from the White House without the State Department's help.

Whether or not anything of substance would emerge from this, Nixon could take satisfaction from the fact that few American politicians could have opened a dialogue with the Chinese Communists, pilloried in the U.S. press as bloodthirsty heathens for twenty-two years, as risklessly as he. Nixon's long record of anti-Communism was too well known to subject him to the ideological dangers that would have befallen a liberal Democrat.†

But beyond this, the visit of the ping-pong team to China, from April 10 to 17, accompanied by the first U.S. news correspondents to enter China in a generation, evoked a wholly unexpected sense of

---

*Actually, Nixon had referred to the People's Republic of China in a White House dinner party toast to visiting President Ceaucescu of Rumania on October 26, 1970, but it escaped attention.

†But Vice President Spiro Agnew, following his renewed hard line, told nine reporters in an off-the-record session at the Republican Governors' Conference in Williamsburg, Va., on April 19, that Nixon's move was dangerous to the future of the United States. Agnew had made the same criticism at a National Security Council meeting after April 6, but when his April 19 remarks, inevitably, were published by reporters not at the off-the-record meeting, the President was displeased. Communist China had become his pet project and he did not like his judgment questioned by his Vice President.

good cheer in a nation starved for just such cheer. Unrealistic it might have been, but Nixon and his White House aides were not the only Americans somewhat desperately hoping for glad tidings of any sort. After Laos, after the sluggish economy, and after the morbid Calley case, it was good news indeed.

China, in fact, ushered in a rush of good news by mid-1971 in the President's long quest to transform confrontation into negotiation. As Richard Nixon began to look toward the 1972 Presidential campaign, he could perceive promising shafts of light in several directions on the foreign policy horizon: China, where he kept sending out public signals to Peking on trade, culture and travel;* Berlin, where the prospect of settling a persistently and dangerously contentious trouble spot was growing brighter; SALT, in which President Nixon and Soviet leaders, working through secret correspondence started in the winter, agreed to agree on a first arms-limitation step in a statement each side issued simultaneously on May 20; and, finally, mutual reduction of troops from Europe, with the Communists to thin out its Warsaw Pact forces and the allies to thin out the North Atlantic Treaty forces (a surprise offer by the Kremlin in May 1971, matching a long-standing NATO proposal).

Of all these shafts of light, the most important was SALT. On its face, the Washington-Moscow agreement to negotiate an agreement was a sharp retreat from the President's persistent demand for a comprehensive nuclear agreement not limited to defensive missile systems, as the Soviets wanted. The agreement-to-agree was weighted heavily on the ABM side, only marginally on the offensive side. What it would almost surely encompass, when it reached the final decision state probably late in 1971 or early 1972, was this: ABMs to protect Washington and Moscow and to "safeguard" not more than two offensive long-range missile sites in each country.

But if Nixon bowed to the Russians on the form of the agreement-to-agree, its substance promised rich political rewards for

*The long list of nonstrategic goods approved for export to Communist China on June 10 looked impressive, but White House experts estimated its maximum value to the Chinese at no more than $200 million—a pittance in a country of 800 million. The purpose of the list was not nearly so much trade per se but politics; it was Nixon's way of telling Peking he wanted to continue and expand the indirect dialogue.

1972. When the President actually got his agreement (and as of the summer of 1971 there was little doubt that he would), it would mark the first time in their long hostility that the two superpowers had agreed not only to limit but to *reduce* existing nuclear armaments (the United States already having started ABM work on more than the two sites to be agreed to).

Nixon would not be shy about advertising that dramatic fact when it came to signing the expected ABM limitation treaty with the Russians. At the very least, a Presidential trip to Vienna or Helsinki, the sites of the SALT negotiations, looked highly probable. If not Vienna or Helsinki, Moscow itself might become the site for signing the treaty. That signing session with the Soviet leaders could also be used as a springboard for the talks on mutual reduction of Warsaw Pact and NATO troops, a negotiation that would last many months, possibly several years. Thus, if the Western powers could agree among themselves on a common goal for cutting NATO forces, President Nixon then might be ready to announce the start of that negotiation at the same time he signed the ABM treaty at a summit meeting with the Russians.

That, at least, was one scenario being spun in the White House during the summer of 1971 when, with bad news still piling up on the economic homefront, White House politicians clearly perceived the vital importance of putting Nixon on display in the 1972 Presidential election campaign as the Peace President. The scenario was not the exclusive property of the politicians. Even the skeptical Henry Kissinger, who had repeatedly warned about the dangers of summit meetings (every one of which since World War II, he told Nixon, had been followed by rapid deterioration), saw the possibility of formalizing the East-West thaw in Europe, together with an American-Soviet nuclear limitation treaty, into an international arrangement approaching real stability. This was, clearly, Richard Nixon's ace-in-the-hole: a unique opportunity finally to clear away the wreckage of World War II and end the upward nuclear-arms spiral that threatened the future. If the President could play that ace he would immeasurably strengthen his claim to run for reelection as the Peace President, increasingly obvious as his best hope to retain the Presidency.

His posture as Peace President was strengthened dramatically on July 8, when Kissinger, supposedly taken ill in Rawalpindi, Pakistan, in the midst of a hurried round-the-world fact-finding tour for the President, sneaked off to a historic rendezvous in Peking. Unknown to all but a handful of top officials, Kissinger's mission had been painstakingly planned and perfectly executed. Kissinger, the first U.S. government official to visit the Forbidden City since the Communist takeover of mainland China twenty-one years earlier, stayed in Peking for forty-nine hours—twenty hours of them in consultation with Chou En-lai.

The full scope and success of the Kissinger-Chou conversation were not immediately known, but one result was revealed on July 15, after Kissinger had flown to San Clemente to meet Nixon following the completion of his mission. When the President asked for national television time to address the nation that night, the secret had been so well kept that everybody assumed Nixon was about to respond to the latest Communist proposal in the Vietnam peace negotiations. Instead, speaking for five minutes from the NBC studios in Los Angeles he stunned the nation by announcing that he had been invited to Peking by Chou and had accepted, with the visit to take place sometime before May 1, 1972.

Except for the far right, the reaction was universally favorable. All good things seemed to beckon—peace, a reopening of the sentimental old friendship with China, possibly a peace settlement in Vietnam. Beyond that, Americans were heartened to see their President doing something with flair, precision and mastery after so many dreary years of loss of confidence. And whatever its worldwide implications, Nixon's coming visit to Peking would provide powerful political medicine in an election year.

Richard Nixon himself was pleased with his coup. It had all the ingredients that Nixon liked most: surprise, novelty, shattering of precedence, high-level international politics. He showed his pleasure the evening of July 15 by breaking his usual iron isolation—a sure sign that the course of events had bolstered his normally sagging self-confidence. Instead of returning to San Clemente after the telecast, he dined at Perino's Restaurant (having a gourmet meal and a forty-dollar bottle of French wine). As he left the restaurant, a crowd gathered outside in the balmy California evening to cheer and applaud the smiling President.

In late winter 1971, when confidence in the Nixon Presidency was dipping ever lower, William Safire, the President's irrepressible speech writer, had a word of advice for Democrats, for new corre-

spondents and even for some of his gloomy colleagues at the White
House: "The gloom and doom will lift when the cherry blossoms
appear."* A President's fate, in short, is cyclical: the hard long
winter gives way to spring, and things are never as bad as they seem.

Confidence in Richard Nixon kept dropping even with the ad-
vent of the cherry blossoms. But Safire's theory was saved by that
unlikely game of diplomatic ping-pong with Communist China that
Richard Nixon had started with such verve in the early spring of
1971. Although it temporarily restored a spirit of confidence, it was
soon forgotten in the rush of bad news: an unresponsive economy,
the President's falling ratings in the polls, the intensity of opposition
to Nixon's Vietnam policy. But on July 15 the dramatic disclosure
of the President's visit to Peking once again heartened the administration, bolstering it for the last eighteen months of power.

In nearly thirty months in office, however, Richard Nixon, who
had known bitter defeat, frustration and impotence in the vagaries
of political seasons long before he came to the White House, had
suffered deep wounds and so had the men around him. They could
never regain the mood of high exuberance—the almost innocent
assumption that grand undertakings would be grandly accomplished
—which raised their hopes and expectations in that long-ago time at
the Pierre Hotel.

They had confronted one of the darkest times in American
history: a cancerous war that could not be done away with; an
incipient anarchy at home whose roots were deeply embedded and
which did not easily respond to any remedy; a foreboding public
skepticism† about governmental institutions; a powerful, resourceful
antagonist abroad, the Soviet Union.

Although those first thirty months had indeed been a time of

---

*Later, in mid-May 1971, when Nixon's fortunes seemed on the rise again, Safire
amended his aphorism to read as follows: "The gloom and doom will lift when the
cherry blossoms appear and descend again after the blossoms are gone and forgotten." He was emphasizing the cyclical nature of Presidential popularity, forecasting
that Nixon would have downs as well as ups prior to the 1972 election.

†That skepticism was fed by sensational disclosures of top-secret documents in
June 1971, when the *New York Times* published internal Johnson administration
memoranda and option papers on the Vietnam war. War critics seized on these as
evidence of massive duplicity and calculated deceit of the American people during
Johnson's escalation of the war in 1965 and 1966.

grave trouble, it was trouble always just short of real calamity. Thus, if there was a way to judge a President's response to some future catastrophe that threatened the republic, Richard Nixon had not yet revealed it in himself. What he had revealed was a tendency, no more, often to fall short in the use of his power in particularly trying circumstances, a certain lack of fortitude and skill in managing and directing the Presidency's vast political resources, an inability to lead a tightly coordinated administration. Thus the unanswered question was whether Richard M. Nixon could summon the strength and astuteness to handle the far greater challenges that would surely confront him in the days ahead.

And Richard Nixon the man had changed remarkably little in the Presidency. He remained essentially the same lonely, introspective poor boy from Yorba Linda who had clawed his way to the peak of power against the rich and well-born, and having reached it, remained suspicious and uneasy. Although, in truth, the press attacks on Nixon did not approach in vehemence and consistency the assaults on Lyndon B. Johnson in 1967 and 1968, Nixon told Howard K. Smith on March 29, 1971: "It is true that of all the Presidents in this century, it is probably true, that I have less, as somebody has said, supporters in the press than any President." In that one sentence he revealed both his tendency toward self-pity and his phobia about the press—two unchanging characteristics.

Despite his heralded change toward a new concentration on domestic affairs, his political aides complained that he did not stir himself on key Congressional votes in Congress as he did on foreign policy questions. Republican Congressmen still muttered about an isolated President and an arrogant staff. Relations between the White House and the regular party organizations around the country had grown no more cordial. At bottom, little had changed.

Nixon's political tactics were also unchanging. His courting of the South, in line with John Mitchell's strategy, was unceasing. On a visit to Birmingham, Ala., on May 25, 1971, he praised the South and spanked the North: ". . . . I have nothing but utter contempt for the double hypocritical standard of Northerners who look at the South and point the finger and say 'Why don't those Southerners do something about their race problems?' " Contending there had been "no progress in the North" toward school desegregation the preceding three years, he contrasted that with "significant progress in the

South." But returning to Washington, he declined to use his national forum as a pulpit for preaching racial amity. When he was asked at a news conference on June 2 about his Birmingham statement, the President passed up an opportunity to exhort greater efforts toward desegregation, either in the North or the South.

At that June 2 press conference, Nixon followed his new practice of standing behind a podium instead of a naked microphone, as he had done during his first two years. He told his aides that he liked the podium and felt more secure with it. But symbolically the effect on others was the opposite. It made him seem less self-confident, less sure of himself. In his public television appearances, Richard Nixon was still nervous, still less than masterful.

With eighteen months remaining in his term of office, he had accomplished much of what he had worked at hardest, inexorably winding down the Vietnam war and reaching the fringes of success in dealing with the Communist world. But he seemed farther than ever from any sort of warm and easy relationship with the American people, a lack of empathy which, when combined with the still-ailing economy, raised the question whether he would become the first President since Herbert Hoover to seek and be denied a second term.

SOURCE NOTES

The vast majority of primary source material in this book which is not available on the public record was obtained from interviews with public figures, most of them officials of the administration. These include some fifty conducted especially for this book, and hundreds of other interviews which were a routine part of the daily reporting for our column. Since all of these interviews were conducted on a confidential basis, any listing of complete source notes for the information in this book not contained in the public record would comprise a tedious series of interviews with anonymous sources. It goes without saying, then, that the following list of secondary sources by no means represents a comprehensive listing of sources.

CHAPTER II
11. "I've always thought"—Theodore H. White, *The Making of the President 1968* (New York: Atheneum, 1969), p. 147.
15. "this fellow Moynihan"—*ibid.*, p. 146.
30. "one of the best political craftsmen"—Richard M. Nixon, *Six Crises* (New York: Pocket Books, 1962), p. 347.
31. The 1966 difficulties between Nixon and Bliss are taken in part from Jules Witcover, *The Resurrection of Richard Nixon* (New York: Putnam's Sons, 1970), pp. 167–169.

CHAPTER VI
136. "I had been one of the most"—Nixon, *op.cit.*, p. 391.
148. "The trouble was"—Leon Panetta and Peter Gall, *Bring Us Together* (New York: Lippincott, 1971), p. 76.
152. The Baker-Brock pressure on HEW—*ibid.*, p. 114.
154–55. The account of the August 23 meetings—*ibid.*, p. 258.
157. "The South, the South"—*ibid.*, p. 111.

CHAPTER VII
179. "Inflation, in the past four years"—White, *op.cit.,* p. 425.
179 *n*. "As in other inflations"—*ibid.,* pp. 425–426.
180. "Unfortunately, Arthur Burns turned out"—Nixon, *op.cit.,* p. 334.
206–7. The account of the firing of Mayo is based in part on a syndicated column by Joseph Slevin of June 25, 1970.

CHAPTER IX
246. "keyed up and ready for battle"—Nixon, *op.cit.,* p. xv.

CHAPTER XI
307. "My impression is"—Daniel St. Albin Greene, "Agnew, Man and Boy—and the Phenomenon," *National Observer,* November 2, 1970.
323. "privileged elite of the Northeast"—Kevin P. Phillips, *The Emerging Republican Majority* (New Rochelle, N.Y.: Arlington House, 1969), pp. 469–470.
324. "It was change that some few Americans"—Richard W. Scammon and Ben J. Wattenberg, *The Real Majority* (New York: Coward-McCann, 1970), p. 44.

Epilogue

. . . my strong point is not rhetoric, it isn't show-manship, it isn't big promises—those things that create the glamour and the excitement that people call charisma and warmth. My strong point, if I have a strong point, is performance. I always do more than I say. I always produce more than I promise.

—Richard M. Nixon, in a televised interview
with Dan Rather of CBS, January 2, 1972.

The mood in the White House—from Presidential aides on down to stenographers—was surprise bordering on shock the morning of Friday, January 28, 1972, when Barbara Walters of the National Broadcasting Company's *Today* program turned up at 1600 Pennsylvania Avenue with an NBC film crew in tow. Even Herb Klein, the director of communications for the Nixon administration, who was supposed to know about such matters, was taken by surprise. Nor could anybody have guessed Miss Walters' highly improbable mission: to interview Harry Robert Haldeman himself, the cloistered keeper of the Presidential keys and preeminent master of the White House inner sanctum. For the first time, Bob Haldeman was to be exposed to the outer world.

There was no particular crisis in the administration of Richard Nixon, now entering its fourth year, requiring Haldeman to strip aside the veils of anonymity and publicly proclaim the virtues of his chief. Far from it. An aura of optimism, of almost smug satisfaction, had drenched the White House ever since Nixon's two great surprises of the surprising summer of 1971: the announcement on July 15 of his China trip and the announcement on August 15 of his New Economic Policy. The former, in a single stroke, had disarmed Nixon's foreign policy critics on the left and given the nation a forceful demonstration of daring and imaginative management of foreign policy; the latter, temporarily at least, had seemed to arrest both inflation at home and deterioration of the dollar abroad while robbing Democrats of ammunition for their economic attack against the President that had been building in velocity and effect. Nixon's long decline in popularity had ended, and the curve was now upward. Nine months before the election, his chances for a second term seemed to be improving. And apart from popularity polls and long-range election forecasting, the glowing self-confidence of the President and the men around him was both obvious and justified. Nixon's dramatic action on China and the economy the previous summer had been fine political tonic, arresting the decline of his administration into frustration and ineffectiveness. To much of Washington, Richard Nixon was exercising Presidential power in the grand manner.

The mood of euphoria was particularly thick at the White House the morning Miss Walters taped her Haldeman interview. Just three nights earlier, on January 25, Nixon had once again gone to the country on nationwide television with another stunning surprise, though less so than the twin shockers of China and the New Economic Policy. The impact was similar: Nixon had preempted the staggering Democrats on a key issue.

On that evening, the President revealed that the ubiquitous Henry A. Kissinger had conducted private, informal peace negotiations with North Vietnamese envoys on the outskirts of Paris on twelve occasions between August 4, 1969, and August 16, 1971. On May 31, 1971, Nixon revealed, Kissinger had offered a total American withdrawal from Vietnam in return for the release of all American prisoners and a cease-fire. In reply, he said, Hanoi's diplomats "insisted that we overthrow the Government of South Vietnam." He then revealed that after more fruitless negotiations between Kissinger and the Communists, the United States had prepared a new proposal: an offer of free elections one month *after* the resignation of General Nguyen Van Thieu as President of South Vietnam and after the withdrawal of American forces. Instead of an answer, Hanoi declined even to meet Kissinger again in Paris, reported the President.

The more militant members of the Senate peace bloc—Edward M. Kennedy of Massachusetts, George McGovern of South Dakota, and Frank Church of Idaho in the forefront—lashed out at the President's revelations. But they were alone. Nixon's new peace plan was termed "a long step forward" by Senator Mike Mansfield, the Democratic leader of the Senate and a critic of America's Indochina policy for long years. Republican politicians, fearful of an election-year indictment in which the Democrats would charge them with being the war party for refusing to make concessions that would free American P.O.W.'s, sighed in relief. The President's disclosures seemed to eliminate that possibility. Now the United States looked magnanimous, the Communists intractable, Nixon reasonable and the complaining Democrats petty and peevish. Whatever impact Nixon's performance of January 25 might have on the final outcome of the Vietnamese ordeal, for the time being it had transformed the political atmosphere at home. Once again, Richard Nixon had extracted maximum benefits from a proper exercise of Presidential power.

But inside the White House, this sense of political well-being was diminished by the President's irritation, obvious to close aides, over the criticism of the Senate doves. And no aide was closer than the faithful Haldeman, who reflected his President's moods as accurately as a thermometer reflects the temperature. Without careful thought, Haldeman's reflection mechanism went to work, inevitably magnifying out of all reasonable proportions the criticism from Capitol Hill that was so irritating Nixon. That the criticism was in the forefront of his mind became swiftly apparent when Miss Walters and the NBC crew entered his neat-as-a-pin Williamsburg-style office in the White House where so few journalists, politicians and even administration officials had ever been admitted.

The interview was the result of many months of effort by the aggressive Miss Walters, who realized she would score a major coup if she could lure the most inaccessible man in the most inaccessible White House onto her *Today* show. Haldeman's precise motives in succumbing were unclear. Answering to nobody but the President, he was not in the habit of explaining himself to his colleagues. Presumably, at some point or other in their countless, businesslike exchanges, Haldeman had informed Nixon about the interview; he might well have sought his advice. But elsewhere in the White House, the public unleashing of H. R. Haldeman was not even disclosed, much less discussed. Haldeman did not mention it at the daily White House staff meeting over which he presided early each morning. Nor did he consult John Mitchell, who was getting ready to step down as Attorney General to manage Nixon's reelection campaign, or any political or public relations aide on the White House staff. Some Presidential aides speculated that Haldeman might have been touched with envy of Kissinger, whose secret mission to Peking the previous summer had suddenly transformed him from anonymous adviser to a familiar, rather glamorous figure on television. Certainly, based on her earlier *Today* interviews with Dr. Kissinger, Mrs. Nixon and Nixon himself, Barbara Walters gave Haldeman no reason to expect hostile questioning.

The result was memorable. With the cheery blaze in Haldeman's office fireplace providing a cozy background, Haldeman was asked by Miss Walters what kind of criticism upset President Nixon. Haldeman replied: criticism "that can get in the way of what he's doing," and immediately offered a case in point—the President's new peace plan. Before that plan had been revealed on January 25, he explained, the President's critics were *"unconsciously* echoing the line that the enemy wanted echoed."* But now that the President had fully revealed the nature of Kissinger's secret negotiations, Haldeman went on, "the only conclusion you can draw is that the critics now are *consciously* aiding and abetting the enemy of the United States. . . ." With Haldeman skating perilously close to the thin ice of the definition for treason, the startled Miss Walters reminded him that these critics included United States senators. But Haldeman skated on. "In this particular posture," he said evenly, "I think they are *consciously* aiding and abetting the enemy."†

The tape was not shown on the *Today* program until some ten days later, on February 7, and the instantaneous result was one of those angry furors that so delight Washington. "Back us, says Mr. Haldeman of the White House staff," wrote James Reston in the

---

*The emphasis in Haldeman's comments is added.

†It was widely assumed that Haldeman's criticism was intended primarily for Senator Edmund S. Muskie of Maine, then the front-runner for the Democratic Presidential nomination. After a few days' silence, Muskie had harshly criticized the Nixon peace plan. In fact, however, Haldeman's interview was filmed before Muskie's criticism, though it was shown on television subsequent to it.

New York Times the next morning, "or you are giving aid and comfort to the enemy. Dissent, even honest dissent, is unpatriotic!" Reston then went on to articulate a common theme heard around Washington that morning—that Haldeman sounded mighty like the "Old Nixon." Haldeman, wrote Reston,

> is still back in the Beverly Hilton Hotel in Los Angeles with Nixon on the morning of November 7, 1962, after he ran Mr. Nixon's campaign to defeat against Pat Brown, blaming everything on the wicked press. . . . He is a loyal Nixon man and sees opposition to his chief as opposition to the nation.

The view was not much different from Reston's that morning when the staff of the "Committee for the Re-Election of the President," the front organization for the President's embryonic 1972 campaign apparatus, met in its office at 1701 Pennsylvania Avenue, catty-corner from the White House. Bitterly these political pros recognized at once that a political blunder of significant dimensions had been committed. The Vietnam critics, Mr. Reston included, who had been on the run were now handed fresh ammunition. The Nixon administration was back on the defensive. The ghost of the old red-baiting Nixon had been conjured up by none other than the President's number one White House aide, whose appearance on his TV debut, crew-cut, unsmiling, slightly bug-eyed, was seen by the Nixon politicians as more than a little menacing. John Mitchell, who was still on the job as Attorney General, did not attend that staff meeting. But privately he made clear he was not at all happy with the Haldeman caper.

But what to do? Haldeman was the ex-officio enforcer on the White House staff. If anybody else made a mistake, he was more than apt to receive an intimidating word of caution from Haldeman. But who could enforce discipline against the enforcer? The only possible answer was the President himself.

On the day the interview was run, Nixon authorized Press Secretary Ron Ziegler to say that Haldeman's comments constituted "his own personal point of view" and not necessarily the President's. But any prospect of a serious disagreement was dispelled two days later at an impromptu press conference called by Nixon in the Oval Office. With the worrisome television cameras barred from the conference, Nixon seemed relaxed, self-confident and in obvious high spirits as he awaited the trip to China a week hence. Asked about Haldeman's interview, the President said "there is nothing further I should say" beyond Ziegler's statement, but then went on to say a great deal further.

Asserting that "I do not question the patriotism, I do not question the sincerity" of his Vietnam critics, he pointed out in some detail that *he*, as a candidate for President in 1968, had not questioned President Johnson's peace plan. Finally, addressing himself to the Democratic Presidential candidates, most of whom were now slashing away at the peace plan, he declared:

> They have to consult their own consciences. They apparently have determined that they wish to take another course of action. I disagree with the course of action. I would strongly urge at this point that all candidates for President, Republican and Democrat, review their public statements and really consider whether they believe they are going to help the cause of peace or hurt it, whether they are going to encourage the enemy to negotiate or encourage him to continue the war.

Later in the press conference, a questioner returned to the subject: "Mr. President, you had some public advice today . . . about how critics of the war should conduct themselves. Do you have any public advice for Mr. Haldeman?" Nixon's geniality vanished, his face clouding over. "I have answered the question," he said sharply. "Anything further?"

He had indeed answered it by saying very much what Haldeman himself had said—far more discreetly, to be sure, but in essence unchanged. Moreover, by now Haldeman had made clear to his colleagues at the White House that he saw not the slightest impropriety in his televised interview. Nobody save the President himself could safely disagree with him, and the President had made it emphatically clear that no disagreement would come from his lips.

The Haldeman incident, like so many transient furors in Washington, was soon forgotten. It is recounted at length because under analysis it reveals a great deal about the administration of Richard Nixon as it entered its fourth year:

1. The mood of being under siege by the liberal establishment that Nixon carried into the White House with him in 1969 still held him and his closest associates in thrall three years later. This mood,

pervasive in their private conversation, popped into public consciousness in Haldeman's "aiding and abetting the enemy" accusation, and in the President's approval of it.

2. Nixon had not broken himself of the irresistible temptation to lash out at his enemies in the most venomous manner, a practice now mimicked by Haldeman. With the political momentum moving in his direction, no assault against essentially ineffective criticism of his peace plan was needed on any pragmatic grounds. Rather, it satisfied an inner compulsion.

3. Loyalty remained the paramount virtue in the upper reaches of the Nixon White House—loyalty upward to the President, loyalty downward from the President. Uncompromising loyalty to Nixon, even to the point of eschewing constructive criticism of him in the privacy of staff meetings, was highly valued among lesser staffers as a worthy characteristic of John Ehrlichman, Chuck Colson and, most particularly, Bob Haldeman. Similarly, loyalty flowed downward to them from the President. For Nixon to have criticized Haldeman for his indiscreet words, either in private or public, would have been a breach of that code.

4. Haldeman, at the apex of the most powerful, highly structured and tightly controlled White House staff system in history, wielded immense power without any accountability. As the *Today* interview showed, no colleague dared challenge him and the President chose not to monitor his activities too closely. Add to this the continuing refusal of Haldeman to give access to influential figures from the outside world—particularly the world of the press and the politicians—and the sacrosanct custom of Executive privilege, which bars Congress from calling him to testify on anything, and Haldeman's awesome power assumes its true dimension.

These four points, moreover, lead to a broader conclusion: sycophantic defenders to the contrary, not all that much had changed in the first three years of the Nixon Presidency. Its strengths and weaknesses, its foibles and its inherent characteristics, were essentially the same as they had been in the beginning.

That conclusion ran against the conventional wisdom of Washington during the first half of 1972. It was widely assumed that sometime late in the summer of 1971 Nixon had finally seized the Presidency and mastered it, implacably bending it to his will. Even some of his aides who, in the early summer of 1971, were despairing now spoke of still another new Nixon that rendered obsolete all judgments about his early years in office.

Indeed, there were some indisputable changes—superficially, far more than normal at the top management levels of the administration. In the spring of 1972 only four members of the original Cabinet remained: Rogers at State, Laird at Defense, Romney at HUD, Volpe at Transportation. More significantly, those renowned figures who competed so aggressively for power and policy in the early days—Dr. Arthur Burns, Bryce Harlow and Dr. Daniel Patrick Moynihan—were now departed. Tempestuous personalities from the outside, such as Dr. Jean Mayer, the food nutritionist from Harvard, no longer stalked the corridors of the White House to promote worthy causes. Robert Finch, long since defeated by the all-powerful Mitchell, had ceased to function as the symbol of social liberalism in the administration. Shelved from power as a Cabinet-level Counsellor, Finch was not even close to policy-making.

In short, the day of the power struggle was over. Aides who sometimes disagreed with the thrust of administration policy, such as liberal White House assistant Len Garment, could do so in the privacy of the White House—if not too vociferously and abrasively —but never, never, take a case to the public. The lines of authority at the White House had hardened. As overseer of the White House bureaucracy, Haldeman was now unchallenged. In policy-making, Ehrlichman and George Shultz amicably divided up the domestic area, Henry Kissinger had strengthened his extraordinary hold over foreign policy and at the Treasury John Connally had now become an economic czar.

As for the president himself, he obviously felt and looked more comfortable in the job, relying somewhat less on staff advice and playing an obviously more activist role in an area he had woefully neglected for so long—the area of domestic and particularly economic policy. The New Economic Policy of August 15, 1971, had been the watershed. Besides offering a dose of much-needed confidence to an unconfident nation, and at least temporary relief from the agonizing price and wage spiral, it also brought a bright measure of confidence to the President himself, and thus visibly affected the nature of the Nixon Presidency. Such an audacious exercise of Presidential power obviously reinforced Nixon's self-esteem, on the wane going into the summer of 1971. However many more days he would spend as President, it was inconceivable that Nixon would again neglect the uses of power to permit a major problem to deteriorate as the economic situation had deteriorated for two and a half years.

But having said that, the myth that an utter metamorphosis had transformed the Nixon Presidency on August 15 was preposterous, and the implication of the Haldeman Incident proved it. A mature politician does not undergo complete transformation so late in life, and the Nixon of 1972 was basically unchanged from the Nixon of 1969.

His emphasis and interests remained heavily on the foreign policy side. His love of ritual and novelty, and his zest for outrageous overstatement, remained undiminished. His hostility toward ancient enemies and hypersensitivity to criticism prevailed. His suspicion of the press was undimmed and his passion for privacy continued to make him the most inaccessible President since Herbert Hoover. The passage into the Oval Office was jealously guarded by Haldeman with the President's thorough approval and deep gratitude. In the spring of 1972 his last televised news conference had been the one in June 1971.

There persisted also an unreality about the inviolability of the Presidency—a fancy propagated in particular by Haldeman and certainly not discouraged by Nixon. When Nixon was interviewed over national television by Dan Rather of CBS on January 2, 1972, he and his senior staff were outraged that Rather should turn "A Conversation with the President" into a penetrating interview with tough (but certainly in no way unfair) cross-examination. The President's senior staff was even more incensed over Alan Drury, the best-selling Washington novelist and a thoroughgoing conservative. Drury had been granted unusual privileges, including private interviews with Nixon and Haldeman and a seat at several White House staff meetings, to help him prepare an illustrated book on the Nixon administration (*Courage and Hesitation,* Doubleday, 1971). Friendly it was, but not friendly enough for Nixon's men. They regarded the occasional critical and unfriendly material as a betrayal of trust, though no objective reader could possibly agree.

What obscured such pettiness was the fact that all indicators of popularity and approval for the President and his administration were moving upward in 1972, whereas they had been in more or less continuous decline for the preceding three years. But in no small part, this stemmed from forces beyond Nixon's control: the deepening crisis of the ideologically splintered Democratic Party, and Nixon's remarkable freedom from misfortune or serious crisis throughout late 1971 and into early 1972.

The question remained: When adversity struck, as indeed it must, would President Nixon be markedly better equipped to deal with it than he had been in his first years as President?

On February 21, 1972, William F. Buckley, Jr., conservative leader and editor-columnist, was seated twenty yards away as a member of the press in Peking's Great Hall of the People when Richard Nixon responded to a banquet toast by Prime Minister Chou En-lai and went strolling among the tables, individually greeting the leaders of Communist China. "It is unreasonable to suppose," an outraged Buckley cabled back for his syndicated column, "that anywhere in history have a few dozen men congregated who have been responsible for greater human mayhem than the gentlemen at the banquet, instruments and mentors of Mao Tse-tung."

Buckley's fury over Nixon consorting with the Communist enemy was isolated to a numerically tiny fringe. In fact, Nixon's eight days in China, more time than had ever been spent before in one country by any President of the United States, had dazzled a nation—Republicans and Democrats, conservatives and liberals, young and old. As communications satellite technology beamed the pictures from China every night, America watched in fascination.* Beyond the revival of old but passionate interest in the mysterious East, there stirred in American hearts a glimmer that peace, after all, might be within grasp of the world.

This was the Presidency, Nixon style—pomp and ceremony, long private conversations with the great men of the world, the intrigue of super world politics on the grandest scale. The China extravaganza was only the culmination of weeks of summitry on an unprecedented scale, weeks that dominated the President's time

---

*Nixon was accompanied to China by eighty-six newsmen. But the selection process of correspondents by the White House raised questions of possible vindictiveness. *Newsday,* which had published an exposé of Bebe Rebozo's finances, was excluded. So was the *Boston Globe,* generally critical of the Nixon administration.

and attention. There had been one conference after another with heads of government: with Heath of Britain in Bermuda, Brandt of West Germany in Florida, Pompidou of France in the Azores, Sato of Japan in California. And in May, if all went well, would come a historic first—a summit meeting in Moscow tailored to exactly the same length as the China visit.

Opening the door to China was the most spectacular initiative in foreign policy taken by an American leader since the start of the Cold War, and the climax of a carefully charted course by the President that began to unfold with his first overtures through Rumania in 1969. His enthusiasm, so manifest in those toasts at the Peking banquet that infuriated Buckley, permeated the entire visit. When asked by a reporter if he was enjoying the cultural and sporting events, Nixon burbled: "Fantastic. . . . The gymnastic events —I have never seen a tumbler like that last one . . . Then the ping pong table, those little girls and teenaged boys! . . . This is certainly the equal of any ballet I have seen."

And at the final banquet of the visit to Shanghai on February 27, the President enthused with his aggressive hyperbole: "This was the week that changed the world." Whether it had or not, the visit certainly seemed a success. After a somewhat hesitant start, the rulers of China gave Nixon dramatic treatment in the controlled press, printing pictures of the President seated beside the deified Mao Tse-tung. And in domestic politics, the immediate impact was overwhelming. While Nixon's prospective Democratic opponents devoured each other in the Presidential primaries, he was world statesman exploring every possible avenue to peace.

Nixon had not yet returned from China, however, when some sour notes sounded. In the joint communiqué issued in Shanghai on February 27, the United States said it "does not challenge" the position that "Taiwan [Formosa] is part of China," adding: "It affirms the ultimate objective of the withdrawal of all U.S. forces and military installations from Taiwan. In the meantime, it will progressively reduce its forces and military installations on Taiwan as the tension in the area diminishes."

What did this mean? Was Nixon betraying Chiang Kai-shek and his Nationalist government on Taiwan? Was there a secret protocol, perhaps tied to the Vietnam war? Nixon and Kissinger denied all such intimations. But the question of just what had been agreed to or accomplished in Peking began to dispel some of the euphoria.

Indeed, Nixon's overall record in foreign policy, though purposefully directed away from confrontation and toward negotiation and the beginnings of détente, had to be punctuated with some elements of doubt:

Soviet Union: Progress toward détente was slower in the spring of 1972 than the President had hoped. No great progress had been made in strategic-arms limitations or mutual reductions of troops in Europe, though a new agreement on rights to Berlin was negotiated. At the Pentagon, Laird privately and repeatedly warned of growing Soviet military strength through an armaments program of massive proportions, particularly in nuclear, missile-armed submarines, hitherto an American monopoly.

Western Europe: Nixon's great hope of restoring intimate ties with the NATO powers had fallen victim to deep economic strains. Western European leaders never quite recovered from the shock of the get-tough international aspects of Nixon's New Economic Policy, including the temporary surcharge on imports into the United States. Although that surcharge had been lifted, Western Europe still looked at economic czar Connally as anti-European, protectionist and chauvinistic.

Japan: U.S.–Japanese relations were still reeling from the two "Nixon shocks" of the summer of 1971—the overture to China and the import surcharge. Relations with this rich and vital nation had deteriorated badly under Nixon.

India: Never had U.S. stock on the subcontinent been lower than in the spring of 1972. Nixon had backed Pakistan, though neither aggressively nor effectively, in a losing war with India in early 1972 that resulted in the secession of East Pakistan as the Republic of Bangla Desh.* The Soviet Union had been India's patron and was now at a peak of prestige and authority there.

Mideast: The truce on the Suez Canal still persisted, thanks in no small part to the Nixon administration. But Nixon's intent to

---

*The publication by syndicated columnist Jack Anderson of minutes of high-level policy meetings revealed that Nixon, while professing a position of neutrality between India and Pakistan, was actually favoring Pakistan. The revelations not only further soured U.S.–Indian relations but did no good for Nixon's credibility at home.

pursue an even-handed policy as between Israel and the Arabs had failed. Thanks to skillful Israeli diplomacy and pressure from the American Jewish community, translated into Congressional influence over policy, Nixon had finally agreed to send Phantom jets to Israel, and U.S.–Arab relations had deteriorated to their pre-Nixon levels.

All such concerns were dwarfed on March 30, 1972, when, under cover of heavy artillery attacks and using powerful armored formations, regular divisions of the North Vietnamese army crossed the Demilitarized Zone separating North and South Vietnam. This was the long-awaited Communist offensive of 1972, the enemy's most important operation since the Tet Offensive of 1968 and by all odds the biggest and potentially most dangerous campaign ever waged by North Vietnamese regulars. Within a week the Communist offensive, using some 80 percent of the North Vietnamese army, was in progress on four separate fronts in South Vietnam, causing an initial falling back by South Vietnamese troops and a bad case of jitters in the Nixon White House.

On the most elemental level, the offensive was a crucial test for Nixon's Vietnamization policy. The President ordered heavy bombing raids by U.S. planes, both in North Vietnam and against the troops invading the South, but there would be no return of U.S. ground troops (now scheduled to be reduced to 69,000 by May 1). Thus, apart from U.S. air—an awesome armada—the ARVN would have to rely on itself to stem the tide from the North. In any event, the Communist offensive had forced the war back onto front pages and network news programs, reviving an election-year issue that Nixon had hoped was dead.

But what really caused the jitters at the White House were the broader implications of the bad news from Vietnam. What did it portend for détente—U.S.–Chinese détente, to some extent, but far more important, U.S.–Soviet détente? Did all the toasts and smiles at Peking mean anything? And what of the President's forthcoming mission to Moscow? A massive offensive of the size launched by Hanoi, far surpassing the expectations of U.S. intelligence, would not have been remotely possible without massive Soviet weapon support and perhaps technical assistance.

Thus did the Vietnam war, which Nixon entered the White House determined to neutralize as a domestic political issue, come back with a terrible vengeance to haunt him. Nowhere had Nixon's Presidency been more masterly and more successful than in (1) steadily withdrawing U.S. troops from Vietnam without corresponding military deterioration, and (2) moving steadily toward détente both with Moscow and Peking. Now a deeply angered, deeply puzzled President saw the military might of Hanoi's legions threatening to undermine both achievements while his options to react steadily narrowed.

When, on August 15, 1971, Richard Nixon stunned the nation with his New Economic Policy, including a ninety-day wage-price freeze, it was widely assumed that he was making two basic changes in his administration: first, he would now devote much more time to the hitherto neglected economic sphere; second, he had abandoned his old abhorrence of a government-regulated economy and was now embracing the concept of controls.

In truth, the changes proved to be only partial. Although he devoted heavy blocks of time to the economy in the turbulent days immediately following August 15, it was not to last. By the end of 1971, he had again delegated responsibility in this area to Secretary Connally and, to an increasing degree, Dr. Herbert Stein of the Council of Economic Advisers.* As for wage and price controls, Nixon never regarded them as anything more than temporary, reiterating his total resistance to a permanent controls bureaucracy of the kind in which he himself had spent ten unhappy months three decades earlier. Some key figures in the administration responsible for making the controls program work, particularly Stein and George Shultz, were as philosophically and professionally opposed to controls as Nixon was emotionally. The President's true economic philosophy was revealed in his Labor Day radio speech on September 6, 1971, when he declared that only a return to the "work ethic" (described as "the inner drive that has made the American workingman unique in the world")—not government intervention—would bring "a new prosperity without war and without inflation."

But Nixon, by enunciating the New Economic Policy, had

---

*Dr. Paul McCracken, long since eclipsed as a major policy-making force, resigned as Chairman of the Council of Economic Advisers on November 24, 1971 (effective January 1, 1972) and was replaced by Stein.

finally realized that "work ethic" admonitions were not nearly enough. Indeed, the New Economic Policy was the offspring of economic desperation both at home and abroad and was unveiled on August 15 with no real advance planning—no departure, in short, from the way the economy had been managed throughout the Nixon administration. Indeed, not until August 18 did Nixon meet with his economic lieutenants to determine what would happen after midnight, November 13, when the ninety-day wage-price freeze ended.

Whatever de-control fancies the President entertained, once the freeze ended they were quickly erased by his economic advisers, who explained the freeze would immediately be followed by a surge in prices. The question for the postfreeze period—Phase II of the New Economic Policy—quickly became not whether but how to control wages and prices. And this essentially became a question of whether the administration would try to control wages with or without the help of organized labor.

That, in turn, evolved into a debate between Connally and Shultz. As a conservative Texas Democrat, Connally had fought organized labor throughout his career and now felt that Nixon should go over the heads of the labor leaders to the workingman to seek his cooperation. If Big Labor refused to cooperate, Connally said, that was labor's misfortune. George Shultz, who had maintained friendly contacts with union leaders even after leaving the Labor Department, vigorously disagreed. An organized labor boycott, said Shultz, would cripple any wage-price control program. The AFL–CIO's George Meany asserted that any wage board that did not include labor members—"fascist" in nature, said Meany—would be boycotted. Meany, waxing to the fight, demanded a tripartite board with labor, business and public members but refused even to consider serving on such a board unless Nixon pledged that it would be autonomous, free from all administration control and direction. That was also the substance of debate between Connally and Shultz. Connally opposed autonomy, contending the President must exercise ultimate control; Shultz urged autonomy as the price necessary for Meany's cooperation. In a close decision, bitterly regretted by some top White House aides, Shultz won. A tripartite Pay Board, including George Meany, and a separate Price Commission were named.

But if Nixon deferred to Shultz for reasons of practicality, his heart was with Connally. Although he did not want to risk a general strike by setting wages without labor's cooperation, Nixon still relished the prospect of appealing to workers over the heads of their union leaders, a battle in which he thought his political ally would be the American people and their instinctive animosity against Big Labor.

So, with Phase II controls barely a week old, Nixon decided to address the AFL–CIO convention at Bal Harbour, Fla., on November 19, to beard Big Labor in its den. He got what he bargained for: a reception so icy that it bordered on disrespect. When the network evening news programs portrayed Meany and the labor delegates laughing derisively at the President, the White House knew it had won a political and psychological victory. But the bitter realization by organized labor of exactly why Nixon had come to Bal Harbour did nothing to improve the cooperation between the administration and Big Labor on Phase II that Shultz felt was essential.

Although Meany continuously complained that the Pay Board's public and business members were ganging up on the outnumbered labor members with secret White House connivance, labor won some early victories. Despite Meany's continuous complaints, the direction of the Board's early negotiations on wage increases was quite the opposite: the alliance was not business and public members but business and labor members, with some business members taking labor's side for purely parochial, self-interest economic reasons—they did not want to affront their own big unions by taking too strong an anti-union stance.

So obvious did this sub rosa alliance become that Arthur Burns, enthroned in the gleaming marble palace of the Federal Reserve Board, worried that runaway wage increases threatened to undermine the President's whole anti-inflation program. Whereupon Burns summoned the business members of the Board to his office, singly and together, to put some steel in their spines. Burns minced no words. The business members, he said, were not only selling out to the unions, they were also selling out the anti-inflation campaign, the result of which was predictable: a stronger pattern of controls based on runaway wages and cost-push inflation that would bring the government even deeper into the business of American business.

Whether Burns could claim credit or not, the Pay Board soon

began to reflect a new balance of power, with business joining public members and rolling back some big new wage increases negotiated by labor, first in the aerospace industry and then on the West Coast docks. The end was near. Finally, on March 22, 1972, Meany and two other AFL–CIO labor members (followed shortly by the United Auto Workers' Leonard Woodcock) walked off the Pay Board with a blast that its majority was controlled by the White House and that the Price Commission had been too soft on policing big business.* In truth, Nixon was happy that Big Labor's grudging cooperation had lasted this long.

But there was sentiment inside the White House that Meany's criticism of the Price Commission was not entirely unfounded. Besides, the labor walkout had come at a time when food prices, particularly beef, uncontrolled under Phase II, were going through the roof. Despite White House claims that price stability was just around the corner, the high hopes that the New Economic Policy would be able to curb inflation was far from realized in the spring of 1972.

Nor was inflation the only economic headache. Recovery following the 1970–71 recession was slow, and unemployment stubbornly stayed around the 6 percent mark. The administration was not only running immense budget deficits of close to $40 billion a year, but the shaky state of the economy and an incipient tax revolt barred any prospect of tax increases. The international aspects of the New Economic Policy had neither solved the balance-of-payments crisis nor stifled demand for protectionism.

Thus, the President was in only marginally less economic trouble in the spring of 1972 than the summer of 1971. The future might indeed turn out brighter, but the marked improvement in his political prospects still did not have an economic base.

On October 8, 1971, Richard Nixon met with top legal and political aides at the White House to discuss the return of a familiar problem: Supreme Court vacancies. The resignation of two of the Court's most prestigious members, Hugo Black and John Marshall Harlan, both old and mortally ill, had opened up two more chairs for Nixon to fill. The Haynsworth-Carswell debacle of 1969 and

---

*One of the five labor members, Frank E. Fitzsimmons of the Teamsters, did not join Meany's walkout and was named to the new, reconstituted Pay Board as the only labor member.

1970 had surely fulfilled Nixon's 1968 campaign promise to name two Southern conservatives to the Court, even though both were rejected by the Senate. Now, some aides hoped, he could satisfy other demands. Prominent Jewish Republicans felt a Jew had been absent from the Court long enough; amid increasing feminist militancy, there were demands for a woman member; some lawyers, less than impressed by the credentials of the two Nixon appointees who had been confirmed by the Senate, wanted the President to opt more for quality and less for ideology this time.

All were to be disappointed. At that October 8 meeting, Nixon made clear he was again in the market for a Southerner. When blatantly mediocre names were mentioned, one aide warned of a veto by the American Bar Association. "Screw the ABA," Nixon snapped back. In his never-ending quest to ingratiate himself with the South, the President did not mind thumbing his nose at the Establishment—including the elite of the legal profession, which had never taken him in.

Deputy Attorney General Richard Kleindienst, in charge of the search for two new Justices, had clear directions: one was to be a conservative Southerner, and the other a staunch exponent of law-and-order. Quality was not even a secondary consideration. The name of Edward Levi, president of the University of Chicago, was summarily rejected when suggested by one administration official. Levi's impressive legal background meant nothing; he was neither a Southerner nor a law-and-order champion.

The results of Kleindienst's search astonished legal scholars and politicians alike. One was Herschel H. Friday, a Little Rock, Ark., attorney best known as Governor Orval Faubus' lawyer in fighting school integration in the 1950s. The other was Judge Mildred L. Lillie of the California State Court of Appeals, known as a hanging judge in dealing with juvenile offenders, and a staunch foe of the Warren Court's civil libertarian decisions. Neither had the slightest national reputation. Neither was viewed as remotely qualified for the Supreme Court. Yet, Attorney General Mitchell quickly approved Kleindienst's shocking selections, and so did Nixon. From there, they went to the ABA for a check.*

*Their names were submitted to the ABA with four others (including Senator Robert Byrd, the conservative Democrat from West Virginia), but the additional names were merely camouflage intended to hide the selection of Friday and

Members of the ABA Committee on the Federal Judiciary could scarcely believe their eyes when they saw the President's selections. But before they voted to reject them, a source in the ABA leaked them to the press. When the names of Friday and Mrs. Lillie became public on October 14, Nixon, Mitchell and Kleindienst were ill prepared for the fury from the bar and the press. Two days later, the ABA leaked its formal finding that both were unqualified.

Nixon was outraged. Inside the White House, he stormed at aides that the Eastern Establishment—both the bar and the press —had invoked its hated brand of elitism once again. Nor did anybody inside the administration dare disagree. Len Garment, the self-styled house liberal in the White House, rejected pleas from his liberal lawyer friends in New York that he intercede with the President. Give the President's choices a chance before you shoot them down, Garment pleaded. Similar advice came from Clark Mac-Gregor to his old liberal Republican friends on Capitol Hill. A friend who tried to convince Mitchell of the folly of the selections was rudely and abruptly cut off. This matter had been decided, beyond the peradventure of any appeal.

Nixon's own first angry inclination was to fight the Friday and Lillie nominations through the Senate, win or lose. But as he sat alone in his hideaway in the Executive Office Building next door to the White House, his fury diminished. He still could not bring himself to admit that his selections were thoroughly unqualified. But in the cool quiet of his office, he realized that he might wind up with yet two more Senate rejections of his own Supreme Court nominees, a catastrophic blow that could not possibly do him any good. Reluctantly, Nixon finally asked Mitchell for two new names, stressing only that they *must* be conservatives. On that point, he would not budge.

The two choices finally submitted to Nixon and accepted by him were brilliant conservative lawyers: Lewis F. Powell, Jr., a distinguished attorney from Richmond, Va., and former national president of the ABA, and Assistant Attorney General William H. Rehnquist. Powell at age sixty-four violated Nixon's age standards;

Mrs. Lillie. Originally, the camouflage list included Judge Arlin Adams of the U.S. Court of Appeals in Philadelphia. But his name was withdrawn when Kleindienst realized that a boom might be inadvertently generated for Adams, a Jew with excellent connections in Philadelphia Republican and legal circles.

Rehnquist violated the President's inclination against naming members of his administration to the Court. But he was long past sticking to the letter of his specifications. Both were easily confirmed, though not until Senate liberals gave Rehnquist a going-over because of his conservative ideology.

It was a remarkable recovery for Nixon from a most difficult situation. Yet, the incident was revealing of what it told about the President and his closest aides—his resentment against the Establishment, the limitation on dissent within the White House, the strange contempt for quality on the Court, the passion to redeem yet again that campaign commitment for a Southern conservative on the Supreme Court. These were enduring characteristics of the President and his men after almost three years of Presidential experience.

Even if Richard Nixon had let the opportunity of the double vacancy go by without naming a Southerner, his position in the South was secure. Ever since his election to a new term as governor of Alabama in 1970, George Wallace had been handled with kid gloves by the President and his political advisers in hopes that he would not run again as a third-party candidate. Whereas in 1969 and 1970 the White House painted the Wallace menace in the most lurid terms, in his January 2 interview with Dan Rather, Nixon passed up an opportunity to attack: "It is not the problem here of our party. As far as Mr. Wallace is concerned, he is now seeking the Democratic nomination, and that is . . . going to have to be worked out within their own party."* With Wallace not leading a third party, Nixon could well capture all eleven states of the Old Confederacy against any nominee the Democratic Party might select —an incalculable advantage for reelection. The Southern Strategy, with roots in the Goldwater disaster of 1964, had finally matured in the first Nixon administration. John Mitchell's grand design of wedding the Nixon and Wallace votes of 1968, so often derided by the press and liberal Republicans, was within sight.

Only one cloud darkened the horizon. Court-ordered busing of pupils for purposes of school integration was spreading through the country, particularly in the great cities of the South where

*There were reports in 1972, denied by both sides and unsubstantiated, that Nixon and Wallace had made a deal whereby Wallace would not run for President in return for an unstated quid pro quo.

Nixon had always been so popular—Charlotte, Jacksonville, Dallas, Nashville. Nixon's anti-busing position was unequivocal and of long standing. Yet, in the 1971–1972 school year, white citizens of Dallas and Nashville were outraged over racial busing, and the President was getting his share of the blame. To be sure, no Democrat with any chance to win his party's Presidential nomination could accuse Nixon of being inadequately militant against busing. But there remained the possibility that Wallace might yet sweep into the South as a third-party candidate, accusing the President of softness on busing and robbing him of precious electoral votes. Besides, busing was becoming a major issue in many Northern states—Michigan especially—where a strong stand by Nixon might conceivably take votes from the Democrats.

Thus, in the late winter of 1972, there developed a deep but quiet schism over busing within the administration—a pale descendant of the furious civil rights conflicts between Mitchell's Justice Department and Finch's HEW three years earlier. Secretary Elliot Richardson at HEW and Len Garment at the White House urged caution and recommended that the President stay aloof. Their most effective agent was HEW's General Counsel, Wilmot R. Hastings. But politically minded aides at the White House were insisting that Nixon must actively promote some anti-busing legislation—if possible, a Constitutional amendment to prohibit busing. Not surprisingly, Harry Dent, still Nixon's chief political ambassador to the South, took this view. But it also was strongly supported by Dick Cook, a pragmatist rather than a conservative, who had worked his way up the ladder to become the President's top lobbyist in the House.

Inevitably, Nixon inclined toward the Dent–Cook view. Just before his departure for China in February, Cook persuaded the President to squeeze in a meeting with key anti-busing leaders in Congress, along with the regular Republican leadership. It was decided to study the matter and avoid specific proposals until the return from China. But nobody could have left that meeting without being absolutely certain that the President would act.

Upon his return the President found nearly unanimous opposition to a Constitutional amendment. Instead, a committee on the busing question (headed by Mitchell) recommended legislation putting a moratorium on new busing plans. Also recommended were extra federal funds for predominantly black schools, a proposal correctly viewed as little more than a sop to liberals both in and out of the administration.

The question now was how the Nixon anti-busing program should be presented to the nation. The liberals preferred a simple press release with no hoopla. But Cook and Dent, convinced that this was *the* social issue of the day, wanted an extravaganza—perhaps even an address to a joint session of Congress, at least a television address to the people.

The issue was decided by Wallace's landslide win on March 14, in the Florida Democratic Presidential primary, where busing was the preeminent issue. Two days later, Nixon went to the public on nation-wide television once again to attack busing and lay out his remedies. On the next day, March 17, he told a bipartisan meeting of Congressional leaders that he was ready to crack the whip against bureaucrats in HEW who had been covertly supporting busing around the country.

The citizens of Dallas, Nashville and other busing centers, unaffected by the moratorium, were displeased by the Nixon program. There was not even assurance that Congress would pass the moratorium in the election-year confusion on Capitol Hill. One leading Southern Democrat, Representative Joe Waggonner of Louisiana, castigated the Nixon program privately to his friends as a "Yankee relief measure." When the White House telephoned Senator James Eastland of Mississippi, the chairman of the Judiciary Committee, to seek his sponsorship of the Nixon program, Eastland gave an immediate and unequivocal no. He would neither sponsor nor speak for the legislation, said Eastland.

Still, Nixon was on the popular side of an emotional issue, and in good position to capture Democratic votes on the busing issue. The school desegregation issue had been a recurrent theme throughout the first three and a half years of Nixon's Presidency. All that time, he had braked the efforts by Court and government to integrate public schooling. On this issue, there had been no deviation or leftward drift. Thus if his efforts were less than successful in the face of court rulings, Nixon could nevertheless expect high marks for trying come November 7.

On Monday morning, November 30, 1971, Richard Nixon met with John Mitchell and his Congressional lobbying staff to consider a political time bomb that Congress was about to send him.

Both the House and Senate had eagerly passed his tax cuts to stimulate the sluggish economy as part of his New Economic Policy. But
on November 22, the Senate added to the bill a pet project of
Democratic National Committee Chairman Lawrence F. O'Brien:
a scheme to finance Presidential campaigns from the U.S. Treasury,
thereby relieving the virtually bankrupt Democratic Party of its
fiscal agony and eliminating a major 1972 campaign advantage for
the lushly financed Republicans. What's more, O'Brien had assurance from Representative Wilbur D. Mills that he would accept
the Senate amendment in behalf of the House conferees.

It was a tidy scheme for the Democrats. The political financing
plan, passed by itself, would have been vetoed by Nixon without a
moment's hesitation. But O'Brien and the party's Congressional
leaders, Mills included, were certain the President would not be so
reckless as to veto the tax bill and bring the shaky economy to its
knees merely for the sake of maintaining a political advantage in
the 1972 campaign. Even Nixon's own economic advisers shuddered
at the mere suggestion of a veto.

But his economic advisers were not present at that November
30 meeting, and Nixon was not in the market for advice anyway.
Rather, he informed Mitchell and his Congressional advisers that
his mind was made up: he intended to veto the tax bill if it contained the Democratic scheme no matter what the economic consequences. He would have Ron Ziegler make the announcement that
very afternoon.

Nixon explained it this way: if Congress could blackmail him
on this issue, it could blackmail him on other issues for the rest of
his term. Besides, he revealed he had always regretted signing the
eighteen-year-old vote into law in 1970 rather than veto an extension of the Equal Voting Rights Act to which Democratic leaders
had attached it. Never again, he said. On the tax bill, Nixon told
his Congressional lobbyists, the next move was to mobilize the
business community to press Congress to remove the offensive
political fund rather than endanger the economy.

The Democratic leaders could not believe the President was
serious when they heard his veto threat that afternoon. Mills told
newsmen he was certain that Nixon was bluffing. But private word
relayed to him and other key Democrats that the President meant
exactly what he said changed his mind. The auto industry went into
shock. Relying on a retroactive repeal of auto excise taxes contained

in the bill, it had adjusted auto prices downward. Veto of the tax bill, panicky lobbyists for the automotive industry told Mills, would be a catastrophe.

Mills was convinced. The economy, he felt, simply could not withstand the veto of the tax bill. And so on December 2, the Senate–House conferees capitulated. The President had stared down Congress, and politicians and lobbyists in Washington knew that the image of Nixon floundering on Capitol Hill was no more. In contrast to his conspicuous misuse of the veto in 1970, he had now effectively exercised what little power a Republican President can exert against a Democratic Congress.

To be sure, much of his legislative program was dead by mid-1972. The ambitious program of reform outlined to Congress by Nixon in January 1971 had been ignored, just as everyone predicted it would be (though the President had an excellent chance to win passage of revenue sharing).

Moreover, communications gaps between White House and Republican cloakrooms on Capitol Hill still turned up. Senator Robert Dole of Kansas, though chairman of the Republican National Committee and a party leader from a heavily Republican agricultural state, had not even been consulted before Nixon named the controversial Dr. Earl Butz of Purdue University on November 11, 1971, as the new Secretary of Agriculture. Other farm-state Republicans were also overlooked and they grumbled that the President had risked alienating the farm vote with the selection of an academician reputed to be against his farm prices.*

On balance, however, the climate had changed on Capitol Hill. The combination of guts and skill shown in stripping the political fund-raising scheme from the tax bill impressed members of both parties on Capitol Hill. Congress was no longer so clear a net liability for Nixon. Considering the record of 1969 and 1970, that constituted progress indeed.

As the cherry blossoms bloomed in Washington in the spring of 1972, the state of Richard Nixon's political health seemed stronger than at any time since his election.†

*Butz was confirmed by the Senate on December 2 by a 51 to 44 vote, with many farm state Republicans opposing him.

†In the late winter and spring of 1972, a political menace to Nixon whose extent could not be immediately measured suddenly appeared. Columnist Jack

A Republican Presidential-primary challenge from the right by Representative John Ashbrook of Ohio, reflecting the anger of the Buckleyite conservatives that Nixon had drifted too far leftward (particularly in foreign policy), was picking up no popular support. When Nixon broadly hinted over national television on January 2, 1972, that Sipro T. Agnew probably would be his running mate again in 1972, millions of conservatives were pacified.

In the national opinion polls, Nixon for the first time since 1969 was running far ahead of any possible Democrat, although some of his political aides well understood that much of this advantage derived from the disarray of the Democratic Party and its disorderly struggle to find a nominee.

Nevertheless, after nearly three and a half years in office, the underlying frustrations of Richard Nixon's Presidency persisted:

Instead of quietly going away, the Vietnam war continued to threaten all that Nixon had attempted and accomplished both at home and abroad.

The delicate diplomacy to establish a true era of negotiations with the Soviet Union and Communist China remained a treacherous tortuous affair with only moderate progress recorded.

The economy continued to resist administration remedies, the twin evils of inflation and unemployment persisting and the workingman increasingly discontented.

Though considerably tamer than it had been in 1969, the Democratic Congress was maddeningly balky in dealing with the President's proposals.

And finally, despite all his efforts, Richard Nixon remained an essentially unloved President—more respected and admired, surely, than three years earlier, but still unloved. Bearing that burden, he persisted in the traits that had always dogged his career of adversity: suspicion, hostility toward enemies, aloofness, and

---

Anderson published a memorandum indicating that the Justice Department had settled an anti-trust suit out of court against the huge conglomerate International Telephone and Telegraph Corp., because ITT had made a $400,000 contribution to permit the 1972 Republican National Convention to be held in San Diego, Calif., as the President desired. Senate Judiciary Committee hearings on the matter turned into a sensational, highly partisan affair that titillated the nation. It was clearly an embarrassment for the administration; it remained to be seen whether it would become a full-blown political scandal and raise an old and dangerous specter—the specter of big-business domination over a Republican administration.

that curious inability to reach a state of empathy with his country-men.

Perhaps if he were reelected, the second term might be different. Then, for the first time in his political life, there would not be yet another election to prepare for and other worlds to conquer.

Index

Index

ABOUT THE AUTHORS

ROWLAND EVANS, JR., was born in White Marsh, Pennsylvania, and attended Yale University. From 1953 to 1955 he covered the Senate for the Associated Press. Next he covered Congress and then national and international politics for the Washington bureau of the *New York Herald Tribune*.

ROBERT D. NOVAK was born in Joliet, Illinois, and is a graduate of the University of Illinois. In 1957 he became a Capitol Hill correspondent for the Associated Press, and in 1961 Congressional correspondent for the *Wall Street Journal*.

In May 1963 Messrs. Evans and Novak teamed to write *Inside Report*, the well-known political column which is syndicated by *The Chicago Sun-Times* in over 212 newspapers worldwide.

Mr. Novak is the author of *The Agony of the G.O.P. 1964* (1965). He and Mr. Evans co-authored *Lyndon B. Johnson: The Exercise of Power* (1966). They publish a bi-weekly newsletter, the *Evans-Novak Political Report*, and both appear regularly on TV and the lecture platform.

They and their families live in Washington, D.C.